Internet Research Ethics for the Social Age

Steve Jones
General Editor

Vol. 108

The Digital Formations series is part of the Peter Lang Media and Communication list.
Every volume is peer reviewed and meets
the highest quality standards for content and production.

PETER LANG
New York • Bern • Frankfurt • Berlin
Brussels • Vienna • Oxford • Warsaw

Internet Research Ethics for the Social Age

New Challenges, Cases, and Contexts

Edited by Michael Zimmer
and Katharina Kinder-Kurlanda

PETER LANG
New York • Bern • Frankfurt • Berlin
Brussels • Vienna • Oxford • Warsaw

Library of Congress Cataloging-in-Publication Data

Names: Zimmer, Michael, editor. | Kinder-Kurlanda, Katharina, editor.
Title: Internet research ethics for the social age: new challenges, cases, and contexts / edited by Michael Zimmer and Katharina Kinder-Kurlanda.
Description: New York: Peter Lang, 2017.
Includes bibliographical references.
Identifiers: LCCN 2017015655 | ISBN 978-1-4331-4266-6 (paperback: alk. paper)
ISBN 978-1-4331-4267-3 (hardcover: alk. paper) | ISBN 978-1-4331-4268-0 (ebook pdf)
ISBN 978-1-4331-4269-7 (epub) | ISBN 978-1-4331-4270-3 (mobi)
Subjects: LCSH: Internet research—Moral and ethical aspects.
Classification: LCC ZA4228 .I59 2017 | DDC 174/.90014—dc23
LC record available at https://lccn.loc.gov/2017015655
DOI 10.3726/b11077

Bibliographic information published by **Die Deutsche Nationalbibliothek.**
Die Deutsche Nationalbibliothek lists this publication in the "Deutsche Nationalbibliografie"; detailed bibliographic data are available on the Internet at http://dnb.d-nb.de/.

29 Broadway, 18th floor, New York, NY 10006
www.peterlang.com

Table of Contents

Foreword

Grounding Internet Research Ethics 3.0: A View from (the) AoIR

CHARLES ESS

Michael Zimmer and Katharina Kinder-Kurlanda have brought together a carefully organized and critically important anthology – important for its own sake and, as I will try to show, as this volume both indexes and inaugurates a third wave of Internet Research Ethics (IRE). That is, we can think of the first era of IRE – IRE 1.0 – to emerge alongside the initial IRE guidelines developed and issued by the Association of Internet Researchers (AoIR) in 2002 (Ess & AoIR Ethics Working Committee). To be sure, as Elizabeth Buchanan makes clear here in her magisterial overview of the past 20 years of IRE, the first AoIR document rests on considerably older roots. At the same time, it served as at least a partial foundation for the second AoIR document, "Ethical Decision-Making and Internet Research: Recommendations from the AoIR Ethics Working Committee (Version 2.0)" (Markham & Buchanan, 2012). As Buchanan shows, this second document – what many of us take as central to IRE 2.0 – was catalyzed by the multiple shifts affiliated with "the era of social computing took hold, circa 2005." This shifts included first and foremost the rise of social networking sites (SNSs) such as MySpace, Friendster, and the now hegemonic Facebook, followed by an explosion of diverse venues and forms of social media that more or less define contemporary communication venues (e.g., Twitter, Snapchat, WhatsApp, and Instagram, just to name the primary usual suspects). These shifts further included dramatically expanded possibilities for "users" to actively engage in internet-facilitated communication venues, e.g., in the form of blogs, certainly, but also by creating and uploading content to sites such as YouTube. Many of the ethical questions and dilemmas taken up by IRE 2.0 were further occasioned by the rise of mobile internet access – i.e., the introduction and diffusion of smartphones, beginning roughly in 2008. Last but certainly not least, as Buchanan notes, the era of Big Data research, beginning ca. 2010, likewise issued in a new range of issues and possible resolutions addressed in the AoIR 2.0 document.

The current volume does nothing less than inaugurate and critically ground an emerging IRE 3.0. To be sure, the volume takes social media as its defining thread: but several of the individual contributions make equally clear that "social media" encompass a staggering range of venues, communicative possibilities, and thereby research interests, methodologies, and so on. To my eye, they thereby highlight and help initiate the still richer and more extensive ethical discussions that will constitute IRE 3.0.

To begin with, it is important to notice that just as IRE 2.0 was an extension, not a rejection of IRE 3.0 – so IRE 3.0 continues to build upon these previous documents and now rather extensive affiliated literatures. Indeed, I have argued that in some cases of IRE 2.0, "what is old is new again" – i.e., IRE 1.0 considerations surrounding informed consent can prove useful in 2.0 Big Data research projects (Ess, 2016). In these directions, it is not surprising to see in the current volume that concerns with *privacy* remain paramount. That is, privacy intersects with the most basic obligations of Human Subjects Protections at the foundations of IRE – namely, obligations to preserve anonymity, confidentiality, and informed consent. So privacy concerns figure large in the contributions here from Ishani Mukherjee; Ylva Hård af Segerstad et al; Amaia Eskisabel-Azpiazu, Rebeca Cerezo-Menéndez, and Daniel Gayo-Avello; Lisbeth Klastrup; Robert Douglas Ferguson; Patrick Sweeney; and Martina Wengenmeir.

But of course, these concerns are often dramatically transformed – not only by the rise of social media and big data, as IRE 2.0 already recognized. In addition, what I see as the most significant novelties here, i.e., what can be taken on board as signature themes and concerns for IRE 3.0, rest on a growing recognition of perhaps the most profound shift affecting IRE – namely, the shift from a primarily *individual* conception of selfhood and identity towards a more *relational* conception This shift emerges early in the volume in the title of the chapter by Tobias Matzner and Carsten Ochs, "Sorting Things Out Ethically: Privacy as a Research Issue Beyond the Individual." Matzner and Ochs rightly point out that strictly individualistic conceptions of privacy have shaped by far the greatest bulk of philosophical and ethical theorizing, at least until relatively recently. Taking on board more relational understandings of selfhood means, however, that our understandings of privacy likewise become more relational, i.e., as implicating both the individual and his/her close-tie relationships. Their account of "Post-Individualist Privacy in Internet Research" points correctly to Helen Nissenbaum's now central theory of privacy as "contextual integrity" (2010). At the same time, their discussion is in some ways importantly anticipated in the (Norwegian) National Committee for Research Ethics in the Social Sciences and the Humanities (NESH, 2006; cf. Ess, 2015; Ess & Fossheim, 2013).

Broadly speaking, responsibility in ethics depends upon agency: I am directly responsible (only) for what I can enact, and not responsible for what I cannot initiate or affect ("*ought* implies *can*"). Hence relational selfhood – especially as literally distributed across networked communications – entails a (comparatively) new sense of ethical responsibility, i.e., one that understands that responsibility is *distributed* across the relationships that shape and define us. So Jonathon Hutchinson, Fiona Martin, and Aim Sinpeng, in their "Chasing ISIS: Network Power, Distributed Ethics and Responsible Social Media Research," call for "new professional standards, such as the AoIR guidelines, and to advocate for social media research in context – based on an understanding of the limits of distributed responsibility and the different meanings of social visibility for diverse social media agents, human and non-human." By the same token, in their "How Does It Feel to Be Visualized?: Redistributing Ethics," David Moats and Jess Perriam further explore a *distributed ethics* as a way of resolving the challenges evoked by the technologies of networked interconnection, including algorithms, APIs, and related research tools.

Finally, this shift towards more relational understandings of selfhood in Western societies directly intersects the attention to Confucian and Buddhist concepts of relational selfhood taken up here by Soraj Hongladarom, as part of his considerations of how an IRE might function across both Western and Eastern cultural differences. Hongladarom's chapter thereby highlights an IRE 1.0 theme that will become all the more significant for IRE 3.0. That is: from the earliest days of developing the AoIR 2002 document, we were acutely aware of the ethical challenges further evoked by the internet as a communication technology more or less oblivious to national borders and thereby the diverse national/cultural backgrounds and traditions that deeply shape and inflect our ethical sensibilities. Our awareness and deliberations in these directions were fostered by many committee members – including the venerable Soraj Hongladarom. Here, Hongladarom highlights the importance of *ethical pluralism* as a primary way of conjoining shared ethical norms and principles with resolute insistence on the importance of sustaining the multiple and diverse approaches and traditions rooted in distinct cultures: as he notes, such ethical pluralism is already in play in IRE 1.0 (Ess & AoIR Ethics Working Committee, 2002, pp. 29–30). At the same time: one of the most striking dimensions of the AoIR 2016 ethics panels was that, for the first time in our history, both the majority of presentations and participants represented countries and culture domains outside the United States. Both presentations and subsequent discussion made clear that more and more countries and cultures are taking up new initiatives and/or expanding extant initiatives in developing an IRE within their distinctive national and cultural domains. Manifestly, an IRE 3.0 will become ever more informed by these rapidly expanding initiatives.

More immediately, Hutchinson et al identify an increasingly significant topos that emerges from this relational-distributed focus – namely, that "social media research is often located between corporations and governments, which is often a zone within which an individual researcher has limited power." As they point out, a primary ethical problem resulting from these sorts of entanglements is how researchers are to maintain rigorous standards of scientific integrity, objectivity, accuracy, and so on, vis-à-vis corporate and government agendas that may run contrary to these standards. That these issues are of growing concern can be seen in their prominence in the 2016 AoIR ethics panels: so Franzke, 2016; Locatelli, 2016; and Schäfer & van Schie, 2016.

EXPANDING THE FRAMEWORKS: FEMINISM, VIRTUE ETHICS, AND SOFTWARE ENGINEERS

In both IRE 1.0 and 2.0, feminist approaches to both methodology and ethics played a significant role (e.g., Ess & AoIR Ethics Working Committee, 2002, ftn. 5, p. 29; Hall, Frederick, & Johns, 2004; see Buchanan & Ess, 2008, 276f. for additional discussion and examples). These feminist orientations and approaches are both represented and importantly extended in this volume by Mary Elizabeth Luka, Mélanie Millette and Jacqueline Wallace. Their "A Feminist Perspective on Ethical Digital Methods" pursues the critical ambition to further "the integrated nature of an ethics of care with feminist values that include respecting diversity, understanding the intention of research as a participant and as a researcher, and paying attention to our responsibility as researchers to do no harm in the communities within which we work, even as we aim to generate potentially transformative engagements."

In foregrounding a feminist ethics of care, Luka et al add to an increasing number of researchers and, more importantly, research communities that likewise – but only very recently – turn to an ethics of care in order to better come to grips with the ethical challenges evoked by networked technologies and the relationships they facilitate and afford. To be sure, since Sara Ruddick's inauguration of care ethics (1980), care ethics has been closely interwoven with both feminist ethics and virtue ethics as these emerged in the 1970s and 1980s. Broadly, virtue ethics centered Norbert Wiener's foundational text ([1950] 1954) in Information and Computing Ethics (ICE); virtue ethics has become increasingly central to both (ICE) in general and especially in recent years (e.g., Vallor, 2016) – as it has also become more prominent in approaches to the *design* of ICTs, perhaps most notably in the work of Sarah Spiekermann (2016). Indeed, Spiekermann's implementations of virtue ethics in ICT design underlies nothing less than the critical new initiative of the IEEE, "Global Initiative for Ethical Considerations in the Design of Autonomous Systems" (<http://standards.ieee.org/develop/indconn/ec/autonomous_systems.html>)

As this IEEE initiative makes clear, what is most striking here is how virtue ethics broadly and care ethics in particular have been taken up and endorsed by our colleagues in software engineering, networked systems design, and related, centrally "technical" fields. As a further example: at the conclusion of a global, two-year project of seeking to discern the ethical frameworks best suited to the technically-intensive field of networked systems research, Bendert Zevenbergen and his colleagues concluded nothing less than that "… virtue ethics should be applied to Internet research and *engineering* – where the technical persons must fulfil the character traits of the 'virtuous agent'" (Zevenbergen et al., 2016, p. 31: emphasis added, CME; cf. Zevenbergen, 2016). Similarly, Jackson, Aldrovandi, & Hayes (2015) have endorsed both virtue ethics and ethics of care as primary frameworks for the Slándáil Project (2015). The project exploits big data techniques to harvest and analyze social media data during a natural disaster, for the sake of improving the efficiencies of emergency responders. The project is also cross-cultural, involving institutes and agencies from four (Western) countries – Ireland, Italy, Germany, and the U.K. – and thereby invokes an explicit ethical pluralism. The turn to virtue ethics and care ethics begins with an account of the self as *relational.* In these ways, Jackson et al. directly draw from IRE 1.0 and 2.0 – and instantiate an application of virtue ethics and care ethics directly parallel to the approach articulated here by Luka et al.

Simply as an indication of the growing influence and importance of feminist ethics, such these examples would be heartening enough. Even more importantly: these examples index a still more profound development and thereby characteristic of IRE 3.0. That is, it is an understatement to say that efforts over the past five decades or so to overcome the profound disciplinary boundaries between applied ethics, on the one hand, and the more technical fields of engineering, computer science, software engineering, and so on, on the other, have been fundamentally challenging on multiple grounds. The recent two decades or so have shown some progress as our more technical colleagues have come to more enthusiastically embrace primary ethical frameworks such as utilitarianism and deontology. But for these colleagues to now go still further and endorse, primarily as a result of their own initiatives and insights, both virtue ethics and care ethics, as clearly feminist, is the disciplinary equivalent of the fall of the Berlin Wall.

Both within and beyond this volume, then, we could hardly ask for better starting points for IRE 3.0. To be sure, there are additional issues and topics that will require (re)new(ed) attention in this third wave. For example, the relational-distributed focus foregrounds the increasingly central issue of the need to protect *researchers* as much as (if not more than) our informants, as their research risks exposing them to the full array of hate speech, threats, and acts that are now routinely directed at them – especially if they are women researching predominantly male hate behaviors (e.g., Massanari, 2016). Another increasingly central issue, brought forward here by Katrin Weller and Katharina Kinder-Kurlanda ("To Share or Not to Share? Ethical Challenges in Sharing Social Media-based Research Data"), concerns the multiple ethical issues confronting researchers who increasingly depend on commercial sources for "big data" – and/or "grey data," i.e., data that has been leaked and made public by hackers: so Nathaniel Poor's "The Ethics of Using Hacked Data: Patreon's Data Hack and Academic Data Standards." For relational selves, "sharing is caring" – but such sharing is often ethically fraught in ways that remain to be fully explored and at least partially resolved.

Of course, still more issues – and, ideally, possible resolutions – will fill the agenda of our developing IRE 3.0. But as I hope these comments make clear: if anyone needs or wants to know what IRE 3.0 will look like – s/he can do no better but to begin with this volume.

REFERENCES

Buchanan, E., & Ess, C. (2008). Internet research ethics: The field and its critical issues. In K. Himma & H. Tavani (Eds.), *The handbook of information and computer ethics* (pp. 273–292). Hoboken, NJ: John Wiley & Sons.

Ess, C. (2015). New selves, new research ethics? In H. Ingierd & H. Fossheim (Eds.), *Internet research ethics* (pp. 48–76). Oslo: Cappelen Damm. Retrieved from Open Access: http://press.nordicopenaccess.no/index.php/noasp/catalog/book/3

Ess, C. (2016, October 6). *Introduction, Internet research ethics roundtable I: New problems, new relationships.* Panel presentation, Association of Internet Researchers annual Internet Research conference, Berlin.

Ess, C., & AoIR Ethics Working Committee. (2002). *Ethical decision-making and Internet Research: Recommendations from the AoIR Ethics Working Committee.* Retrieved from http://www.aoir.org/reports/ethics.pdf

Ess, C., & Fossheim, H. (2013). Personal data: Changing selves, changing privacy expectations. In M. Hildebrandt, K. O'Hara, & M. Waidner (Eds.), *Digital enlightenment forum yearbook 2013: The value of personal data* (pp. 40–55). Amsterdam: IOS Amsterdam.

Franzke, A. (2016). *Big data ethicist: What will the role of the ethicist be in advising governments in the field of big data?* (MA thesis in applied ethics). Utrecht University. Retrieved from http://tinyurl.com/h2g3s2n

Hall, G. J., Frederick, D., & Johns, M. D. (2004). "NEED HELP ASAP!!!": A feminist communitarian approach to online research ethics. In M. Johns, S. L. Chen, & J. Hall (Eds.), *Online social research: Methods, issues, and ethics* (pp. 239–252). New York, NY: Peter Lang.

Jackson, D., Aldrovandi, C., & Hayes, P. (2015). Ethical framework for a disaster management decision support system which harvests social media data on a large scale. In N. Bellamine Ben Saoud et al. (Eds.), *ISCRAM-med 2015* (pp. 167–180), LNBIP 233. doi:10.1007/978-3-319-24399-3_15.

Locatelli, E. (2016, October 6). *Social media and erasing the boundaries between academic/critical and corporate research.* Panel presentation, Association of Internet Researchers annual Internet Research conference, Berlin.

Markham, A., & Buchanan, E. (2012). *Ethical decision-making and Internet Research, Version 2.0: Recommendations from the AoIR Ethics Working Committee.* Retrieved from www.aoir.org/reports/ethics2.pdf

Massanari, A. (2016, October 6). *The changing nature of research in the age of #Gamergate.* Panel presentation, Association of Internet Researchers annual Internet Research conference, Berlin.

NESH (National Committee for Research Ethics in the Social Sciences and the Humanities). (2006). *Forskningsetiske retningslinjer for samfunnsvitenskap, humaniora, juss og teologi* [Research ethics guidelines for social sciences, the humanities, law and theology]. Retrieved from http://www.etikkom. no/Documents/Publikasjoner-som-PDF/Forskningsetiske%20retningslinjer%20for%20samfunnsvitenskap,%20humaniora,%20juss%20og%20teologi%20%282006%29.pdf

Nissenbaum, H. (2010). *Privacy in context. Technology, policy, and the integrity of social life.* Stanford, CA: Stanford University Press.

Ruddick, S. (1980). Maternal thinking. *Feminist Studies,* 6(2), 342–367.

Schäfer, M. T., & van Schie, G. (2016, October 6). *Big data and negotiating the blurring boundaries between academic, corporate, and public institution research.* Panel presentation, Association of Internet Researchers annual Internet Research conference, Berlin.

Spiekermann, S. (2016). *Ethical IT innovation: A value-based system design approach.* New York, NY: Taylor & Francis.

Vallor, S. (2016). *Technology and the virtues: A philosophical guide to a future worth wanting.* Oxford: Oxford University Press.

Wiener, N. ([1950] 1954). *The human use of human beings: Cybernetics and society.* Boston, MA: Houghton Mifflin (2nd Revised ed.). New York, NY: Doubleday Anchor.

Zevenbergen, B. (2016). *Networked systems ethics.* Ethics in networked systems research: Ethical, legal and policy reasoning for Internet Engineering. Oxford Internet Institute, University of Oxford. Retrieved from http://networkedsystemsethics.net/

Zevenbergen, B., Mittelstadt, B., Véliz, C., Detweiler, C., Cath, C., Savulescu, J., & Whittaker, M. (2015). Philosophy meets Internet engineering: Ethics in networked systems research. (GTC workshop outcomes paper). Oxford Internet Institute, University of Oxford.

Introductory Material

Introduction

MICHAEL ZIMMER AND KATHARINA KINDER-KURLANDA

The internet and related social media technologies and platforms have opened up vast new means for communication, socialization, expression, and collaboration. They also have provided new resources for researchers seeking to explore, observe, and measure human opinions, activities, and interactions. Increasingly, social media tools are used to aid traditional research: subjects might be recruited through Facebook or Twitter, surveys are administered and shared online, and data is often stored and processed on social and collaborative webbased platforms and repositories. Social media has also emerged as a preferred domain for research itself: ethnographies take place within massively online social environments, entire collections of Facebook profile pages are scraped for data analysis, and the content of public Twitter streams is routinely mined for academic studies. And we have now entered the era of big data, where researchers can access petabytes of transactional data, clickstreams and cookie logs, media files, and digital archives, as well as pervasive data from social networks, mobile phones, and sensors.

In short, academic research has begun to fully embrace what Maria Azua, a Vice President of Technology and Innovation at IBM, describes in her book, *The Social Factor: Innovate, Ignite, and Win through Mass Collaboration and Social Networking*, as "the social age," the leveraging of the internet and pervasive connected devices to enhance communication, information exchange, collaboration, and social interactions (Azua, 2009, p. 1). As a result, researchers studying the internet and big data find themselves immersed in a domain where information flows freely but is also potentially bound by contextual norms and expectations, where platforms may oscillate between open and closed information flows, and where data may be usergenerated, filtered, algorithmically-processed, or proprietary.

As a result, just as in its offline counterpart, internet and social mediabased research raises critical ethical concerns about the role of the "subject" in such research endeavors. Various disciplines with a history of engaging in human subjects research (such as medicine, anthropology, psychology, communication) have longstanding ethical codes and policies intended to guide researchers and those charged with ensuring that research on human subjects follows both legal requirements and ethical practices, and often ethical review boards are charged with approving, monitoring, and reviewing research involving humans to ensure the rights and welfare of the research subjects are protected. But in the socalled "social age" – where individuals increasingly share personal information on platforms with porous and shifting boundaries, the aggregation of data from disparate sources is increasingly the norm, and webbased services, and their privacy policies and terms of service statements change too rapidly for an average user to keep up – the ethical frameworks and assumptions traditionally used by researchers and review boards alike are frequently challenged and, in some cases, inadequate.

Researchers using the internet as a tool or a space of research – and those tasked with facilitating and monitoring ethical research such as ethical review boards – are confronted with a continuously expanding set of ethical dilemmas: What ethical obligations do researchers have to protect the privacy of subjects engaging in activities in "public" internet spaces? Which national or international ethical standards apply when researching global networks, communities, or information flows? How is confidentiality or anonymity assured online? How is and should informed consent be obtained online? How should research on minors be conducted, and how do you prove a subject is not a minor? Is deception (pretending to be someone you are not or withholding identifiable information) in online spaces a norm, or a harm? Is "harm" possible to someone existing online in digital spaces? What are researchers' obligations in spaces which are governed by platform providers? How should we contend with inequalities in data access and uncertainties about data provenance and quality?

In recent years, a growing number of scholars have started to address many of these open questions within this new domain of internet research ethics (see, for example, Buchanan, 2004; Buchanan & Zimmer, 2016; Heider & Massanari, 2012; Markham & Baym, 2008; McKee & Porter, 2009). As regulatory authorities responsible for the oversight of human subject research are starting to confront the myriad of ethical concerns internetbased research brings to light (see, for example, SACHRP, 2013), numerous scholarly associations have drafted ethical guidelines for internet research, including the American Psychological Association's Advisory Group on Conducting Research on the Internet, the Association of Internet Researchers (AoIR) Ethics Working Group Guidelines, and the Norwegian National Committee for Research Ethics in the Social Sciences and the Humanities.

Yet, even with increased attention and guidance surrounding internet research ethics, significant gaps in our understanding and practices persist. Across the research community, for example, there is disagreement over basic research ethics questions and policies, such as what constitutes "public" content and at what stage computational research becomes human subjects research (see, for example, Carpenter & Dittrich, 2011; Metcalf & Crawford, 2016; Zimmer, 2016). Further, media attention surrounding Facebook's "emotional contagion" experiment (Kramer, Guillory, & Hancock, 2014) sparked widespread concern over how internet companies conduct research on their own users, and big data research generally (see, for example, Fiesler et al., 2015; Goel, 2014; Schroeder, 2014).

Our goal with *Internet Research Ethics for the Social Age: New Challenges, Cases, and Contexts* is to directly engage with these discussions and debates, and to help stimulate new ways to think about – and work towards resolving – the novel ethical dilemmas we face as internet and social media-based research continues to evolve. The chapters within this volume – which present novel ethical challenges, case studies, and emerging research contexts from a collection of global scholars and researchers – accomplishes this in three critical ways:

First, as internet tools and social platforms continue to evolve at a rapid pace, *Internet Research Ethics for the Social Age* highlights new research contexts and case studies that introduce readers to unique uses – and related ethical concerns – of the current state-of-the-art technologies and platforms, including crowdsourcing on Amazon Mechanical Turk, the health sharing platform PatientsLikeMe, new forms of data visualization and facial recognition platforms, and automated tools for flagging potentially suicidal behavior online.

Second, *Internet Research Ethics for the Social Age* recognizes the broad disciplinary terrain impacted by internetbased research, and brings together discussions of ethical issues from the familiar domains of the social sciences (such as communication studies, sociology, and psychology) alongside perspectives from computer science, data science, gender studies, museum studies, and philosophy. The result is a more inclusive umbrella of domains that can learn from each other and collaborate to confront the challenges of internet research ethics.

Third, *Internet Research Ethics for the Social Age* provides a global approach to the challenges of internet research ethics, bringing together contributions from researchers in diverse regulatory environments, as well as those dealing with the complex ethical dimensions of researching platforms and users in geographically diverse locations. Global regions and cultures represented within the volume include Australia, Canada, Denmark, Germany, the Netherlands, New Zealand, South Asia, Spain, Sweden, Thailand, the United Kingdom, and the United States.

ORGANIZATION OF THE BOOK

To set the stage for the current state of internet and social media research ethics, immediately following this Introduction is a short historical essay, "Internet Research Ethics: Twenty Years Later," where Elizabeth Buchanan, the leading expert in the field, outlines the trajectory internet research ethics has taken since its emergence in the mid-1990s. Buchanan reflects on the myriad of changes in technologies, users, research disciplines, and ethical considerations that have evolved over the last two decades.

In order to include the broadest range of voices, perspectives, and research domains, *Internet Research Ethics for the Social Age: New Challenges, Cases, and Contexts* has three main forms of contributions: *Challenges*, *Cases*, and *Contexts*.

The opening *Challenges* section features nine chapters, each providing an in-depth discussion of new conceptual challenges faced by researchers engaging in internet and social media-based research, organized into three categories of *Conceptual Challenges*, *Data Challenges*, and *Applied Challenges*. In an attempt to highlight that many of the addressed issues are subject to ongoing, lively and often controversial discussions within various research communities and to ensure the broadest set of viewpoints, each of the ten *Challenges* is followed by a brief *reaction*. These reaction pieces were provided by leading thinkers in the field, who often looked at the issue from a complimentary – or even contrasting – point of view. The second part of the book includes ten *Cases*, brief discussions of unique social media and internet-based research projects that generated novel ethical challenges for the investigators. The final section, *Contexts*, presents five short descriptions of new research contexts that describe emerging technologies and platforms that present new ethical dilemmas for researchers.

CHALLENGES

The first of four *Conceptual Challenges* is "Recasting Justice for Internet and Online Industry Research Ethics," where Anna Lauren Hoffmann and Anne Jonas argue for a broadening of how we conceive of the principle of justice within research ethics, especially in the face of increased industry-sponsored research activities that impact vulnerable or disadvantaged user populations. The next chapter, "A Feminist Perspective on Ethical Digital Methods" by Mary Elizabeth Luka, Mélanie Millette, and Jacqueline Wallace, makes a similar demand for deriving more rigorous ethical protocols, working from feminist epistemological and methodological foundations. In the third *Conceptual Challenge*, "Sorting Things Out Ethically: Privacy as a Research Issue beyond the Individual", Tobias Matzner and Carsten

Ochs argue that, given the explosive use of "social data" within digital research, the longstanding concern over privacy within research ethics must be re-conceptualized beyond a traditional individualist notion, and recognize that privacy is inherently social, relational, and sociotechnical in the context of internet-based research. Jonathon Hutchinson, Fiona Martin, and Aim Sinpeng continue this impetus for reconceptualizing traditional research ethics in the face of new social and digital research methods and environments. Building from a case study of the communicative activities of Islamic State (IS) agents, their contribution, "Chasing ISIS: Network Power, Distributed Ethics and Responsible Social Media Research," argues that ethical review boards must move beyond purely normative approaches and embrace more procedural approaches to ethical decision-making, while also recognizing the networked and distributive nature of internet-based research environments and actors.

Three important *Data Challenges* follow, led by Rebekah Tromble and Daniela Stockmann's chapter, "Lost Umbrellas: Bias and the Right to be Forgotten in Social Media Research," which outlines how the so-called right to be forgotten creates new challenges for scholars conducting internet research, including research subjects' privacy rights if data originally made public on social media platforms is later deleted, or when consent might be withdrawn. The next chapter is "Bad Judgment, Bad Ethics? Validity in Computational Social Media," where Cornelius Puschmann argues that concerns over data quality in empirical social media research are more than just a methodological issue, but also have considerable ethical ramifications. The third *Data Challenge* comes from Katrin Weller and Katharina Kinder-Kurlanda, whose contribution, "To Share or Not To Share: Ethical Challenges in Sharing Social Media-based Research Data," reports on the ethical decision-making processes of social media researchers confronted with the question of whether – and under what conditions – to share datasets.

Finally, two *Applied Challenges* are presented. In "'We Tend to Err on the Side of Caution': Ethical Challenges Facing Canadian Research Ethics Boards When Overseeing Internet Research," Yukari Seko and Stephen Lewis report on the ethical challenges faced by Canadian ethical review boards face when reviewing internet research protocols, illuminating various gaps in both the regulatory framework and the underlying ethical assumptions that need to be addressed to ensure proper guidance is taking place. Challenges in pragmatically applying research ethics is further explored in Soraj Hongladarom's contribution, "Internet Research Ethics in a Non-Western Context," which demands increased sensitivity to cultural norms and traditions when internet-based research extends across one's local environment, and suggests that traditional ethical frameworks and guidelines must need to be flexible to adaptation when applied outside of the Western context.

CASES

The second part of the book includes ten *Cases*, brief discussions of unique social media and internet-based research projects that have generated novel ethical challenges for the investigators. In "Living Labs – An Ethical Challenge for Researchers and Platform Operators," for example, Philipp Schaer introduces the "living labs" paradigm, where industry-based researchers conduct experiments in real-world environments or systems – such as the ill-fated Facebook emotional contagion experiment – and outlines numerous ethical concerns that researchers must address in such scenarios. Another helpful case study comes from Matthew Pittman and Kim Sheehan, who discuss the growing use of crowdsourcing in scholarly research in "Ethics of Using Online Commercial Crowdsourcing Sites for Academic Research: The Case of Amazon's Mechanical Turk."

The unique case of engaging in digital ethnography within online museum communities presents numerous ethical challenges related to privacy, publicness, and consent, according to Natalia Grincheva's contribution "Museum Ethnography in the Digital Age: Ethical Considerations." This discussion of digital ethnographies is continued in "Participant Anonymity and Participant Observations: Situating the Researcher within Digital Ethnography," where James Robson engages with the ethical challenges of ensuring participant anonymity, as well as researcher integrity, in digital environments.

In "The Social Age of 'It's Not a Private Problem': Case Study of Ethical and Privacy Concerns in a Digital Ethnography of South Asian Blogs against Intimate Partner Violence," Ishani Mukherjee presents her study of blogs focusing on violence against immigrant women within the South Asian-American diaspora, revealing various ethical concerns that stem from publishing testimonies of participants within these digital spaces, which might act as identity markers and broadcast information that is private, sensitive, and controversial. Consideration of such ethical challenges with studying sensitive online communities is continued in "Studying Closed Communities On-line: Digital Methods and Ethical Considerations beyond Informed Consent and Anonymity," by Ylva Hård af Segerstad, Christine Howes, Dick Kasperowski, and Christopher Kullenberg. In their case study of closed Facebook groups for parents coping with the loss of a child, the authors point to ways of modifying our research methods when studying vulnerable communities online, including the use of various digital tools and techniques to help protect subject anonymity.

The next case, "An Ethical Inquiry into Youth Suicide Prevention Using Social Media Mining" by Amaia Eskisabel-Azpiazu, Rebeca Cerezo-Menéndez, and Daniel Gayo-Avello, discusses the increasing interest in mining social media feeds for clues about the feelings and thoughts of potentially-suicidal users, and highlights the related ethical concerns of privacy, anonymity, stalking, and the algorithmic challenges of trying to profile sensitive online activities. In "Death, Affect and the Ethical Challenges of Outing a Griefsquatter," Lisbeth Klastrup shares a unique case where, while researching Facebook memorial pages for recently deceased users, she came across an imposter creating public memorial pages for people he did not know, apparently in order to attract attention. Klastrup discusses the ethical dilemma of whether to go public with the name of this imposter, and the resulting aftermath.

Lee Humphreys, in her case on "Locating Locational Data in Mobile and Social Media," addresses how locations as immensely meaningful information are increasingly a byproduct of various interactions on the internet but are accompanied by inequalities in the ability to access and understand locational data. And in the final case, "How Does It Feel to Be Visualized?: Redistributing Ethics," David Moats and Jess Perriam delve into the world of visualizations of data on social media platforms and explain the need for distributed ethics that also consider the growing role of tools, APIs, and algorithms in the research process.

CONTEXTS

The final section of the book presents five short *Contexts*, descriptions of new research domains, technologies, and platforms that present new ethical dilemmas for researchers. Robert Douglas Ferguson reflects on the use of online health data in his ethnographic study in the contribution "Negotiating Consent, Compensation, and Privacy in Internet Research: PatientsLikeMe.com as a Case Study," and discusses issues around informed consent, compensation and privacy. In "The Ethics of Using Hacked Data: Patreon's Data Hack and Academic Data Standards," Nathaniel Poor shows the ethical dilemmas and complex decision making processes required to deal with an opportunity to used hacked data for research.

Jeff Shuter and Benjamin Burroughs, in their contribution "The Ethics of Sensory Ethnography: Virtual Reality Fieldwork in Zones of Conflict," explore the ethical issues of using virtual reality devices in ethnographic fieldwork and show how sensory ethnography may need to be redefined. In "Images of Faces Gleaned from Social Media Used as Experimental Stimuli" Patrick Sweeney raises concerns about using images of human faces downloaded from social media profiles for the use in experiments that ask participants to assess sexual orientation. He concludes that social psychologists are struggling with the blurring of what counts as private or public content on the internet. And, Martina Wengenmeir's example of "Twitter Research in the Disaster Context – Ethical Concerns for Working with Historical Datasets" shows how Twitter users may, for example, during crises such as earthquakes, publicly post messages without any consideration of privacy implications – which requires researchers to reflect on the circumstances of origination of a dataset when making decisions about how to present or clean the data.

ACKNOWLEDGEMENTS

We would like to thank our authors for their thoughtful, innovative, and stimulating contributions, revealing how varied the perspectives are from which individual researchers approach the internet and social media as an object of study. The ethical challenges you faced were often idiosyncratic, unexpected, or tricky to deal with, and the work presented here confirms your commitment to engaging in ethically-informed research. We particularly would like to thank Charles Ess and Elizabeth Buchanan for helping "set the scene" for the book, and our generous colleagues who provided short reaction pieces: your valuable insights have greatly improved the volume. We would also like to thank the editorial team at Peter Lang for their advice and excellent collaboration in getting making this book a reality. Last, but certainly not least, we thank Rebekka Kugler, our editorial assistant, who, with the help of Marcel Gehrke, did a fantastic job proofreading and formatting the manuscripts.

REFERENCES

Azua, M. (2009). *The Social Factor: Innovate, Ignite, and Win through Mass Collaboration and Social Networking*. Boston, MA: Pearson Education.

Buchanan, E. (Ed.). (2004). *Readings in virtual research ethics: Issues and controversies*. Hershey, PA: Idea Group.

Buchanan, E., & Zimmer, M. (2016). Internet research ethics (revised). In E. N. Zalta (Ed.), *The Stanford encyclopedia of philosophy* (Fall 2016 Edition). Retrieved from http://plato.stanford.edu/entries/ethics-internet-research/

Carpenter, K., & Dittrich, D. (2011). *Bridging the distance: Removing the technology buffer and seeking consistent ethical analysis in computer security research*. 1st International Digital Ethics Symposium. October 28, Chicago, IL.

Fiesler, C., Young, A., Peyton, T., Bruckman, A. S., Gray, M., Hancock, J., & Lutters, W. (2015). Ethics for studying online sociotechnical systems in a big data world. *In Proceedings of the 18th ACM Conference Companion on Computer Supported Cooperative Work & Social Computing* (pp. 289–292). New York, NY.

Goel, V. (2014, August 12). As data overflows online, researchers grapple with ethics. *The New York Times*. Retrieved from http://www.nytimes.com/2014/08/13/technology/the-boon-of-online-data-puts-social-science-in-a-quandary.html

Heider, D., & Massanari, A. L. (Eds.). (2012). *Digital ethics: Research and practice*. New York, NY: Peter Lang.

Kramer, A. D. I., Guillory, J. E., & Hancock, J. T. (2014). *Experimental evidence of massive-scale emotional contagion through social networks*. Proceedings of the National Academy of Sciences, 111(24), 8788–8790.

Markham, A., & Baym, N. (Eds.). (2008). *Internet inquiry: Conversations about method*. Los Angeles, CA: Sage Publications.

McKee, H. A., & Porter, J. E. (2009). *The ethics of Internet research: A rhetorical, case-based process*. New York, NY: Peter Lang.

Metcalf, J., & Crawford, K. (2016). Where are human subjects in Big Data research? The emerging ethics divide. *Big Data & Society*, 3(1), 1–14.

Schroeder, R. (2014). Big data and the brave new world of social media research. *Big Data & Society, 1*(2), 1–11.

Secretary's Advisory Committee on Human Research Protections (SACHRP). (2013). *Considerations and Recommendations Concerning Internet Research and Human Subjects Research Regulations, with Revisions*. SACHRP meeting March 12–13, 2013. Retrieved from http://www.hhs.gov/ohrp/sachrp/mtgings/2013%20March%20Mtg/internet_ research.pdf.

Zimmer, M. (2016, May 14). OkCupid study reveals the perils of big-data science. *Wired.com*. Retrieved May 29, 2016 from https://www.wired.com/2016/05/okcupid-study-reveals-perils-big-data-science/

Internet Research Ethics

Twenty Years Later

ELIZABETH BUCHANAN

INTRODUCTION

It has been twenty years since the seminal issue of *The Information Society* which opened the scholarly discourse on internet research ethics in an expansive way. At that time, Rob Kling commented that "research ethics are normally a specialty topic with relatively little public interest" (1996, p. 103). Little did anyone suspect that in less than twenty years, a technological revolution would occur and such platforms and tools as American Online, Facebook, Google, Twitter, and countless others would make research ethics a topic of near daily conversation. Research ethics would grow beyond a narrow consideration for predominately medical/biomedical researchers to directly include social-behavioral-educational and computational researchers; these researchers would define and engage with "research subjects" or "research participants" in novel ways. Indeed, the notion of a "research participant" itself has been redefined. And, the fields or locales of research settings moved beyond traditional field sites, physical spaces, or labs, to online spaces, virtual worlds, chat rooms, profiles, and massive open courses. In twenty years, the internet has contributed to a new paradigm in the research enterprise, contesting long-standing tenets and principles of research methods and praxis; but, has internet research changed the foundations from which considerations of traditional research ethics principles begin? Researchers have reflected and debated these questions many times and in many different ways: Is there something unique about internet research and are there new ethical standards or principles that apply?

Since that 1996 issue and its influential articles that demanded attention to such myriad issues as identification and representation of subjects and participants, informed consent, tensions and discrepancies between public and private spaces, and rights and responsibilities of researchers in online spaces, the internet research ethics landscape has grown; discrete disciplinary approaches have developed, and, so has the inter- and cross-disciplinary field of internet studies, complete with its own methods and ethics. Researchers from across the disciplines, and their research ethics boards, have debated what is "ethical" and how ethics are determined in light of new methods and new spaces. Who, or what, determines those ethics, and for whom? Along these twenty years, the role of ethics boards has been disputed, as standing definitions of core principles themselves, for example, "human subjects," or "private information" have faced multiple, and inconsistent, interpretations. In these twenty years, the research enterprise became dispersed, with more stakeholders with competing interests, and competing ethics.

There is, at least, one constant sentiment, which began in the 1996 *Information Society* papers, and continues through the chapters herein, and across internet research as a whole: Internet research complexities more often than not end with the following conclusions: "We need more ethical understanding;" "we need more ethical training;" "we need more ethics in our research;" "we need more ethics in our computing practices;" "we need to explore the ethics of [social media, big data, algorithms …]."

Are these conclusions sufficient, now that ethical controversy has become commonplace, routine, with a new case, a new dilemma, arising consistently and persistently? How many Facebook experiments, or reidentifications need to occur before researchers are able to answer with confidence "a" correct, ethical response and reaction? What has the past twenty years of internet research ethics taught the research enterprise, and how does it progress into the next decade? The past twenty years has produced countless volumes, papers, workshops, regulatory responses, and yet, researchers across disciplines continue to seek answers or remedies. Researchers borrow from different ethical frameworks to explain an issue, but still often conclude with "more exploration is needed."

To understand where internet research ethics is circa 2016, and to understand why it is so incredibly challenging to respond with certainty to the ethics of […], consider how experientially and epistemically different the internet is today. It is fundamentally different than it was in the mid-1990s when there was no Google, no Facebook, no Twitter, and there was much weaker computing and algorithmic processing, much less manipulation of data, and much less social data, and much fewer sources and consumers of "public" data. We were not in an era of ubiquitous and pervasive connectivity; there were fewer stakeholders in the fields and locales of internet research. That concept of the internet as a medium or locale was sufficient; individuals "got online," and chose the who, what, where, and when of participation. There was an active researcher role and more often than not, a clearly delineated research frame (Buchanan, 2016). Then, the operational definition of internet research was established, and suited the times:

> Internet-based research, broadly defined, is research which utilizes the Internet to collect information through an online tool, such as an online survey; studies about how people use the Internet, e.g., through collecting data and/or examining activities in or on any online environments; and/or, uses of online datasets, databases, or repositories. (Buchanan & Zimmer, 2016)

By extension, internet research ethics was deemed "the analysis of ethical issues and application of research ethics principles as they pertain to research conducted on and in the Internet" (Buchanan & Zimmer, 2016). The ethical foundation chosen early on, from the inception of "internet research ethics," was modeled after traditional principles of research ethics, namely justice, beneficence, and respect for persons (Frankel & Siang, 1999). This seemed logical, and appropriate, as these concepts were considered somewhat universal, having their origins in the Declaration of Helsinki and later the UN Declaration of Human Rights. But, Frankel and Siang pointed to areas of contestation in the applicability of the principles to internet research, and there were legitimate reasons to question this applicability, as these principles were grounded in biomedical research, and are applied to research in a very precise way in the biomedical model. Not only has their application in and to social-behavioral-educational-computational research in general been questioned, but internet research in particular pushed direct alignment and applicability even further. Obvious reasons, such as epistemological and ontological differences in the disciplines and their methods, account for some of the disagreements, but has the prevalence of these three principles clouded clarity around internet research ethics? We are, some twenty years into the field, still asking those fundamental questions about the ethical specificity of internet research.

Twenty years later, fundamental issues and questions linger, albeit in different modalities. Internet research in the late 1990s, early 2000s was dominated by online surveys, participant observations, online interviews and focus groups, great interest in newsgroups, support groups, and online communities. Researchers were actively engaging participants, observing participants, and communities; large-scale data surveillance and scraping from those communities were still a few years away. This early phase of internet research saw ethical conundrums in relation to basic research considerations: "Is this human subjects" "research," "is an avatar a human subject," "is consent needed," "is an internet message board a public space," and "is an IP address identifiable private information?" (AoIR, 2002). Researchers in this first phase of internet research would quickly see these questions as somewhat straightforward, once the era of social computing took hold, circa 2005. Social computing and social media became interchangeable with "the internet."

Looking back, the transition to the era of social was swift. Ethical reflections grounded in the 1999 internet were not necessarily fitting, but, newfound questions were already at play. The 1990s internet, now, seems immature, unsophisticated, in comparison to the intricacies and strengths of Facebook, Google, and Twitter, and the powerful analytics that drive them. The early processes for conducting and participating in research, those that required a conscious and intentional act, were changing. Analytical processes were quickly growing and expanding, becoming more dominant. Simultaneously, while individuals had greater means to create and share their data, there was also less awareness of the pervasiveness of data analytics and the omnipresent research that was underway. From cloud-based ubiquity, to mobile to wearable devices and the internet of things, the second phase of internet research ethics, the social era, would dominate, and would eventually overlap with the era of big data research, circa 2010.

As 2016 closes, the era of big data continues to push the research enterprise in pioneering ways; the rate with which knowledge production and scientific findings occur is unprecedented. Social knowledge, citizen science, crowd-based solutions, and a global knowledge enterprise characterize this time. Internet research has become so multi-faceted that a congruous definition eludes any particular discipline or methodological approach. And, as for ethics, the discourse of big data points to at least four major trends: The rise of large-scale data sets and correspondingly immense processing power available to *some* stakeholders; non-consensual or minimally-consensual access to and sharing of individual data; data misappropriation; and, different values and ideologies between and among creators, processors, distributors and consumers of data.

Not surprisingly, the regulatory arm of the research enterprise has struggled over the past twenty years, as the concept of "human subjects" merges with "data subjects." The research industry, too, looks and acts differently today than it did twenty years ago. In the United States, for example, research regulations have not kept up with the methods and stakeholders as those involved with the Facebook Contagion Study. There was no regulatory response despite the significant debates about the ethics of the methods and procedures used. But, to some researchers, there was nothing ethically dubious about the methods or procedures – they were simply a sign of the times, characteristic of big data research.

While readying themselves for the next frame of internet research, researchers across the globe face significant regulatory changes, including the ways in which ethics review and approval *is and should be* sought and obtained; fundamental definitions of privacy and identification have been, and are under revision, in the European Union's Right to Be Forgotten Act and the proposed changes to the US Common Rule.

Twenty years later, research ethics *have* become commonplace; discussions about misaligned data releases or violations of personal privacy are hardly shocking because of the degree to which we are all now data subjects, the participants in or of some social experiment. Twenty years from now, we will look back at this time of social data and big data, and think, how simple. If only respect, beneficence, and justice were so simple.

REFERENCES

Ess, C. and AoIR. (2002) Ethical decision-making and Internet research: Recommendations from the aoir ethics working committee. Retrieved from http://aoir.org/reports/ethics.pdf

Buchanan, E. (2016). Ethics in digital research. In M. Nolden, G. Rebane, & M. Schreiter (Eds.), *The handbook of social practices and digital everyday worlds* (pp. forthcoming). Springer.

Buchanan, E. A., & Zimmer, M. (2016). Internet research ethics. In E. N. Zalta (Ed.), *The Stanford encyclopedia of philosophy* (Fall 2016 Edition). Retrieved from http://plato.stanford.edu/archives/fall2016/entries/ethics-internet-research/

Frankel, M. S., & Siang, S. (1999, June 10–11). *Ethical and legal aspects of human subjects research in cyberspace.* A Report of a Workshop. Washington, DC: American Association for the Advancement of Science.

Kling, R. (1996). Letter from Rob Kling. *The Information Society, 12*(2), 103–106.

PART ONE

Challenges

CHAPTER ONE

Recasting Justice FOR Internet AND Online Industry Research Ethics

ANNA LAUREN HOFFMANN AND ANNE JONAS

INTRODUCTION

The rise of behavioral research and experimentation by online companies and, in particular, social networking sites presents new challenges for internet research ethics (IRE) today. It has also reinvigorated conversations about respect, autonomy, and consent in online research, especially as it relates to users who may not know that their data is being used for research purposes. Compared to these values, however, the value of justice for online industry research has received relatively little attention.

In this chapter, we revisit feminist and other discussions of conventional research ethics that argue for a conception of justice in research that goes beyond matters of subject selection and distribution of benefits and burdens. After doing so, we explore the implications of a more expansive notion of justice for industry researchers who have greater access to – and power to influence – the design, practices, and (often proprietary) systems of online platforms that are often hostile or violent environments for vulnerable or otherwise disadvantaged populations. As we discuss below, conditions of harassment and abuse on social networking sites systematically affect women and people of color. Consequently, these groups shoulder a greater share of the social, political, and emotional burden of online participation – the very thing that generates the sorts of data that support the efforts of industry researchers. In view of this, we argue that researchers have – specifically as a matter of research ethics – an obligation not only to avoid replicating or compounding existing injustices in their research but to foreground the needs and safety of vulnerable users and attend to those conditions and practices that give rise to injustice in the first place.

JUSTICE AND RESEARCH ETHICS

Justice occupies a precarious position in the history of research policy and ethics. In some instances, concerns of justice are explicitly detailed, as in ideals of fairness in subject recruitment and in the distribution of research's burdens and benefits. In other ways, justice seems implicit in all values relevant to research ethics, like respect for persons, informed consent, and beneficence. For example, informed consent is – in part – an expression of classical liberalism's prioritization of individual liberty and autonomy in considerations of justice. However, despite its explicit and implicit value, justice has received comparatively less explicit attention than other values, especially informed consent and beneficence. Arguably, the sub-domain of internet research ethics has inherited this relative blind spot; while justice is by no means absent in discussions of IRE, it has received considerably less attention than issues of consent, privacy, and data security.[1] Below, we briefly map this tension – between implicit and explicit considerations of justice – in both IRE and research ethics generally. Along the way, we demonstrate some of the various ideas of justice employed in research ethics conversations, and we articulate some of the challenges to these ideas advanced by critics.

Justice in a research context refers largely to social justice, that is, the articulation of fair or equitable relations between individuals and between individuals and institutions in a given society.[2] Though social justice has been articulated in different ways at different times, the term as we use it today owes its meaning to political and scholarly movements from the early and mid-20th century. In the United States context, efforts by labor unions in the 1930s brought attention to unfair and oppressive practices of employers and were influential in gaining protections and benefits for American workers (Goldfield, 1989). During the 1960s and 1970s, activist and student movements in both the United States and in other countries brought a number of social issues to the forefront of public consciousness, in particular race, gender, and poverty. For example, organizing and activism around issues of racism sought greater rights and political liberties as well as the alleviation of oppression and liberation of self-respect for marginalized racial groups (Boxill, 1992; Thomas, 1983). Parallel to these social and political developments, discussions of social justice gained increasing prominence in scholarly contexts, as exemplified by John Rawls' *A Theory of Justice* (published in 1971). Rawls' (1971) work offered "a standard whereby the distributive aspects of the basic structure of society are to be assessed" (p. 8) and has sparked decades of debate over the fair distribution of the benefits and burdens of social cooperation (see, for example: Nozick, 1974; Okin, 1989; Sen, 2009; Walzer, 1984; Young, 1990).

In United States' federal research policy, concerns over social justice are made explicit in discussions related to the selection of subjects and the distribution of the benefits and risks of research practice. The first concern – selection of subjects – represents a protective conception of justice, one that aims to shield or guard the vulnerable against the imposition of significant or undue risk (Powers, 1998, p. 151). Importantly, this conception recognizes that informed consent may not be sufficient for protecting all research subjects and, therefore, further ethical oversight is required, as through ethical review boards or other formalized processes. For these review boards, "the emphasis is on protecting those who are perceived as vulnerable to coercion or manipulation, exploitation, or deception, or persons otherwise thought to be less capable of relying on their own judgments to protect their own interests" (Powers, 1998, p. 151). The second concern – fair distribution of the benefits and burdens of research – goes beyond the protective conception of justice to also consider issues of fairness in access to research. This dimension relates to the protectionist conception through a consideration of subjects and potential beneficiaries, but goes beyond it by requiring researchers to consider future applications and benefits of the research in question. As the Belmont Report frames the connection, "research should not unduly involve persons from groups unlikely to be among the beneficiaries of subsequent applications of the research" (National Commission, 1978, p. 10).

Eventually, however, this second, distributive conception of justice in research ethics was expanded to include considerations not of protection, but of inclusion in research. In the 1980s, in particular, certain vulnerable or marginalized groups began demanding greater access to participation in research. Chief among them were gay men and other people suffering from the AIDS epidemic and seeking access to possibly beneficial clinical trials for innovative drugs and therapies (McCarthy, 1998, pp. 26–27). In addition, advocates for women's health – sparked by an increasingly visible and influential feminist movement – demanded that more women be included in the research process. Paternalistic rules preventing any woman capable of bearing children (regardless of whether or not one was pregnant) from participating in drug trials resulted in a situation where many therapies eventually approved by the Food and Drug Administration (FDA) were not adequately tested on women. Rather than protecting women's interests, women simply became "guinea pigs" not during but *after* the research and trial stages, as they were exposed to undue risk once a therapy hit the market (Merton, 1993). Against the protectionist strain of early conceptions of justice in research ethics, exclusion from research came to be seen as itself a kind of discrimination and injustice (McCarthy, 1998, p. 27). In addition, considerations of dissemination of research raise further questions of distributive justice. Availability (or unavailability) of research findings can "have significant influence on establishing future research priorities, including the development of future research questions and the populations in which they will be explored" (Kahn, Mastroianni, & Sugarman, 1998, p. 170).

This evolution points to broad and unresolved issues articulated by feminist and other scholars critical of the ways research ethics debates frame justice. In different ways, both AIDS and feminist activism demonstrated that research and researchers do not exist in a vacuum – rather, their work is embedded in (and has implications for) a larger social and political context of power and vulnerability, privilege, and oppression. But, as Susan Wolf (1999) has argued in the context of bioethics, "even when the racism, ethnocentrism, and sexism haunting key events have been acknowledged, they have usually been treated as a layer of extra insult added into [a] more fundamental harm" – an approach that fails to fully appreciate the ethical significance of difference (pp. 65–66). We submit that this is true not only of bioethical analyses, but of broader research ethics analyses generally. Following Sherwin (2005): "No sooner does the Belmont Report note that injustice affects social groups in many complicated ways than it reverts back to warning that it is easy accessibility that exposes groups (or classes) to high risk of exploitation" (p. 152). As a result, the Belmont Report reinforces the limited view that injustice in research is primarily a problem of accessibility (Sherwin, 2005, p. 152). Ultimately, this focus on issues of accessibility and selection of research subjects fails to take into account a broader range of vulnerabilities and risks associated with membership in disadvantaged groups.

At times, informed consent and respect for autonomy are invoked as a way of compensating for the shortcomings of justice's place in research ethics discussions. As Rogers and Lange (2013) note, the Belmont Report's "treatments of minority vulnerability have focused on mandating informed consent and protecting against the exploitation and over-representation of minorities in research. But precisely identifying the nature, source, and best response to minority vulnerability has been more difficult" (p. 2146). But focusing on respect and consent can ultimately prevent researchers from grappling with broader social and political implications of their research demanded by justice. In a health context, for example, "justice may require steps to eliminate the more fundamental sources of inequality that result in the inequalities in medical research" (Kahn et al., 1998, p. 158).

Moreover, subsuming some justice concerns under the umbrella of informed consent prevents research ethics from reaching beyond the narrow scope of research design and processes. As King (2005) points out, accounting for justice issues does not mean that "all concerns about consent [can] be alleviated by modifying the consent process or the interaction between institution or researcher and subject. For example, it may be necessary to improve conditions in prisons before permitting prisoners to participate in research" (p. 136). Instead of prioritizing individual autonomy, alternative approaches to justice and research ethics could position subjects' vulnerabilities as a starting – rather than stopping – point for research. Doing so allows for the recognition that individuals face distinct risks as a result of distinct features of their identities; accordingly, "research should address specific sources of vulnerability in minority populations, rather than taking the vulnerability of minority groups to be homogenous" (Rogers & Lange, 2013, p. 2144). Regardless of the approach, however, it is clear that "significantly more must be said about the risks of exploitation that are associated with membership in an oppressed social group" (Sherwin, 2005, p. 152).

NEW CHALLENGES: JUSTICE AND ONLINE INDUSTRY RESEARCH

Outstanding questions of justice and research ethics take on new urgency as online companies and platform operators – spurred by a larger "big data" movement – conduct more data-intensive and (at times) social scientific kinds of research. It also presents new problems given the particular position and nature of this kind of work. Industry research has a long history and comes in different forms – from the sorts of basic research being conducted at large industrial research labs to narrowly applied research that aims to improve or increase engagement with an existing product (boyd, 2016). In either case, researchers' work is constrained in at least some way by the companies that employ them. Even those conducting basic research with relative freedom "know that they will be rewarded for helping the company. As a result, researchers in these institutions often balance between their own scholarly interests and their desire for corporate recognition in deciding which projects to pursue" (boyd, 2016, p. 6).

As with basic research for industrial companies, social scientific and behavioral research is integral to online companies. Social networking site Twitter, online dating site OKCupid, and the data-rich transportation network company Uber all actively advertise and share parts of their research in more or less accessible ways, through blogs, informational webpages, and academic publications (OKCupid, 2016; Twitter, 2016; Uber Design, 2015). OKCupid's Christian Rudder has, in particular, been a vocal proponent of online industry research and what it can contribute to broader understandings of human sociality, through both his company's OKTrends blog and elsewhere (see: Rudder, 2014a, 2014b). Academic research is also integral to Facebook's institutional culture – the company's data science division has extensive ties to academia (Grimmelmann, 2015, p. 222; see also, Research at Facebook, 2016). As Eytan Bakshy, Dean Eckles, and Michael S. Bernstein (2014) – Facebook researchers themselves –point out, A/B tests and randomized field experiments "play a central role throughout the design and decision-making process" for many organizations (p. 1).

Online research conducted by internet companies like Facebook present new challenges to our conceptions of research ethics and, in particular, internet research ethics. As Shilton and Sayles (2016) describe our current moment: "Never before have data about human interactions been so available to researchers. Public attention to research ethics in this space has grown as reports of the amount and intensity of research using data from digital and social media platforms have appeared" (p. 1909). Research being conducted outside of academia by online platforms and internet companies is no longer limited to simple A/B testing, but "now encompasses information about how humans live, eat, sleep, consume media, move about, and behave in the seclusion of their home" (Polonetsky, Tene, & Jerome, 2015, p. 337). In addition, the lack of clear oversight mechanisms and the use of proprietary systems and algorithms in corporate settings add another layer of concern beyond the usual concerns that have come to mark discussions of IRE in the last 25 years. Moreover, recent research has suggested that there is notable disagreement between how researchers in academia and researchers in industry perceive the ethical practices of the other; academics are more likely to think ethics in industry is lacking, whereas researchers in industry are more likely to consider their ethics to be comparable to academics (Vitak, Shilton, & Ashktorab, 2016).

The now infamous Facebook emotional contagion study is perhaps the paradigmatic example of these new concerns. Published in 2014, the study reported on efforts by Facebook researchers (along with researchers from Cornell University) to better understand the possible effects the site's NewsFeed algorithm might have on users' mood or mental health (Kramer, Guillory, & Hancock, 2014). The experiment – which ran for one week in 2012 – split a small set of users into two groups. One group's NewsFeeds were tailored to show more positive posts from friends and family (that is, posts with language that was deemed to have an emotionally positive valence); the other group's feeds were tailored to show more negative posts (that is, posts with language that was deemed to have an emotionally negative valence). The researchers then measured whether or not the modified NewsFeed had an impact on the emotional valence of the posts of the research subjects. Both academics and the public forcefully questioned the ethics of an experiment designed to emotionally manipulate users without consent or post-experiment debrief (Flick, 2016; Gray, 2014; Puschmann & Bozag, 2014). Others, especially those more sympathetic with industry research, defended the study as ultimately posing little risk to subjects or even as a responsible move on Facebook's part (Meyer & Chabris, 2015; Watts, 2014).

As Mary Gray (2014) detailed during the aftermath of the study's publication, "social media platforms and the technology companies that produce our shared social playgrounds blur the boundaries between practice and research" (n.p.) in order to understand and improve the products and services they provide users. Moreover, this blurring is not incidental but often necessary, as it exposes the limits of our extant understandings, methods, and ethical frameworks. "Indeed," Gray (2014) rightly points out, "'ethical dilemmas' are often signs that our methodological techniques are stretched too thin and failing us" (n.p.). While the terrain of these new challenges is still unsettled, it is nonetheless uncontroversial to say that internet service providers are conducting research that may have ethical and political consequences for the lives and online experiences of users. And, since data frequently involves persons – either directly or indirectly – "consideration of principles related to research on human subjects may be necessary even if it is not immediately apparent how and where persons are involved in the research data" (Markham & Buchanan, 2012, p. 4). Moreover, the particularities and additional challenges of industry research and online experimentation may ultimately require a more or less radical rethinking of research ethics and oversight (Fiske & Hauser, 2014); but "although the options and the necessary procedures may differ from those seen in traditional experiments, experiments' responsibility to protect users from harm remains as strong as ever" (Felten, 2015, p. 201).

Advocates of online industry research point to the fact that online platforms – and their attendant algorithms – are already impacting users' lives on a daily basis and, consequently, it would be unethical not to research their effects. Commenting on the Facebook emotional contagion study, Duncan Watts (2014) argues that "we should insist that companies like Facebook – and governments for that matter – perform and publish research on the effects of the decisions they're already making on our behalf. Now that it's possible, it would be unethical not to" (Watts, 2014, n.p.). As boyd (2016) puts it, "Facebook algorithmically determines which content to offer to people every day. If we believe the results of this study, the ongoing psychological costs of negative content on Facebook every week prior to that one-week experiment must be more costly" (p. 9). Overly burdensome or ill-fitting ethical or legal regulation would possibly stunt this important work or, worse, drive it underground altogether (Meyer, 2014).

In addition, social networking sites are part of a broader online ecosystem of social data generation and dissemination enabled by the web – a system that some commentators and evangelists believe marks the "end of theory," as knowledge production today simply involves "[throwing] numbers into the biggest computing clusters the world has ever seen and [letting] statistical algorithms find patterns where science cannot" (Anderson, 2008, n.p.). This particular historical moment seems to demand the work and insight of industry researchers – especially in the form of data scientists – who are in the best position to deploy the tools, methods, and expertise necessary to make sense of all this data. Though claims as to the "end of theory" are ultimately misguided or shortsighted (see: Boellstorff, 2013; Bowker, 2014), the era of Big Data nonetheless "ushers in new forms of expertise and promises to render various forms of human expertise increasingly unnecessary" (Bassett, 2015, p. 549). As Robert W. Gehl (2015) sardonically summarizes, "a common refrain … is that we are in for a revolution, but only if we recognize the problem of too much data and accept the impartial findings of data science for the good of us all" (p. 420).

As Bakshy et al. (2014) describe, "the Internet industry has distinct advantages in how organizations can use experiments to make decisions: developers can introduce numerous variations on the service without substantial engineering or distribution costs, and observe how a large random sample of users (rather than a convenience sample) behave when randomly assigned to these variations" (p. 1). Moreover, these sorts of tests and experiments can have profound implications for the design and direction of a service, both now and into the future: "Some of the most effective experiments directly inform decisions to set the parameters they manipulate, but other well-designed experiments can be effective through broader, longer-term influences on beliefs of designers, developers, scientists, and managers" (Bakshy et al., 2014, p. 9). Even clear proponents recognize the unique position of power these companies are in with regard to research and the development of their platform; writing on the Facebook emotional contagion study, Meyer (2015) notes that "the company alone was in a position to … rigorously determine the mental health effects of [the] News Feed" (p. 275).

As discussed in the preceding section, however, justice in research ethics has, especially in recent decades, focused on more and more inclusive research. Consequently, claiming that conventional research ethics have always been overly protectionist and would constrain industry research in undue ways fails to recognize the value of justice for opening up new conversations about inclusion and the moral imperative of research. Simply dismissing the concerns of critics as merely reactionary and hindering responsible innovation is not a genuine representation of the landscape of research ethics discussions. Claims that academics, legislators, and the public view research and experimentation without consent as inherently dangerous and absolutely unethical are not fairly representative of broader research ethics discussions that prioritize the problem of inclusion and the social and political responsibility of researchers.

The relative underdevelopment of discussions of justice in this emerging research ethics domain is, in part, a consequence of the conceptions of justice that dominate both conventional research ethics and IRE. Though researchers at companies like Facebook need to think carefully about particular features of users' identities – gender, race, sexuality, and beyond – in study design and analysis, it is not necessarily an issue of subject recruitment. After all, these sites have a built-in pool of subjects and their data – they have, in some ways, already been "recruited" simply by agreeing to use the site. As a consequence, one of the phases of research where justice provides guidance – the recruitment of subjects – is not applicable, at least not in a conventional sense.

This is not to say, however, that these built-in subject pools do not raise other questions regarding fairness. From the Menlo Report (Homeland Security

Department, 2012) to discussions of possible consumer subjects ethics oversight mechanisms (Calo, 2013; Polonetsky et al., 2015), researchers and practitioners have highlighted the importance of avoiding discrimination and ensuring that vulnerable populations are not unfairly targeted in research. For example, while many users are simply "opted-in" as research subjects when they sign up to use a site, other users are systematically excluded from signing up for other reasons. For example, sites may be inaccessible or unusable for people with certain disabilities; "real name" policies that require people to use a legally or administratively-recognized name may prevent other vulnerable populations from joining the site, like transgender users or domestic violence survivors. In addition, as users of any given social network tend not to reflect global demographics, findings or insights from research on social media users are likely not generalizable (Hargittai, 2015).

The relevance of the second explicit concern of justice – the distribution of the burdens and benefits of research – is also tentative. If we accept the claims of the most ardent defenders of online industry research, A/B testing and online experiments are inherently good in this regard, as they help designers and developers better understand the impact of their services and make adjustments and improvements that benefit all users simultaneously. Meyer (2015) argues that this "tight fit between the population upon whom (no more than minimal) risks are imposed and the population that stands to benefit from the knowledge produced by a study" is integral to responsible innovation and part of what makes A/B tests like Facebook's emotional contagion experiment ethically permissible (p. 278). But this "tight fit" relies on a narrow conception of burden and benefit – one that minimizes the commercial and commodified aspects of research by online companies. Saying that "it is not the practitioner who engages in A/B testing but the practitioner who simply implements A who is more likely to exploit her position of power over users or employees" (Meyer, 2015, p. 279) ignores the fact that online platforms exert power and may be exploitative even if they engage in A/B testing. Online experimentation might indeed be an important marker of responsible innovation or necessary to the development of trust between users and platforms, but this does not at the same time forestall or render exploitation impossible or even unlikely. After all, responsible innovation still raises questions of whom companies should be responsible to and for what reasons. For instance, it can be argued that the very mechanisms that make online experimentation possible – impenetrable terms of service agreements, active user bases, and proprietary algorithms – alienate people from their data and online activities in ways that might best be described as "data colonialism" (Thatcher, O'Sullivan, & Mahmoudi, 2016; see also Ogden, Halford, Carr, & Earl, 2015).

But one need not accept the more forceful view of corporate data practices by corporations as wholly exploitative in order to accept that, at a minimum, the owners, developers, and researchers of online platforms are in a position of power relative to users (Proferes, 2016). This lack of power afforded users by many platforms is not only a broader political problem – it should also be viewed specifically as a problem of research ethics for those companies that build and maintain social platforms. Inversely, the affordances and features of the internet and online platforms may magnify or exacerbate the harms and injustices that some internet users face. Digital information is easily transmittable and doggedly persistent; harmful or abusive photos, records, or online exchanges may be transmitted far beyond a user's control and persist in far-flung servers or databases despite deletion elsewhere. Similarly, harmful or shaming content (like tweets or Facebook posts) may "go viral" and trigger an onslaught of harassment that is hard to escape and even harder to erase. Moreover, while these features of online communication can impact anyone, they are particularly damaging when mapped on to deeply-rooted problems of racism and sexism – in this way, the internet and online platforms not only reproduce but magnify or intensify already existing injustices.

Given the radically different experiences and vulnerabilities of different types of users – who exist at the intersections of a range of marginalized identities – online research conducted by internet services should, in order to be just, also attend to conditions of harassment, abuse, and oppression that exist on many social networking sites. In this sense, we can learn a great deal from feminist and other critics of conventional research ethics that demand greater attention not just to the ways in which we should avoid reproducing existing injustices in our research but also to alleviating the conditions that give rise to oppression and injustice in the first place. Consequently, fully understanding the value and importance of social justice in the context of online research requires going beyond conventional concerns of subject recruitment and distribution of research's burdens and benefits.

ONLINE HARASSMENT AND VULNERABLE POPULATIONS

Since online industry research resists easy capture under conventional conceptions of justice and research, it may be necessary to revisit and reassert critiques of conventional research ethics that argue for a more expansive conception of justice. We can begin this process by pointing to well-documented vulnerabilities of certain groups in online spaces and digital platforms. Legal scholar Danielle Citron (2014) has extensively detailed the widespread sexism and harassment of women, an issue that has also received coverage in mainstream publications (for example: Buni & Chemaly, 2014). Designer and engineer Alyx Baldwin (2016) has reviewed in detail the ways in which automated systems based on machine learning are encoded with racial and gender biases. Both Google and Facebook, two of the largest internet corporations, have been criticized for enforcing aforementioned "real name" policies that disproportionately targeted vulnerable populations, disabling accounts of individuals or forcing them to conform to standards that might either put them at risk for harassment and abuse or that misrepresent their identities (boyd, 2011; Haimson & Hoffmann, 2016; Hassine & Galperin, 2015).

The response to these concerns from the relevant platforms has generally been to attempt to tweak policies to minimize explicit harm, without engaging with the broader and more complex social and political dynamics that generate certain harms in the first place. Law student Kendra Albert (2016) argues that "defamation" is commonly invoked in the terms of service for online platforms as shorthand for amorphous forbidden bad speech about another person. However, truthfulness, the quality at the heart of defamation cases, is rarely what is most at stake when it comes to harmful speech acts online. Legal scholar and journalist Sarah Jeong (2015) suggests that platforms generally pay too much attention to harmful *content* in these cases, rather than considering patterns of *behavior* which might require greater attention and interaction.

Social media platforms often exacerbate these problems by relying on users to report one another, thus shifting the onus for policing behavior off of the company and onto individual users without recognition of their differential positions of power and uneven experiences of harm (Crawford & Gillespie, 2014). For example, Gamergate and related campaigns of misogynist harassment exploit site features like algorithms and reporting buttons to target specific users for repeated and sustained anti-feminist harassment (Massanari, 2017). Tinder user Addison Rose Vincent (2016), for example, describes being alerted of an inordinate number of reports and "blocks" from other Tinder users – a problem Vincent attributes to their non-normative, transfeminine genderqueer identity. In this case, Tinder's reliance on a relatively unsupervised user base to determine what counts as offensive tilts normative expectations towards the dominant group (even when that group is displaying egregious discrimination and structural violence). These examples can further be viewed as online analogs to other failures of justice where technological interventions ostensibly intended to support vulnerable groups ultimately serve to further victimize them, as when video footage from police body cameras is used as evidence against victims (most often people of color) of police brutality.

While some feminist activists have called for easier access to mechanisms of punishment via social media, others understandably remain concerned that these very "protections" will be weaponized against them. The fear that mechanisms intended to empower users will ultimately undermine or be used against vulnerable individuals takes on additional force in a broader social and political system that targets those who speak out against particular injustices and oppressions. For example, feminists of color who have critiqued racism among white feminists are often labeled in the popular press as "toxic" and "bullies" (Ross, 2014). Similarly, black faculty members have been reprimanded by their institutions for discussing structural racism (McMillan Cottom, 2013). As Tressie McMillan Cottom (2014) has argued in regards to the "trigger warnings" for material dealing with racism, sexism, and similar topics, flagging mechanisms do not support but rather prevent or actively block discussions of larger, systemic social problems. Ultimately, by shifting the responsibility for flagging and reporting onto individuals users, these mechanisms simply "rationalize away the critical canon of race, sex, gender, sexuality, colonialism, and capitalism" (McMillan Cottom, 2014, n.p.).

It is thus not enough to develop methods for flagging practices or content of concern – there must be a greater push towards shifting the underlying systems of oppression that produce inequality and systemic violence. While, as Joan Donovan (2016) argues, the coerciveness of online platforms may not be equivalent to the carceral abilities of the state, being excluded from social networks and prevented from effective online participation nonetheless has real consequences for individuals, including the potential for isolation and for one's reputation to be tarnished without recourse.

CONCLUDING REMARKS

Unlike conventional academic research that has to carefully consider the selection and recruitment of subjects, researchers working for online platforms are able to harness the massive amounts of behavioral and digital trace data produced by users to create value for site owners and develop new insights into human sociality. Without these troves of data, the unique and increasingly lauded research performed by online companies is not possible. At the same time, users' experiences on these platforms are not uniform or monolithic – for many users, these platforms are sites of (often racial or gendered) violence. These experiences are in part the result of platform norms or mechanisms that produce new opportunities for racial or gendered harm, enable new strategies or methods by which these harms may be enacted, and too often work to legitimate and reify the values and expectations of dominant or privileged groups over others. These problems of injustice and violence online must be accounted for within an internet research ethics framework if such a framework is to be politically relevant today and in the foreseeable future.

The anemic responses of online companies to the dangers faced by vulnerable subjects online have not only failed to stem problematic or violent behavior but ultimately reinforce and amplify existing hierarchies and biases. Consequently, targeted or vulnerable individuals along certain lines (for example, racial or gendered) may remove themselves from the user pool of online platforms. These groups then bear the burden of being reified into the margins through research, without benefiting from continued access to the products. While reminiscent of conventional conversations of justice and research ethics that emphasize a fair distribution of the burdens and benefits of research, it breaks from conventional discussions in its persistence.

Whereas other forms of research might need to consider justice in the selection of subjects to test an already outlined research question, online industry researchers capture the ongoing activity of users prior to inquiry. The result is an ever-present pool of captive subjects – represented by their personal and social data – that, in the meantime, are exposed to ongoing problems of harassment and abuse. Ultimately, then, realizing justice in internet and industry research ethics must go beyond issues of representation in research or selection of subjects, it must also incite broader social and political transformation.

NOTES

1. Consider, for example, recent special issues from two journals on ethics and industry research after the Facebook emotional contagion experiment controversy: *Colorado Technology Law Journal*, vol. 13, no. 2 (see: Jeans, 2015) and *Research Ethics*, vol. 12, no. 1 (see: Hunter & Evans, 2016). Both issues cover a wide-range of topics – from privacy to informed consent to autonomy – but none of them explicitly attend to matters of justice. At best, we can infer implications for justice from the few articles that discuss issues of power and control online.
2. Other forms of justice may attend to other relations (as with environmental justice, which focuses on fair or good relationships between humans and the rest of the natural world) or a specific subset of social justice issues (like criminal justice or reproductive justice).

REFERENCES

Albert, K. (2016, April). *Put down the Talismans: Abuse-handling systems, legal regimes and design*. Presented at the Theorizing the Web, New York, NY. Retrieved from http://theorizingtheweb.tumblr.com/2016/program

Anderson, C. (2008, June 23). The end of theory: The data deluge makes the scientific method obsolete. *Wired*. Retrieved from http://www.wired.com/2008/06/pb-theory/

Bakshy, E., Eckles, D., & Bernstein, M. S. (2014). Designing and deploying online field experiments. In C. Chung, A. Broder, K. Shim, & T. Suel (Eds.), *WWW'14: 23rd International World Wide Web Conference* (pp. 1–10). Seoul, KR: ACM.

Baldwin, A. (2016, April 25). The hidden dangers of AI for queer and Trans people. *Model View Culture*. Retrieved from https://modelviewculture.com/pieces/the-hidden-dangers-of-ai-for-queer-and-trans-people

Bassett, C. (2015). Plenty as a response to austerity? Big data expertise, cultures and communities. *European Journal of Cultural Studies, 18*(4–5), 548–563.

Boellstorff, T. (2013). Making big data, in theory. *First Monday, 18*(10), n.p.

Bowker, G. (2014). The theory/data thing. *International Journal of Communication, 8*, 1795–1799.

Boxill, B. (1992). Two traditions in African American political philosophy. *Philosophical Forum, 24*(1–3), 119–135.

boyd, d. (2011, August 4). *"Real names" policies are an abuse of power*. Retrieved from http://www.zephoria.org/thoughts/archives/2011/08/04/real-names.html?utm_source=feedburner&utm_medium=-feed&utm_campaign=Feed%3A+zephoria%2Fthoughts+%28apophenia%29

boyd, d. (2016). Untangling research and practice: What Facebook's "emotional contagion" study teaches us. *Research Ethics, 12*(1), 4–13.

Buni, C., & Chemaly, S. (2014, October 9). The unsafety net: How social media turned against women. *The Atlantic*. Retrieved from http://www.theatlantic.com/technology/archive/2014/10/the-unsafety-net-how-social-media-turned-against-women/381261/

Calo, R. (2013). Consumer subject review boards: A thought experiment. *Stanford Law Review, 66*, 97–102.

Citron, D. K. (2014). *Hate crimes in cyberspace*. Cambridge, MA: Harvard University Press.

Crawford, K., & Gillespie, T. (2014). What is a flag for? Social media reporting tools and the vocabulary of complaint. *New Media & Society, 18*(3), 410–428. Retrieved from http://doi.org/10.1177/1461444814543163

Donovan, J. (2016, April). *The Ferguson effect*. Presented at the Theorizing the Web, New York, NY. Retrieved from http://theorizingtheweb.tumblr.com/2016/program

Facebook. (2016). *Research at Facebook*. Retrieved from https://research.facebook.com

Felten, E. (2015). Privacy and A/B Experiments. *Colorado Technology Law Journal, 13*(2), 193–201.

Fiske, S. T., & Hauser, R. M. (2014). Protecting human research participants in the age of big data. *PNAS, 111*(38), 13675–13676.

Flick, C. (2016). Informed consent and the Facebook emotional manipulation study. *Research Ethics, 12*(1), 14–28.

Gehl, R. W. (2015). Sharing, knowledge management and big data: A partial genealogy of the data scientist. *European Journal of Cultural Studies, 18*(4–5), 413–428.

Goldfield, M. (1989). Worker insurgency, radical organization, and new deal labor legislation. *American Political Science Review, 83*(4), 1257–1282.

Gray, M. L. (2014, July 9). When science, customer service, and human subjects research collide. Now what? *Culture Digitally*. Retrieved from http://culturedigitally.org/2014/07/when-science-customer-service-and-human-subjects-research-collide-now-what/

Grimmelmann, J. (2015). The law and ethics of experiments on social media users. *Colorado Technology Law Journal, 13*(2), 219–271.

Haimson, O. L., & Hoffmann, A. L. (2016). Constructing and enforcing "authentic" identity online: Facebook, real names, and non-normative identities. *First Monday, 21*(6), n.p.

Hargittai, E. (2015). Is bigger always better? Potential biases of Big Data derived from social media data. *The Annals of the American Academy of Political and Social Science, 695*, 63–76.

Hassine, W. B., & Galperin, E. (2015, December 18). *Changes to Facebook's "real names" policy still don't fix the problem*. Retrieved from https://www.eff.org/deeplinks/2015/12/changes-facebooks-real-names-policy-still-dont-fix-problem

Homeland Security Department. (2012). *The Menlo report: Ethical principles guiding information and communication technology research*. Washington, DC: Author.

Hunter, D., & Evans, N. (2016). Facebook emotional contagion experiment controversy. *Research Ethics, 12*(1), 2–3.

Jeans, E. D. (2015). From the editor. *Colorado Technology Law Journal, 13*(2), viii–ix.

Jeong, S. (2015). *The Internet of garbage*. Jersey City, NJ: Forbes Media.
Kahn, J. P., Mastroianni, A. C., & Sugarman, J. (1998). Implementing justice in a changing research environment. In J. P. Kahn, A. C. Mastroianni, & J. Sugarman (Eds.), *Beyond Consent: Seeking Justice in Research* (pp. 166–173). Cary, NC: Oxford University Press.
King, P. A. (2005). Justice beyond Belmont. In J. F. Childress, E. M. Meslin, & H. T. Shapiro (Eds.), *Belmont revisited: Ethical principles for research with human subjects* (pp. 136–147). Washington, DC: Georgetown University Press.
Kramer, A., Guillory, J., & Hancock, J. (2014). Experimental evidence of massive-scale emotional contagion through social networks. *Proceedings of the National Academy of Sciences, 111*(24), 8788–8790.
Markham, A., & Buchanan, E. (2012). *Ethical decision-making and Internet Research Recommendations from the AoIR Ethics Working Committee (Version 2.0)*. Association of Internet Researchers. Retrieved from http://aoir.org/reports/ethics2.pdf
Massanari, A. (2017). #Gamergate and the Fappening: How Reddit's algorithm, governance, and culture support toxic technocultures. *New Media & Society, 19*(3), 329–346.
McCarthy, C. R. (1998). The evolving story of justice in federal research policy. In J. P. Kahn, A. C. Mastroianni, & J. Sugarman (Eds.), *Beyond consent: Seeking justice in research* (pp. 11–31). Cary, NC: Oxford University Press.
McMillan Cottom, T. (2013, December 3). *The discomfort zone*. Retrieved from http://www.slate.com/articles/life/counter_narrative/2013/12/minneapolis_professor_shannon_gibney_reprimanded_for_talking_about_racism.html
McMillan Cottom, T. (2014, March 5). *The trigger warned syllabus*. Retrieved from https://tressiemc.com/2014/03/05/the-trigger-warned-syllabus/
Merton, V. (1993). The exclusion of pregnant, pregnable, and once-pregnable people (a.k.a. women) from biomedical research. *American Journal of Law and Medicine, 19*, 369–451.
Meyer, M. N. (2014). Misjudgements will drive social trials undergound. *Nature, 511*, 265.
Meyer, M. N. (2015). Two cheers for corporate experimentation: The A/B illusion and the virtues of data-driven innovation. *Colorado Technology Law Journal, 13*(2), 273–332.
Meyer, M. N., & Chabris, C. F. (2015, June 19). Please, corporations, experiment on us. *The New York Times*. Retrieved from http://www.nytimes.com/2015/06/21/opinion/sunday/please-corporations-experiment-on-us.html
National Commission for the Protection of Human Subjects of Biomedical and Behavioral Research. (1978). *Belmont report: Ethical principles and guidelines for the protection of human subjects of research*. Washington, DC: United States Government Printing Office.
Nozick, R. (1974). *Anarchy, state, and Utopia*. New York, NY: Basic Books.
Ogden, J., Halford, S., Carr, L., & Earl, G. (2015). This is for everyone? Steps towards deconolonizing the web. *ACM Web Science Conference*, Oxford, UK, 2015. New York, NY: ACM.
OKCupid. (2016). *OKTrends*. Retrieved from http://oktrends.okcupid.com
Okin, S. M. (1989). *Justice, gender, and the family*. New York, NY: Basic Books.
Polonetsky, J., Tene, O., & Jerome, J. (2015). Beyond the common rule: Ethical structures for data research in non-academic settings. *Colorado Technology Law Journal, 13*(2), 333–367.
Powers, M. (1998). Theories of justice in the context of research. In J. P. Kahn, A. C. Mastroianni, & J. Sugarman (Eds.), *Beyond consent: Seeking justice in research* (pp. 147–165). Cary, NC: Oxford University Press.
Proferes, N. (2016). Web 2.0 user knowledge and the limits of individual and collective power. *First Monday, 21*(6), n.p.

Puschmann, C., & Bozag, E. (2014, June 30). *All the world's a laboratory? On Facebook's emotional contagion experiment and user rights.* Retrieved from http://www.hiig.de/en/all-the-worlds-a-laboratory-on-facebooks-emotional-contagion-experiment-and-user-rights/

Rawls, J. (1971). *A theory of justice* (Revised ed.). Cambridge, MA: Belknap Press.

Rogers, W., & Lange, M. M. (2013). Rethinking the vulnerability of minority populations in research. *American Journal of Public Health, 103*(12), 2141–2146.

Ross, T. (2014, May 30). Mikki Kendall and her online beefs with white feminists. *Vice.* Retrieved from https://www.vice.com/read/their-eyes-were-watching-twitter-0000317-v21n5

Rudder, C. (2014a). *Dataclysm: Who we are (When we think no one is looking).* New York, NY: Crown Publishing Group.

Rudder, C. (2014b, July 28). *We experiment on human beings!* Retrieved from http://blog.okcupid.com/index.php/we-experiment-on-human-beings/

Sen, A. (2009). *The idea of justice.* Cambridge, MA: Belknap Press.

Sherwin, S. (2005). Belmont revisited through a feminist lens. In J. F. Childress, E. M. Meslin, & H. T. Shapiro (Eds.), *Belmont revisited: Ethical principles for research with human subjects* (pp. 148–164). Washington, DC: Georgetown University Press.

Shilton, K., & Sayles, S. (2016). "We aren't all going to be on the same page about ethics:" Ethical practices and challenges in research on digital and social media. In T. X. Bui & R. H. Sprague (Eds.), *49th Hawaii International Conference on System Sciences (HICSS),* (pp. 1909–1918). Hawaii, HI: IEEE.

Thatcher, J., O'Sullivan, D., & Mahmoudi, D. (2016). Data colonialism through accumulation by dispossession: New metaphors for daily data. *Environment and Planning D: Society and Space, 0*(0), 1–17.

Thomas, L. (1983). Self-respect: Theory and practice. In L. Harris (Ed.), *Philosophy born of struggle: Anthology of Afro-American philosophy from 1917.* Dubuque, IA: Kendall/Hunt.

Twitter. (2016). *Research at Twitter.* Retrieved from https://engineering.twitter.com/research

Uber Design. (2015, September 23). *Field research at Uber: Observing what people would never think to tell us.* Retrieved from https://medium.com/uber-design/field-research-at-uber-297a46892843#.lw0u604wj

Vincent, A. R. (2016, March 25). Does Tinder have a transphobia Problem? *The Huffington Post.* Retrieved from http://www.huffingtonpost.com/addison-rose-vincent/does-tinder-have-a-transp_b_9528554.html

Vitak, J., Shilton, K., & Ashktorab, Z. (2016). Beyond the Belmont principles: ethical challenges, practices, and beliefs in the online data research community. In D. Gergle, M. Ringel Morris, P. Bjørn, & J. Konstan (Eds.), *CSCW'16: Proceedings of the 19th ACM Conference on Computer-Supported Cooperative Work & Social Computing* (pp. 941–953). San Francisco, CA: ACM.

Walzer, M. (1984). *Spheres of justice: A defense of pluralism and equality.* New York, NY: Basic Books.

Watts, D. J. (2014, July 7). Stop complaining about the Facebook study. It's a golden age for research. *The Guardian.* Retrieved from http://www.theguardian.com/commentisfree/2014/jul/07/facebook-study-science-experiment-research

Wolf, S. (1999). Erasing difference: race, ethnicity, and gender in bioethics. In A. Donchin & L. M. Purdy (Eds.), *Embodying bioethics: Recent feminist advances* (pp. 65–81). Lanham, MD: Rowman and Littlefield.

Young, I. M. (1990). *Justice and the politics of difference.* Princeton, NJ: Princeton University Press.

REACTION BY CÉLINE EHRWEIN NIHAN

The discussion conducted by Hoffmann and Jonas makes it clear that ethical framing of online research cannot be reduced to a strictly private matter. Neither users – who are put in a position of powerless captive subjects, nor online industries – that are caught in the defence of their market shares, nor researchers – who are trapped in loyalty conflicts and financial dependencies towards their employers – seem to be able to provide alone freely and impartially designed principles of conduct in order to ensure greater justice, and to apply them.

In this context and in the light of the challenges mentioned by the authors, it appears even more necessary not only to advocate for the development of "an internet research ethics framework" that takes into account "the injustice and violence online" and to call for a "broader social and political transformation", but to support also the strengthening of the legal framework that is supposed to regulate research work in order to achieve a better balance of powers between its different actors (users – vulnerable/dominant; researchers – academics/working for on-line platforms; online industry/public institutions; etc.) and thus combat inequalities and injustices arising therefrom.

More specifically, this might lead us, for instance, to question the relevance and legitimacy of setting up the following:

- a multi-party system (managed by online industries, users, state institutions, etc.) designed to control the content of online platforms;
- an obligation for online industries to make their research data fully and freely available to all researchers;
- an authorization and control system designed to define what kind of researches might be conducted with online data.

Céline Ehrwein Nihan, PhD, is a Professor in Ethics at the School of Management and Engineering Vaud (HEIG-VD), University of Applied Sciences and Arts Western Switzerland (HES SO).

CHAPTER TWO

A Feminist Perspective on Ethical Digital Methods

MARY ELIZABETH LUKA, MÉLANIE MILLETTE,
AND JACQUELINE WALLACE

INTRODUCTION

From big data to thick data, social media to online activism, bloggers to digital humanities, evolving digital technologies have gained prominence over the last two decades in humanities and social science research. Scholars seek to refine tools, techniques, and tactics for examining the cultural, social, economic, political, and environmental entanglements between these forms and our everyday lives (e.g. Couldry & van Dijck, 2015; Hine, 2015; Kozinets, 2010). These approaches vary widely across the field. They include the emergence of ethical review boards and concomitant requirements to share vast data sets scraped from seemingly public environments (Mauthner, 2012). The development of highly technical quantitative methods for capturing the meaning of expansive data sets and social networks is sometimes subject to questionable ethical practices rather than substantive understandings about the underpinnings of the technological systems on display (Kim, 2014; Shepherd & Landry, 2013). Fraught debates over the ethics of collecting and analyzing digital qualitative data in online spaces where questions of privacy, safety, and veracity linger (boyd & Crawford, 2012; Housley et al., 2014) find resonance in established feminist scholarly examinations of the historical binary between quantitative methods, often seen as more objective, rational, or masculine, versus qualitative methods, framed as subjective and intuitive (Haraway, 1988; Hughes & Cohen, 2010). In this chapter, we seek to problematize assumptions and trends in the context of feminist digital research, to help expand the disciplinary terrain upon which the ethics of internet studies rests. Here, a commitment to an "ethics of care" approach can help to suggest a broader range of methodological and equity concerns (Miller, Birch, Mauthner, & Jessop, 2012). This leads to the identification of overlaps and blind spots from which to articulate how a set of coherent feminist digital methods and a corollary epistemology is being developed. Echoing feminist work on materiality (Asberg, Thiele, & van der Tuin, 2015), our argument is articulated through an analysis of digital labor, which aims to incorporate "practices of care" in research and a reassertion of the importance of "situated knowledge" from a feminist perspective (Haraway, 1988; Hughes & Lury, 2013) in relation to digital sociality and lively data.

In a broader sense, our aim is to lay out the potential for more rigorous ethical protocols for feminist digital research methods as a contribution to strengthening the relevance of scholarly research to contemporary networked life. We also intend for our investigative framework to be fluid and responsive, able to accommodate iterative discoveries and explorations. The commitment to equity, however, is firm. To operationalize this work on an ongoing basis, we recognize and rely on contributions from our own international research group in the field of feminist digital research methods, as well as similar assemblages in scholarly and scholar-activist traditions.[1] The international Fembot Collective based in the United States (http://fembotcollective.org/) is one such example, as are more loosely affiliated clusters of interest such as those represented in Miller et al. (2012), in the collaborative work of Housley et al. (2014), or of Mountz et al. through practices of "slow scholarship" (2015). So is the work of professionalizing the field of digital research ethics, including that of the international Association of Internet Researchers (Markham & Buchanan, 2012).

TOWARDS AN EPISTEMOLOGY OF FEMINIST DIGITAL RESEARCH ETHICS

Traditional analogue qualitative and quantitative methods are in the midst of being transferred and transformed into digital tools, including interviews, focus groups, oral histories, participant observation, and audience research (Luka, 2014; Mahrt & Scharkow, 2013). While digital methods articles, workshops, conferences, and books are becoming more popular (e.g. Kitchin, 2014; Kozinets, 2010), there is a need to continue to critically interrogate the underlying politics and ethics of these increasingly interdisciplinary and cross-sectoral projects. In this section, we take these challenges as an opportunity to demarcate some crucial ethical dimensions of a feminist digital epistemology, addressing today's politics of access concerning research on the internet through an ethics of care, practices of care, and "lively" data. In other words, we consider the implications of embedding *ethics* mobilized in *practices* associated with triangulations of "dissonant *data*" (Vikström, 2010, p. 212). We reflect on these elements through a feminist lens, stemming from related yet distinct perspectives – including critical race, feminist, queer, trans, decolonial, and disability studies.

To undertake inclusive and reflective research, we argue that ethical concerns have to be taken into account at every stage. Mobilizing Sandra Harding's work in philosophy of science regarding gender disparities (1983), Joey Sprague (2005) distinguishes between epistemology, methodology, and methods. Epistemology "is a theory about knowledge" and observing it reveals under "what circumstances knowledge can be developed" (p. 5). Methods are techniques we design and apply "to gathering and analyzing information" (idem). Methodology is the complex process between these two stages, constituting the "researcher's choices of *how* to use these methods" (idem, italics in original). While emphasizing that our biases come into play at every stage, Harding and Sprague simultaneously note that methodology is key because it is "the terrain where philosophy and action meet. [R]eflecting on methodology … opens up possibilities and exposes choices" (2005, p. 5).

Consequently, we mobilize *ethics of care* as an epistemological framework with commitments to equity and explicate below how practices of care act as a methodology to bridge between methods and a feminist epistemology. Finally, we examine what is meant by lively data to reinforce how feminism can ethically inform big, small, and thick data in digital research.

ETHICS OF CARE AS A COMMITMENT TO EQUITY IN RESEARCH

To move towards feminist digital ethics, then, we draw attention to strengths offered by a well-established qualitative and reflexive feminist "ethics of care" (Miller et al., 2012; Mountz et al., 2015), emerging from the work of feminist psychology, sociology, and cultural studies from the 1980s onwards. Ethics of care is grounded in the ethnographic work of Carol Gilligan (1982), Norman K. Denzin (1997) and ongoing work by Angela McRobbie (2015), among others. Miller et al. (2012) recently republished a collection of essays on feminist ethics to incorporate maturing digital research. The updated essays continue to emphasize the integrated nature of an ethics of care with feminist values that include respecting diversity, understanding the intention of research as a participant and as a researcher, and paying attention to our responsibility as researchers to do no harm in the communities within which we work, even as we aim to generate potentially transformative engagements (Edwards & Mauthner, 2012). Consequently, an ethics of care is a core approach in qualitative feminist research, but also finds strong application in other settings. More recently, these include professional standards articulated by AoIR respecting quantitative *and* qualitative datasets (Markham & Buchanan,

2012), and research justice methodologies that embrace social change, thus generatively "queering" (p. 47) the research endeavor (Zeffiro & Hogan, 2015).

According to Gillies and Aldred (2012), an ethics of care is built on three separate and related epistemologies: "representing women" (p. 49) (which includes finding ways to include dominant colonial and other perspectives), "initiating personal change through action research" (p. 51), (which relates to practices of care) and "deconstructing and undermining 'knowledge' structures" (p. 55). Today, all three elements find agreement in critical work on digital labor (e.g. McRobbie, 2015), digital sociality (e.g. Cardon, 2015), and the false assumption of "neutrality," (discussed below).

Practices of Care

Practices of care in research actually articulate what we intend to embody in an ethics of care (see Hughes & Lury, 2013; Mountz et al., 2015). What we do matters, and so does what we say. Talking about patterns, reflections, and imbrications "speaks" of the "situatedness" of political and ethical positions of both the researcher and the researched (Hughes & Lury, 2013, p. 797). A useful example can be found in the increasingly iterative need to negotiate and respect *informed consent processes*. Moya Bailey (2015) and Tina Miller (2012) discuss the role of ethical review boards in North America over the last two decades, lauding the principle of ethical oversight, but cautioning researchers and ethics boards alike to pay attention, especially "in the digital landscape, [to] a more nuanced and fluid understanding of the way power flows between researcher and researched" (Bailey, 2015, para. 16). In Bailey's view, "social media users are not the traditionally infantilized research subjects that the IRB assumes" (idem, para. 17). Simultaneously, as Sanjay Sharma (2013) points out in her discussion of black Twitter:

> Modalities of race wildly proliferate in social media sites such as Facebook, YouTube and Twitter: casual racial banter, race-hate comments, "griefing", images, videos and anti-racist sentiment bewilderingly intermingle, mash-up and virally circulate; and researchers struggle to comprehend the meanings and affects of a racialized info-overload. (p. 47)

Miller (2012) also describes the delicate, sometimes-public dance that emerges from the "answering back" (p. 37) affordances of social media for participants and researchers alike, noting that a participant who blogs "is not subject to any of the [...] professional codes of ethical practice [that academics are]" (2012, pp. 36–37). This begs the question: If an understanding of the evolving power dynamics in research is neither mandatory nor surfaced during scholarly ethics reviews, and if mutual responsibility (researcher/researched) is not a foundation of ethics practices, then we may find ourselves not just complaining about the bureaucracy of such processes, but also becoming willing participants – even instigators – in reinforcing posthumanist systems of surveillance on populations we wish to support or observe.

Taking Diversity into Account: New Materialism's Implications for "Lively" Data

Moreover, Housley et al. (2014) make explicit some of the many social, political, and cultural assumptions embedded in data collection, particularly distributed data analysis. What they term the gathering of "lively data" (p. 3) – that is, the iterative collection and interpretation of "big and broad" (p. 1) digital data from social media sites over time, such as Facebook, etc. – indicates the fluid and often non-representative nature of interpretation as it is practiced by some big data researchers. Analyses of hate speech, racism, and related topics suggest that what we have so far determined is mixed evidence about whether social media can radically reshape civic society to become more equitable (idem, p. 25), or as Sharma (2013) and boyd and Crawford (2012), among others, make clear, some fairly negative evidence that social media may be implicated in quite the opposite. It is helpful, then, to consider the influence of new materialist approaches that have emerged in the last decade in tandem with digital research, and particularly those that have touched on ethical concerns emanating from feminist commitments. Asberg et al. (2015) suggest that new feminist materialisms (that is, a focus on the *posthumanist object* as an object of study) "is not a move away from but rather a renewed move towards the Subject" (p. 164). They draw on legacies of "difference" (p. 154) in feminism (including earlier work by Elizabeth Grosz and Donna Haraway) as a set of practices as well as an object of study incorporating critiques, ontologies, and linked systems of knowledge. Asberg et al. (2015) reassert the necessity of "connectivity, power-imbued co-dependencies … and other similar concepts for the formative topologies of force and power that cause us to materialise" (p. 149). Such an approach opens the door to understanding why "blind" (seemingly value-neutral) big data claims are fallacious (Kitchin, 2014), as discussed further below. Furthermore, the ethical challenges of promulgating blind data is complicated enormously in a digital research environment where big data is supported by billions of research dollars annually, predominantly in the domains of science, technology, engineering, and math (STEM).

Investigating Digital Labor: Practices of Care in the Knowledge Economy

Digital labor is a key site for the critical study of networked technologies, given that networked creative and computational practices not only alter existing forms of work but also engender new modes of labor that are often invisible or undervalued as an element of technical infrastructures (McRobbie, 2010; Wallace, 2014).

Attending to such invisible forms of labor entails understanding the persisting inequalities in gendered, raced, and classed divisions of labor that inform workplaces in a globalized knowledge economy (Bailey, 2015; Roberts, 2016). In today's convergent online media era, social (science) research is undergoing vast transformations in terms of how to study the pervasive digital labor that underpins a globalized knowledge economy. Networked technologies have engendered an "always on" work culture (Wallace, 2014) that is changing the very nature of work and its relationship to social and leisure time. Feminist scholar Tara McPherson (2009) explains how this merged work/lifestyle is deeply entangled with discourses of electronic culture, which "simultaneously embody prohibition and possibility" (p. 383). These discourses

> [let us] feel we can control our own movements and create our own spaces, shifting our roles from consumers to producers of meaning. Such moments of creation and making can be quite heady and personally powerful, but we'd do well to remember that this promise of transformation is also something the web (and electronic culture more generally) concertedly packages and sells to us. From my "personal" account on numerous web pages to my DVR to countless makeover shows on cable, electronic culture lures us in with its promises of change and personalized control.… Although transformation and mutability may be inherent in digital forms, an aspect of their *ontology*, transformation is also a compelling *ideology* that can easily stitch us back into the workings of consumer capital. (p. 383; emphasis in original)

Moreover, the ability to negotiate technological infrastructures and networks requires certain capacities and literacies that arguably replicate hegemonic structures and privileges. In turn, these structures need epistemological and methodological frameworks that pursue critical study of these new modes of labor. In the digital environment, digital research methods must also acknowledge and make space for a relationship between material and immaterial labor. Following the ethics of care model, we argue for a feminist perspective on digital labor that engages "practices of care" to shed light on inequality and reveal the *invisible* labor behind contemporary networked technologies (McRobbie, 2010; Roberts, 2016). Ensuring practices of care are built into research design from conceptualization through analysis to writing up of findings is vital to ensuring knowledge production. Such an approach goes beyond the standard scientific research model that positions the researcher as impartial authority and is conventionally predicated on a masculinist rationality and objectivity. Instead, we argue for feminist approaches that acknowledge individual standpoints, stress the importance of specificity of context, make space for negotiation and dialogue, and advocate for partial stances and situated knowledges (Edwards & Mauthner, 2012; Haraway, 1988).

Feminist practices of care ensure methods that open up critical pathways for an ethical unraveling of the power dynamics of digital labor, including making visible a bias toward youth, masculinity, and technical savvy that punctuates the celebratory "work hard, play hard" rhetoric of digital culture. The "new" economy is often celebrated for the emancipatory potential of creative work that is typically associated with digital labor. In this idealized conception of work, the independence of flexible work (e.g. freely setting one's own hours and work schedule), and the "cool-factor" of producing for such cultural sectors as gaming, design, digital journalism, social media, or tech start-ups are said to chart a more exciting, creative, and fulfilling path than traditional industries. Dubbed "no collar," and "meccas for the creative class" (Florida, 2002; Ross, 2004) these work environments claim to value freedom, fun, and equality among employees and management often depicted by the flattening of organizational structures. They also consider workers' creative capacities as a prized resource to be cultivated. However, by employing care-based practices that critically interrogate the so-called emancipatory potential of creative digital labor, we can probe the persistent inequalities that mark its underbelly. Significant is that an ethics of care enables a foregrounding of questions of gender, race, ability, sexuality, and class that are so often overlooked in methodological design, but essential to understanding the power dynamics and politics of digital labor.

These ethical considerations help to shed light on the considerable amount of unaccounted affective and immaterial labor of the digital age, including, for instance, such repetitive tasks as data entry, tagging, or keywording, or the constant work of updating web profiles, social media, and ecommerce storefronts that meld together traditionally feminine service-sector work with the continual stream of "always on" digital labor. McRobbie (1998, 2010) refers to this political-economic phenomenon as defining a precarious feminized sector. Weigel and Ahern (2013) go as far as to argue that:

> Today the economy is feminizing everyone. That is, it puts more and more people of both genders in the traditionally female position of undertaking work that traditionallypatriarchal institutions have pretended is a kind of personal service outside capital so that they do not have to pay for it. When affective relationships become part of work, we overinvest our economic life with erotic value. Hence, "passion for marketing"; hence, "Like" after "Like" button letting you volunteer your time to help Facebook sell your information to advertisers with ever greater precision.[2]

Digital Labor, Digital Dilemmas: Messiness at Work

To understand what approaches are best suited to understanding the digital labor force, given the implicit and explicit ethical considerations generated by working in precarious and increasingly transnational mobile workplaces, we must not rush to simply use the latest digital adaptation of an analogue method, but instead critically interrogate the power dynamics and technological affordances embedded in new modes of digital labor. Moreover, when seeking to uncover the practices of digital labor, rather than idealizing research design and its framework as tidy and clean, a feminist approach wrestles with the two-headed dragon of deploying digital methods to gather data while recognizing that these practices are messy, contingent, and situated.

John Law (2004) develops his notion of "messiness," as a means to seek knowledge in the social world where things are often elusive and multiple, intentionally countering a tradition of methods that seek absolute clarity and precision. He argues for "methodological assemblages" that "detect, resonate with, and amplify particular patterns of relations in the [...] fluxes of the real" (p. 14). In other words, he argues for practices of care that embody a clear ethical stance. Sawchuk (2011) takes up Law's position, reinforcing how we become a part of the processes we study. In our desire to understand contemporary cultural phenomena,

> We are constantly stopping the flow of events and activities, and as soon as we write about a subject, it already seems out of date … Law (2004) suggests that the chaotic messiness of the social world demands not just one method, but a knowledge of a set of methods [… to] allow researchers to write about their subjects intelligibly, creatively and rigorously … methods are a delightfully messy business that asks us to take pleasure in uncertainty and to confidently learn to be accountable, even if we are not revealing a truth that will hold for all people, at all times, in all places. (Sawchuk, 2011, p. 339)

This is evident, for example, in the study of DIY production cultures, which are a delightfully messy business of creativity and commerce, of ever-changing technologies and networks, of identities and standpoints, as shown in research on the cultural economy of craft, including the ascendance of Etsy and digitized marketplaces (Wallace, 2014). Such research aims to make process visible and also the people and the multiplicity of threads that bind us to one another. It is also evident in adaptations of conventionally analogue methods with digitally-enabled tools and techniques, such as digital ethnography, immersive online participant-observation, discourse analysis of social media content and data sets, blogs as a discursive tradition, hashtagged images and threads, among others. Practices of care moves well beyond quantitative capture of posts, keyword analysis, or splicing of metadata tables toward not only recording the qualitative outcomes of digital production but investigating the labor and technical affordances behind it.

Studying Online Sociality: Reflecting (on) the Human in Digital Traces

French sociologist Dominique Cardon (2015) illustrates how algorithms, which come with very powerful and prescriptive affordances, are ideologically loaded. Google's Page Rank, Facebook's Edge Rank, and other systems of reference format content and behavior, ensuring that algorithms reflect political views – mostly neoliberal, capitalist ones – governed by calculation and probability. His analysis finds agreement in political economy analyses of big data such as that of Shepherd and Landry (2013), who take up Lawrence Lessig's argument about how the values of the dominant society are reflected in the writing, sorting, and coding of data itself (p. 262). Shepherd and Landry hail "agency and the absence of restrictions" as a kind of freedom (p. 269), embedded in the modes of resistance they enumerate (e.g. hacktivism, pp. 268–270) in response to their own categorizations of oppression (pp. 260–267). Even so, the elegant simplicity of the typologies that Shepherd and Landry offer is challenged by experiences on the ground, where the participants involved may damage themselves or others, or suffer from a system of oppressions that they themselves reinforce or accept. This can be seen, for example, in the 2016 political race for the Republican leadership in the United States, where surges in Donald Trump's popularity with working and middle-class Americans both correlates and stands in opposition to what he says about racism and also with "deindustrialization and despair" (Frank, 2016).

Consequently, more equitable, and "lively" (or responsive) digital methods can be developed by opening the "black boxed" processes of data-driven research (Mansell, 2013). When it comes to sociality as an object of research, there are always two layers involved: the object of study and the researcher as interpreter. The latter includes academic, professional, and personal relationships, and, thus, includes relationships developed in the field, with interviewees, etc. In digital life, as in "real" life, we paradoxically deal with deterministic views (utopic or dystopic) about technique and its supposed neutrality: There are ongoing debates about the empowering capacities of the internet for civil society. For example, as suggested earlier, digital mediation is never neutral nor is it necessarily empowering; social media and Internet use often reproduce offline power dynamics (e.g. boyd & Crawford, 2012; Mansell, 2016; Sharma, 2013). The most recent research in this field concerns embodied bias in online sociability and algorithms, including posts and likes on Facebook, Snapchat exchanges, or "hashtag-mediated assemblages" on Twitter (Rambukkana, 2015). From an ethics of care perspective, we must keep in mind that the meaning generated by these digital traces can only be grasped if we reconnect it to its social context of production and circulation. As Rambukkana puts it, these traces:

> [...] inherit their character neither solely from the social material poured into them nor from their specific nature as technology or code alone but from the singular composition of each of their "continuous locality" (Latour, 1996, p. 6): in how they are crafted; for what purpose; among what other actants and actors, individual, technical, communal or corporate; as well as in what spaces, through what technologies; with what coverage; and finally articulated with which effects, with what temporality and through which history. (p. 5)

By making digital data lively, Rambukkana implies that the black box metaphor developed by Bruno Latour (1987) reinforces how technological devices and scientific facts are presented as autonomous, not open, and usually create the illusion of being ineluctable. Understanding how they were conceived, funded, and deployed is never a given. Twisted by the pressures of dominant ideologies, the methodology is often a part of the black box. By being explicit about our own methodology and methods, we can be open and outspoken about what there is to know about the relationship between our own epistemology and the results generated. Academic research requires us to explain how to reproduce our protocols – but this is often reduced to a limited report: number of interviews, lists of variables, perhaps time spent on the field, yet all the struggles and failures, the e-mails to manage and make sense of, and all the help we sought are not part of it. A lot of what was challenging, inexplicable, hard, or unfair, is left out. Yet these messy details quite often *shape* the research, what is kept in and left out, and what the results will and will not say.

Similarly, Miller (2012) points out the difficulty of anticipating where the research starts and ends when it comes to the "official" data covered by ethical accreditation. E-mail exchanges can become a more consistent source of information than an initial interview (the "doorknob disclosures" of digital research, p. 33), and sampling imbalances are caused by requirements for participants to self-select into a study. How many times has a researcher understood more about a social experience when an interviewee made a seemingly minor correction in an e-mail, rather than during an interview? For example, Millette (2015) faced this situation when she first contacted interviewees during her research on French-Canadian minority communities, who pointed out via e-mail that they were not sure they could call themselves "communities," preferring to talk about themselves as "francophonies" outside Quebec because of their scattered nature and very different political, historical, and cultural backgrounds. These exchanges indicated her own bias and the politics of her field, but also the need to document data collection and the iterative, often serendipitous (Verhoeven, 2016) and situated nature of data-based research. As discussed below, understanding how a social media dataset is collected, which decision-making processes are used for cleaning and processing the dataset, and where the data originated (including who has access to the platforms used and the affordances of those platforms), are all crucial considerations (Langlois, Redden, & Elmer, 2015).

Not only does the digital environment have situated and embedded power relationships but the specificity of identities matter more than ever when we conduct digital research on any aspect of social life. Massive quantitative data sets on Facebook and social media may inform us about some trends, networks, and patterns of uses. But the *meaning* of digital uses for these people will never be fully understood if we do not trace it back to the particularities of their situation. In 1988, long before big data, mobile phones, and social media, Haraway argued for a plurality of "situated knowledges" (p. 581) instead of a singular, dominant "manufactured-knowledge" (p. 577). Prefiguring the emergence of a digital feminist materialism (Asberg et al., 2015), Haraway (1988) suggested that objectivity could only exist through the embodiment of knowledge, by ensuring that those who are studied are involved in how their lives are being examined. In other words, equitable social science must emerge through dialogue and the observation of situated knowledges. For methodological design, this standpoint requires us to embody both an ethics and practices of care, putting ourselves in vulnerable and often messy positions, where each researcher looks her or his own biases in the eye. Being deeply aware of our own identity and agency is critical to being able to understand marginalized subjects without romanticizing or appropriating their experiences. These are real and present dangers, according to Haraway and others noted above. An ethical feminist methodology takes into consideration the context within which the data was created. This holds true, whether for traditional interviews or data collection with users, or for those involving digital traces where the researcher brings the data collected online to the people, who produced it, in order to trigger dialogue about the context of its creation and purpose (Dubois & Ford, 2015; Kozinets, 2010). That is not all that is required, but it is a good beginning.

CONCLUSION: AN ETHICAL ENGAGEMENT

To consolidate these three elements (ethics of care, practices of care, and the growth of lively data), it is helpful to consider what Gibson-Graham (2015) has termed an "ethical economical and ecological engagement" (p. 47). While new materialists focus on immanence, including the relationship to spirit, "language, the symbolic order and so on" (Asberg et al., 2015, p. 166), Gibson-Graham rethinks what the economics of research and value-based social engagement could mean, and how that rethink harks back to a feminist understanding of multiple and fluid identities, requiring mutual commitment and care. Gibson-Graham (2015) refers to self-positionality in the "everyday economy" as informative:

> People are involved in many other identities in excess of that of employee, business owner, consumer, property owner, and investor; that is, those associated with capitalist practice that are theorized as motivated by individual self-interest. There are, for example, volunteers who want to offer their services "free"...; workers-owner-cooperators who want to make enough returns to live a good life, sustain the cooperative, and contribute to the community; consumers who want to reduce, recycle, reuse; [and] property owners who want to care for a commons. (p. 56)

Such an approach points towards "the possibility of ethical rather than structural dynamics" (idem, p. 57), which in turn could ameliorate the tensions between demands for open data and ongoing calls to protect big data collections, and the already established pattern of parsing out high-powered computing contracts primarily to STEM projects, in corporate as well as government-funded digital research. Mauthner (2012) describes the increasing tension between maintaining confidentiality of data and the growing number of public funders with the requirement to make big data reusable and shareable (including through ethical review boards). This is problematic for sensitive or power-laden research, as well as for the development of long-term relationships with participants, communities, and organizations. Even while noting that, above all, "we do research" (p. 171), Mauthner (2012) elucidates ethical tensions:

> Digital data sharing methods are reshaping the research environment and research practices; … seeking informed consent, anonymizing data, and reusing digital data reconfigure the relationships we develop with our respondents, our moral responsibilities and commitments to respondents, [and] our moral ownership rights over the data we produce. (p. 158)

A brief survey of recent innovative feminist digital research suggests several directions for how to expand the disciplinary terrain upon which a feminist ethics of internet studies rests. These include, for example, Bivens on Facebook (2015), Harvey's work on video games (2015), Hogan's examination of data centres and digital archives (2015), and the work of Luka (2014, 2015) and Matthews and Sunderland (2013) on media-based narratives and networks. In the domain of ethnographic digital sociality and digital labor, it includes Latzko-Toth, Bonneau, and Millette (2017) on thick data, as well as Gajjala and Oh (2012), Roberts (2016), and Wallace (2014) on feminized digital labor practices.

As a starting point for developing an epistemology of feminist digital ethics, it is clear that an ethics of care, practices of care, and the situatedness of lively – rather than simply big – data, involve ongoing negotiations of power relations. Our preliminary delineation of the current field suggests how science and humanities alike gain from such perspectives in terms of inclusion and studying original knowledge from the field. In many ways, research on emerging digital technologies requires greater academic consideration of the value and, increasingly, necessity of ongoing collaborative engagements with community, business, non-profit, activist, artistic, and other public partners (Luka, 2014; Wallace, 2014; Zeffiro & Hogan, 2015). This aligns with our own commitments to social and epistemic well-being enabled by networked digital technologies. By working together on a feminist epistemological and methodological foundation for such research, we aim in turn to provide new means for civil society, government, and industry to benefit from scholarly research. In this sense, then, the chapter has aimed to elucidate underlying ethical opportunities and challenges in collaborative projects, including those with non-academic partners, including industry, community, governmental, NGO, activist, artist, and other institutions. A consideration of feminist perspectives in the context of digital methods to address social phenomena and labor practices does not only help to frame a feminist epistemology that can incorporate considerations of race, gender, queer, trans, decolonial, and disability studies. It also enables us all to move towards a more ethical, reflexive, and situated way to carry out research on contemporary digital life.

NOTES

1. Other than the authors, our research group includes: Rena Bivens, Alison Harvey, Mél Hogan, Jessalyn Keller, Koen Leurs, Joanna Redden, Sarah Roberts, Tamara Shepherd, Samantha Thrift, Andrea Zeffiro.
2. The New Inquiry: http://thenewinquiry.com/essays/further-materials-toward-a-theory-of-the-man-child/ (accessed August 1, 2013)

REFERENCES

Asberg, C., Thiele, K., & van der Tuin, I. (2015). Speculative before the turn: Reintroducing feminist materialist performativity. *Cultural Studies Review, 21*(2), 145–172. Retrieved from http://dx.doi.org/10.5130/csr.v21i2.4324

Bailey, M. (2015). #transform(ing)DH writing and research: An autoethnography of digital humanities and feminist ethics. *Digital Humanities Quarterly, 9*(2), n.p. Retrieved from http://www.digitalhumanities.org/dhq/vol/9/2/000209/000209.html

Bivens, R. (2015). Under the hood: The software in your feminist approach. *Feminist Media Studies, 15*(4), 714–717. doi:10.1080/14680777.2015.1053717.

boyd, d., & Crawford, K. (2012). Critical questions for big data. *Information, Communication & Society, 15*(5), 662679. Retrieved from http://doi.org/10.1080/1369118X.2012.678878

Cardon, D. (2015). À quoi rêve les algorithmes? Nos vies à l'heure des *big data.* Paris: Seuil.

Couldry, N., & van Dijck, J. (2015). Researching social media as if the social mattered. *Social Media & Society, 1*(7), 1–7. doi:10.1177/2056305115604174.

Denzin, N. K. (1997). *Interpretive ethnography: Ethnographic practices for the 21st century.* Thousand Oaks, CA: Sage Publications.

Dubois, E., & Ford, H. (2015). Qualitative political communication. Trace interviews: An actor-centered approach. *International Journal of Communication, 9*(0), 2067–2091.

Edwards, R., & Mauthner, M. (2012). Ethics and feminist research: Theory and practice. In T. Miller, M. Birch, M. Mauthner, & J. Jessop (Eds.), *Ethics in qualitative research* (2nd ed., pp. 14–28). Thousand Oaks, CA: Sage Publications.

Florida, R. (2002). *The rise of the creative class and how it's transforming work, leisure, community and everyday life.* New York, NY: Basic Books.

Frank, T. (2016, March 8). Millions of ordinary Americans support Donald Trump. *The Guardian.* Retrieved from http://www.theguardian.com/commentisfree/2016/mar/07/donald-trump-why-americans-support

Gajjala, R., & Oh, Y. J. (Eds.). (2012). *Cyberfeminism 2.0.* New York, NY: Peter Lang.

Gibson-Graham, J. K. (2015). Ethical economic and ecological engagements in real(ity) time: Experiments with living differently in the anthropocene. *Conjunctions: Transdisciplinary Journal of Cultural Participation, 2*(1), 47–71. Retrieved from http://www.conjunctions-tjcp.com/article/view/22270

Gillies, V., & Aldred, P. (2012). The ethics of intention: research as a political tool. In T. Miller, M. Birch, M. Mauthner, & J. Jessop (Eds.), *Ethics in qualitative research* (2nd ed., pp. 43–60). Thousand Oaks, CA: Sage Publications.

Gilligan, C. (1982). *In a different voice*. Boston, MA: Harvard University Press.

Haraway, D. (1988). Situated knowledges: The Science question in feminism and the privilege of partial perspective. *Feminist Studies, 14*(3), 575–599. Retrieved from http://doi.org/10.2307/3178066

Harding, S. (1983). Why has the sex/gender system become visible only now? In S. Harding & M. B. Hintikka (Eds.), *Discovering reality: Feminist perspectives on epistemology, metaphysics, methodology, and philosophy of science* (pp. 311–324). Dordrecht: D. Reidel Publishing Company.

Harvey, A. (2015). *Gender, age, and digital games in the domestic context*. New York, NY: Routledge.

Hine, C. (2015). *Ethnography for the Internet: Embedded, embodied and everyday*. London & New York, NY: Bloomsbury Academic.

Hogan, M. (2015). Water woes & data flows: The Utah Data Center. *Big Data and Society, 2*(2), 1–12. Retrieved from http://dx.doi.org/10.1177/2053951715592429

Housley, W., Procter, R., Edwards, A., Burnap, P., Williams, M., Sloan, … Greenhill, A. (2014). Big and broad social data and the sociological imagination: A collaborative response. *Big Data and Society, 1*(2), 1–15. Retrieved from http://dx.doi.org/10.1177/2053951714545135

Hughes, C., & Cohen, R. L. (2010). Feminists really do count: The complexity of feminist methodologies. *International Journal of Social Research Methodology, 13*(3), 189196. Retrieved from http://doi.org/10.1080/13645579.2010.482249

Hughes, C., & Lury, C. (2013). Re-turning feminist methodologies: From a social to an ecological epistemology. *Gender and Education, 26*(6), 786–799. Retrieved from http://dx.doi.org/10.1080/09540253.2013.829910

Kim, D. (2014). Social media and academic surveillance: The ethics of digital bodies. *Model View Culture*. Retrieved from https://modelviewculture.com/pieces/social-media-and-academic-surveillance-the-ethics-of-digital-bodies

Kitchin, R. (2014). Big Data, new epistemologies and paradigm shifts. *Big Data & Society, 1*(1), 1–12. Retrieved from http://doi.org/10.1177/2053951714528481

Kozinets, R. (2010). *Netnography: Doing ethnographic research online*. London: Sage Publications.

Langlois, G., Redden, J., & Elmer, G. (2015). *Compromised data: From social media to big data*. New York, NY: Bloomsbury.

Latour, B. (1987). *Science in action: How to follow scientists and engineers through society*. Cambridge, MA: Harvard University Press.

Latour, B. (1996). On actor-network theory. A few clarifications plus more than a few complications. *Soziale Welt, 47*, 369–381.

Latzko-Toth, G., Bonneau, C., & Millette, M. (2017). Small data, thick data: Thickening strategies for trace-based social media research. In A. Quan-Haase & L. Sloan (Eds.), *SAGE handbook of social media research methods* (pp. 199–213). Thousand Oaks, CA: Sage Publications.

Law, J. (2004). *After method: Mess in social science research*. New York, NY: Routledge.

Luka, M. E. (2014). The promise of crowdfunding in documentary filmmaking and audience development. In R. DeFillipi & P. Wikstrom (Eds.), *International perspectives on business innovation and disruption in the creative industries: Film, video, photography* (pp. 149–176). Northampton, MA & Cheltenham: Edward Elgar Publishing.

Luka, M. E. (2015). CBC ArtSpots and the activation of creative citizenship. In M. Mayer, M. Banks, & B. Conor (Eds.), *Production studies, Volume II* (pp. 164–172). New York, NY: Routledge.

Mahrt, M., & Scharkow, M. (2013). The value of big data in digital media research. *Journal of Broadcasting & Electronic Media, 57*(1), 20–33. doi:10.1080/08838151.2012.761700.

Mansell, R. (2013). Employing digital crowdsourced information resources: Managing the emerging information commons. *International Journal of the Commons, 7*(2), 255–277.

Mansell, R. (2016). Power, hierarchy and the internet: Why the internet empowers and disempowers. *Global Studies Journal, 9*(2), 19–25. Retrieved from http://gsj.cgpublisher.com/

Markham, A., & Buchanan, E. (2012). *Ethical decision-making and Internet research. Recommendations from the AoIR Ethics Working Committee (Version 2.0).* Retrieved from http://aoir.org/reports/ethics2.pdf

Matthews, N., & Sunderland, N. (2013). Digital life story narratives as data for policy makers and practitioners: Thinking through methodologies for large-scale multimedia qualitative datasets. *Journal of Broadcasting and Electronic Media, 57*(1), 97–114. doi:10.1080/08838151.2012.761706.

Mauthner, M. (2012). Accounting for our part of the entangled webs we weave: Ethical and moral issues in digital data sharing. In T. Miller, M. Birch, M. Mauthner, & J. Jessop (Eds.), *Ethics in qualitative research* (2nd ed., pp. 157–175). Thousand Oaks, CA: Sage Publications.

McPherson, T. (2009). Response: "Resisting" the Utopic-Dystopic Binary. In Blair, K., Gajjala, R. and C. Tulley (eds.) *Webbing Cyberfeminist Practice: Communities, Pedagogies and Social Action.* Cresskill, NJ: Hampton Press Inc. 379–384.

McRobbie, A. (1998). *British fashion design: Rag trade or image industry?* New York, NY: Routledge.

McRobbie, A. (2010). Reflections on feminism, immaterial labor and post-Fordist regimes. *New Formations, 17*, 60–76.

McRobbie, A. (2015). Notes on the perfect. *Australian Feminist Studies, 30*(83), 1–20. doi:10.1080/08164649.2015.1011485.

Miller, T. (2012). Reconfiguring research relationships: Regulation, new technologies & doing ethical research. In T. Miller, M. Birch, M. Mauthner, & J. Jessop (Eds.), *Ethics in qualitative research* (2nd ed., pp. 29–42). Thousand Oaks, CA: Sage Publications.

Miller, T., Birch, M., Mauthner, M., & Jessop, J. (Eds.). (2012). *Ethics in qualitative research* (2nd ed.). Thousand Oaks, CA: Sage Publications.

Millette, M. (2015). *L'usage des médias sociaux dans les luttes pour la visibilité: le cas des minorités francophones au Canada anglais* (Doctoral dissertation). Université du Québec à Montréal, Montreal, Canada.

Mountz, A., Bonds, A., Mansfield, B., Loyd, J., Hyndman, J., Walton-Roberts, M., … Curran, W. (2015). For slow scholarship: A feminist politics of resistance through collective action in the neoliberal university. *ACME: An International E-Journal for Critical Geographies, 14*(4), 1235–1259. Retrieved from http://ojs.unbc.ca/index.php/acme/article/view/1058

Rambukkana, N. (2015). *Hashtag publics. The power and politics of discursive networks.* New York, NY: Peter Lang.

Roberts, S. T. (2016). Commercial content moderation: Digital laborers' dirty work. In S. U. Noble & B. Tynes (Eds.), *Intersectional Internet: Race, sex, class and culture online* (pp. 147–159). New York, NY: Peter Lang.

Ross, A. (2004). The golden children of razorfish. In *No-collar: The humane workplace and its hidden costs* (pp. 55–86). Philadelphia, PA: Temple University Press.

Sawchuk, K. (2011). Thinking about methods. In W. Straw, S. Gabriele, & I. Wagman (Eds.), *Intersections of media and communications: Concepts, contexts and critical frameworks* (pp. 333–350). Toronto, ON: Emond Montgomery.

Sharma, S. (2013). Black Twitter?: Racial hashtags, networks and contagion. *New formations: A Journal of Culture/Theory/Politics, 78*, 46–64. doi:10.1353/nfm.2013.0006.

Shepherd, T., & Landry, N. (2013). Technology design and power: Freedom and control in communication networks. *International Journal of Media & Cultural Politics, 9*(3), 259–275. Retrieved from http://dx.doi.org/10.1386/macp.9.3.259_1

Sprague, J. (2005). *Feminist methodologies for critical researchers: Bridging differences*. Oxford: Rowman Altamira.

Verhoeven, D. (2016). As luck would have it: Serendipity and solace in digital research infrastructure. *Feminist Media Histories, 2*(1), 7–28. doi:10.1525/fmh.2016.2.1.7.

Vikström, L. (2010). Identifying dissonant and complementary data on women through the triangulation of historical sources. *International Journal of Social Research Methodology, 13*(3), 211–221. doi:10.1080/13645579.2010.482257.

Wallace, J. (2014). *Handmade 2.0: Women, DIY networks and the cultural economy of craft* (Doctoral dissertation). Concordia University, Montreal, Canada.

Weigel, M., & Ahern, M. (2013). Further materials toward a theory of the man-child. *The New Inquiry*. Retrieved from http://thenewinquiry.com/essays/further-materials-toward-a-theory-of-the-man-child/

Zeffiro, A., & Hogan, M. (2015). Queered by the archives: No more potlucks and the activist potential of archival theory. In A. J. Jolivétte (Ed.), *Research justice: Methodologies for social change* (pp. 43–55). Bristol: Policy Press.

REACTION BY ANNETTE N. MARKHAM

The authors of *A Feminist Perspective on Ethical Digital Methods* articulate nicely how feminist epistemologies exemplify an ethic of care. The examples in this piece contribute nuance to how ethics are (and can be) enacted by social researchers looking at digital media. Taking ethics to the level of practice, the authors emphasize the importance of situated knowledge (à la Donna Haraway) as a foundation for building "methods that open up critical pathways for an ethical unraveling of the power dynamics of digital labor" (p. 9 draft). From my perspective on internet research ethics, this begins with a bottom-up and context-sensitive rather than top-down approach to decision making throughout all stages of research. Below, I augment the points made in this chapter by mentioning two closely aligned frameworks I've developed in the past few years: ethics as method and ethics as impact.

A method- or practice-centered approach to ethics in researching digitally-saturated social contexts (Markham, 2003, 2005a) highlights the epistemological and political privilege of the researcher to make decisions on behalf of other actors in the context of study (Markham, 2005b) as well as the dangers of relying on inflexible disciplinary approaches. A methods-centered approach to ethics allows the researcher to notice and then reflect on critical junctures or decision points rather than the overall conceptual approach to method. Focused reflexivity is strongly associated with consciousness raising, which is one of many ways to bring integrity to the surface for introspection and scrutiny. One of the results of such reflexive practice is to make more transparent the ways in which modernist legacies for conduct and evaluation of scholarship tend to "flatten, depoliticize, and individualize our research" (Fine & Gorden, 1992, p. 14). Reflexivity facilitates mindfulness "from start to finish. By mindful, I mean present, prepared, honest, reflexive, and adaptable" (Markham, 2003, p. 52). Whether or not this means we focus on issues of labor or questions of what counts as data, a mindful attitude is one that is more readily able to flexibly adapt to the situation, to let both the research question and the larger cultural questions help determine the approach, rather than the discipline, method, or norm. The challenge, I have long argued, is one of recognizing, resisting, and then reframing the situation of inquiry to better match the goals underlying an ethic of care.

To the end of reframing how we might operationalize an "ethics as choices at critical junctures" approach, I have begun to develop a framework that shifts our basic vocabulary from ethics to impact, so that we can take a more future-oriented, speculative perspective, on the various ways in which our everyday research, as well as the outcomes our studies, have impact (Markham, 2015). Adding temporality to the ethic of care, we can begin to experiment with various "what if" scenarios. These speculative fabulations, in the way Haraway (2007) discusses, eventually allow us to move beyond critical description of "what is" to the critical interventionist ethic of analyzing multiple possibilities for what we might become.

REFERENCES

Fine, M., & Gorden, M. (1992). Feminist transformations of/despite psychology. In M. Fine (Ed.), *Disruptive voices: The possibilities of feminist research* (pp. 1–25). Ann Arbor, MI: University of Michigan Press.

Haraway, D. (2007). *Speculative fabulations for technoculture's generations: Taking care of unexpected country*. Catalog of the ARTIUM Exhibition of Patricia Piccinini's Art, Vitoria-Gasteiz (Spain), pp. 100–107.

Markham, A. (2003). Critical junctures and ethical choices in internet ethnography. In M. Thorseth (Ed.), *Applied ethics in internet research* (pp. 51–63). Trondheim: NTNU University Press.

Markham, A. (2005a). Ethic as method, method as ethic. *Journal of Information Ethics*, 15(2), 37–54.

Markham, A. (2005b). The politics, ethics, and methods of representation in online ethnography. In N. Denzin & Y. Lincoln (Eds.). *The SAGE handbook of qualitative research* (3rd ed., pp. 793–820). Thousand Oaks, CA: Sage.

Markham, A. (2015). Assessing the creepy factor: Shifting from regulatory ethics models to more proactive approaches to 'doing the right thing' in technology research. Colloquium lecture given at Microsoft Research New England, May 8, 2015, Boston, MA. Video available online at: https://www.microsoft.com/en-us/research/video/assessing-the-creepy-factor-shifting-from-regulatory-ethics-models-to-more-proactive-approaches-to-doing-the-right-thing-in-technology-research/

***Annette Markham** is Professor of Information Studies at Aarhus University, Denmark & Affiliate Professor of Digital Ethics in the School of Communication at Loyola University, Chicago. She researches how identity, relationships, and cultural formations are constructed in and influenced by digitally saturated socio-technical contexts.*

CHAPTER THREE

Sorting Things Out Ethically

Privacy as a Research Issue beyond the Individual

TOBIAS MATZNER AND CARSTEN OCHS

INTRODUCTION

Manifold approaches within the academic social sciences aim at raising the treasure of "social data" generated on the internet for the purpose of enhancing social knowledge. E.g. Bruno Latour (2007) notes that thanks to the internet:

> [t]he precise forces that mould our subjectivities and the precise characters that furnish our imaginations are all open to inquiries by the social sciences. It is as if the inner workings of private worlds have been pried open because their inputs and outputs have become thoroughly traceable. (p. 2)

However, while some researchers have dealt with the problematics that come with this new potential to force open the "inner workings of private worlds" (boyd, 2010; boyd & Crawford, 2011; Heesen & Matzner, 2015; Ochs, 2015a) most undertakings are rather focused on analyzing and tapping the potential that is created by digitally networked interactions, and the traces they leave (Manovich, 2012; Rogers, 2014; Venturini, 2012; Venturini & Latour, 2009). This article aims to contribute to theoretically characterize the comparatively novel sociotechnical situation by asking for ethical problematics that threaten to arise from a non-reflexive application of the methods in question. More precisely, we will analyze the ethical challenges that these developments bring about for the modern social ordering mechanism called *privacy*. How to relate to "privacy" in research environments harnessing digital methods? Why are there privacy-related ethical questions to be posed, and how so?

To approach these issues our starting point will be an assessment of the role privacy plays for *processes of subject formation*. The first step of our argument (Section "Privacy as Individual Control: The Bourgeois Legacy of Privacy Discourse") will be decidedly sociological in that it specifies (roughly) the entwined social history of privacy and subjectivity from the 18th century onwards. The role of privacy in bourgeois practices of subject formation is to protect the subject from revelation of her innermost personal individuality. Such protection is based on historically quite specific, thoroughly individualistic ideas of subjective personality (having an essential core), but also of data (having a representational character), and privacy (protecting from revelation via individual retreat and/or control). In a second step we will show how the current sociotechnical situation renders increasingly difficult the practicing of a bourgeois subject, who as an individual retreats form the social or controls "his" information (Section "Why Individualistic Privacy Discourse Fails to Match Current Practices"). The third step of the analysis will be more conceptually minded and designate the outlines of the novel problem space as constituted by current sociotechnical practices: We will argue that, while novel problems tend to exceed the individual dimension and transgress well-known privacy practices, such as individual control, informed consent, de-/re-anonymization etc., the latter concepts still retain elements of a bourgeois notion of individuality. As current practices entail novel notions of personality (being performed in sociotechnical *relations*), data (*enacting* subjects rather than representing some "truth" about them), and privacy (fostering subject *performance* rather than revelation) they at the same time effectively shift the very basis for ethical considerations (Section "Post-Individualist Privacy in Internet Research: Data Enacting Subjects"). This shift results in a number of novel ethical orientations internet research is bound to consider, which we will specify in the conclusion (Section "Conclusion: Novel Ethical Orientations for Internet Research"). Our critique of an overly individualist notion of privacy thus does not merely aim at emphasizing the social value of privacy (Regan, 1995) but at the inherently social character of the individual value of privacy – with internet research being bound to take this into consideration.

PRIVACY AS INDIVIDUAL CONTROL: THE BOURGEOIS LEGACY OF PRIVACY DISCOURSE

Privacy is one half of the public/private distinction, and the practicing of this distinction goes back as far as to the city state of Ancient Greece (e.g. Arendt, 1958). The distinction belongs to the "fundamental ordering categories in everyday life" (Bailey, 2000, p. 384) structuring social aggregates of various kinds. Privacy is not only multidimensional and extremely scalable, in that it may be applied to diverse phenomena from individual minds to social spheres; it also covers the whole of

Euro-American cultural history from antique to contemporary social formations. Still, though, while social and cultural history lays quite some stress on the role of public/private occurring in the form of *oikos/polis* in Ancient Greece (Veyne, 1989), there is only little research on the status and practice of the distinction between, say, privacy in the years 600 and 1600 (an exception is Duby, 1990). Moreover, influential socio-historical reconstructions, such as Elias' (1969) work on the "civilizing process", at least implicitly suggest that the distinction for a while was of minor relevance before starting to reemerge around 1600 when multiple processes of social differentiation took off, and shifted ever more aspects of human bodies and bodily functions to some unobservable "private realm" (Elias, 1969).

We will consider privacy's genealogy here only, roughly, from the 18th century onwards, i.e. historical starting point of our reconstruction is the advent of the *Bürgertum*. The bourgeoisie interests us predominantly as a fraction of modern society that manages to distribute its own idea of *subjectivity* up to a point where it becomes the dominant subject culture. The reason for setting out from this observation is that the particular understanding of privacy coined at that time still haunts today's discourses with fresh notions appropriate for current sociotechnical conditions only having begun to develop recently. In this spirit, we follow Reckwitz (2006, p. 34) in also conceiving of subjectivity as a historically contingent product of symbolic regimes. The latter contain "subject codes" (Reckwitz, 2006, p. 42) materially and semiotically performed in the course of everyday practices.

According to Reckwitz, around the 18th century bourgeois culture, including its subject code, became dominant in European societies, and it remained so until the beginning of the 20th century (Reckwitz, 2006, p. 75) followed by firstly, post-bourgeois organized modernity's employee culture and later on by Postmodernity's "creative class." Bourgeois culture may be understood as a cultural training program, cultivating subjects who feature three characteristics: autonomy, inwardness, and morality. These characteristics are to be attained, amongst others, by making extensive use of "technologies of the self" (Reckwitz, 2006, p. 58), i.e. script-based and printed media technologies, such as letters, diaries, and novels – leading to the creation of "inward-oriented" subjects (Reckwitz, 2006). The triad autonomy/inwardness/morality and its relationship to media technologies is also highlighted by Habermas (1991) who believes that the practices in question make subjectivity "the innermost core of the private" (p. 49). In sum, the form of privacy occurring here is thus to a certain extent the contingent outcome of a culturally specific style of using media technologies, a style that is part of a more encompassing subject culture. The latter manages to establish its own blueprint of subjectivity as societal role model: Humans in general are considered to feature the threefold bourgeois characteristics noted above, which is why there is an implicit normative claim directed at everyone to feature these traits (Habermas, 1991). Quite obviously, privacy discourse is massively influenced by such ideas. E.g. Warren and Brandeis

(1890) state at the outset: "That the individual shall have full protection in person and property is a principle as old as the common law" (p. 193), and they explicitly argue to extend this protection to "products and processes of the mind" (p. 194).

What is striking is that the reproduction of basic elements of this bourgeois interlocking of subject formation mode and privacy notion stretches into post-bourgeois historic phases, i.e. into an era in which, according to Reckwitz, (2006), bourgeois culture has already ceased to provide the dominant subjectification mode. While organized modernity's "employee culture" gains dominance in 1920, it is the creative class of post-modern culture that provides the blueprint for subject formation from the 1970s onwards (Reckwitz, 2006). However, if we turn to Westin's privacy theory, we see how basic features of bourgeois subjectivity still inform privacy theory in the late 1960s. For Westin (1967), perfect privacy is achieved in the seemingly non-social situation of solitude, and as far as the secluded individual is concerned Westin holds that "In solitude he will be especially subject to that familiar dialogue with the mind or conscience" (p. 31). Privacy-as-retreat thus allows the individual to constitute inwardness, which in turn enables individualized actors to develop autonomy, "The most serious threat to the individual's autonomy is the possibility that someone may penetrate the inner zone and learn his ultimate secrets, either by physical or psychological means" (p. 33). While having achieved autonomy via privacy, the individual is called upon to govern itself by becoming a moral human being, "The evaluative function of privacy also has a major moral dimension – the exercise of conscience by which the individual 'reposseses himself.' (…) it is primarily in periods of privacy that [people] take a moral inventory" (p. 37).

Thus, there is far-reaching congruity of bourgeois subject culture on the one hand, and privacy discourse on the other. In bourgeois culture, privacy seems to concern the essential core of the subject, the "inner zone" of her subjective personality. The latter may be threatened if the outside world learns about the subject's "ultimate secrets", hence data about the essential personal core are conceived as representational. The role of privacy, then, is to protect the *representational data* speaking the truth about subjects' *essential personal core* from *revelation*; as there is a constant threat of revelation, subjects protect themselves by way of retreating from the social (Sennett, 1992), or by way of controlling personal information. In this respect, Westin's famous nutshell definition of privacy as "the claim of individuals, groups or institutions to determine for themselves when, how, and to what extent information about them is communicated to others" (Westin, 1967, p. 7) is prototypical for theoretical (e.g. Rössler, 2004 defines individual control over information as one dimension of privacy) as well as juridical definitions of privacy (e.g. the German Federal Constitutional Court's "Census Ruling" in which the judges specified the *Right to Informational Self-Determination* as individual right to determine who knows what about oneself on what occasion).

It is therefore only consistent that influential scholars have characterized privacy as bourgeois and individualistic a concept (Bennett, 2011). Now, is there anything wrong with such an individualism?

WHY INDIVIDUALISTIC PRIVACY DISCOURSE FAILS TO MATCH CURRENT PRACTICES

In this section we will render plausible the claim that individualistic privacy notions are inadequate to grasp current practices of digital networking. To illustrate our claim, we will draw on two types of sociotechnical practices.[1]

The first set of practices, that we will deal with here is the one constituting subjectivities in *Online Social Networks* (OSN). Considering the wide distribution and central role of these practices for subject formation (Paulitz & Carstensen, 2014) they can be deemed paradigmatic when focusing on what Reckwitz (2006) in the style of Foucault calls "technologies of the self" (p. 58), i.e. media technologies used to constitute the subjectivity of the self. As was explained above, the bourgeois ideal type of the subject withdraws at times from company, to generate and consume script-based media. It is especially novels being read and discussed in the "world of letters" (Habermas, 1991, p. 51) that they make use of so as to constitute themselves as subjects: *collectively developed practices*, however, practices that can be, and are, performed in solitude. This use of media technologies features two traits: The quiet reading of literary products creates a self-referential modern subject, and thus the inner core of subjective personality (Reckwitz, 2006, p. 58); and the semantics of these media are deeply moral (Reckwitz, 2006, p. 67). Thus, if the paradigmatic media practice of the bourgeois subject is the reading of moral content in privacy-as-isolation, this situation at once allows subjects to be trained in autonomy (temporary cutting off of social relations, and emotional release from the burden of playing social roles (Westin, 1967, pp. 34–35)), inwardness (quietly reading in seclusion, a dialogue only with oneself), and morality (consuming the semantics of morally uplifting writings).

Now, if the "writing culture" of the 18th/19th century is paradigmatic for the constitution of the bourgeois subject, today it is rather OSNs, digitally networked sociality *par excellence*, that may count as a media practice central for subject constitution. And obviously the conditions for constituting subjectivity in OSNs are thoroughly different to those of bourgeois media practice. Right from the outset, current subjectivity does not require a retreat from the social but its complete opposite: *social networking* by digital means. As a result, the constitution of the subjectivity at hand is not based on self-referential inwardness, but on other-referential expressiveness. It is only consistent, then, that also the basis of autonomy is affected by this shift:

> Increasingly, social networking is becoming the condition through which to pursue individual goals, by connecting people with the resources (information, other people, opportunities, etc.) necessary to act autonomously – that is, to be able to follow their particular agenda for life. (…) by providing personal information generously and without too much worrying about privacy, individual autonomy – and the ability to act in groups – can be increased. (Stalder, 2011, pp. 510, 511)

Stalder here has a bourgeois meaning of privacy in mind, just to establish that such privacy runs fundamentally counter to the practices of digital networking. However, from an empirical point of view, there are in fact privacy problems within OSNs, insofar as users still tend to perceive and address problems concerning information flows as privacy issues – it is just the bourgeois conception of privacy that is overburdened with grasping them.

In this sense, privacy as a precondition for autonomy has principally ceased to be about retreat from the social. But what about individual control over information? The second set of practices that we refer to illustrates how practicing individual control becomes difficult, too. Those practices concern what we call *Calculating Spaces* (Ochs, in press). The latter term is meant to point out the transformed relationship between space and digital networking. In the early stages of the internet, a lot of effort was spent on simulating space within the digital medium. In the 1990s terms, such as "cyber-space" or "web-sites" became common, and the virtual landscape of *Second Life* by the beginning of the 2000s attracted a lot of attention due to the spatial experience it allowed for. While internet access at this time still predominantly happened via desktop computers, today it is rather mobile technologies (smart phones, tablets) that are used. Networked sensor technologies pervade physical space, a tendency that is likely to be intensified by, say, the *Internet of Things*, *Cyberphysical Systems*, *Smart Homes*, or *Wearable Computing*.

The question arises, how individual control over information in such densely networked environments might still be possible – how to give "informed consent" to all these services? The problem is, of course, well-known. Framing the setting in terms of individual rights renders it practically impossible for the individual to effectively exercise her rights, for only legal scholars disposing of sufficient time are able to read and understand all the inscriptions materializing in services' terms and conditions. The advent of Calculating Spaces is suited to further aggravate the problematic: The technologies in question tend to operate below the threshold of perception, and it is difficult to see how the individual subject is in a position to make decisions concerning her personal information in such a situation. Moreover, wearable technologies, such as the now-failed *Google Glass,* seem to further take away individual control over information. The resistance *Glass* raised, leading to the freezing of the project as a mass market device, is quite telling. To illustrate the whole affair we may refer to an anecdote documented by the New York Times when Glass was in its introduction phase:

> The 5 Point Cafe, a Seattle dive bar, was apparently the first to explicitly ban [Google] Glass. [...] the bar's owner, Dave Meinert, said there was a serious side. The bar, he said, was "kind of a private place." (Stretfield, 2013)

The banning of the technology from the bar space implies that the owner does not act on the assumption that anyone will be able to exercise individual control over information once Google Glass (wearers) are present. There is a turn to collective rules instead, safeguarding the particular privacy of the place. Spatial technologies such as this one thus provide a taste of the difficulties that arise when living in completely networked surroundings. boyd (2012) drives this point home eloquently:

> Expecting that people can assert individual control when their lives are so interconnected is farcical. Moreover, it reinforces the power of those who already have enough status and privilege to meaningfully assert control over their own networks. In order to address networked privacy, we need to let go of our cultural fetishization with the individual as the unit of analysis. We need to develop models that position networks, groups, and communities at the center of our discussion. (p. 350)

We are well aware that privacy research has already begun to realize the shortcomings of individual notions (Nissenbaum, 2010; Rössler & Mokrosinska, 2015), and our ultimate goal is to contribute to this shift. With a view to the thrust of the article, however, we would like to establish at this point only that the bourgeois legacy of privacy, and especially its individualistic framing, as it plays out in ideas, such as retreat and individual control, is not adequate to grasp current digital practices; and there are good reasons to expect, that, at least in online environments, it will be even more difficult in the future to practice bourgeois privacy.

As a result, also established strategies of privacy protection are pressurized, with ethical implications not least for internet research. This is what we will turn to next.

POST-INDIVIDUALIST PRIVACY IN INTERNET RESEARCH: DATA ENACTING SUBJECTS

Whereas bourgeois subject conceptions, as implicated by the prevalent discourse on privacy, are no longer viable, such conceptions nevertheless still constitute the basis for a range of privacy protection strategies, including those protecting the privacy of research subjects in internet research.

One such strategy is asking the research subject for "informed consent," a provision to be found in many common research settings. Making sure that the subject actually is informed is usually the responsibility of the researcher, e.g. by providing leaflets, explanations, or conversations. Consequently, the subject signs a form or otherwise declares consent. The underlying assumption is that the subject is enabled to control his information in the sense that he makes a conscious decision based on what he is told about the research setting by the researcher. Thus, the research setting suggests that the subject is a person that can understand the information provided and the consequences of the use of data for herself and others. Correspondingly, the researcher would be a person able to estimate probable risks of the data collection and processing, and to care for the orderly conduction of the research. Similarly, using pseudonyms for interlocutors and removing directly identifying information from statements enacts an ethnographer as a responsible, privacy respecting researcher.

We will see below that the control thus suggested is no longer effective, neither for researches nor their subjects. Still the practices of informed consent (as well as of anonymization and pseudonymziation) are widely accepted since they cohere with notions of the individual that we have been trained to adopt for several centuries. The force of these established discourses, which makes individual control a matter of course, then structures the subject positions of researcher and subject – however, without actually safeguarding the actual control they have over the data. From this perspective, provisions, which are meant to protect individuals' privacy, actually contribute to who the subjects and the researchers are. So, rather than protecting persons, they contribute to the creation of this subject position in the first place. This way, an illusion of control, which is essentially an illusion of privacy, is created. Bottom line is that the research setting helps to reproduce bourgeois modes of subject formation, while at the same time failing to grant effective bourgeois privacy (in the sense of control over information to the subjects). This is related to the way privacy breaches are conceptualized in this context. Usually, affordances to ensure the privacy of subjects have to ensure that no "personally identifiable" information leaks. This means that no information about the autonomous individuals who have consented to the use of "their" data should become available.

But why is individual control over information no longer effective? This is above all due to the transformed character of data. Advances in data analytics, sometimes dubbed "Big Data," promise an exploratory approach to data (Kitchin, 2014). Generally speaking, they promise that the data will tell us what to look for rather than looking for something in the data. Thus, data are seen as a resource, where relations, correlations, patterns, rules, and associations can be detected. This entails a shift in the idea of data itself. In the context of information technology[2] data has long been used in the way established by (relational) databases. There are fields for particular entries – name, age, blood type, Twitter handle, etc. Thus, each field contains a particular, determined piece of information, which can be queried, sorted, tagged, and recombined. New methods in data analysis treat data as a resource for very different modes of inquiry – rather than as entries with fixed meanings. As a resource data are something that our actions leave in the (digital) environment and which can be appropriated ("mined") in very different ways. This way of inquiry and the context, in which the data are put, determines its significance. Cheap computing power allows researchers to experiment with all kinds of algorithms and tools for analysis to see which one brings interesting results. Against this background, the bourgeois concept of privacy, entailing a view on personality with fixed features that are represented by personal data such as names, addresses etc. is insufficient for in the right context, using an appropriate tool, any data can become personal information.

This renders, say, anonymizing statements collected from social media or blogs utterly difficult. Any string longer than a few words will do to find the original statement using a search engine, no matter how its source is concealed. The ease of searching and parsing the web also makes it very convenient to procure additional contextual information necessary for data analytics. E.g., approvedly, it was possible to identify people in a data set that just contained anonymized movie ratings (Narayanan & Shmatikov, 2008). Other researchers managed to predict the sexual orientation by analyzing Facebook friendships (Jernigan & Mistree, 2009). Many more attempts at de-anonymizing datasets attest to this set of problems. And there are still more issues. What people post on social media does not only reveal things about them, but might also allow deriving insights about their "friends", followers, or similarly associated users. Even if the individualist setting worked in a perfect fashion with every individual carefully reflecting on what they put on their social media sites before allowing researchers to use these data, the resulting research could create an aggregate allowing to infer information that none of the subjects provided individually – and thus was not part of the things they pondered before giving consent.

Such possibilities of aggregative, inductive, or explorative data analysis also change the meaning of "privacy breach." When research data are released (e.g. in anonymized or aggregate form) or when security measures are circumvented and unauthorized, persons gain access to the data, third parties still might not be able to identify individuals – in the sense that they know names, addresses etc. However, quite often this is not their aim in the first place. It might be enough if they can send targeted ads, or perhaps verbal abuse, or tailored viruses at subjects' (rather anonymous) e-mail address or Twitter handle. Thus, a lot of morally or legally negative actions may happen to persons *without identifying their essential personality*: Having said this, a lot of data analytics is not about knowing *who you are*, but *what you are like* (Matzner, 2014). It is not about personal identification or revealing the essential core of one's personality, but about sorting people into groups. And depending on who performs the sort, this group may consist of valuable customers or suspected political activists. It is for these reasons that also mathematical approaches to maintaining privacy threaten to fail. E.g., concepts, such as "differential privacy" (Dwork, 2008) or "k-anonymity" (Sweeney, 2002) are valuable tools that provide mathematical guarantees for the impossibility to identify members of a database when selectively revealing information from it. But they are still tailored towards identifying *the individuals* and do not concern other information which can be learned from the aggregate database.

The thesis to be derived from these observations is that ethical considerations of privacy as regards internet research must be based on novel notions of subjective personality, of data, and also of privacy. For, at least some of the problems privacy protection currently faces have nothing to do with personality understood as essential core of the subject; data are not necessarily problematic because they represent facets of this essential core; and privacy does not generally amount to protecting the core of a subject's personality from being revealed through public representation of personal data. But how to conceive, then, differently of subjectivity, data, and privacy in internet research settings?

For a start, we may point out that the classification or sorting of people – the way we appear to each other on the internet – is not just determined by information representing facts about subjects, i.e. our understanding of data must not be reduced to the information they contain or allow to derive; likewise, algorithms must not be reduced to their functionality. They must be understood as embedded in social practices. Thus Gillespie (2014) writes:

> What users of an information algorithm take it to be, and whether they are astute or ignorant, matters. [...] This means that, while the algorithm itself may seem to possess an aura of technological neutrality, or to embody populist, meritocratic ideals, how it comes to appear that way depends not just on its design but also on the mundane realities of news cycles, press releases, tech blogs, fan discussion, user rebellion, and the machinations of the algorithm provider's competitors. (p. 182)

Similar considerations hold concerning data. In particular social media sites, blogs, and similar resources from the internet come with a sheen of authenticity. It is where persons perform themselves. This sheen of the information is central to the social networking based mode of individuality described above. In contrast, using sophisticated analytical tools can add a layer of objectivity to information derived from data (Gillespie, 2014), in particular in the context of science and research. Quite generally, data and the algorithms used to analyze them enact subject positions. And this potential to enact goes beyond the information or facts contained in the data (the veracity of which the critics of big data rightfully contest). In this sense, *data have to be conceived as performative*: To an increasing extent *our personalities are enacted* using data and digital communication (Matzner 2016). When data or results released by researchers enable that the subjects appear in a different, negative light, the damage is done – even if that is not a fact but depends on "what users of an information algorithm take it to be" as Gillespie writes. For instance when social media research data arouse suspicions concerning sexual orientation, then the issue is not only, whether this information is correct in a representational sense – but whether and how the research contributes to the appearance of a person.[3] Research, then, might put a subject into a position where she has to (publicly) deal with a justified, private issue – and this issue is not necessarily about the revelation of a subject's personal core by way of stripping the subject off her control over personal data that represent facets of this core. In such a case data, and the way they are manipulated, rather enact a type of subjectivity that is unwanted by the person; preserving privacy in such a case means to preserve the person's subject performance. And as such a type of privacy is beyond the individual control of the subject, but forms part of collective data practices instead, ethical considerations have to set out from a relational (subjectivity), enactment type (data), and performative (privacy) perspective.

The conclusion will translate the outlines of this novel problem space into ethical considerations internet research is supposed to take into account.

CONCLUSION: NOVEL ETHICAL ORIENTATIONS FOR INTERNET RESEARCH

Most of the newly arising issues are not reflected upon in individualistic research settings. Neither researchers nor subjects can sensibly claim to identify the type and extent of information used in internet research. Neither can they foresee all the uses of that data that will potentially be possible. For these reasons, internet research settings should abstain from configuring the subject and the researcher as self-contained individuals that have rational oversight over a determined situation. Instead, they should consciously reflect the openness and transience of data-analytics. Rather than asking what will be known about the subject and who might control this knowledge, the ethical question should be: *Will the data allow to enact a subject in a problematic manner?* Thus, researchers should act the role of a person that potentially interferes with the way in which persons appear to others (peers, advertisers, criminals, etc.). They should take into account what the context of the research, the researcher's discipline and personality, the institutional setting, etc. add to this appearance, to the performativity of data – beyond the facts and knowledge derivable from it. This means that researchers should

- change their notions of privacy breaches from releasing personal information to releasing enough information to create meaningful aggregates.
- avoid creating the illusion of control by maintaining research settings that perpetuate bourgeois individualist notions of privacy. Rather they should reflect on and point out the openness and the possibility of permanent resignification of data.

- reflect that avoiding identification is not the only issue of anonymous databases: privacy issues may not only be constituted by knowing who a person is, but also by knowing what this person is like.
- conceive of data not only as digital representations of the world but as performing various meanings according to use and context.
- orient their research not on facts and personal information (what becomes known about the person) but on their appearance in a networked world: will the research allow to enact the subject in a problematic manner?

This is *not* to say, of course, that existing provisions to preserve privacy should be abandoned for good, but that they should be supplemented by caring for how the research results allow enacting the subjects in a problematic manner. This should also include considerations that persons who are completely uninvolved in the research are probably among those concerned. Finally, the openness of potential uses of data and the group of people concerned should be made an explicit part of privacy provisions. While research in times of social data has to be seen as a risk for privacy that cannot be fully mitigated, these orientations can be a first step to re-invent privacy-related research ethics for future internet research.

NOTES

1. Due to space limitations we provide here a very condensed analysis. Elaborated treatments of the issues dealt with can be found in Ochs (2015b, in press).
2. For a more general discussion of the concept of data see Rosenberg (2013).
3. This is not to imply that there is anything suspicious about any sexual orientation, but regarding the discriminatory reality of our societies, sexual orientation is considered private for good reasons.

REFERENCES

Arendt, H. (1958). *The human condition*. Chicago, IL: University of Chicago Press.

Bailey, J. (2000). Some meanings of "the private" in sociological thought. *Sociology, 34*(3), 381–401.

Bennett, C. (2011). In defense of privacy: The concept and the regime. *Surveillance and Society, 8*(4), 485–496.

boyd, d. (2010). *Privacy and publicity in the context of Big Data*. Retrieved from http://www.danah.org/papers/talks/2010/WWW2010.html

boyd, d. (2012). Networked privacy. *Surveillance and Society, 10*(3/4), 348–350.

boyd, d., & Crawford, K. (2011). *Six provocations for Big Data*. Retrieved from http://papers.ssrn.com/sol3/papers.cfm?abstract_id=1926431

Duby, G. (Ed.). (1990). *Geschichte des privaten Lebens. 2. Band: Vom Feudalzeitalter zur Renaissance*. Frankfurt a. M.: S. Fischer.

Dwork, C. (2008). Differential privacy: a survey of results. In M. Agrawal, D. Du, Z. Duan, & A. Li (Eds.), *Theory and applications of models of computation: 5th International Conference, TAMC 2008, Xi'an, China, April 25–29, 2008. Proceedings* (pp. 1–19). Berlin: Springer. Retrieved from http://dx.doi.org/10.1007/978-3-540-79228-4_1

Elias, N. (1969). *The civilizing process. Vol. I: The history of manners.* Oxford: Blackwell.

Gillespie, T. (2014). The relevance of algorithms. In T. Gillespie, P. Boczkowski, & K. Foot (Eds.), *Media technologies* (pp. 167–194). Cambridge, MA: MIT Press.

Habermas, J. (1991). *The structural transformation of the public sphere. An inquiry into a category of bourgeois society. Translated by Thomas Burger with the assistance of Frederick Lawrence.* Cambridge, MA: MIT Press.

Heesen, J., & Matzner, T. (2015). Politische Öffentlichkeit und Big Data. In P. Richter (Ed.), *Privatheit, Öffentlichkeit und demokratische Willensbildung in Zeiten von Big Data* (pp. 151–167). Baden-Baden: Nomos.

Jernigan, C., & Mistree, B. (2009). Gaydar: Facebook friendships expose sexual orientation. *First Monday, 14*(10). Retrieved from http://firstmonday.org/article/view/2611/2302

Kitchin, R. (2014). Big Data, new epistemologies and paradigm shifts. *Big Data & Society, 1*(1), 1–12.

Latour, B. (2007, April 6). Beware, your imagination leaves digital traces. *Times Higher Education Literary Supplement.* Retrieved from http://www.bruno-latour.fr/sites/default/files/P-129-THES-GB.pdf

Manovic, L. (2012). Trending: The Promises and the Challenges of Big Social Data. In M.K. Gold (Ed.), *Debates in the Digital Humanities* (pp.. 460–471). Minneapolis: University of Minesota Press.

Matzner, T. (2016). Beyond data as representation: The performativity of Big Data in surveillance. *Surveillance and Society* 14(2), 197–210.

Matzner, T. (2014). Why privacy is not enough privacy in the context of "ubiquitous computing" and "big data." *Journal of Information, Communication and Ethics in Society, 12*(2), 93–106.

Narayanan, A., & Shmatikov, V. (2008). Robust de-anonymization of large sparse datasets. In *Proceedings of the 2008 Security and Privacy, IEEE Symposium on* (pp. 111–125). Oakland, CA: IEEE Computer Society.

Nissenbaum, H. (2010). *Privacy in context. Technology, policy, and the integrity of social life.* Stanford, CA: Stanford University Press.

Ochs, C. (in press). Rechnende Räume: Vier Merkmale der digitalen Transformation von (räumlichen) Privatheit(en). *Zeitschrift für theoretische Soziologie. ZTS 3. Sonderband: "Raum & Zeit".*

Ochs, C. (2015a). BIG DATA – little privacy? Eine soziologische Bestandsaufnahme. In P. Richter (Ed.), *Privatheit, Öffentlichkeit und demokratische Willensbildung in Zeiten von Big Data* (pp. 169–186). Baden-Baden: Nomos.

Ochs, C. (2015b). Die Kontrolle ist tot – lang lebe die Kontrolle! Plädoyer für ein nach-bürgerliches Privatheitsverständnis. *Mediale Kontrolle unter Beobachtung, 4*(1). Retrieved from http://www.medialekontrolle.de/wp-content/uploads/2015/11/Ochs-Carsten-2015-04-01.pdf

Paulitz, T., & Carstensen, T. (Eds.). (2014). *Subjektivierung 2.0. Machtverhältnisse digitaler Öffentlichkeiten.* Wiesbaden: Springer VS.

Reckwitz, A. (2006). *Das hybride Subjekt. Eine Theorie der Subjektkulturen von der bürgerlichen Moderne zur Postmoderne.* Weilerswist: Velbrück.

Regan, P. (1995). *Legislating privacy. Technology, social values, and public policy.* Chapel Hill, NC: The University of North Carolina Press.

Rogers, R. (2014). *Digital methods.* Cambridge, MA: MIT Press.

Rosenberg, D. (2013). Data before the fact. In L. Gitelman (Ed.), *Infrastructures series. Raw data is an oxymoron.* Cambridge, MA: MIT Press.

Rössler, B. (2004). *The value of privacy.* Cambridge: Polity Press.

Rössler, B., & Mokrosinska, D. (Eds.). (2015). *Social dimensions of privacy. Interdisciplinary perspectives.* Cambridge: Cambridge University Press.

Sennett, R. (1992). *The fall of public man.* New York, NY: W. W. Norton.

Stalder, F. (2011). Autonomy beyond privacy? A rejoinder to Bennett. *Surveillance & Society, 8*(4), 508–512.

Stretfield, D. (2013). Google Glass picks up early signal: Keep out. *The New York Times.* Retrieved from http://www.nytimes.com/2013/05/07/technology/ personaltech/google-glass-picks-up-early-signal-keep-out.html?nl=todaysheadlines&emc=edit_th_20130507&_r=1&

Sweeney, L. (2002). K-anonymity: A model for protecting privacy. *International Journal of Uncertainty, Fuzziness and Knowledge-Based Systems, 10*(5), 557–570.

Venturini, T. (2012). Building on faults: How to represent controversies with digital methods. *Public Understanding of Science, 21*(7), 796–812.

Venturini, T., & Latour, B. (2009). *The social fabric: Digital traces and quali-quantitative methods.* Retrieved from http://www.medialab.sciences-po.fr/publications/Venturini_Latour-The_Social_Fabric.pdf

Veyne, P. (Ed.). (1989). *Geschichte des privaten Lebens. 1. Band: Vom Römischen Imperium zum Byzantinischen Reich.* Frankfurt a.m.: S. Fischer.

Warren, S. D., & Brandeis, L. D. (1890). The right to privacy. *Harvard Law Review, 4*(5), 193–220.

Westin, A. F. (1967). *Privacy and freedom.* New York, NY: Atheneum.

REACTION BY CÉLINE EHRWEIN NIHAN

Matzner and Ochs forcefully demonstrate the limits and weaknesses of bourgeois privacy used as a moral principle to frame Internet researches and developments. Therefore they prompt us to radically rethink the meaning and scope of this notion. In this perspective, it appears to me that the thought of Hannah Arendt, and more specifically her reflections on plurality in its relation to the private realm, might be particularly fruitful.

In her writings, Arendt recognizes and highlights the importance of privacy for subject formation and the construction of his/her autonomy. However, it seems to me that her vision of the private sphere differs quite significantly from that of the bourgeois tradition.

According to her, privacy is (1) neither devoid of otherness (2) nor the one and only place of self-fulfilment and self-disclosure.

1) In the solitude of his/her thoughts (the place of privacy par excellence), the individual is never completely lonely nor detached from the world to which he/she belongs. Namely, his/her personal judgment is forged through a fictitious dialogue with partners on the surrounding world. And even his/her self-consciousness constitutes him/her as a being inhabited by plurality. Yet, it is this inner plurality, as well as the permanent relation to others and to the world (that are both close and distant), which allows the subject to form his/her personality.

(2) This being said, according to Arendt, the subject personality is also built and, in fact, only reveals itself in the confrontation of the political and public plurality. "In acting and speaking, men show who they are, reveal actively their unique personal identity and thus make their appearance in the human world [...]. This disclosure of "who" in contradistinction to "what" somebody is [...] implicit in everything somebody says and does. It can be hidden only in complete silence and perfect passivity, but its disclosure can almost never be achieved as a wilful purpose, as though one possessed and could dispose of this "who" in the same manner he has and can dispose of his qualities. On the contrary, it is more than likely that the "who", which appears so clearly and unmistakably to others, remains hidden from the person himself" (Human Condition, University of Chicago Press, 19582, 179).

Hannah Arendt's thoughts lead me to think that, in the Internet age, it is perhaps not so much privacy that we should seek to preserve as the conditions of realization of plurality which permit the revelation of our singularities and common humanity.

Céline Ehrwein Nihan, PhD, is a Professor in Ethics at the School of Management and Engineering Vaud (HEIG-VD), University of Applied Sciences and Arts Western Switzerland (HES SO)

REACTION BY CHRISTIAN PENTZOLD

References to privacy cannot, it seems, escape normative generalizations when it comes to defining who should be entitled to which sort of privacy. In principle, the right to privacy pertains to all human beings. Yet, the problems already start when it comes to say what privacy actually is – and thus what historical, social or cultural frameworks should be mobilized in order to account for its peculiar status and the demands that could be derived from it. Therefore, Matzner and Ochs develop a poignant critique of the bourgeois legacy within the privacy discourse. But the quaint location of privacy within reclusive realms of autonomous isolation and moral devotion is not only empirically outdated in industrialized societies and a post-modern world. Whether or not this patrician vision once held true for well-to-do people, it never accounted for the reality of privacy practice and privacy concerns among the majority of the people at all times.

Of course, this ideal had and still might have a considerable force in setting expectations of what privacy is about and through which measures it could be secured. In addition, some studies have shown that internet users in different nations seem to have similar attitudes toward privacy (Dutta, Dutton, & Law, 2011). Yet precisely such spurious dominance should encourage our creativity to seek out as many environments and circumstances as possible for contextualizing concepts of privacy instead of assuming some homogenous model. In making the case for such a much more nuanced understanding of privacy in terms of the performative qualities of data, Matzner and Ochs aim at providing an adequate and updated understanding and management of privacy issues of digitally networked people. However, by asking to whom their thoughtful considerations apply we might also be able to challenge the uneven terms and conditions under which people become enrolled in these dynamics – or are left out. This would allow seeing the new model of privacy as again one, again perhaps particularly Western model of privacy, which needs to be complemented by experiences, and paradigms that would otherwise again be marginalized.

Dutta, S., Dutton, W. H., & Law, G. (2011). The New Internet World. INSEAD Faculty and Working Paper. Retrieved from https://flora.insead.edu/fichiersti_wp/inseadwp2011/2011-89.pdf

***Christian Pentzold** is an Associate Professor (Junior professor) for Communication and Media Studies with a focus on Media Society at ZeMKI, Centre for Media, Communication and Information Sciences, University of Bremen, Germany.*

REACTION BY D. E. WITTKOWER

Matzner and Ochs do an excellent job of situating the liberal individualist conception of the research subject in Euro-American culture and history. We can certainly point to other cultural conceptions of persons that have relatedness to others and to communities at their core – relational ideas of the self that are primary in, for example, East Asian cultures influenced by Confucianism, or in African cultures as seen through the community ideals of *ubuntu*.

From the perspective of feminist ethics of care, we can see how the liberal individualist conception of the self that remains itself in disconnection from others is not only a particularly Euro-American conception, but a typically male Euro-American conception. Women in Euro-American culture more often than men describe their fundamental self in relation to others. Who am I? A daughter; a wife; a mother. Men are enculturated to view these relationships as modifications of a separable, core self that exists prior to and essentially unchanged through the development of these relationships – often to men's social, psychological, and moral detriment. But while women are enculturated to view their core selves in their caring relationships with others, the standard conception of the "human" in a Euro-American cultural context adopts the typically masculine self-conception. We see this in the conceptualization of the research subject, and in many other places as well – the way that interviews with successful women (but not men) nearly invariably ask about the sacrifices and tensions of having (or not having!) spouses and children, or the way that having children or having had multiple marriages can become a source of concern about female politicians where it is typically a non-issue for male politicians.

The isolatable "core self" is also a typically white conception of self in Euro-American culture. Consider John Rawls's famous "veil of ignorance" thought experiment, in which we are asked to imagine what kind of distribution of rights, opportunities, and goods we would want if we didn't know our position in society, including our age, gender, race, socio-economic status, sexual orientation, able/disabled status, etc. This presumes that we would still be ourselves in a meaningful sense apart from these aspects of the self, which are framed, as a hidden assumption, as secondary and accidental to rather than primary and constitutive of who we are. Critics have rightly pointed out that this hidden assumption is questionable, and that women, non-white persons, and other marginalized persons often view our identities as inseparably bound up with who we are and how we conceive of ourselves and others.

How can we conceive of the research subject outside of these liberal individualist, Euro-American, white/male/het/cis/able background assumptions? What practices of care and respect are demanded of the ethical researcher by the relational self?

***D. E. Wittkower** is an Associate Professor of Philosophy & Religious Studies at Old Dominion University. He is a philosopher of technology and culture.*

CHAPTER FOUR

Chasing ISIS

Network Power, Distributed Ethics and Responsible Social Media Research

JONATHON HUTCHINSON, FIONA MARTIN, AND AIM SINPENG

INTRODUCTION

Of all the ethical dilemmas facing internet researchers in the so-called "social age" (Azua, 2009) the most difficult is negotiating the expansion of actors and risks in distributed communicative environments, particularly where actors have unequal power over the terms and conduct of research. As digital media ethicist Charles Ess (2013) notes academic research ethics have historically focused on the duties of individual, institutional researchers to protect vulnerable human subjects from harm – a focus that is destabilized in studies of social media environments. Social media users, bots, communities, platform providers, and governments all possess degrees of creative and legal autonomy that pose problems for ensuring traditional procedural research controls such as consent or confidentiality. Some users may deliberately mask their identities and troll their observers. Terms of service and privacy controls may change mid-study. States may surveil and control certain data transactions. The proliferation of non-human actors alone challenges scholars to reimagine the concepts of subject, sociality, and social responsibility. Intellectual property and data protection laws are evolving too, provoking difficult questions about the terms of research access to platforms and their responsibilities to the creators of that information. Thus the contingent nature of internetworked power relations complicates the identification of risks, evaluation of benefits, and assessment of social implications for those involved in any social media study.

In this chapter we review normative, procedural, and practice-based challenges to negotiating this complexity, based on our work in media and communications research and political science. We also discuss ethical dilemmas scholars face when researching a contemporary and highly controversial research on the Islamic State (IS). Over the past decade academics in these fields, and the ethics review committees that approve their work, have looked to guidelines developed by professional organisations such as the Association of Internet Researchers (AoIR), the European Society for Opinion and Market Research (ESOMAR), and the British Psychological Society (BPS) (BPS, 2013; ESOMAR, 2011; Markham & Buchanan, 2012) for guidance on best practice ethical approaches to social media research. However, conceptions of what actions might be inappropriate or harmful, for whom and in what context, are not always shared or agreed by all stakeholders of these environments, particularly where proprietary and government interests dominate, consumer protections are limited, and users may have already consented to market research as part of their platform use contracts. Facebook's "emotional contagion" study (Kramer, Guillory, & Hancock, 2014), which tried to manipulate users' emotional states without their specific informed consent, is an infamous case in point. It triggered global debate about the principles of corporate social media research, such as the need for opt out provisions for users who could not anticipate the scope or consequences of that company's intended research (Bowser & Tsai, 2015; Carter et al., 2016). In practice then, research reflexivity is central to conceiving and administering network-aware, respectful, and just social media inquiries. It is also critical to informing and revising ethics review processes in light of research recruitment, data collection and analysis (see Guillemin & Gillam, 2004).

Drawing on Manuel Castell's (2011) four-fold conception of network power and ideas of "distributed morality" (Floridi, 2013, p. 728) or "distributed responsibility" (Ess, 2013, p. 21) among network agents, we explore how we might apply reflexive ethical thinking to map the shifting ethical roles and relations of the social media systems we are studying and to negotiate the procedural and practice based aspects of the ethical process. As a case study we consider how the pursuit of socially contentious knowledge, such as the identities and communicative activities of Islamic State (IS) agents, might lead us to question normative research ethics approaches and processes. Finally, with a mind to innovation in social media studies we make recommendations to university ethics bodies about productive ways to strengthen ethical consultation, decision-making, and review processes.

NORMATIVE APPROACHES TO SOCIAL MEDIA RESEARCH ETHICS

While there are many conceptions of social media research in this collection, we find that academics use social media platforms in four ways:

1. to find and recruit participants;
2. to gather information about people, communities, their activities and/or their discursive engagement;
3. to observe social actor behaviors and relations; or
4. to analyse the environments in which actors interact (eg. as code, interfaces or systems).

Human ethics research approval is required for studies that involve interaction with identifiable living human subjects or interventions into their activities, social environments and communication flows. Ethical reviews are a procedural guarantee that normative principles of research integrity have been considered and codified in the research methodology, as well as a forum for ongoing debate about ethics in practice.

In the West, our general understanding of human ethics principles is based on canonical international declarations, including The Belmont Report (Department of Health, Education, and Welfare, 1979), the United Nations Declaration of Human Rights (United Nations, 1948), and the Declaration of Helsinki (World Medical Association, 1964). These documents represent humanity's understanding of basic human rights, which have emerged from medical science, and have been widely adopted across the scholastic disciplines. They collectively highlight the need for human dignity, justice, safety, protection, respect for persons, and participant autonomy. They also emphasize that human research subjects should always be part of research in a voluntary condition. A core ethical consideration with any research is the maximization of benefits that the project can potentially produce, alongside the minimization of harm to the participants. These guiding principles provide the foundation for ethical decision-making, from which scholars then need to assess, evaluate, and prioritize their actions.

The primary rights based ethical framework for social media scholars in media and communications disciplines was developed by the Association of Internet Research (AoIR) Ethics Working Committee in 2002 (Ess & AoIR Ethics Working Committee, 2002), and revised in 2012 (Markham & Buchanan, 2012). In AoIR's *Ethical Decision-Making and Internet Research* report, internet research encompasses the collection of data from web, mobile, locative, and social media platforms; establishing an understanding of how people access and use the internet and how they design systems (via software, code and interface studies); the storage of internet research datasets; the analysis (semiotic, visualisation, or other) of images, text and media; and the large-scale use and regulation of the internet (Markham & Buchanan, 2012). Importantly the report notes that "the fields of internet research are dynamic and heterogeneous" (Markham & Buchanan, 2012, p. 2), and as such any rules or recommendations for research conduct can never be static. A field of research whose objects and relations are in a constant state of innovation, therefore, requires perpetually new ethical approaches that accommodate technological and regulatory *étalonnage*. With that in mind, the report recommends contextual flexibility in ethical decision making based on key recommendations and rights-based principles.

First, it proposes that the more vulnerable the study population, the greater the obligation of the researcher to protect them. Second, it argues that a "one size fits all" approach is unhelpful in internet research because harm should be considered as contextual. Third, it notes human research principles should be considered even where identifiable individuals' presence or involvement in the research data is not obvious, for example, in platform or interface studies. Fourth, it emphasizes that social media users have rights and agency "as authors, research participants and people" (p. 4) and as such the social benefits of any study should outweigh the risks of the research and fifth, that ethical decision-making should be followed at each step of the research from data collection through to dissemination. Finally, it advocates that ethical research should be a deliberative or consultative process that incorporates input from many stakeholders including other researchers, review boards, and the research participants themselves. This final recommendation is of interest in that it embodies a notion of distributed power and responsibility in ethical decision-making that is fundamental to digital media studies.

DISTRIBUTED MORALITY AND ETHICS

Notions of distributed ethics, exemplified in the work of Luciano Floridi (2013) and Charles Ess (2013), explore the consequences of the interconnected, shared and reciprocal actions that constitute networked digital communications. Floridi's concept of "distributed morality" considers whether "'big' morally-loaded actions" can also be "the result of many, 'small' morally-neutral or morally-negligible interactions" (2013, p. 729), undertaken by human, artificial or hybrid agents. In distributed environments, Floridi argues "good" actions can be aggregated and "bad" actions can be fragmented, but the interdependent operation of moral agents means that the ethical impacts of any actions need to be evaluated in terms of the consequences for systemic and individual well-being. Many academics and corporate researchers have assumed that publicly visible and legally accessible data streams such as Tweets or Instagram posts can be collected and analysed without the informed consent of the creators or communities. However, the analytical judgements made about this material may not only lack qualitative substance, but also have unseen consequences for those deemed to be part of a contentious social movement (e.g. political extremists or anti-government activists) or responsible for transgressive behaviors (e.g. sexting or racism).

Distributed ethical decision-making relies on a first order framework of *infraethics*, agreed expectations, attitudes, values, and practices that can foster coordination for morally good ends, as well as socio-technological mechanisms or *moral enablers* that support and promote positive actions. For example, social media platforms ordinarily have standards that guide users in how they should communicate with each other and a community manager who might "block" or "delete" those who deviate from these norms. Here good outcomes are the result of an ensemble of ethical facilitation with coordinated investment from as many communicative agents as possible.

Ess (2013) describes "distributed responsibility" across a network as "the understanding that, as these networks make us more and more interwoven with and interdependent upon one another, the ethical responsibility for a given act is distributed across a network of actors, not simply attached to a single individual" (Ess, 2013, p. xii). That is, some responsibility for research relations and outcomes may lie beyond academics, with other moral agents in a social network – with those communicating in a network and their choice of platform, privacy tools, and form of address; with the platform provider in enabling public data streams or effective privacy settings; or with regulatory bodies in ensuring user rights are not breached by illegal uses of data.

This notion sees unethical practices as the burden of all system agents and in that respect demands researchers recognize and deliberate their methodology and ethical strategy with all those stakeholders. Ideally then, as ethics is a moving feast, researchers should also share in progress findings, along with any changes to ethical decision-making. There is an element of action research to this approach in that both researcher and research participant are collaborating to improve process, with the benefits and risks of a study debated and made more apparent to all. Communicative reciprocity, a key concept in online communities literature (Bonniface, Green, & Swanson, 2005; Papadakis, 2003), is critical to this process of consultation and to researchers' goal of consulting effectively with their network agents.

Distributed models have obvious limits in terms of motivating agent participation (persuading powerful players such as platforms or government to take part in research design), and engaging non-human participants or vulnerable and hidden populations, such as pro-anorexia communities or hackers. In some cases it may not be practical, appropriate, or safe for other research subjects to share every ethical decision or all findings with all stakeholders. As a result social media researchers cannot defer or deflect their primary ethical obligations to other agents in a social network.

Rather we are challenged to consider the effective moral agency of any participant and the characteristic power relations of specific network contexts to better understand how otherwise seemingly morally neutral research actions may interact/

aggregate with unjust and/or damaging outcomes. Mapping the operation of network power and ethical obligation is a key procedural step in finalizing research design and securing ethics approval and remains a factor throughout any study.

NETWORK POWER, ETHICAL PROCEDURE, AND ETHICS IN PRACTICE

Social media systems involve diverse social identities, many forms of agency and complex, shifting social connections. Often the rights and interests of different parties may be in conflict, particularly where platforms and governments have the power to dictate access to data, the terms under which one can conduct one's study, or the rights of the participants. In order to define the research relations with one's study cohort, and to ensure their rights and safety as far as is possible, it is helpful to conceptualize these power relations and to map the scope of the ethical process.

Castells (2011) proposes there are four models for exercising power within human actor networks, each of which can be used to consider the ethical roles and responsibilities of those agents involved in a research project during the procedural phase of seeking ethics approval:

1. *Networking power* operates as a form of gatekeeping, to include or exclude actors based on their potential to add value to or jeopardise the network;
2. *Network power* is used to coordinate the protocols of communication or the rules for participation within the network;
3. *Networked power* the collective and multiple forms of power, referred to by Castells as "states", within the network; and finally,
4. *Network-making power*, critical as it is "(a) the ability to constitute network(s) and to program/reprogram the network(s) in terms of the goals assigned to the network; and (b) the ability to connect and ensure the cooperation of different networks by sharing common goals and combining resources while fending off competition from other networks by setting up strategic cooperation." (2011)

The last model indicates, for example, the critical institutional role of university ethics review committees in mediating between powerful interests and for the rights of participants and researchers. Switchers "control the connecting points between various strategic networks," for example, "the connection between the political networks and the media networks to produce and diffuse specific political-ideological discourses" (Castells, 2011, p. 777). Review boards can critically assess researchers' commitment to participant rights and protections, while advocating for academic rights in relation to claims by corporations, governments or hostile agents.

The review board also provides a forum for investigating contentious fields of study, where normative ethical strategies are unworkable and may threaten academic freedom or participant rights. For example, in the case study below of ISIS and its social media recruitment strategy, distributing some responsibility for ethical conduct to extremist organisations or foreign combatants publishing on social media is unviable, as they are a hidden population being studied without informed consent. Similarly, sharing research strategy or results with those organisations (a common aspect of procedural ethics) may reduce the likelihood of researchers capturing authentic communications and increase risks for other parties identified as being part of an IS network, while adding no demonstrable social advantage.

The difficulty is that ethics review committees may have little or no training in ethical review of new methodologies (Carter et al., 2016). In the dynamic state of social media research, this places added emphasis on the researchers capacity to promote shifts in ethical thinking brought about by research practice. As the AoIR guidelines suggest "ethical concepts are not just hurdles to be jumped through at the beginning stages of research" (Markham & Buchanan, 2012, p. 4), but ground ongoing enquiry during any study and lead revision of norms and procedures.

PRIVACY, CONFIDENTIALITY, AND SOCIAL VISIBILITY

One important dimension of social media ethics is investigating the privacy and confidentiality of research participants – that is, the extent to which any social media study cohort has made their data open to collection or assents to being monitored by others outside their social networks with awareness of the attendant risks and benefits of being research subjects. Privacy has a normative ethical dimension in defining constraints on the use of personal information, but as the AoiR guidelines indicate understandings of "publicness" or "privateness" may vary from person to person and shift as the research progresses. Recent studies suggest cultural differences in the way users express privacy concerns and manage personal information and changes to their perception of privacy over time (Trepte & Masure, 2016; Tsay-Vogel, Shanahan, & Signorielli, 2016). As Nissembaum (2010) notes privacy is also contextually mediated, and its integrity differently framed according to relational expectations, social norms and contracts.

We propose that a users' intention to disclose information with (or beyond) their social network can be understood in terms of the value they place on *social visibility* and the benefits they perceive, or power that accrues, through recognition and connectedness. Social visibility refers to the degree of privacy and confidentiality participants might assume in different uses of social media, such as sharing content with close friends, making a statement of political allegiance, or engaging in civil disobedience. Brighenti (2007) notes that visibility "lies at the intersection of the two domains of aesthetics (relations of perception) and politics (relations of power)" (p. 324). The ways that different stakeholder groups behave on social media platforms reflect how they conceive and value the "publicness" or aesthetic visibility of their activities and the impact on this attention on their self-perception and network status. Within youth cultures, online celebrity or popularity equate with positive visibility, while negative connotations are associated with less widely lauded activities like sexting or doxing (Berriman & Thompson, 2015). In organisational communications Uldam (2016) argues "management of visibility in social media plays a key role in securing corporate legitimacy" (p. 203) and in deflecting crisis narratives. Certain types of visibility then are productive, while others may attract opprobrium, particularly where information that was not intended for public consumption is widely distributed through activities like outing, revenge porn or cloud account hacking (Meikle, 2016, p. 93). As Meikle notes:

> The cost of this creativity, sharing and visibility is that the user loses control over what is done with their personal information, loses control over the new contexts into which others may share it, and loses control over to whom the social media firms might sell it. (p. x)

The problem for social media researchers is understanding a user's intention of visibility within any research relationship, alongside their expectations of privacy and information control. Academics cannot presume that social media users are aware of how accessible their communications are to longitudinal tracking and professional scrutiny, or how their activities may be interpreted as part of broader social movements or patterns of use.

In our examination of peer reviewed journal articles on IS use of social media, we find some disagreement about what forms of social media data are verifiable, how users might be identified, and what aspects of their communications are intentionally public and performed for political affect.

RESEARCHING THE ISLAMIC STATE ONLINE

Studying the use of social media by the Islamic State (IS or ISIS for Islamic State of Iraq and al-Sham)[1] presents a fascinating focus for understanding the rise and operation of today's transnational terrorist organisations. Social media platforms, once simplistically dubbed a "liberation technology" in connection with the Arab Spring protests (Diamond, 2010, p. 70) are now pivotal to the recruitment strategy and propaganda machine of ISIS, an organisation whose pursuit of a caliphate has resulted over 1,000 civilian casualties, beyond the hundreds of thousands lost on the battlefields of Syria and Iraq (Yourish, Watkins, & Giratikanon, 2016). IS use of social media far outstrips that of any other terrorist organisation known to date, with each IS-linked Twitter account having an average of 1,000 followers – far higher than regular Twitter users (Berger & Morgan, 2015). Beyond the Twittersphere, IS also famously employed YouTube to show their disturbing beheading videos, many of which went viral, as a way to recruit supporters. The video, "There is No Life without Jihad," released in 2014, was a strategy for online radicalization aimed at recruiting young Western-based future foreign fighters. Abdel Bari Atwan (2015) refers to IS activities online as "the digital caliphate."

After the Paris and Brussels attacks in 2016, which led to over 160 deaths, governments in the United States and Europe have been pouring considerable resources into countering so-called homegrown extremism, including working with social media companies to identify individuals with active recruitment accounts. In 2016 Twitter reported having deleted 125,000 accounts believed to be tied to violent extremism – many of which belonged to IS agents (Calamur, 2016). Despite this, extremist accounts continue to proliferate (Karam, 2016). Indeed a 2015 report by the Brookings Institute argues that closing accounts is unlikely to be very effective in combating extremist activity:

> Account suspension isolates ISIS and can increase the speed of radicalization for those who manage to enter the network, and hinder organic social pressures that could lead to de-radicalisation." (p. 3)

With this in mind, researching the Islamic State's online strategy is now a political priority for the West – the European Union alone having increased its counter terrorism budget from €5.7 million (in 2002) to €93.5 million (in 2009) (European Parliament, 2016). A Google search of the terms "ISIS," "research," and "media" returns 25 million results, while Google Trends shows "ISIS" and "social media" searches peaking at times of key attacks on Western citizens, such as beheadings.[2] In recent years governments, foundations, and universities in North America and Europe have funded an increasing number of projects investigating the understanding of extremism online.[3] Given the continued intensity of military engagements in Iraq and Syria, IS attacks across the Middle East and Europe and the protracted Syrian civil war, research on IS will remain important in the foreseeable future.

Despite the clear policy importance of studying IS activities online, there are a number of ethical challenges to doing this from a distributed ethical perspective. First, while the research needs and interests of nations and research institutions take priority over those of IS protagonists, there will be little concern for any potential negative research impacts on the broader network of IS communicants, including potential child recruits. Yet, given the degree of security interest in this community, identifying social media users as IS-connected may make them vulnerable to ongoing surveillance and legal prosecution. The Islamic State fighters are among the most wanted terrorists in many countries, and some governments have gone to great lengths to locate their identity of their supporters. The astonishing revelation over the U.S. National Security Agency's (NSA) "spying" program shows it has access to details of every American's call history, real time phone and Internet traffic and received cooperation from tech giants like Google and Facebook in obtaining that data (Electronic Frontier Foundation, n.d.). In March 2016 the UK parliament introduced the *Investigatory Powers Bill*, condemned by lawyers for breaching international standards on civilian surveillance that will give the security agencies wide ranging powers to intercept and access electronic data (Bowcott, 2016). Similarly new data retention laws in Australia, passed in 2015, permit the intelligence and law enforcement agencies immediate access to all telephone and Internet metadata without a warrant. Under the scope of such government-sanctioned surveillance programs, it is imperative that IS researchers debate how and whether they are able to protect those they study.

Second, given that these subjects are a hidden population, legally and socially stigmatized by membership, and often represented by bots and apps (Berger & Morgan, 2015, p. 42), there is little chance that they will respond to an ethical framing consultation and so share some degree of individual or shared responsibility for the way social media research is framed and conducted. Thus, while an automated social media network analysis of IS Twitter supporters could provide tremendous empirical insights into the organisation's campaign strategy, including identification of its close and wide support bases and key issues that gain currency among followers and potential recruits, in the absence of informed consent, researchers and review committees must still assume the responsibility for weighing the risks to those identified as part of that network. In the most comprehensive analysis of ISIS supporters on Twitter to date (Berger & Morgan, 2015) the authors present a strong public policy case for their research, while poorly attesting to the risks faced by research subjects. The only concern they note is the potential negative consequences of Twitter intervening to suspend suspected IS-linked accounts.

Third, in the absence of distributed engagement with research subjects, there is little consensus about what constitutes valid, ethical data collection and analysis in IS studies. Most scholarly research examining IS use of new media technologies has emerged from political science and related disciplines.[4] An examination of university and non-profit funded published studies has shown that researchers have taken two approaches to discussing ethical research conduct.

The first is choosing to investigate only "publicly available" data in order to avoid any involvement in government surveillance and intervention. Twitter is the most studied platform because of its openly accessible data streams and culture of promotion, networking, and amplification. Yet, Twitter studies of IS differ in defining what constitutes verifiable "public" data and ISIS identities. Lorenzo Vidino and Seamus Hughes (2015) from the Center for Cyber and Homeland Security at George Washington University, sought to explain the upsurge in American jihadi recruits by investigating IS activity. They conclude that the majority of online supporters are men and show their support by introducing new, pro-ISIS accounts to the online community. However, the authors conducted a qualitative analysis of "known" ISIS supporters already identified by the U.S. authorities, and did not examine the social networks of these identified individuals, instead relying heavily on information from newspapers and published government reports. In contrast Jytte Klausen (2015) first identified the Twitter accounts of 59 "potential" foreign fighters in Syria, based on "news stories, blogs, and reports released by law enforcement agencies and think tanks" (2015, p. 5) and, then, conducted a social network analysis of the 29,000 accounts they followed or that followed them. Carter, Maher, and Neumann (2014) took a similar approach in identifying 190 Syrian foreign fighter Twitter accounts and, then, applying the snowball method to analyse patterns among their followers.

The second approach to IS studies ethics is to omit that discussion entirely. This was commonplace among the literature surveyed from both political science and media and communications. It is possible that political scientists perceive the public policy implications of IS research to be so great and "evident" beyond the potential risks to individuals studied, that the consequences do not warrant discussion in the space of a 8,000-word article. Even so, why then would Berger and Morgan's 68-page report, which has a section called "challenges and caveats" (2015, p. 41), lack discussion of ethical risks? Such oversight, intentional or not, points to the need for more debate about distributed ethics principles to inform research design and critique. Centrally researchers need to interrogate more closely how social media users understand and practice social visibility in different cultural contexts as a means to building or reinforcing their networking power.

CONCLUSION

In researching social media systems we advocate ethical approaches that acknowledge the relational aspects of agency and obligation that characterize our new online communities and that problematize the assumption that all network agents have equivalent moral agency. In this chapter distributed responsibility functions less as an attributive framework for determining fixed ethical obligations in networked environments and more as a means of locating and analysing the sometimes conflicting expectations of scholars, users, user communities, platform and internet service providers, governments, and research institutions about how inquiries might be designed and conducted. Distributed ethics can be used to conceptualize the scope of networked agents and their relations in globally connected, transcultural, proprietary environments and to surface conflicts over infraethical meaning or enabling strategies. It cannot provide researchers a blueprint for fully weighing participant interests, rights, and capacities, or evaluating research impacts, where those entities are unable to engage in a deliberative ethical consultation. This leaves hidden populations and transgressive agents like IS promoters.

Social media research takes place in commercially oriented environments, governed by less than transparent corporate communication paradigms and variable forms of nation state regulation. In this respect the job of developing fair and effective procedural research ethics for these complex social systems falls to researchers and university review committees, which can act as forums for ethical debate. It is not uncommon though for review boards to be dominated by individuals unfamiliar with trends in social network studies and digital media research methodologies, or to be cautious about approving innovative research projects. This is why we urge social media researchers to promote new professional standards, such as the AoIR guidelines, and to advocate for social media research in context – based on an understanding of the limits of distributed responsibility and the different meanings of social visibility for diverse social media agents, human and non-human.

What we offer in this chapter, based on our empirical evidence of research that has been conducted on social media associated with IS, are two recommendations for university ethics boards. First, university boards need to understand the normative approach towards social media research better, building on the AoIR ethics procedural approach towards ethical decision-making. Second, university ethics boards should undertake the role of network-making power agents and engage in "switching" activities during the application of the social media research. These two recommendations are designed to be applied to the field of internet research, which remains in constant flux as new cultures and technologies emerge at a rapid pace. These recommendations should be applied to existing university ethics boards processes, while also beginning a transformation of the role of these boards within the research process. As we see it, university ethics boards, should remain active in the research process until the completion of the research, which is inclusive of the dissemination of findings.

Our first recommendation notes that university boards need to understand the publicness versus the private nature of the social media conversation before approving research projects. Social media research projects apply to a variety of disciplines where some will have significantly different outcomes compared with others. normative ethics approach for decision-making only works when the university ethics board has a transparent understanding of the specific conversation the researcher is attempting to understand. Our second recommendation calls for university ethics boards to embody an ongoing active role within the ethical decision-making process by becoming what Castells terms a network-making power agent, or a switcher. As we noted earlier, social media research is often located between corporations and governments, which is often a zone within which an individual researcher has limited power. However, an institutional approach, which is spearheaded by a university ethics board, has more capacity to "control the connecting points between various strategic networks" (Castells, 2011, p. 777). We suggest ethics review bodies take a continuing interest in the evolution of social media research and in educating members in innovative methodologies. Their supportive and constructive engagement will enable scholars to safely navigate disputed research territories, where their work is not fully sanctioned by platform hosts and their independence is not guaranteed by governments.

NOTES

1. In Arabic, the group is known as Al-Dawla Al-Islamiya fi al-Iraq wa al-Sham, which is a geographical construct that includes territories stretching from southern Turkey through Syria to Egypt. The group seeks to build an Islamic state, or a caliphate, in this area.
2. Google trends: ISIS + social media. Peak searches: September 2014, February 2015 and November 2015.
3. For example, see the projects being funded by the Minerva Institute, a research arm of the US Department of Defence from 2013 to 2018.
4. According to CrossSearch results across scholarly databases, the majority of results on key word searches of "ISIS" and "media" since January 2013 were articles in political science journals, which include the fields of international relations, security and military studies.

REFERENCES

Atwan, A. B. (2015). *Islamic state: The digital caliphate.* London: Saqi.

Azua, M. (2009). *The social factor: Innovate, ignite, and win through mass collaboration and social networking.* San Francisco, CA: IBM Publishing.

Berger, J. M., & Morgan, J. (2015). The ISIS Twitter census: Defining and describing the population of ISIS supporters on Twitter. *The Brookings Project on US Relations with the Islamic World.* No. 20, March 2015. Retrieved from https://www.brookings.edu/wp-content/uploads/2016/06/isis_twitter_census_berger_morgan.pdf

Berriman, L., & Thompson, R. (2015). Spectacles of intimacy? Mapping the moral landscape of teenage social media. *Journal of Youth Studies, 18*(5), 583–597.

Bonniface, L., Green, L., & Swanson, M. (2005). Affect and an effective online therapeutic community. *M/C Journal, 8*(6), n.p. Retrieved from http://journal.media-culture.org.au/0512/05-bonnifacegreenswanson.php.

Bowcott, O. (2016). Investigatory powers bill not fit for purpose, say 200 senior lawyers. *Guardian Online.* March 14 2016. Retrieved from http://www.theguardian.com/world/2016/mar/14/investigatory-powers-bill-not-fit-for-purpose-say-200-senior-lawyers

Bowser, A., & Tsai, J. Y. (2015). *Supporting ethical web research: A new research ethics review.* Paper presented at the WWW 2015 conference, Florence, Italy.

Brighenti, A. (2007). Visibility: A category for the social sciences. *Current Sociology, 55*(3), 323–342.

British Psychological Society. (2013). *Ethics guidelines for internet-mediated research.* British Psychology Society. Leicester. Retrieved from: http://www.bps.org.uk/system/files/Public%20files/inf206-guidelines-for-internet-mediated-research.pdf.

Calamur, K. (2016). *Twitter's new ISIS policy*. Retrieved from http://www.theatlantic.com/international/archive/2016/02/twitter-isis/460269/

Carter, C. J., Koene, A. R., Perez, E., Statache, R., Adophs, S., & O'Malley, C. (2016). Understanding academic attitudes towards the ethical challenges posed by social media research. *ACM SIGCAS Computers and Society, 45*(3), 202–210.

Carter, J. A., Maher, S., & Neumann, P. R. (2014). #Greenbirds: Measuring importance and influence in Syrian foreign fighter networks. *The International Centre for the Study of Radicalisation and Political Violence.*

Castells, M. (2011). A network theory of power. *International Journal of Communication,* 5, 773–787.

Department of Health, Education, and Welfare. (1979, April 18). *The Belmont Report: Ethical principles and guidelines for the Protection of Human Subjects of Research U.S. National Commission for the Protection of Human Subjects of Biomedical and Behavioral Research.*

Diamond, L. (2010). Liberation technology. *Journal of Democracy, 21*(3), 69–83.

Electronic Frontier Foundation. (n.d.). *How the NSA's domestic spying program works.* Electronic Frontier Foundation. Retrieved from https://www.eff.org/nsa-spying/how-it-works

ESOMAR. (2011). *Guideline on social media research.* Amsterdam: World Association for Market, Social and Opinion Research. Retrieved from https://www.esomar.org/uploads/public/knowledge-and-standards/codes-and-guidelines/ESOMAR-Guideline-on-Social-Media-Research.pdf

Ess, C. (2013). *Digital media ethics* (2nd ed.). Cambridge: Polity Press.

Ess, C., & AoIR Ethics Working Committee. (2002, November 27). *Ethical decision-making and Internet research: Recommendations from the AoIR Ethics Working Committee.* Approved by AoIR. Retrieved from http://aoir.org/reports/ethics.pdf

European Parliament. (2016, March 8). *Counter-terrorism funding in the EU budget.* Retrieved from http://www.europarl.europa.eu/thinktank/en/document.html?reference=EPRS_BRI(2016)580904

Floridi, L. (2013). Distributed morality in an information society. *Science and Engineering Ethics, 19*(3), 727–743.

Guillemin, M., & Gillam, L. (2004). Ethics, reflexivity, and "ethically important moments" in research. *Qualitative Inquiry, 10*(2), 261–280.

Karam, J. (2016, February 9). Twitter, ISIS and social media whack-a-mole. *Foreign Policy.* Retrieved from http://foreignpolicyblogs.com/2016/02/09/twitter-isis-social-media-whack-mole/

Klausen, J. (2015). Tweeting the jihad: Social media networks of Western foreign fighters in Syria and Iraq. *Studies in Conflict & Terrorism,* 38(1), 1–22.

Kramer, A. D., Guillory, J. E., & Hancock J. T. (2014). Experimental evidence of massive-scale emotional contagion through social networks. *Proceedings of the National Academy of Sciences, 111*(24), 8788–8790. Retrieved from http://www.pnas.org/content/111/24/8788.full

Markham, A., & Buchanan, E. (2012). *Ethical decision-making and Internet research. Recommendations from the AoIR Ethics Working Committee (Version 2.0).* Retrieved from http://aoir.org/reports/ethics2.pdf

Meikle, G. (2016). *Social media: Communication, sharing and visibility.* New York, NY: Routledge.

Papadakis, M. (2003). *Computer-mediated communities: The implications of information, communication, and computational technologies for creating communities online.* Arlington, VA: SRI International.

Trepte, S., & Masure, P. K. (2016). *Cultural differences in media use, privacy and self disclosure.* Research report on a multicultural survey study. Germany: University of Honenheim.

Tsay-Vogel, M., Shanahan, J. E., & Signorielli, N. (2016). Social media cultivating perceptions of privacy: A five-year longitudinal analysis of privacy attitudes and self-disclosure behaviors among Facebook users. *New Media & Society.* Online first August 2. doi:10.1177/1461444816660731.

Uldam, J. (2016). Corporate management of visibility and the fantasy of the post-political: Social media and surveillance. *New Media & Society, 18*(2), 201–219.

United Nations. (1948). *The universal declaration of human rights.* General Assembly resolution 217 (III) International Bill of Human Rights. Paris: United Nations. Retrieved from http://www.un.org/en/ga/search/view_doc.asp?symbol=A/RES/217(III)

Vidino, L., & Hughes, S. (2015). *ISIS in America: From retweets to Raqqa.* The George Washington University.

World Medical Association. (1964). *WMA declaration of Helsinki – Ethical principles for medical research involving human subjects.* Adopted by the 18th General Assembly, Helsinki, Finland, June 1964, amended October 2013. Retrieved from http://www.wma.net/en/30publications/10policies/b3/

Yourish, K., Watkins, D., & Giratikanon, T. (2016). Where ISIS has directed and inspired attacks around the world. *New York Times.* Retrieved from http://www.nytimes.com/interactive/2015/06/17/world/middleeast/map-isis-attacks-around-the-world.html?_r=0

REACTION BY KATLEEN GABRIELS

The field of internet research ethics requires constant revisions and updates in order to adequately address the rapid changes. New technologies lead to shifting understandings, amongst others concerning informed consent and the researcher-informant relation. A world of big data also entails other rules and guidelines than one of "small" data; for instance, big data makes re-identification of alleged "anonymous" datasets easier. And even though we are still dealing with the transitions of the social age, we already face the ethical challenges of conducting research in the era of the Internet of Things (IoT).

Institutional review boards and researchers need to be flexible and dynamic to keep track of these challenges. In fact, to make the already multifaceted "networked digital communications" even more complex, the notion of "distributed responsibility" should be extended to students as well. Worldwide, numerous students conduct internet research for their Bachelor or Master's theses. The relational aspects of agency and ethical obligation, which are addressed in this chapter, also apply to students. The OkCupid incident in May 2016 disclosed the consequences of what can happen if ill-informed students follow their "gut feelings" about alleged public data. Two Danish students released identifiable datasets of 70,000 users of the dating website OkCupid, arguing that the data were already publicly available. This incident furthermore reveals that students as well can exert power over users, who did not give their consent for the release.

By integrating internet research ethics in students' curricula, potential risks and harms can be reduced. This is not only essential in order to diminish the likelihood of another OkCupid scenario, but also because a growing number of MA theses can be consulted online. If ethical principles are ignored or handled in a careless manner – for instance in terms of sloppy data protection, not obtaining an *informed* consent, or by not respecting confidentiality – undesirable effects are probable. Students need to be educated in order to become responsible and cautious researchers, to meet professional standards, and to raise their overall awareness. By making them more attentive for internet research ethics, core values and principles can be better protected.

Katleen Gabriels *is currently working as a postdoctoral researcher at the Department of Philosophy and Moral Sciences of the Vrije Universiteit Brussel (VUB), Brussels, Belgium. She is specialized in media ethics and computer ethics.*

REACTION BY CHRISTIAN PENTZOLD

The care researchers give to their ethical considerations is very much based on the assumption that the partners and participants of their endeavors dispose of inalienable entitlements. But what if inquiries have to make decisions in a social and political culture that contests the genuine moral agency of those people that should form part of their examination? Actually, such a situation opens up in the case presented by Hutchinson, Martin, and Sinpeng. On a normative level, it is thus provoked by the question if we should acknowledge the ethical claims of ISIS (Islamic State) combatants and followers at all. For sure, social science research has turned to delinquents and the legally and socially stigmatized and features already a long debate of how to respect their rights. At times, this bridging position between social circles of quite different public esteem has provoked considerable friction, for instance with prosecutors who wanted to access the confiding scholarly records and relations. Yet, with ISIS, investigations are confronted with a collective that not only antagonizes the systems of value and civic virtues considered to be at the heart of modern Western societies, but it also largely negates the very right to exist of the research drawn out there.

In addition to this fundamental challenge research dealing with ISIS also faces a practical problem. Even if it agrees to consider the ethical claims and moral rights of ISIS partisans, for example, when making use of their tweets or Facebook accounts, how could it possibly secure some sort of informed consent? Empirical research that wants to get close to people's orientations, sensitivities, relations, and modes of life usually relies on a minimal form of cooperation, compliance or at least connivance of those researched. In their contribution, Hutchinson, Martin, and Sinpeng thus advocate for a practice-based approach that helps to translate these complex considerations into procedural steps again. Yet, establishing informed consent, this promises to be hardly ever a neat affair that arrives at indisputable solutions. Rather, it might be better portrayed as a tentative and always preliminary deliberation, but only with those who want to engage in it.

Christian Pentzold *is an Associate Professor (Junior professor) for Communication and Media Studies with a focus on Media Society at ZeMKI, Centre for Media, Communication and Information Sciences, University of Bremen, Germany.*

CHAPTER FIVE

Lost Umbrellas

Bias and the Right to Be Forgotten in Social Media Research

REBEKAH TROMBLE AND DANIELA STOCKMANN

Since the European Court of Justice handed down its ruling in the 2014 *Costeja* case – finding that Google and other search engine operators must consider requests made by individuals to remove links to websites that contain the requesting party's personal information – scholars, policymakers, legal practitioners, media commentators, and corporate representatives around the globe have been vigorously debating the so-called "right to be forgotten." In the American context, many worry that recognizing such a right would undermine the First Amendment's protections for freedom of speech and press. In the European Union, a renamed "right to erasure" has become law as part of the EU's General Data Protection Regulation in 2016. The right to erasure "prevent[s] the indefinite storage and trade in electronic data, placing limits on the duration and purpose for which businesses" can retain such data (Tsesis, 2014, p. 433) and holds that individuals may request the deletion of data when those data have become irrelevant, are inaccurate, or cause the individual harm that is not outweighed by a public benefit in retaining the data (Koops, 2011).

Though most of the discussion surrounding the right to be forgotten and the right to erasure has focused on the limits and responsibilities of corporate and media data "controllers," internet users' basic right to remove and have removed content they personally generate – including content that they believe may have a detrimental effect on how they are publicly viewed – also needs to be taken seriously by scholars conducting internet research. At a minimum, the right to be forgotten points to important ethical concerns about research subjects' privacy, as well as how and when a subject's consent is given and withdrawn. Indeed, if we accept the common argument that formal consent needs not to be obtained from research subjects who have made their content entirely open to the public, the corollary would suggest that we have a responsibility to delete their data from our datasets when it is has been removed from the public domain.

And yet, to do so could undermine the validity and reliability of social scientific research findings, introducing bias and undercutting reproduction and replication efforts. Indeed, respecting and observing the right to be forgotten has the potential to hamper ongoing movements for greater social science data sharing and transparency. Hoping to increase the accessibility of publicly funded research, thwart data falsification, and improve the reproducibility and replicability of social science studies, researchers and policymakers have vowed to make data even more widely available. Thus, we face a dilemma: Do we protect the rights of research subjects by deleting their data when it is no longer in the public domain? Or do we safeguard the scientific process and the integrity of our research results – sharing data widely and making the right to erasure effectively impracticable?

In order to understand and address this dilemma, we first need a better grasp of just how serious the implications of honoring the right to erasure would be for social science research. That is, we need a clearer understanding of whether and to what extent inferences might be biased and basic scientific replicability undermined if deleted internet content were indeed removed from our datasets. To this end, we examine two Twitter datasets related to the 2014 Hong Kong protests, often referred to as the "umbrella revolution" or "umbrella movement." We collected these data from Twitter's historical archive using the same search parameters at two points in time – in December 2014, just as the Hong Kong protests were winding down, and one year later in December 2015 – and we use these datasets to assess the number of tweets deleted, as well as how these deletions impact social network metrics derived from the data.

As a case study, the umbrella movement presents an excellent opportunity to gauge, in concrete and practical ways, how the right to erasure might impact a large, growing, and influential body of work on the use of social media by social movement activists (cf. González-Bailón, Borge-Holthoefer, Rivero, & Moreno, 2011; Hanna, 2013; Harrigan, Achananuparp, & Lim, 2012; Tremayne, 2014). The Hong Kong protests represent a case in which the subjects being studied are likely to have compelling reasons to exercise their right to be forgotten. Though somewhat freer to express their views than are those in mainland China, Hong Kong residents have reason to be concerned about state censorship and repression and may wish to delete content to avoid monitoring, detention, or other forms of state control. The Hong Kong protests therefore represent exactly the type of case that should stimulate ethical concerns among internet researchers.

In laying out this analysis, we begin by offering a more detailed discussion of the umbrella movement, elucidating its context and developments. We then present a brief overview of Twitter, its archive, and the rules the company lays out for data use, including data deletion. Next, we provide a short description of the methods used to collect our Twitter data before moving on to an analysis of the differences between our two datasets and a discussion of the implications of these differences for social scientific research.[1]

THE HONG KONG UMBRELLA MOVEMENT

Protest erupted in Hong Kong on September 22, 2014 in reaction to a decision by the National People's Congress (NPC) of the People's Republic of China regarding electoral reform for the Chief Executive in Hong Kong. Currently, the Chief Executive is chosen by an election committee.[2] For the 2017 elections, the NPC decided that voters should be able to choose from a list of two or three candidates selected by the election committee and that each nominee would be eligible to run if he or she secured the support of more than 50% of that committee.[3] Critics argued that the election committee overrepresented the interests of Beijing and that without democratizing the selection of the election committee itself, the popular vote for the Chief Executive constituted mere window dressing. Because the Basic Law of the Hong Kong Special Administrative Region expressed the ultimate aim of selecting the Chief Executive upon nomination by a broadly representative election committee "in accordance with democratic procedures," protesters called for Beijing to fulfil its promise to implement genuine universal suffrage in this process.[4] Supporters of the decision argued that the letter of the law leaves room for interpretation and does not specify the timing of gradual electoral reforms.

During the protests, students and other citizens occupied a central square in Hong Kong, often referred to simply as "Central," as well as a few shopping streets. The occupation and protests came to be known as the "umbrella movement" or "umbrella revolution" after the pro-democracy protesters held up umbrellas as a protection against tear gas fired by police. Yellow ribbons also emerged as a symbol for peace worn by supporters and were seen fluttering in the city to condemn the use of tear gas and violence by the Hong Kong police.

But not everyone in Hong Kong agreed with the umbrella movement and some began displaying blue ribbons to support the authorities and the police (the latter of whom wear blue uniforms). Blue-ribbon supporters accused student protesters of engaging in violent protests and of severely disrupting social order.[5] The blue ribbon counter-movement also took to the streets, and numerous clashes took place between yellow and blue ribbon supporters until the occupation ended on December 15, 2014. Ultimately, the umbrella movement protests failed to secure revisions to the NPC Standing Committee's electoral procedures.

While the Chinese government avoided direct contact with the protesters, it kept a close eye on how Hong Kong officials handled the protests and sought to direct the response from behind closed doors.[6] As early as September 28, the Propaganda Department, State Council Information Office, and related institutions issued directives to strictly manage interactive media and delete all harmful information regarding "occupy central."[7] Words such as "Hong Kong," "barricades," "occupy central," and "umbrella" were censored on Sina Weibo, a popular Twitter-like social media platform in mainland China.[8] The official line of Chinese media was to cover the protests, but focusing on blue-ribbon themes. The main state broadcaster, China Central Television, focused on the negative consequences of the protests on the economy and the responsibility of the protesters to end the illegal occupations. Elections and protesters' demands were framed as a foreign intervention in Chinese domestic affairs. People's Daily, the mouthpiece of the central Chinese Communist Party, claimed that protesters were trained by foreign forces in order to undermine the authority of the government.[9]

Not surprisingly, then, protesters in Hong Kong predominantly used social platforms outside of the so-called "Great Chinese Firewall," platforms such as Facebook and Twitter, to spread information and mobilize support. Our analysis of Twitter therefore provides insights into the network connections formed between and among both citizens located in Hong Kong and international observers of the movement.

TWITTER'S TERMS OF SERVICE

Twitter, its tools for data collection, and its terms for third-party data use provide an excellent opportunity to explore the implications of the right to be forgotten for social scientific research. Twitter maintains an historical archive of all tweets and associated metadata generated since its inception in 2006 to which scholars and others may gain (paid) access. However, Twitter removes any tweet from the historical archive that has been deleted from the platform for any reason. Thus, if a user deletes an individual tweet or closes an entire account, the associated data no longer appear in the archive. The same is true if Twitter suspends an account or removes spam. Even retweets are removed when the original tweet is deleted. In short, substantial amounts of historical Twitter data disappear or "decay" over time.

Moreover, as part of its terms of service agreement, Twitter requires that third parties "respect users' control and privacy" by deleting any "Content that Twitter reports as deleted or expired," as well as any content that has been changed from public to private.[10] As such, Twitter's terms of service require that researchers recognize the right of users to control access to their personal data at any point in time, regardless of whether it was once available to the public. This, in turn, places a researcher's data in a constant state of flux. With data perpetually decaying, pure reproducibility – whereby one verifies results using the same set of data and following the same analytical procedures – is by very definition impossible. And if one is interested in examining the same issue or event, it may also impact replicability – or the process of testing one study's results using similar research procedures and conditions, but employing new data. That is, the robustness of our findings may be called into question by subsequent studies relying on incomplete and potentially biased data.

THE UMBRELLA MOVEMENT TWITTER DATA

Just how much might we expect the data to vary over time? And how different might the conclusions we draw from these data be? In order to answer these questions we have gathered two Twitter datasets. Both capture tweets, including retweets sent between October 1st and October 15th, 2014 containing one or more of the following popular hashtags: #HongKong, #OccupyCentral, #UmbrellaRevolution, #OccupyAdmiralty, #HK929, and #HKStudentStrike.[11] The first dataset was obtained by purchasing tweets from Twitter's historical archive via Sifter, one of a handful of third-party applications licensed to search, retrieve, and re-sell archive data.[12] We collected the archive data on December 21, 2014, just after the Hong Kong occupations ended. However, the fact that we obtained the data two months after their origination means that even this dataset does not represent a complete record of relevant Twitter activity. Indeed, only Twitter's so-called "Firehose" application programming interface (API) offers real-time capture of the full stream of public tweets, but, as of writing, access to the Firehose costs around $3,000 per month and requires substantial technical and infrastructural support, placing it out of reach for the vast majority of social scientists. Because we were interested in how many and which tweets had been deleted over time, we used the archive dataset as the starting point for the second round of data collection. Each tweet contains a unique ID number that can be used to capture the tweet and its associated metadata from another Twitter API, the REST API, which is open to the public and free of charge. Thus, on December 30, 2015, we queried the REST API with the full list of tweet IDs found in the 2014 data. Any tweets that had not been deleted as of December 30, 2015 were thereby recaptured.

The archive dataset contains 556,412 tweets, while the recapture dataset comprises 506,356 tweets, or 91.0% of the original data. This finding is in line with previous research suggesting that internet data decays by about 10% annually (SalahEldeen & Nelson, 2012). Thus, it does not seem that inordinate amounts of data rapidly disappear, even when related to an inherently contentious event such as the Hong Kong umbrella movement. Under many circumstances, we might be satisfied with the recapture dataset. Following the law of large numbers, and because we are working with such high-volume data, when 91% of the data remain intact, many basic descriptive measures should remain acceptably close. Take, for example, the hashtags found in each dataset. The archive contains 24,500 unique hashtags, the recaptured dataset, 23,248, or 93.0%. The average number of times each hashtag appears in the archive data is 49.88, while average frequency is 46.72 in the recaptured data. Indeed, a t-test reveals there is no difference in the means between the two datasets.

BIAS IN SOCIAL NETWORK ANALYSIS

However, few social scientists will be interested in such broad, aggregate findings alone. Indeed, a great many scholars are particularly interested in the social networks resulting from social media data, including Twitter. Communication researchers studying discourse and framing, for instance, frequently analyze hashtag co-occurrence networks. Hashtags are often used to signal topics or to otherwise express intent and meaning within a tweet. Take the six hashtags we used to collect our own Twitter data: Each conveys, at a minimum, that the tweet is associated with the events occurring in Hong Kong. However, when these hashtags appear in the same tweet with additional hashtags, we are often able to identify deeper meaning and intent. We might expect, for instance, that when #OccupyCentral co-occurs in a tweet with #Democracy, the Twitter user sees the movement as a campaign for democratic freedom and likely supports the movement's agenda. On the other hand, a tweet that contains both #OccupyCentral and #BlueRibbon likely denies the legitimacy of and supports the police response to the Hong Kong protests. Thus, hashtag co-occurrence networks might be used to examine the topics discussed online during a given event, to analyze how frames spread via social media, to explore how discourse and framing shift over time, and so on.

Many scholars also construct and analyze user and mentions networks in order to examine digital leadership dynamics within organizations, events, or both. Directed user-mention networks reproduce the connections formed when one Twitter user mentions another by using the latter's @username in the body of the tweet. Users who frequently mention others often serve as diffusers in a social movement network, helping to spread information to or about many others. Those who are frequently mentioned, on the other hand, are often key leaders within a movement. Similarly, mention co-occurrence networks (i.e., two mentions appear in the same tweet) may help to uncover movement or group leaders, including brokers – or those actors who serve as key links between otherwise unconnected, or at least distantly connected, actors.

Unfortunately, however, social network analyses are particularly vulnerable to biases generated by missing values. That is, when analyzing social networks, a very large sample may still produce considerable biases in our findings. In a study of digitally-gathered social networks, Wang, Xiaolin, McFarland, and Leskovec (2012) investigated the impact of measurement error introduced as a result of missing nodes and edges (edges are another term for the connections or ties between nodes). Randomly removing ever larger numbers of nodes and edges from these digital networks, they found that networks with positively skewed degree distributions often tolerate low levels of measurement error. In such networks a small proportion of nodes have a large number of connections, while many have just one connection. As such, if even a small number of highly-connected nodes or, similarly, a small number of edges tied to highly-connected nodes, are removed, the relative position of all the nodes within the network can change rather significantly.

And this is precisely the type of network we are most likely to observe from Twitter data. Because, for example, only a small handful of users tweet at high volume, very few hashtags trend, and so on, most Twitter networks are likely to have positively skewed degree distributions. Thus, even if Twitter data decays somewhat slowly, just a small amount of missing data may result in significantly biased network measures.

We test this expectation empirically by analyzing several network graphs and metrics generated from our two datasets. Each graph corresponds with one of the three commonly applied networks described above: hashtag co-occurrence, mention co-occurrence, and directed user-mention networks. In the latter case, a person tweeting (the user) "directs" or "sends" a connection to each person or entity s/he mentions in a given tweet; the person mentioned therefore "receives" this connection.

For all three network types we compare the number of nodes and edges, as well as three common node-level network measures – degree, betweenness, and eigenvector centrality – across our two datasets. Degree centrality represents a count of the number of ties each node has. Thus, in the hashtag co-occurrence network, if #HongKong occurs in tweets alongside 20,000 other hashtags, its degree centrality measure is 20,000. Note that in our data these are not unique observations. If #HongKong appears with #Democracy 2,000 times, each of these co-occurrences counts as a tie (in social network terminology, we therefore have "weighted edges"). In our user-mention directed networks, we measure both in-degree centrality (i.e., the number of mentions *received*) and out-degree centrality (i.e., the number of mentions *sent*). Thus, if User A sends 20 total tweets, each of which mentions User B (and only User B), User A's out-degree centrality is 20. And if User B receives only these mentions, her in-degree centrality is also 20.

Our second network metric, betweenness centrality, is a measure of brokerage or gatekeeping. It measures how often a given node falls along the shortest path between two other nodes. Nodes with high betweenness centrality are typically presumed to control access and information within a network. At the very least, they have the potential to significantly disrupt the flow of information (Borgatti, Everett, & Johnson, 2013, p. 174). In hashtag co-occurrence networks, hashtags with high betweenness centrality connect multiple concepts to one another and thus are key to interpreting the broader discourses, concepts, and frames surrounding a given issue or event.

The third metric, eigenvector centrality, is a variation on degree centrality that takes into account a node's own ties, plus the ties of its neighboring nodes, plus the ties of the neighbors' neighbors, and so on. The reasoning here is that a node is especially influential if those to which it is connected are also influential. In other words, a node that has many ties to nodes that are otherwise unconnected is much less important than a node that has many ties to nodes that are themselves highly connected. Eigenvector centrality is thus a measure of *relative* influence or popularity within a network (Borgatti et al., 2013, p. 168).

We are ultimately interested in the robustness of each of these metrics as we move from the archive to the recaptured dataset. We evaluate robustness in two key ways: first, by calculating the relative difference, or error, between the centrality score observed for a given node in the archive and recapture networks; second, by comparing the ordered rankings of nodes by each centrality measure. We describe both of these procedures and their results in detail below.

FINDINGS

First, however, let us take a look at some of the basic network characteristics. Table 1 offers a set of descriptive statistics for all six network graphs drawn from the archive and recaptured data. Across all graphs, the vast majority of nodes and edges are present in the recaptured data. At the lowest end, 84.07% of edges were recaptured in the hashtag co-occurrence network, and 88.58% of nodes were recaptured in the mentions co-occurrence network. The table also confirms that each of the networks derived from the archive data have positively skewed degree distributions. The positive skew is particularly high in the hashtag and user-mention graphs. We therefore expect all three networks to be highly susceptible to bias, but the hashtag and user-mention networks especially so.

Network Measurement Error

The first calculation we use to assess the robustness of our social network metrics is measurement error. In statistics, measurement error is understood as the difference between the true value of an item and its observed value. Because we do not

Table 1: Descriptive statistics for the archive and recapture networks.

		Nodes		Edges		
		Count	% Recaptured	Count	% Recaptured	Degree Skewness
Hashtags	Archive	24,500	94.89	1,494,751	84.07	117.88
	Recapture	23,248		1,256,621		114.90
Mentions	Archive	15,301	88.58	207,509	90.36	30.04
	Recapture	13,553		187,504		20.00
User-Mention	Archive	145,728	91.84	586,738	90.76	158.02
	Recapture	133,833		532,486		153.80

have the full population of tweets meeting our data collection criteria, we cannot assess the centrality measures generated by recaptured data against their true values. However, we are able to use the archive data as a near approximation, treating it as a baseline for comparison.

In what follows, we assess network measurement error by comparing across data sets. We gauge the relative error generated in the recaptured data by calculating the difference between the centrality scores observed in each network for a given node and dividing by the node's score in the archive network. Take, for example, the degree centrality scores for #HongKong in the hashtag co-occurrence networks. In the archive network graph, this hashtag has 20,595 ties. In the recapture graph, #HongKong has 19,508 ties. Its relative error is therefore 0.0528, or ((20,595–19,508)/20,595). In other words, #HongKong's degree centrality score in the recapture network is 5.28% lower than that of the archive.

To more fully illustrate these calculations, Table 2 provides a comparison of the degree, betweenness, and eigenvector centrality scores, as well as their relative errors, for the top five nodes in the archive mentions co-occurrence network. Note that the top mention in terms of both degree centrality and betweenness centrality does not appear at all in the recaptured data. For those nodes that do not appear, we assign the maximum relative error value observed across the networks. For degree centrality, the maximum value is 1.00. No node can have more connections in the recaptured graph than it does in the archive, and a completely disconnected node has degree 0. However, for betweenness and eigenvector centrality, where missing nodes and edges can substantially lower or raise the centrality of other nodes, relative error can be much higher. As Table 3 – which presents the mean relative error for all nodes in the hashtags, mentions, and user-mention networks – shows, the maximum values associated with betweenness centrality are particularly high.

Table 2: Relative error, mentions co-occurrence networks.

Degree Centrality			
	Score		
Mention	Archive	Recapture	Relative Error
rightnowio_feed	1,072	–	1.0000
hkdemonow	699	645	0.0773
oclphk	572	551	0.0367
tomgrundy	426	374	0.1221
scmp_news	377	353	0.0637
Betweenness Centrality			
	Score		
Mention	Archive	Recapture	Relative Error
rightnowio_feed	13,976,953	–	36,625.1523
hkdemonow	5,923,100	4,920,030	0.1693
oclphk	5,636,451	5,794,951	–0.0281
hk928umbrella	3,881,635	2,989,842	0.2297
wsj	3,420,049	3,020,590	0.1168
Eigenvector Centrality			
	Score		
Mention	Archive	Recapture	Relative Error
hkdemonow	1.0000	1.000	0.0000
williamsjon	0.9915	0.9915	0.0000
panphil	0.1907	0.1900	0.0041
france7776	0.0739	0.0738	0.0016
kemc	0.0636	0.0637	–0.0014

Following Wang and colleagues (2012), we presume that the bias introduced by very low levels of error, 0.0500 or less, is likely to be "trivial" (p. 407). But above this level, bias is likely to have a more substantial impact on one's findings. As Table 3 shows, the mean relative error is above 0.0500 for all but the in-degree centrality scores found when comparing the user-mention networks. Degree centrality proves to be the most robust measure for each network category. In comparison, betweenness centrality proves exceedingly prone to error, with the mention co-occurrence networks demonstrating an average relative difference of 0.6207 and the hashtag networks a remarkable 4.2908.

Table 3: Mean relative error.

		Mean Relative Error	Standard Deviation	Maximum
Degree Centrality	Hashtags	0.0665	0.2309	1.0000
	Mentions	0.1411	0.3259	1.0000
	User-mention, In-degree	0.0210	0.1297	1.000
	User-mention, Out-degree	0.0805	0.2669	1.0000
Betweenness Centrality	Hashtags	4.2908	276.4510	36,625.1523
	Mentions	0.6207	21.0771	2,207.8168
	User-mention	0.1254	15.4421	3,398.5269
Eigenvector Centrality	Hashtags	0.1412	0.2166	1.0000
	Mentions	0.2000	0.3313	2.9997
	User-mention	0.0510	0.1959	2.6848

Correlation of Centrality Rankings

These results already raise serious concerns about biases resulting from analysis of the recaptured data. However, comparing general results across data sets, or calculating the mean relative error, does not provide the whole picture. The distribution of these differences across a network also matters. Even when the mean error for all nodes is quite low, if that error is distributed unevenly – and particularly if larger errors are associated with the most central actors – it is likely to have serious consequences for our findings. When interpreting network data, one is usually particularly interested in the most central nodes. Using the hashtags data, one might focus on the most prominent hashtags and their connections in order to unpack and understand the dominant topics or discourses. Examining the mentions or user-mentions networks, our interest is likely to be in the most influential actors and their roles in the networks. But, if we are misidentifying who those actors are due to measurement error, our conclusions will be fundamentally flawed.

With this in mind, the second method we use to assess the robustness of our social network metrics employs Kendall's tau correlations of rank ordered lists for each of the centrality measures. Kendall's tau gauges the ordinal association, or the similarity of the rank orderings, between two lists. Thus, the lower Kendall's tau, the more likely we are to misidentify the most central actors or hashtags when using the recaptured data. In order to illustrate some of these rank orderings as they appear in the Hong Kong data, Table 4 offers a comparison of the top 10 nodes in the mentions co-occurrence networks for each centrality measure.

To calculate Kendall's tau, we take the archive data and the rank orderings that result from those data as baseline. As with the relative errors, we use 0.0500 as the cutoff point, presuming that correlations of 0.9500 or higher are likely to result in minimal levels of bias. Table 5 displays the correlation coefficients for each centrality measure based on lists of the top 10, 25, 50, 100, 250, 500, and 1000 nodes in each network.

In total, only 12 out of 70 (17.14%) correlation coefficients are 0.9500 or higher and most fall substantially below this threshold. Degree centrality is again most robust, with an average correlation coefficient across all three networks of 0.8662, and it is particularly robust for in-degree rankings in the user-mention network. Indeed, this is the only metric for which the mean correlation for all lists – from top 10 to top 1000 – is higher than 0.9500. On the other hand, with an average coefficient of 0.6858 across the hashtags, mentions, and user-mention networks, betweenness centrality is again least robust.

Table 4: Top 10 nodes in the mentions co-occurrence networks.

Degree Centrality					
Archive			Recapture		
Rank	Node	Score	Rank (archive)	Node	Score
1	rightnowio_feed*	1,072	2	hkdemonow	645
2	hkdemonow	699	3	oclphk	551
3	oclphk	572	4	tomgrundy	374
4	tomgrundy	426	5	scmp_news	353
5	scmp_news	377	6	wsj	294
6	wsj	323	7	bbcworld	273
7	bbcworld	291	8	williamsjon	245
8	williamsjon	257	9	time	231
9	time	249	11	hk928umbrella	221
10	krislc	245	10	krislc	217
Betweenness Centrality					
Archive			Recapture		
Rank	Node	Score	Rank (archive)	Node	Score
1	rightnowio_feed*	13,976,953.11	3	oclphk	5,794,951.49
2	hkdemonow	5,923,100.21	2	hkdemonow	4,920,030.04
3	oclphk	5,636,450.54	5	wsj	3,020,590.47
4	hk928umbrella	3,881,634.82	4	hk928umbrella	2,989,841.99
5	wsj	3,420,048.63	8	scmp_news	2,772,167.87

6	tomgrundy	3,190,610.81	6	tomgrundy	2,595,443.44
7	time	2,946,749.75	7	time	2,294,809.83
8	scmp_news	2,803,754.42	9	krislc	2,235,635.71
9	krislc	1,998,297.65	10	nytimes	1,703,180.23
10	nytimes	1,954,599.23	11	bbcworld	1,703,159.88

Eigenvector Centrality					
Archive			Recapture		
Rank	Node	Score	Rank (archive)	Node	Score
1	hkdemonow	1.0000	1	hkdemonow	1.0000
2	williamsjon	0.9915	2	williamsjon	0.9915
3	panphil	0.1907	3	panphil	0.1900
4	france7776	0.0739	4	france7776	0.0738
5	kemc	0.0636	5	kemc	0.0637
6	zuki_zucchini	0.0607	6	zuki_zucchini	0.0605
7	raykwong	0.0400	7	raykwong	0.0402
8	lisahorne	0.0236	8	lisahorne	0.0241
9	paddycosgrave	0.0180	9	paddycosgrave	0.0182
10	Afp	0.0148	10	afp	0.0152

*Node does not appear in the recaptured data.

Table 5: Kendall's tau correlations.

Degree Centrality				
			User-mention	
	Hashtags	Mentions	In-degree	Out-degree
Top 10	1.0000	0.6000	1.0000	0.5111
Top 25	0.9583	0.7893	0.9933	0.7179
Top 50	0.9289	0.7911	0.9763	0.7843
Top 100	0.9303	0.8563	0.9595	0.8619
Top 250	0.9071	0.8473	0.9133	0.8567
Top 500	0.9016	0.8610	0.9060	0.8605
Top 1,000	0.8852	0.8727	0.9152	0.8705
Mean	0.9302	0.8025	0.9519	0.7804

	Betweenness Centrality		
	Hashtags	Mentions	User-mention
Top 10	1.000	0.4222	0.2000
Top 25	0.9733	0.6000	0.3733
Top 50	0.9118	0.6424	0.5673
Top 100	0.8040	0.6962	0.5875
Top 250	0.8253	0.7291	0.6739
Top 500	0.7739	0.7066	0.7133
Top 1,000	0.7591	0.7046	0.7373
Mean	0.8639	0.6430	0.5504
	Eigenvector Centrality		
	Hashtags	Mentions	User-mention
Top 10	0.9111	1.0000	0.3778
Top 25	0.9333	0.9867	0.5400
Top 50	0.8173	0.9755	0.6686
Top 100	0.7515	0.9455	0.7160
Top 250	0.7723	0.9194	0.7365
Top 500	0.8375	0.8922	0.7372
Top 1,000	0.8652	0.8735	0.7112
Mean	0.8412	0.9418	0.6410

Interestingly, the correlation coefficients for eigenvector centrality in the user-mention network are very low – ranging from 0.3778 to 0.7365, with an average of 0.6410. This occurs despite the fact that the average relative error for user-mention eigenvector centrality was just 0.0510. As it turns out, this discrepancy occurs precisely because the error is distributed unevenly across the network. The ten most central nodes have an average relative error of 0.3606.

The Kendall's tau results for the hashtag networks are also surprisingly weak. Given the fact that we collected our data by querying tweets containing one or more of six hashtags, we would expect the Kendall's tau coefficients to be very high, especially in the small (i.e., top 10, top 25) lists. Though the correlations are above the 0.9500 threshold for the top 10 and top 25 nodes based on degree and betweenness centrality, the hashtags network actually proves much less robust than the mentions network for eigenvector centrality, never rising above 0.9333.

CONCLUSION

Taken together, these findings suggest that honoring the right to be forgotten in social media research is likely to have substantial consequences for social scientists. Should we acknowledge that, when obtained without formal consent, we have little right to maintain – and, in particular, to *share* – data once they are removed from the public domain, the inferences drawn from such "decayed" data are likely to be considerably biased.

This seems particularly true if we are using decayed data to conduct social network analysis – though the magnitude of the impact does vary by the network metric in question. As we have seen, measurement error is extremely high for betweenness centrality measures. A year after the Hong Kong protests ended, it is clear that key data regarding brokers and the links they provide between concepts and actors in our Twitter networks were lost. Moreover, this extremely high degree of error promotes flawed conclusions regarding the relative prominence of various hashtags, users, and mentions.

Degree centrality, on the other hand, is the most robust network metric. The degree of error across all the networks proved relatively low, and the ranking correlations comparatively high. And yet, only the in-degree centrality measures, drawn from the user-mention networks, fall within generally acceptable ranges of error.

The last metric, eigenvector centrality, rests between the first two metrics. Relative error is much lower than that associated with betweenness, but is still substantial. Because eigenvector centrality scores are based not just on the ties of a given node itself but on those ties, plus the ties of its neighbors, plus the ties of its neighbors' neighbors and so forth, a small amount of missing data can quickly distort our understanding of influence and popularity within a network (Wang et al., 2012, p. 401). The eigenvector centrality results also provide a clear portrait of the impact that the distribution of errors can have on our findings. Even when the mean error across all nodes is quite low, if larger errors are associated with the most central actors – precisely as occurs in the user-mention network – we are likely to reach flawed conclusions regarding which nodes are most central. To be sure, looking across the Kendall's tau results for all network metrics, it is clear that focusing on just the top 10 or 25 nodes would generally be ill-advised. However, even as we reach deeper into the data – looking all the way to the top 1000 nodes – rank correlations remain troublingly low.

Of course, these findings are based on limited data. We would ideally like to be able to compare recaptured data to the full population of tweets meeting our selection criteria. And yet, measurement error will always be present to some extent in empirical data. Even had we been able to obtain tweets in real time from Twitter's Firehose API, technical and infrastructural perturbations on both the data sending and receiving ends would result in some degree of error. Moreover, we believe that the archive data we employ in our study represent a reasonable compromise between accessibility (i.e., they were not too costly and did not require vast technical and infrastructural resources) and proximity to the population of relevant data. These parameters place such data within reach of other social scientists who might like to explore this line of questioning.

Indeed, we believe this is a line of inquiry worth further pursuit. Our analysis has provided a set of initial findings using a single case study – the 2014 Hong Kong umbrella movement – and considered the implications for a popular, but still singular, methodology – social network analysis. Nonetheless, the implications are clear: If we wish to take the right to be forgotten seriously, scholars must begin discussions about how to best protect both the rights of their research subjects and the integrity of social scientific processes. A full-speed-ahead approach to data sharing makes the former impossible, but, conversely, a total embrace of the right to be forgotten seems likely to introduce substantial bias and undercuts efforts to ensure replicability in our research.

NOTES

1. This research has received funding from the European Research Council under the European Union's Seventh Framework Programme (FP/2007-2013)/ERC Grant Agreement n. [338478].
2. For details of the composition of the election committee, see Annex I of Basic Law at http://www.basiclaw.gov.hk/en/basiclawtext/images/basiclaw_full_text_en.pdf, accessed on August 8, 2016.
3. http://news.xinhuanet.com/politics/2014-08/31/c_1112298240.htm, accessed on April 16, 2016; http://www.bbc.com/news/world-asia-china-27921954, accessed on April 16, 2016.
4. See Article 45 of the Basic Law at http://www.basiclaw.gov.hk/en/basiclawtext/images/basiclaw_full_text_en.pdf, accessed on August 8, 2016.
5. http://cpc.people.com.cn/n/2014/1003/c87228-25774432.html, accessed on April 16, 2016; http://www.rfa.org/mandarin/yataibaodao/gangtai/xl2-10022014102343.html, accessed on April 16, 2016.
6. http://www.nytimes.com/2014/10/18/world/asia/china-is-directing-response-to-hong-kong-protests.html?_r=0, accessed July 24, 2015. http://www.ejinsight.com/20150326-has-leung-really-secured-beijings-blessing-to-seek-second-term/, accessed July 24, 2015.
7. China Digital Times, http://chinadigitaltimes.net/2014/09/minitrue-delete-harmful-information-hong-kong/, accessed July 24, 2015.
8. http://www.nytimes.com/2014/10/01/world/asia/chinese-web-censors-struggle-with-hong-kong-protest.html, accessed July 24, 2015.
9. http://opinion.people.com.cn/n/2014/0929/c1003-25761887.html, accessed July 24, 2015. http://www.nytimes.com/2014/09/01/world/asia/hong-kong-elections.html, accessed July 24, 2015. See also http://cmp.hku.hk/2014/10/10/36410/, accessed July 24, 2015.
10. Twitter Developer Policy, https://dev.twitter.com/overview/terms/policy, latest version effective May 18, 2015.
11. The hashtag queries were not case sensitive.
12. See http://discovertext.com/sifter/.

REFERENCES

Borgatti, S. P., Everett, M. E., & Johnson, J. C. (2013). *Analyzing social networks*. Thousand Oaks, CA: Sage Publications.

González-Bailón, S., Borge-Holthoefer J., Rivero, A., & Moreno, Y. (2011). The dynamics of protest recruitment through an online network. *Scientific Reports, 1*(197), 1–6.

Hanna, A. (2013). Computer-aided content analysis of digitally enabled movements. *Mobilization: An International Quarterly, 18*(4), 367–388.

Harrigan, N., Achananuparp, P., & Lim, E.-P. (2012). Influentials, novelty, and social contagion: The viral power of average friends, close communities, and old news. *Social Networks, 34*(4), 470–480.

Koops, B.-J. (2011). *Forgetting footprints, shunning shadows: A critical analysis of the "right to be forgotten" in big data practice*. Retrieved from http://papers.ssrn.com/abstract=1986719

SalahEldeen, H. M., & Nelson, M. L. (2012). Losing y revolution: How many resources shared on social media have been lost? In P. Zaphiris, G. Buchanan, E. Rasmussen, & F. Loizides (Eds.), *Theory and practice of digital libraries* (pp. 125–137). Berlin: Springer.

Tremayne, M. (2014). Anatomy of protest in the digital era: A network analysis of Twitter and Occupy Wall Street. *Social Movement Studies, 13*(1), 110–126.

Tsesis, A. (2014). Right to erasure: Privacy, data brokers, and the indefinite retention of data. *Wake Forest Law Review, 49*(2), 433–484.

Wang, D. J., Xiaolin S., McFarland, D. A., & Leskovec, J. (2012). Measurement error in network data: A re-classification. *Social Networks, 34*(4), 396–409.

REACTION BY ZOETANYA SUJON

The question of protecting and safeguarding research subjects is at the heart of every ethics code in most human and social sciences, a question that must be balanced with research integrity and validity. Internet-based research raises new challenges for how to navigate these issues. The ethical consequences for the choices global platforms like Google make around the management of personal data are still becoming known and are likely to be uneven. The "right to be forgotten" is also complex. Take, for example, "Celebgate" and the release of 500+ hacked nude photos of dozens of celebrities in 2014 that resulted in an almost immediate lawsuit being threatened against Google for not removing photos, URLs and other internet content fast enough. Ordinary people do not have that kind of power or resources for removing personal, hacked, or unwanted content. In terms of big datasets, a similar inequity grows between researchers who can afford access to data and those who cannot (Zelenkauskaite & Bucy, 2016).

Yet, in terms of safeguarding research subjects, the bigger issue for researchers is how we manage the balance between transparency and protecting research subjects. The authors of "Lost Umbrellas", make a really valuable point about bias and decay in internet research, yet like many others in the field, publish easily locatable Twitter handles to active Twitter accounts. The complexities of internet data raise conflicts between markers of quality research like transparency and accountability to safeguarding research subjects through confidentiality, anonymity, privacy, and informed consent. Publishing Twitter handles, tweets, and other identifiable content means personal information becomes fixed permanently in publicly accessible text which is an issue that must be addressed prior to broader issues related to global platforms. Before asking about the right to be forgotten, we need to work out how to effectively manage privacy, anonymity, and transparency in our own research.

Zelenkauskaite, A., & Bucy, E. P. (2016). A scholarly divide: Social media, big data, and unattainable scholarship. *First Monday, 21*(5), http://ojphi.org/ojs/index.php/fm/article/view/6358

Zoetanya Sujon *is a Senior Lecturer in Media Theory at Regent's University London and HEA Fellow, specializing in new technologies, digital media and culture.*

REACTION BY ARVIND NARAYANAN

The authors show that deleting a small fraction of tweets from a corpus used for social science research can lead to a significant change in the conclusions drawn. The point is important and well taken, especially for research that looks back at historical events. Yet for research that seeks to derive generalizable, scientific insights from the data, this finding is an opportunity rather than a threat. If a research conclusion is drastically affected by withholding a small number of inputs, it suggests that the finding may not have been statistically robust in the first place. Matthew Salganik (2017) calls big data "digital exhaust" and points out that it is often "incomplete, inaccessible, non-representative, drifting, algorithmically confounded, inaccessible, dirty, and sensitive". Using such data for research is inherently tricky. Even researchers who don't face the possibility of withdrawn data should look for ways to improve scientific validity. One method could be to simulate withdrawal of data from the public sphere and measure the effect on the conclusions.

Salganik, M. J. (2017). *Bit by bit: Social research in the digital age.* Princeton, NJ: Princeton University Press. Open review edition.

Arvind Narayanan *is an Assistant Professor of Computer Science at Princeton. He leads the Princeton Web Transparency and Accountability Project to uncover how companies collect and use our personal information.*

CHAPTER SIX

Bad Judgment, Bad Ethics?

Validity in Computational Social Media Research

CORNELIUS PUSCHMANN

Data quality is a key concern in empirical social science. In quantitative research paradigms, data quality reflects the ability of a variable to allow valid inferences about social processes or entities (Trochim & Donnelly, 2006, p. 20). In this chapter, I discuss the role of data quality in relation to research ethics. I frame data quality as an ethical issue (in addition to being a methodological one) because a particular set of assumptions about what data is shapes both the methodological and ethical considerations of researchers. I draw on several cases that have been critically discussed by the scientific community in relation to their operationalization, including Google Flu Trends (Carneiro & Mylonakis, 2009) and the so-called Facebook emotional contagion study (Kramer, Guillory, & Hancock, 2014). I close by showing how the field is progressing in terms of both ethical and methodological considerations.

INTRODUCTION

How valid are the results of analyses that rely on the digital breadcrumbs that all of us leave behind when we use the internet? While initially this hardly seems to be a question related to ethics,[1] I argue that in computational research, data quality and operationalization are equally methodological and ethical issues that impact both academia and industry research. Billions of users log on to their preferred platforms on a daily basis, generating petabytes of what is sometimes called digital trace data for its ability to function as the record of interaction with a platform, as well as a basis for inferences about social behavior more broadly (Cioffi-Revilla, 2010; Golder & Macy, 2014; Lazer et al., 2009; Ruths & Pfeffer, 2014; Strohmaier & Wagner, 2014). These data can be harnessed for a variety of purposes, from disaster prevention to credit scoring and is hoped to shed a new light on well-established social phenomena (Shah, Capella, & Neuman, 2015; Watts, 2015).

The Google Flu Trends (GFT) case discussed by Lazer, Kennedy, King, and Vespignani (2014) is a case in point because it highlights several of these entirely practical problems. GFT's predictions turned out to be inaccurate because of confounded variables or, as the authors wryly acknowledge, "the initial version of GFT was part flu detector, part winter detector" (p. 1203). Mahrt and Scharkow (2013) highlight this difficulty, phrased in slightly different terms, when they caution that "scholars should be careful to take data for what it truly represents (e.g., traces of behavior), but not infer too much about possible attitudes, emotions, or motivations of those whose behavior created the data" (p. 24), while Giglietto and Rossi argue somewhat more optimistically that "the idea of using user-generated content for sociological research may be considered an extension of traditional study based on the content analysis of data produced by mass media" (p. 34). Yet the operationalization in GFT that equates fluctuations in search queries with flu outbreaks was clearly inaccurate, because too many sources of error stand between the human expression via a search query and the ability for its sheer frequency to reliably and robustly predict a particular medical condition. In what follows, I will outline some considerations regarding the quality and qualities of social media data in relation to social research with a computational focus. In particular, I will highlight the unintended consequences of faulty operationalization.

WHERE DOES THE DATA COME FROM, AND WHAT IS DONE WITH IT?

Just as digital data are widely seen as the raw material that fuels social media research, its methods are the tools that transform this raw material into knowledge. The picture of handling physical objects, while evocative, comes with certain limitations. Data in this area of research are often secondary, meaning they are generated for a purpose other than research and later appropriated (or "cooked") for this end, often raising a range of complex ethical questions (Bowker, 2013; boyd & Crawford, 2012; Metcalf & Crawford, 2016; Zimmer, 2010). All data need interpretation, but appropriating content created for other purposes than research is inherently risky. Data from a survey or experiment may be detrimentally affected by biases, such as social desirability in responses, or by the artificiality of a laboratory setting, but experimental data, though cumbersome to produce, are also under much closer control by the researcher than communication or log data that are collected as an afterthought, subjected to post-hoc analysis, and often interpreted at the aggregate level. Judging people by the digital traces that they leave behind is different from following a physical trail. Hypothesis-testing in particular is problematic when the articulation of questions takes place after collecting data, when an incentive exists to confirm a hypothesis, rather than to reject it.

Just as social media research draws on a wide range of data, from tweets and Facebook comments to network data and log files, the methods used by most quantitative computational researchers are collected from a variety of academic fields and from industry research, and assembled depending on the concrete aims involved in a project. Put together, these methods form an eclectic toolbox that leaves much room for interpretation and speculation. An underlying argument in what follows is that the data used in social media research are *signs* rather than *traces*, and that, accordingly, a semiotic perspective on their meaning as relatively flexible is instructive. Social media researchers accordingly are interpreters of signs and the methods at their disposal aim to enable powerful analyses based on large volumes of signs. However, there is something unusual about the understanding of signs in (quantitative) social media research, namely that their malleability is very much productively utilized in research, while the programmatic discourse tends to downplay it. This tension is exemplified by what Jungherr (2015) refers to as *the mirror-hypothesis* and *the mediation-hypothesis*. According to the mirror-hypothesis, digital trace data represent the social world. This analogical view is comparable to that implicit in experiments in disciplines such as economics or social psychology, with the important difference that in those contexts the laboratory setting is generally more similar to that of a controlled trial in the natural sciences. In social media research, data are appropriated and re-conceptualized by scientists from their original context of use and purpose. The mediation-hypothesis, according to Jungherr, posits that media have an inherent logic through which they breed their own self-referential effects; effects which are not based on analogy with the physical social world:

> Following the mirror- hypothesis, we should expect digital trace data to offer a true image of political reality. In contrast, the mediation-hypothesis leads us to expect the reflection of political reality, found in digital trace data, to be biased in accordance with the underlying data generating processes. (Jungherr, 2015, p. 63)

Imagine the notion of friends on Facebook for a moment. A naive interpretation would assume that Facebook friends faithfully represent "actual" friends. But it is common knowledge that this is not true and that Facebook friends are something very different from friends in the traditional sense. Not only this, but also does it become easier with the entrenchment of Facebook to rely on people's knowledge of *Facebook friends* as a distinct concept and to assume that others are familiar with the social conventions that form around Facebook friending. But the original assumption of analogy between a real antecedent and a virtual shadow is perfectly rational before the background of the introduction of computer, the internet and the web. All of these are steeped in metaphors based on physical and familiar processes which are consequently applied to new and unfamiliar environments.

The quantitative methods used in social media research rely on turning information in various formats into numbers, and in applying statistical procedures to these numbers to express relationships among them. Information must be mathematized to be data that can be computationally analyzed and statistical procedures are applied both to inductively discover patterns in the data and to deductively test hypotheses. Far from there being "no theory" needed to interpret these numbers, the devices that record them are powerful mediating devices between social actors and between them and the researchers who study them (Gitelman, 2013; Manovich, 2012; Schroeder, 2014). Data analysis is usually preceded by a sequence of steps that include data acquisition, selection, conversion, restructuring, aggregation, and project-internal presentation. Furthermore, machine learning approaches allow both to discover clusters, mine association rules and construct decision trees from data, and to apply supervised learning where a manual annotation is reproduced by an algorithm. In some cases, the relevant statistical procedures are quite closely related, for example, when logistic regression is applied in supervised machine learning (another example is analysis of variance, or *ANOVA*). Yet, the disciplinary traditions even in the relatively narrow space of statistical analysis are clearly visible, with mathematically similar procedures playing distinctly different roles from one field to the next.

WHAT COUNTS AS DATA (AND TO WHOM)?

Data collection in the social sciences is traditionally an arduous enterprise, or, as Scott Golder and William Macy phrase it "social life is very hard to observe" (2014, p. 130). In addition to the risk of bias in its generation through factors such as social desirability, the sheer cost of data collection needs to be accounted for in every study. Golder and Macy point to longitudinal panel research such as the Framingham Heart Study (1948/2016), which is rare, costly, and often relies on relatively small samples, to underscore this precarious situation. Furthermore, as Murthy and Bowman note, "quantitative sociology has been traditionally driven by manageable, structured data sets" (2014, p. 2), in contrast to the massive volumes of largely unstructured data available online. Social scientists also differ considerably in what they accept as data. Individual fields, from anthropology to political science and sociology to economics, vary significantly in their data practices, often more than text book narratives suggest (cf. Borgman, 2015). Differences are not only patterned along disciplinary lines, but also reflect more granular philosophical distinctions, from the area of research right down to national and local conventions, as well as personal preferences. In spite of these distinctions, to a social scientist data is generally something to be elicited, collected, or observed. It is brought into the world through a series of carefully planned and controlled actions, or culled from a larger body of information using specific sampling criteria. The function of data within the empirical paradigm is to represent the social world, and this is assured by its potential to be valid, reliable, and representative. Qualitative and quantitative research paradigms place very different demands on data and are subject to diverging assumptions and expectations, often by different (and sometimes warring) academic tribes. A broad consensus, however, is that data generation should be a visible part of the research cycle. Data is not natural, but profoundly man-made (Gitelman, 2013). It does not simply come into being by itself, but is either the result of a planned process of elicitation or of purposeful sampling. Such processes are often made to appear more straight-forward in the ideal environment of a text book or an introductory methods class than they turn out to be in actual research.

By contrast, data in computer science are usually considered to be any information in computable form. The ability to process information at scale is perhaps the oldest single research interest in the history of informatics. While the handling and storage of data is of key importance in this perspective, what it represents is not usually essential to the question of how it should be processed. Contrasting the understanding of data in social science and computer science reveals a combination of similarities and differences. A shared assumption is that data are an important resource for generating and transmitting knowledge, though opinions differ on what should be considered knowledge and what should not. Linked to this is the functional understanding of data as a representation of the social world in social science and the formal view of data as any machine-readable information in computer science. A further difference is sheer scale. Social scientists are familiar with data sets in which a few thousand observations are generally considered to be large, while computer scientists have long worked with data bases consisting of millions of records (cf. Schroeder, 2014). Datafication (van Dijck, 2014), or the tendency to create data to reflect more and more things digitally, extends the reach of computation to an ever-growing number of areas. Seen in a historical context, we can consider the high demands placed on the quality of data in the social sciences both as a function of its generation (often some form of dull physical or intellectual labor by the researcher) and its relative scarcity, while the quality of data in computer science is chiefly a formal concern in relation to its processing (previously costly and slow, increasingly cheap, fast, and easily extensible).

While "big data," to computer scientists, can and often does include machine-generated information from remote sensors, such as telescopes, or from internet-enabled devices and the growing "internet of things," what is presently often studied under the banner of social media research is digital discourse, taken from sites such as Wikipedia or from social media platforms such as Twitter, Facebook, or Reddit (Strohmaier & Wagner, 2014; Tufekci, 2014). Images, videos, and other user-generated media increasingly supplement this picture (Procter, Vis, & Voss, 2013), as do geolocation data, server log files, and search queries. Various long and short snippets of text (in practice e-mails, wall posts, tweets, comments, answers, messages) are enveloped by other written information in more structured forms, such as user profiles, and surrounded by a combination of platform signals (friends, followers, faves, likes) and platform-generated meta-data (cookies, time stamps, client software ID strings) that are inadvertently recorded as the user interacts with the platform. This amalgam includes data that users themselves may not be aware of, even outside of any systematic analysis on the aggregate level. The analysis of these different data types requires a complex combination of skills, and this extends beyond mere handling to interpretation. Interpretation is particularly difficult, not only operationally (in terms of required skills) but conceptually (in terms of assumptions about what data represent). This applies to digital trace data such as a series of Facebook messages much more severely than it applies to, for example, a subject's behavior in a laboratory experiment. When the data was produced for a purpose other than research, with a particular audience in mind, and in a social or cultural context unfamiliar to the researcher, this opens the door to misinterpretation and "context collapse" (Marwick & boyd, 2010). Users address "imagined audiences" (Litt, 2012), rather than providing a convenient record of their emotions. Research should always be grounded in domain-specific knowledge, but this parameter is particularly easy to violate when large volumes of data are readily available and the data structurally fulfill properties that make them suitable for analysis with tools that are familiar to the researcher.

These challenges vary from one case to another, and much digital social research being conducted is not automatically subject to issues such as data privacy. Data produced by public institutions with citizens as their intended audience is unlikely to spark much criticism from institutional review boards (IRBs) or the media. A project that analyzes search query logs for popular topics in the US and Germany would ask different questions, use different methods, and have different ethical considerations, than one that investigates manifestations of depression through sentiment analysis of social media messages.

WHO HAS A STAKE IN DATA?

Thinking about how data is generated introduces another stakeholder to the picture, extending our view of the social data ecosystem. While vast troves of information have been digitized in recent years, and more and more traditional sources of data, such as government statistics and public archives are continuously being made accessible online, this volume is dwarfed by what private individuals produce each day on internet platforms. This volume of information rises steadily as more people across the world gain access to cheap mobile devices and successful social media sites close the remaining gaps in their global coverage. Comparative media and communication technologies have taken considerably longer to proliferate to a level that the smart phone has achieved in barely half a decade. All this is not to say that the data from digital platforms offer a comprehensive picture of humanity, nor that they ever will. But the reach of traditional methods, such as surveys, is also severely limited, and their cost means that they must be employed much more selectively (Shah et al., 2015).

Digital traces left by users also underpin a personalization industry that has not only transformed advertising, but is also making inroads into the design of products and services previously unrelated to the internet. Knowing what people are doing and saying in digital media provides a competitive advantage whether it is in predicting sales or in tracking social and political movements. Social media platforms use their data, among other things, to continuously improve their products through intense experimental testing (Sandvig, Karahalios, & Langbort, 2014; Schroeder, 2014). Both these and future business opportunities considered, however, much of what they produce could be more valuable to scholarship than it is to improving products and services (Rudder, 2014). What Amazon knows about the literary preferences of people around the world goes far beyond what it needs to know in order to sell more books, and what Facebook activity reveals about a couple's relationship is at least as relevant to sociologists as it is to the company. While it is clear that global internet companies are ambitious and continuously adapt their business models to newfound innovations on the basis of the information that they have at their disposal, it also seems likely that they are producing more than they need, and that academia is increasingly cut off from their data and insights. Sharing data could result both in privacy headaches and in foregone revenue, which explains the hesitation of companies to engage in it more systematically, in addition to the costs associated with doing so, and the risk of raising ethical concerns (Bozdag, 2013; Puschmann & Bozdag, 2014). Twitter is a case in point for this hesitant approach. After sharing data comparably liberally in the early phase of the service, mostly to attract developers, and inadvertently instigating a veritable barrage of studies that use Twitter data, the company is now imposing increasingly stringent limitations on data access. It appears to regard data as one of its key assets, and sharing that asset too readily with anyone could be detrimental to the interests of shareholders at a time when they are not very forgiving. Before the background of recent media outrage over experiments conducted on social media platforms, it seems likely that collaborations between industry and academia will continue to raise complex legal and ethical questions whose resolution is likely to take even longer than then proliferation of new methods (Puschmann & Burgess, 2013; Schroeder, 2014, p. 3).

Industry research can obviously not be entirely open, otherwise the above-mentioned social media stars risk losing their advantage to competitors. But perhaps it is possible to strike a balance between academic and economic interests. Apart from aiming to find patterns or mechanisms that can be considered even remotely universal, "predictive and analytic techniques can provide insight into, if not directly solve, significant social problems" (Shah et al., 2015, p. 9). Data from a wide range of contexts, from disaster relief and urban poverty to migration patterns and hate crimes, are relevant to research that can have a direct impact on combating social ills and improving government policy.

HOW DIVERSE AND REPRESENTATIVE IS DATA?

The involvement of powerful social media platforms also raises further issues, one of them being that a small number of platforms at present attract by far the most research, creating a skewed picture and risking a social data monoculture (Hargittai, 2015; Tufekci, 2014). Market concentration may well at some point in the future eliminate some of the concerns voiced by scholars. Communication scholars Merja Mahrt and Michael Scharkow (2013), for example, criticize the lack of cross-platform studies in internet research, arguing that "if researchers are interested in social network sites, multiplayer games, or online news in general, it is problematic to include only data from Facebook and Twitter, World of Warcraft and Everquest II, or a handful of newspaper and broadcast news sites" (p. 25). Zeynep Tufekci (2014) voices similar criticism when she speaks of "the model organism problem, in which a few platforms are frequently used to generate datasets without adequate consideration of their structural biases." The reference to newspaper and broadcast sites by Mahrt and Scharkow (2013) warrants emphasis because it suggests that social networking sites as a class are constituted by a large number of individual exemplars, just like individual newspapers or television broadcasters constitute "the news media." But the immense concentration of social media platforms suggests that this analogy is imperfect. Social networking sites as a class may matter less as a concept if in practice people mostly use Facebook. My point is not, by any means, that we should welcome concentration, but rather that our concept of diversity is built on a much less concentrated kind of media, where a diversity of sources differ in content, but hardly in form. Diverse sampling traditionally meant sampling across sources, but how plausible is sampling across different digital platforms? Of course commonalities are crucial, but it seems more honest to assume that the specifics of platforms shape their use, rather than aiming to generalize from one service to others on the grounds that their differences are superficial. Stepping back from claims about generalizability is of course no small theoretical challenge and accepting both the terminology and intra-platform logic of sites such as Facebook and Twitter will no doubt be painful to social scientists.

Sampling is persistently noted in the literature as a thorny issue of social media research (Mahrt & Scharkow, 2013, p. 21). Observational studies that use online data frequently break apart the established cycle of data sampling, collection, and analysis, instead they are providing ex-post interpretations that dramatically overreach the data's validity. Sampling matters on two separate levels: to obtain an initial broad sample of everything that could be relevant to the research question, and for a second, narrower one, drawn to reduce the volume of data while retaining its representativeness. As Mahrt and Scharkow (2013, p. 28) point out, this second step may reduce big data to medium-sized data without a loss of quality, while the first step is the one that needs to be carefully tailored to the research question, and is oftentimes subject to convenience. Working with digital trace data highlights the similarities between traditional content analysis and computational social science. Media and communication research has long recognized that mediated behavior is not merely unmediated behavior that happens to be conveniently recorded in analyzable form. Mahrt and Scharkow (2013) point to a long tradition of studying and classifying messages in communication research and linguistics (p. 27). That this argument is not more widely heard has many reasons, scale being one. That discourse-analyzing computational methods such as sentiment analysis for the most part perform much less reliably than manual content analysis does is not widely acknowledged (González-Bailón & Paltoglou, 2015). Teasing out the exact relationship of sampling strategy and research objectives is crucial to evaluating how much data of what degree of diversity is needed both for adequate prediction and hypothesis-testing. While this is hardly a new issue, the tendency to use much more data than a given question requires is, and whereas in traditional research this involves the elicitation of a larger sample that is associated with more work for the researcher, this is not the case with observational data from digital media platforms. While sampling offline is subject to careful consideration not only to assure research quality, but also, one might suspect, because resources need to be strategically allocated in research projects by their principal investigators, this condition is relaxed considerably with "found" online data. As Carolin Gerlitz and Bernard Rieder (2013) observe: "The majority of sampling approaches on Twitter [...] follow a non-probabilistic, non-representative route, delineating their samples based on features specific to the platform." In other words, most of the studies examined by Gerlitz and Rieder chose varieties of snowball sampling relying on keywords, seed users, or other aspects particular to Twitter. Bruns (2013) makes a similar argument when calling for "non-opportunistic data gathering," by which he means foregrounding data quality in favor of sheer quantity. Obviously, the sample size does nothing to alleviate problems that follow from a strategy of convenience sampling. David Lazer and colleagues (2014), after initially being very optimistic about the potential of computational social science, caution researchers not to succumb to "big data hubris," noting that "most big data that have received popular attention are not the output of instruments designed to produce valid and reliable data amenable for scientific analysis" (p. 1203).

Speaking of *messages* or *discourse*, rather than *behavior*, seems not just to be terminological hairsplitting here, but my insistence to choose words carefully is underpinned by the observation that *behavior* often conjures up an image that is too simple and straightforward to be accurate. The operationalization in GFT that equates fluctuations in search queries with flu outbreaks is simply not a good one because too many sources of error stand between the human expression via a search query and the ability for its sheer frequency to reliably and robustly predict a particular medical condition. The signal sent by Google's users is an arbitrary one, more akin to a smoke sign than a trace.

WHAT DOES DATA SIGNIFY?

It pays off to examine the terminology used to describe what data are and where they come from both closely and critically. Van Dijck notes that "data and metadata culled from Google, Facebook, and Twitter are generally considered imprints or symptoms of people's actual behavior or moods" (2014, p. 199, my emphasis) and Mahrt and Scharkow (2013) speak of "traces [...] automatically left" (p. 24). The term *traces* permeates across much of the literature, as does the analogy to the telescope (Watts, 2015). Golder and Macy (2014) prefer to speak of "digital footprints," while Strohmaier and Wagner (2014) provide the illustrative example of traces in a very physical sense, describing "the wear of floor tiles around museum exhibits as indicators of popular exhibits; the setting of car radio dials as indicators of favorite stations; the wear on library books and rub and fold marks in their pages" (p. 85). The vivid image that they provide makes a resounding point: Data traces are not always as readily interpretable as physical traces. If they were, the level of granularity that they would provide us with would be remarkable. But their potential for misinterpretation is, at least in the present stage, far greater. This need not deter us, but it is a powerful reminder that the interpretation of physical tracks on the ground is performed instantly and inadvertently by the brain, while the interpretation of a tweet's political relevance is a more complicated matter. When characterizing the generation of data, careful attention to detail is also warranted. Shah et al. (2015) refer to digital trace data as "naturally occurring," but put the adjective in quotations, as if wanting to express that such information is in many respects more "natural" than the data from surveys and traditional laboratory experiments, but also less natural than actual physical traces. Strohmaier and

Wagner (2014) discuss different terms, settling for "found data" also to express a situation where the data are generated without the researchers intervention (and chronologically before the researcher appears in the picture). They characterize such data as non-reactive and observational, in other words, as being collected without the possibility of the researcher influencing the research subject. The term is also somewhat suggestive of data as something that naturally occurs (or perhaps, that has been abandoned, and is conveniently discovered by the researcher by the side of the road), backgrounding the variation in the purpose of its creation (say, to communicate with a loved one), its storage (as part of a feature that a social media company hopes will bring more users to its site), and its analysis (by a scientist hoping to publish a paper). Not much is natural about this form of eavesdropping on the conversations of others.

The fact that interaction in digital platforms is mediated should not be equated with the assumption that they are "not real." Golder and Macy (2014) ask rhetorically whether the online world is a parallel universe (p. 143) and go on to argue that it is not. They propose to "turn the tables [...] rather than address the societal implications of the Internet, we survey studies that use online data to advance knowledge in the social sciences" (Golder & Macy, 2014, p. 130). Strohmaier and Wagner (2014) argue in the same direction, but add a qualification: "the World Wide Web represents not only an increasingly useful reflection of human social behavior, but every-day social interactions on the Web are increasingly mediated and shaped by algorithms and computational methods in general." Their comment suggests a double life of platforms (in this case the Web) as reflecting social life and at the same time influencing human behavior and enabling modes of expression that are intricately tied to the design of digital media services. The distinction between real and virtual, or online and offline, obscures the influence of these platforms on data creation. Online interactions are entirely real, but they are also subject to factors that do not exist in unmediated interactions, and that may change rapidly following the changing priorities of platform providers and their reflection in design. Herring (2004) identifies this kind of bias in the pre-social media Web when she argues that "computer-mediated discourse may be, but is not inevitably, shaped by the technological features of computer-mediated communication systems" (p. 338). In terms of their broad usage, their relevance to politics, the economy, and everyday life and the thoughts, emotions and relationships which they enable and support, digital platforms are entirely real. But all of these things take place on a cultural stage, to use the Goffmanian analogy, that is set by the companies running the services that we use – a set that changes with each scene, influencing the performance of the players in a variety of ways. David Lazer and colleagues (2014) seem most keenly aware of this complication, noting that a better understanding of the algorithms underlying Google, Twitter, and Facebook is crucial to both scholarship and civil society. The influence of platform providers on data generation is interchangeably referred to as *platform politics* (Gillespie, 2010), *social media logic* (van Dijck & Poell, 2013), and *blue team dynamics* (Lazer et al., 2014). Lazer et al. note this continuous adjustment in service of the customer, pointing out that "in improving its service to customers, Google is also changing the data-generating process" (p. 1204). The problems caused by analytical feedback loops of the data generating process and subsequent data interpretation should be apparent. Data are only valid if the researcher's actions are not essential for its production. *Red team dynamics*, in Lazer et al.'s parlance, are those where "research subjects (in this case Web searchers) attempt to manipulate the data-generating process to meet their own goals, such as economic or political gain" (p. 1204). It should be conceivable that the distinction between social behavior and "manipulation" is quite a hazy one in many cases. All communication, ultimately, realizes a goal for the communicator, and often goals are determined strategically.

Imagining social media platforms as a stage that is set by the platform provider through the design of the site or app allows us to identify another complicating issue of digital trace data. Social media companies store data in structures that are reflected in the site design, or, turning this around, design the site in a particular way that has implications for what is stored, and how. Facebook likes and Twitter retweets are examples of such units of analysis that find their way into research. Likes and retweets at once serve a function for users and for Facebook and Twitter as companies (Gerlitz & Helmond, 2013). The functions and their utility for users individually is distinct from their function for the provider, particularly to the provider's advertisement-supported business model. But what is their function as indicators of social processes? Tufekci (2014) highlights this discrepancy when she argues that "users engage in practices that may be unintelligible to algorithms, such as subtweets (tweets referencing an unnamed but implicitly identifiable individual), quoting text via screen captures, and 'hate-linking' – linking to denounce rather than endorse" (p. 505). The issue in her examples applies less to algorithms, but to the expectations of platform providers towards users and their "correct" usage of the platform. These expectations may reflect business considerations, or simply result from failing to anticipate the subversive creativity of users. Often, both are at work. The debate around the introduction of a dislike button on Facebook serves to underscore this issue. Such a button does not exist because it would allow the expression of preferences which are not desirable to Facebook and could even result in legal challenges to the company. Some users have voiced their interest in such a button, and others have simply devised other ways of expressing what such a button would express. Subversive behavior is arguably of interest to social scientists, not just "proper" usage, particularly if the considerations at work are driven by what is desirable to companies. But in terms of design, if not expression, the considerations of the platform provider prevail. This simply underscores that Facebook is not a neutral observatory of social interaction. It is not just subject to human biases in what people express, but its very design consciously aims to suppress behavior that could spell out legal or economic detriment to the provider. Among others, van Dijck (2014) notes this conflict between scientific and commercial interests when she speaks of "the paradoxical premise that social media platforms concomitantly measure, manipulate, and monetize online human behavior" (p. 200).

WHAT INTERPRETATIONS DOES DATA PERMIT?

Digital trace data are quite abstract. A physical trace seems for most purposes easier to interpret than a message, tweet, or like. A strategy to counter this problem is to utilize the powers of categorization and comparison. If there is something interesting to compare your data with, even simple descriptive statistics can be enlightening. By contrast, the application of complex methods to a single data set to produce a purely descriptive result can be frustrating because there is no reference point that would allow evaluating the results through a meaningful baseline. This point may seem trivial, but much online research is plagued by producing quantifications which are then left to stand on their own or by making comparisons which are, like sampling, the result of convenience rather than careful research design. Comparing men to women, American users to British ones, highly active individuals to sporadics, and regular weeks with unusual ones achieve this goal. The gender example is chosen deliberately because often comparisons are made without much of a clear motivation, but rather because categorical data are available by which groups can be conveniently compared. But once two groups are contrasted, this implicitly makes the claim that they exist, are sufficiently clear-cut, and play an important role in the analysis. Comparisons facilitate clarity, but what is compared by should be a conscious choice, rather than a matter of convenience. Categorizing people by certain criteria, whether it is gender, race, education, or income, is often useful in social science, but not to claim that they fit unequivocally into convenient ontological boxes, but because aggregation allows quantitative analysis, and quantitative analysis is essential to answering macro-level questions. Categorizing and comparing badly has unintended consequences which are a side effect of the distance that quantitative research creates between a researcher and her subject. That caveat is particularly important in computational social science.

I have previously established that the kind of data that computational social sciences are concerned with comes in many forms. However, for the purpose of most analyses, researchers encounter data in one of two formats in the phase that it is studied: It is usually either numeric or textual. Other formats, such as images and videos, while both immensely popular and increasingly studied, place different demands on researchers in terms of skills, tools, and data processing infrastructure. Numerical data in the aggregate take the shape of counted comments, clicks, friends, likes, or shares. A special significance, however, can be afforded to textual data. As Shah et al. argue (2015): "With much of the core social data now in textual form, changing in central ways how data are acquired and reduced, scholars will need to come to new agreements on what constitutes reliable and valid descriptions of the data; the categories used to organize those data; and the tools necessary to access, process, and structure those data" (p. 12). Textual data has a central role in social media research because so much of what people produce themselves, in contrast to information that is automatically collected about them, is text. Quantifying this in relation to images or video seems pointless, as nobody is likely to dispute the importance of these types of media, which once took dedicated equipment to produce, but can now be created with any common mobile device in excellent quality. Research methods for the analysis of digital images and video will take time to catch up for practical reasons and to make inroads into areas of social science where they are presently not widely used. Textual analysis has a long history in the social sciences and humanities, but it is worth noting that some distinctions made between different levels of analysis that are often conflated in computational approaches are of key importance to such accounts. For example, Herring (2004) distinguishes between four such levels of analysis on which data can be segmented: 1) structure, 2) meaning, 3) interaction, and 4) social behavior (p. 339). Structure covers aspects as orthography, the use of emoticons, or other properties on the level of words or sentences. Meaning relates to what words, speech acts or larger units of discourse express. Thirdly, interaction includes the properties of dyadic discourse such as turn-taking or topic development and other interactional dynamics. The fourth level indicates aspects that can be more abstractly labeled as forms of social behavior, such as expressions of play, conflict, and group membership. Herring's perspective is a linguistic one, therefore her differentiation of structural and socially functional aspects may not resonate with other social scientists (for example, differentiating levels one and two is didactically common in linguistics, but may not be very practical empirically). But it is worth pointing out that much of current research ignores intermediate levels of abstraction, going instead directly from words to social behavior. It is not yet broadly recognized that a word and its meaning is highly context-dependent, and consequently a bad proxy for stable analytical units such as personality traits, social relationships, or public opinion. The reason for the popularity of words as a unit of analysis in computational textual research is to be found in the economics of research feasibility. Words are much more easy to extract than other units, and they are more widely accepted as a form of data than, for example, conversational turns. The approach taken in textual social media research of "operationalizing up" from words to more abstract categories is a lasting challenge to social media research.

WHO OWNS AND CONTROLS DATA?

Finally, questions that go beyond the collection, analysis and interpretation of data also need to be addressed. Who owns digital platform data is a point of ongoing debate among legal scholars. Initially, in many contexts, the answer is "no one", at least not in the sense of legal ownership. Data, apart from a few exceptions, do not constitute intellectual property. While the suggestion has been made that users have a natural right to the data that they produce and the meta-data that surround it, such data are generally not considered to constitute property. Laws protecting the privacy of users apply to social media platforms, but the fact that most information is disclosed willingly in such platforms and that providers are usually granted the right to analyze the data and experiment with the site's features when users sign the terms of service means that companies are under relatively few constraints to make use of the data. Attempts to regulate data about people outside of the frameworks of ownership and privacy protection, such as the "Right to be forgotten" implemented in the European Union and imposed on search results that concern individuals have been met with very mixed responses. Attempts in this and similar directions underscore that data from digital platforms and what is done with it is increasingly seen a human rights issue that transcends national regulation, though political solutions to these problems seem far off.

On the other hand, cases where social media data have been used in large-scale research projects have attracted considerable media attention, particularly when the results have been published in major scientific journals. The Facebook emotional contagion experiment (Kramer et al., 2014) is one such example. Legally, researchers at Facebook had done nothing wrong, despite widespread criticism of the ethics of the study. And while a perceived lack of scrutiny by the institutional review board (IRB) that cleared the research was criticized by some commentators, others did not find the research to breach ethics guidelines. There was, however, a consensus regarding the need to develop better standards and adapt ethical codes to new forms of research. Research in social media research underscores that simply having access to data is much less important than effectively being able to query it. This requires the right tools for infrastructure and analysis, as well as the competence to interpret results. In an environment where data are ubiquitous, their mere existence seems less of an issue than their use and the outcomes of these uses. An ethical use of data in social media research must therefore be more concerned with research results and their potential to clash with the interests of users than with the mere legality of data access. As Shah et al. (2015) argue: "The acquisition and archiving of complex data systems – let alone their manipulation – often involve collecting personally identifiable information [...] this forces some reflection on issues of data privacy and de-identification, especially in an era of increased tracking of expression and action" (p. 8).

SUMMARY

This chapter has examined how data are collected, processed, and interpreted in computational social media research, and how a lack of concept validity frequently dogs ambitious research in this area of study. The flavor of social science that this emerging field embraces is strongly concerned with making scientific inferences on human behavior, yet it has been shown that observational findings based on social media data can frequently not be reproduced (Liang & Fu, 2015). From predicting elections to forecasting consumption, what people do is a key interest of the field. Even when asking very theoretical questions about human sociality, such questions need to be quantifiable in order to fit into the computational paradigm. This is not to say that social media research rejects qualitative insight. Qualitative and quantitative research can be integrated into new approaches and very often this yields the best results (Bastos & Mercea, 2015). Some warn of a crisis of empirical social research if new methods and sources of data are left to computer science and eschewed by social scientists (Savage & Burrows, 2007). But the role afforded in social media research to computation, and therefore some form of quantification, comes with certain limitations. Data are used to answer a set of questions or patterns within data are identified and related to particular behavior. Social media research thrives on data, particularly of the observational kind. These data are generally not produced with research in mind, but accumulate in online platforms as a by-product of a user's actions, sometimes without their knowledge. They are produced for particular purposes and with particular addresses in mind. The researcher ideally has a form of privileged access to these data, putting her under both the methodological and ethical obligation to produce a sound analysis.

NOTE

1. But see Giglietto and Rossi (2012) who also make this connection.

REFERENCES

Bastos, M. T., & Mercea, D. (2015). Serial activists: Political Twitter beyond influentials and the twittertariat. *New Media & Society*. Retrieved from http://doi.org/10.1177/1461444815584764

Borgman, C. L. (2015). *Scholarship in the digital age*. Cambridge: MIT Press. Retrieved from http://doi.org/10.1017/CBO9781107415324.004

Bowker, G. C. (2013). Data flakes: An afterword to "raw data" is an oxymoron. In L. Gitelman (Ed.), *"Raw data" is an oxymoron* (pp. 167–171). Cambridge, MA: MIT Press.

boyd, d., & Crawford, K. (2012). Critical questions for Big Data: Provocations for a cultural, technological, and scholarly phenomenon. *Information, Communication & Society, 15*(5), 662–679. Retrieved from http://doi.org/10.1080/1369118X.2012.678878

Bozdag, E. (2013). Bias in algorithmic filtering and personalization. *Ethics and Information Technology, 15*(3), 209–227. Retrieved from http://doi.org/10.1007/s10676-013-9321-6

Bruns, A. (2013). Faster than the speed of print: Reconciling "big data" social media analysis and academic scholarship. *First Monday, 18*(10). https://doi.org/10.5210/fm.v18i10.4879

Carneiro, H. A., & Mylonakis, E. (2009). Google trends: A web-based tool for real-time surveillance of disease outbreaks. *Clinical Infectious Diseases, 49*(10), 1557–1564. Retrieved from http://doi.org/10.1086/630200

Cioffi-Revilla, C. (2010). Computational social science. *Wiley Interdisciplinary Reviews: Computational Statistics, 2*(3), 259–271. Retrieved from http://doi.org/10.1002/wics.95

Framingham Heart Study. (1948/2016). Retrieved from https://www.framinghamheartstudy.org/

Gerlitz, C., & Helmond, A. (2013). The like economy: Social buttons and the data-intensive web. *New Media & Society, 15*(8), 1348–1365. Retrieved from http://doi.org/10.1177/1461444812472322

Gerlitz, C., & Rieder, B. (2013). Mining one percent of Twitter: Collections, baselines, sampling. *M/C Journal, 16*(2), 1–15. Retrieved from http://www.journal.media-culture.org.au/index.php/mcjournal/article/viewArticle/620

Giglietto, F., & Rossi, L. (2012). Ethics and interdisciplinarity in computational social science. *Methodological Innovations Online, 7*(1), 25–36. Retrieved from http://doi.org/10.4256/mio.2012.003

Gillespie, T. (2010). The politics of "platforms." *New Media & Society, 12*(3), 347–364. Retrieved from http://doi.org/10.1177/1461444809342738

Gitelman, L. (Ed.). (2013). *"Raw data" is an oxymoron*. Cambridge, MA: MIT Press.

Golder, S. A., & Macy, M. W. (2014). Digital footprints: Opportunities and challenges for online social research. *Annual Review of Sociology, 40*, 129–152. Retrieved from http://doi.org/10.1146/annurev-soc-071913-043145

González-Bailón, S., & Paltoglou, G. (2015). Signals of public opinion in online communication: A comparison of methods and data sources. *The ANNALS of the American Academy of Political and Social Science, 659*(1), 95–107. Retrieved from http://doi.org/10.1177/0002716215569192

Hargittai, E. (2015). Is bigger always better? Potential biases of big data derived from social network sites. *The ANNALS of the American Academy of Political and Social Science, 659*(1), 63–76. Retrieved from http://doi.org/10.1177/0002716215570866

Herring, S. C. (2004). Computer-mediated discourse analysis: An approach to researching online behavior. In S. Barab, R. Kling, & J. H. Gray (Eds.), *Designing for Virtual Communities in Service of Learning* (pp. 338–376). New York, NY: Cambridge University Press.

Jungherr, A. (2015). *Analyzing political communication with digital trace data*. Heidelberg: Springer International Publishing. Retrieved from http://doi.org/10.1007/978-3-319-20319-5

Kramer, A. D. I., Guillory, J. E., & Hancock, J. T. (2014). Experimental evidence of massive-scale emotional contagion through social networks. *Proceedings of the National Academy of Sciences of the United States of America, 111*(24), 8788–8790. Retrieved from http://doi.org/10.1073/pnas.1320040111

Lazer, D., Kennedy, R., King, G., & Vespignani, A. (2014). Big data. The parable of Google Flu: traps in big data analysis. *Science, 343*(6176), 1203–1205. Retrieved from http://doi.org/10.1126/science.1248506

Lazer, D., Pentland, A., Adamic, L. A., Aral, S., Barabasi, A.-L., Brewer, D., … Van Alstyne, M. (2009). Computational social science. *Science, 323*(5915), 721–723. Retrieved from http://doi.org/10.1126/science.1167742

Liang, H., & Fu, K. (2015). Testing propositions derived from Twitter studies: Generalization and replication in computational social science. *PLoS One, 10*(8), e0134270. Retrieved from http://doi.org/10.1371/journal.pone.0134270

Litt, E. (2012). Knock, knock. Who's there? The imagined audience. *Journal of Broadcasting & Electronic Media, 56*(3), 330–345. Retrieved from http://doi.org/10.1080/08838151.2012.705195

Mahrt, M., & Scharkow, M. (2013). The value of big data in digital media research. *Journal of Broadcasting & Electronic Media, 57*(1), 20–33. Retrieved from http://doi.org/10.1080/08838151.2012.761700

Manovich, L. (2012). Trending: The promises and the challenges of big social data. In M. K. Gold (Ed.), *Debates in the Digital Humanities* (pp. 460–475). Minneapolis, MN: University of Minnesota Press.

Marwick, A., & boyd, d. (2010). I tweet honestly, I tweet passionately: Twitter users, context collapse, and the imagined audience. *New Media & Society, 13*(1), 114–133. Retrieved from http://doi.org/10.1177/1461444810365313

Metcalf, J., & Crawford, K. (2016, June). Where are human subjects in big data research? The emerging ethics divide. *Big Data and Society*, 1–34. Retrieved from http://doi.org/10.1177/2053951716650211

Murthy, D., & Bowman, S. A. (2014). Big Data solutions on a small scale: Evaluating accessible high-performance computing for social research. *Big Data & Society, 1*(2), 1–12. Retrieved from http://doi.org/10.1177/2053951714559105

Procter, R., Vis, F., & Voss, A. (2013). Reading the riots on Twitter: Methodological innovation for the analysis of big data. *International Journal of Social Research Methodology, 16*(3), 197–214. Retrieved from http://doi.org/10.1080/13645579.2013.774172

Puschmann, C., & Bozdag, E. (2014). Staking out the unclear ethical terrain of online social experiments. *Internet Policy Review, 3*(4), 1–15. Retrieved from http://doi.org/10.14763/2014.4.338

Puschmann, C., & Burgess, J. (2013). The politics of Twitter data. In K. Weller, A. Bruns, J. Burgess, M. Mahrt, & C. Puschmann (Eds.), *Twitter and society* (pp. 43–54). New York, NY: Peter Lang.

Rudder, C. (2014). *Dataclysm: Who we are (When we think no one's looking)*. New York, NY: Crown.

Ruths, D., & Pfeffer, J. (2014). Social media for large studies of behavior. *Science, 346*(6213), 1063–1064. Retrieved from http://doi.org/10.1126/science.346.6213.1063

Sandvig, C., Karahalios, K. G., & Langbort, C. (2014, July 24). *Christian Sandvig, Karrie G. Karahalios, and Cedric Langbort look inside the Facebook News Feed.* Retrieved from http://blogs.law.harvard.edu/mediaberkman/2014/07/24/christian-sandvig-karrie-g-karahalios-and-cedric-langbort-look-inside-the-facebook-news-feed-audio/

Savage, M., & Burrows, R. (2007). The coming crisis of empirical sociology. *Sociology, 41*(5), 885–899. Retrieved from http://doi.org/10.1177/0038038507080443

Schroeder, R. (2014). Big Data and the brave new world of social media research. *Big Data & Society, 1*(2), 1–11. https://doi.org/10.1177/2053951714563194

Shah, D. V., Cappella, J. N., & Neuman, W. R. (2015). Big data, digital media, and computational social science: Possibilities and perils. *The ANNALS of the American Academy of Political and Social Science, 659*(1), 6–13. Retrieved from http://doi.org/10.1177/0002716215572084

Strohmaier, M., & Wagner, C. (2014). Computational social science for the World Wide Web. *IEEE Intelligent Systems, 29*(5), 84–88. Retrieved from http://doi.org/10.1109/MIS.2014.80

Trochim, W., & Donnelly, J. P. (2006). *Research methods knowledge base* (3rd ed.). Mason, OH: Atomic Dog. Retrieved from https://doi.org/10.1515/9783110858372.1

Tufekci, Z. (2014). Big questions for social media big data: Representativeness, validity and other methodological pitfalls. *ICWSM '14: Proceedings of the 8th International AAAI Conference on Weblogs and Social Media* (pp. 505–514).

Van Dijck, J. (2014). Datafication, dataism and dataveillance: Big data between scientific paradigm and ideology. *Surveillance & Society, 12*(2), 197–208.
Van Dijck, J., & Poell, T. (2013). Understanding social media logic. *Media and Communication, 1*(1), 2. Retrieved from http://doi.org/10.17645/mac.v1i1.70
Watts, D. J. (2015). Common sense and sociological explanations. *American Journal of Sociology, 120*(2), 313–351.
Zimmer, M. (2010). "But the data is already public": On the ethics of research in Facebook. *Ethics and Information Technology, 12*(4), 313–325. Retrieved from http://doi.org/10.1007/s10676-010-9227-5

REACTION BY NICHOLAS PROFERES

As Puschmann points out, the assumptions researchers maintain about *what data is* have ethical import. Indeed, reflexive consideration about where we think data comes from, what counts as data to whom, who has a stake in data, how representative we think data is, what data signifies, what interpretations data permits, and who owns and controls data should prompt us to acknowledge the ways in which data is anything but "natural." Puschmann's line of reasoning can be extended further with integration of the work of feminist STS scholar Karen Barad. Barad contends that the presumption that reality can be objectively understood through scientific inquiry repeats the "Cartesian belief in the inherent distinction between subject and object, and knower and known" (2003, p. 813). She argues that techno-scientific discursive practices involving language, measurement, and materiality *produce* phenomena, creating an artificial separation between researcher and the knowable. Layering Barad's ontological and epistemological considerations with Puschmann's work can further our own reflexive practices. Both authors prompt us to consider how data comes into being, how researchers both represent and produce phenomena, and the inherent inseparability of data and observations of it. While Puschmann asks us to consider *what data is*, Barad's work complements by asking us to consider *what researchers do.*

Barad, K. (2003). Posthumanist performativity: Toward an understanding of how matter comes to matter. *Signs, 28*(3), 801–831.

Nicholas Proferes is an assistant professor at the University of Kentucky's School of Information Science. His research focuses on how users experience and navigate the politics of platforms

CHAPTER SEVEN

To Share or Not to Share?

Ethical Challenges in Sharing Social Media-based Research Data

KATRIN WELLER AND KATHARINA KINDER-KURLANDA

INTRODUCTION

Within the broader field of internet research, the analysis of user (inter)actions through different social media platforms has become a major focus of interest, often summarized as "social media research". In particular, the possibilities to use datasets based on user-generated content or user networks from social media platforms have attracted the attention of researchers in a variety of disciplines – including but not limited to computer science, media and communication studies, library and information science, social sciences such as political science or sociology, psychology, linguistics, cultural studies, physics, education, economics, and medicine. Somewhat independently of each other and over the course of time, more and more researchers with different disciplinary backgrounds became interested in data from, for example, Facebook, Twitter, blogs, or Wikipedia; and new researchers are still entering the field. Social media research thus acts as a melting pot for different research interests, a diversity of methodological backgrounds, and, consequently, different methods and tools being applied in research projects. One aspect that unites most scholars involved in social media research is the need to get a hold of data gathered directly from the social media platforms they want to study – although there may again be differences in the data itself with distinctions being made between, for example, user-generated content and network data, textual data and multimedia data, (big) data and qualitative data, or experimental data of different types.

In the context of this chapter, we focus on data collected from social media platforms, for example, tweets and other status updates and messages, user interactions in the form of shares or likes, or whole user networks. Data from social media platforms can be obtained in various ways, including access via application programming interfaces (APIs) or third-party tools that make use of them, by scraping content directly from the platforms, via official resellers (such as GNIP), or via direct supply from social media companies themselves (usually in form of special contracts).

These different ways of obtaining data come with different financial costs (e.g. direct payment to a reseller or costs for personnel to set up collection tools) and are situated within different legal frameworks. Sometimes technical specifications restrict access for specific types of data (e.g. historic data from Twitter cannot be obtained via the API, but can be bought from GNIP). All of this currently contributes to a situation in which the ideal dataset for a specific research question may not be possible to obtain – and in which data are not equally accessible to all researchers alike. Little has changed since boyd and Crawford (2012) criticized the separation of researchers into "data haves" and "data have nots": it remains the case that researchers or research institutes with more financial power or with good personal connections to social media companies have more options to obtain interesting and suitable data. In addition, typically, there is little or no opportunity for others to access the datasets in use for verification or reproduction of the claimed research results. This poses a major challenge to establishing quality standards in social media research (Weller & Kinder-Kurlanda, 2015, 2016).

In this overall situation, data sharing can play an important role as it can help resolve some of the ethical challenges in social media research: Sharing can equalize data access and make current social media research more transparent and reproducible. Yet, social media data sharing also poses considerable ethical challenges. While all research data sharing entails ethical reasoning and decision making, data sharing in the "social age" is subject to specific challenges. The consequences of sharing user data collected from online platforms may be different or more severe than expected. This is particularly the case as researchers are gathering and sharing data within online environments where the degree of publicness of a specific piece of content depends on context.

Within the research community, first cases of sharing gone wrong are starting to cause debates, sometimes even in the general public – such as the example of the release of data from almost 70,000 users of the dating website OKCupid in 2016 by Kirkegaard and Bjerrekær (2016) which led to criticism from academics, journalists, and the interested public. The need for more general and conclusive debates about when to share or not to share social media data is growing.

In this chapter we take a look at the standpoints of researchers engaged in research based on data gathered from social media, focusing on researchers' ethical decision-making when sharing social media datasets. We discuss several perspectives of researchers on the "to share or not to share" question – and will then suggest practical approaches to sharing social media data, assuming that some forms of sharing may invite ethical concerns less than others.

BACKGROUND AND METHOD

Our understanding of the role of data sharing in social media research – and the ethical challenges related to it – are based on two sources: (a) our work in a data archive for the social sciences with a long tradition and expertise in data sharing, the practical experiences with archiving social media datasets in this context, and the thinking and literature in this field; (b) results from a research project based on qualitative interviews with researchers who study social media and work with data collected from social media platforms, in which we capture researchers' perspectives on different ongoing challenges in social media research.

ARCHIVING SOCIAL MEDIA DATA

The specific discussion about sharing social media data needs to be considered within the more general context of sharing and archiving research data, which has a more established tradition, as for example laid out by Borgman (2012). Digital archiving as it is traditionally performed e.g. by digital social science data archives or other repositories has several aims: a) to preserve the data for the long-term, b) to provide data for re-use in the interests of reproducibility, transparency, and economy, and c) to promote ethically reflective, legally sound, and methodologically well-grounded research. Long-term preservation requires that a dataset's significant properties are defined in order to ensure they are preserved across format changes (Recker & Müller, 2015). To ensure that data are easy to reuse, it is documented according to agreed upon metadata standards. To promote good research practices archives often provide data management training and advise research projects, e.g. regarding issues of research data protection when sharing data. Many large scale social science survey projects thus have established long-standing working relationships with specific archives.

Archiving practices are thus well established for research in many fields, but not necessarily for social media research, where new approaches and methods are required, for example, because new issues of indexing and selection arise out of the interlinked, conversational nature of the data:

> Archiving social media as datasets or as big data, however, faces different challenges and requires particular solutions for access, curation, and sharing that accommodate the

> particular curatorial, legal, and technical frameworks of large aggregates of machine-readable data. (Thomson, 2016, p. 11)

Researchers creating social media datasets are often prevented from sharing by the terms of service of social media companies so that archives that traditionally support them are often limited to storing only metadata, such as Tweet IDs. Practices of sharing and archiving social media data are thus still developing and rather little literature is available as guidance. Despite such limitations, however, some archives have successfully curated social media data. A comprehensive overview of current practices as they exist has been provided by Thomson (2016). And as we have shown in previous work, researchers are also already experimenting with different ways of sharing research data collected from social media platforms (Kinder-Kurlanda & Weller 2014; Weller & Kinder-Kurlanda, 2016).

SOCIAL MEDIA RESEARCHERS' PERSPECTIVES

Our research project "Hidden Data" (Kinder-Kurlanda & Weller, 2014; Weller & Kinder-Kurlanda, 2015) aimed to capture the viewpoints of social media researchers on the epistemological, methodological, ethical, and practical challenges of working with social media data. We saw a chance to witness new methods and methodologies in the making and to document the negotiation of emerging best practice and potential standards. To this end we conducted qualitative interviews with researchers at international internet research conferences in which we asked for detailed explanations and focused on open-ended, explorative questions. This enabled us to explore the issues social media researchers faced, their motivations for working with this type of data, and the detailed contexts of specific projects. Interviews were based on an initial interview guide which covered the main topics to be addressed rather than specific questions and which was modified as needed. Following an iterative approach between theory and fieldwork we entered the field with some assumptions based on the discussion of social media and big data in the literature. Findings from our study informed further literature reading which in turn caused adaptations of our interview guide.

We interviewed around 40 researchers from different disciplinary backgrounds, countries, and career levels who all had worked with data gathered from different social media platforms (for details see Kinder-Kurlanda & Weller 2014; Weller & Kinder-Kurlanda, 2015). Interviews were conducted face-to-face, usually together by both authors of this chapter, sometimes by only one of them. All interviewees were recruited from the conference programs of four academic conferences in 2013 and 2014, all of which featured social media research among their conference topics but attracted different audiences.

One topic covered in the interviews was researchers' perspectives on sharing datasets they had collected. Another topic was researchers' ethical concerns (Weller & Kinder-Kurlanda, 2014). Within this chapter we take a closer look at the intersection of these two dimensions.

We found various reasons for why researchers decided to share or not to share social media research data. It very much depended on a) the research field and topic, the specific data collected, the platform data were collected from and b) the ethical frame chosen in the face of this situation and applied in decision making whether sharing seemed advisable from an ethical perspective.

RESULTS AND DISCUSSION

Practices of social media data sharing (similar to data collection practices) turned out, as we had expected prior to our study, to be highly influenced by legal frameworks. In particular, researchers recognized and were aware of the fact that social media companies often imposed restrictions to data sharing in their terms of service. Such restrictions impacted data sharing practices. Therefore, much of the discussion around handling social media data was focused on legal frameworks. However, in the following we want to shift the focus to the ethical considerations that may affect decisions about whether or not to share social media data in research. While ethical considerations were often discussed in connection with legal ones, they go beyond them and, as we will show, also concern a wider range of topics. Of course, ethical considerations also affect different phases of a social media research project; some of the challenges are affecting the entire research process, such as dealing with different ethical review boards (Weller & Kinder-Kurlanda, 2014). Within this chapter we focus on the dimension of data sharing which is often overlooked in the more common discussions around, for example, data collection (Weller & Kinder-Kurlanda, 2015).

TO SHARE: ARGUMENTS FOR DATA SHARING

From the interviews we learned that several researchers were either already sharing some social media datasets they had collected or were considering to do so. The willingness to share data seemed to be related to the specific nature of this type of research data: data only existed because others – namely the users of social media platforms – had created it. Social media data as "found data" thus were seen to differ from other forms of data used to study people and their behaviour, such as survey data or experimental design data. We found that this circumstance seemed to foster a feeling in researchers of not being the actual "owner" of the data underlying their research:

> "We share datasets with everybody, actually. We don't feel we own that."
> "It's all public, it doesn't belong to us, we don't create the data, we don't evoke it, I mean it's natural. I don't think you have the right to really keep other people from it, no."

The perception of not being the data owner engendered a variety of perceived ethical obligations for sharing the data.

Perceived ethical obligations towards the scientific community. In line with concerns about inequalities in data access that have been voiced in the literature (prominently by boyd & Crawford, 2012) researchers in our interviews described the social media research field as highly uneven. They especially criticized that researchers working in or in collaboration with industry had access to bigger and more comprehensive datasets, whereas others were restricted by legal, technical, or financial limitations. Limitations could also arise out of a lack of technical skills and hence no possibility to scrape web data, use APIs, or clean and process collected data (Kinder-Kurlanda & Weller, 2014). Data access often determined which kinds of questions were possible to answer in research. While some efforts were being made to alleviate inequalities in access through interdisciplinary collaborations (Kinder-Kurlanda & Weller, 2014) we still witnessed a situation in which, in the long run, current inequalities in data access opportunities may even increase based on a "rich gets richer" phenomenon: particularly in the computationally oriented big data field, those with access to better datasets may be able to continuously publish in better journals or receive more funding and are thus more likely to again get access to better datasets. We also saw this uneven distribution of opportunities at work in reproducing traditional economies of attention that favour researchers from the "West". Sharing high-quality datasets could thus help to alleviate the inequalities in data access and create a more competitive research landscape, and many researchers found it desirable for this reason.

We found that the current situation not only created unequal possibilities for conducting high-impact research, but researchers also saw it to create inequalities in the ability to judge research quality and to reproduce results:

> "But you can't make your data available for others to look at, which means both your study can't really be replicated and it can't be tested for review."

> "... but again the Twitter rules [...] make it very difficult for us to share the underlying dataset so that someone else can't go and actually do their own analyses and test what we've done."

For some researchers, lack of transparency in review processes was even an argument against buying access to datasets which may not be shared afterwards due to constraints in terms and conditions:

> "... if I'm paying [...] I cannot probably publish it and then if someone wants to repeat that, then that person has to pay for that data, so it's a barrier against the repeatability of my experiment. I shouldn't build this barrier into my research."

We even found a case where sharing was specifically demanded by peers in the research community. This occurred in a project about Twitter use by protesters where data had been obtained from a vendor. The decision not to share (which was in accordance with the vendor's terms of service) led to tensions with other researchers:

> "At the beginning of our […] research there was like a network of researchers […][interested in the topic] who came together online. And some of the people who were in the network really thought that there was like an ethical mandate to share access to data sources. So our access to the Gnip thing was like pretty uncommon. So there was some pressure from people who thought we should just put that online, like, make that accessible to everybody."

In general, data sharing was perceived as a means to securing quality in social media research and to improving standards for good scientific practice. Many researchers thus felt obliged to share their data with the scientific community. While ethical concerns around research transparency and quality can be found in other research fields as well, there are specificities that make sharing in the social media field especially desirable in this sense: Data access was seen as highly unequal; and social media researchers also felt a special responsibility to share data with social media users.

Perceived ethical obligations towards social media users. Social media data had not been created specifically for the purpose of research upon intervention of the researchers, but rather were the result of the authorship of various social media platform users who created data for a variety of reasons in the course of everyday interactions. Most interviewees assumed that users were not aware of their data being used in a specific research project. Only in a few cases had researchers established a direct contact with users. Nevertheless we saw a desire "to give something back" to the users, e.g. to feed results back to studied communities. This was also seen as a means to improve results e.g. by correcting misunderstandings. For example, one researcher felt obliged to publicly share the collected dataset in addition to research findings to recognise all data producers' input and also saw advantages in doing so:

> "… the issue or the question we have had with our work into social movements is that we want to make research available for the people who we are actually studying. So they can look at it and comment and say "yes" – or "no, you got it wrong" or "yes, this is what it was." So we can publish in open access journals. But we still can't make the data available and … we wanted to do projects with people who are involved and say, well, this is what we've got, what we worked together to create."

We found that it depended on the topics and communities of a specific study whether researchers perceived social media users as active authors who they sought to cite and involve, or as more "passive" research subjects. There are additional ethical tensions: As we will see in the next section, obligations to share data with social media users and the research community were often in direct conflict with the desire to protect social media users and specifically their privacy.

Not to Share: Ethical Considerations against Data Sharing

Despite a general willingness to share, in practice still only few social media datasets are officially being shared. At the same time there is evidence of a "grey market" where researchers unofficially pass on datasets to other researchers (Weller & Kinder-Kurlanda, 2015). The lack of officially shared datasets is closely connected to a feeling of insecurity about best practices, often also related to ethical considerations. Probably the most intense discussions are related to the protection of research subjects, a topic that often already arises in discussions about data collection practices (boyd & Crawford, 2012).

Desire to protect research subjects. Data sharing may aggravate the ethical dilemma caused by collecting data from social media users who are not aware that they are becoming research subjects. Much of the discussion is focused on the question of whether or not to share user names or other information that may help to identify the actual users behind the data. In practice, complete anonymization of social media data is hard to achieve (Markham & Buchanan, 2012), and several cases exist where presumably anonymous data have been de-anonymized by others (Zimmer, 2010). Consequently, researchers may prefer not to share any data at all. Researchers were particularly concerned about the consequences of sharing data about certain groups, such as political activists or especially vulnerable communities (e.g. underage persons):

> "And people may get threatened if they expose their identity if they can be tracked or if their political leaning can be identified and they can be personally tracked and identified by the political enemy."

> "… that radically open sharing of the data was extremely dangerous for the activists and a whole bunch of activists got arrested."

From our interviews we also learned that sensitivity towards user privacy seemed to grow over time. For example, some researchers reported that they now refrained from quoting user names in publications while they had done so previously:

> "For a long time, […]. we acted like according to this kind of idea that because something was public that it was ok to use it for research. But that is some kind of strong and unjustified assumption, I mean it doesn't really … if something is public this doesn't mean that the author is ok with you doing research on that specific content."

Although there were some cases where researchers had asked social media users for consent to their data being shared, we found that many of them were uncertain about the topic of consent to data sharing. Points of unclarity and often also dissent were whether researchers should attempt to specifically ask for consent to the specific research project; how formal or implicit consent to research in general (e.g. by agreeing to a platform's terms of service) was to be interpreted; and how asking for consent may be possible or feasible. Furthermore, even informed consent may not be enough to fully protect social media users in some data sharing scenarios: Data collected for research may be used for unexpected purposes and by players outside of research contexts, e.g. governmental players or the police. For example, in the US research data may even be requested under the Freedom of Information Act. Research data may also be combined with other data and, then, reveal more information than initially considered, and users might "inadvertently reveal things" they did not intend to reveal.

Lack of clarity about legal constraints and their role in good research practice. The desire to protect research subjects was influenced by the lack of clarity with regard to the legal situation around social media data. Often researchers were not knowledgeable about the details of legislations such as local data protection legislation. On the other hand, there are currently several open challenges in the legal environment, as legislation is not keeping up with new technical developments on the internet, so that what is allowed and what is not and which laws apply is often still being negotiated (e.g. Ströbel, 2016). The lack of clarity in legal frameworks goes beyond questions of e.g. privacy protection. Many researchers were aware that even in their approaches to data collection they may be breaking social media companies' terms of service – and possibly additional legal constraints ("Probably, possibly we'd be actually operating outside the spirit if not the letter and the law of the latest Twitter API"). They were also aware that additional restrictions applied for sharing even in cases where data collection had been conducted in accordance with legal requirements ("Because when you buy this data from GNIP they tell you that you can't re-publish this data"). We found that some researchers were willing to accept the uncertainty or even the certainty of possibly breaking legal constraints in their own research projects. But many were worried about consequences if they shared the resulting datasets:

> "Our university has strict policies about research data and, in the excitement of doing science, you don't always follow those things, I guess. If people ask us for a data set because they are working on something similar by email, then we might share it, but we can never publicly do that."

In some cases sharing did not happen because a researcher was afraid of personal consequences for her/himself, others were afraid of putting their university or those researchers who may reuse the data at risk. Ethical considerations came into play once a researcher had to decide about whether or not to violate legal contracts in order to conduct a specific research project and continued when he/she realized that others may also be affected by this decision. A researcher may explicitly decide against putting others at risk of also breaking some legal constraints. Overall, data sharing in this context faced the major challenge of balancing between following principles of good scientific practice which included openness and transparency and between respecting legal constraints, some of them imposed by social media companies who may have agendas that researchers do not agree with or even actively would like to resist due to ethical considerations. The fact that researchers faced these challenges when studying social media data had also led to critique of social media companies' policies that often hindered efficient and good research practices. One researcher even considered sharing research data as problematic as it facilitates the use of social media data for research and thus does not motivate platform providers, who may also profit from research as free publicity, to work on improving accessibility of data for researchers.

Lack of clarity in data collection and negative effects on data analysis. Finally, we found another and probably less obvious argument against data sharing when researchers were worried about misinterpretation of data. Currently, there is little or no best practice for documenting data collection processes for social media data, and it is therefore often very hard to retrace and understand how a specific dataset has been created (Weller & Kinder-Kurlanda, 2015). Some researchers do not reuse datasets collected by others for the very reason that they have no means to fully understand how the data have been collected and prepared:

> "I actually only use [other researcher's datasets] where I'm very sure about where it comes from and how it was processed and analyzed. There is too much uncertainty in it."

Sometimes it was not even feasible to describe every detail of a data collection process or the context in which data collection had occurred, which led to researchers being hesitant to share data that can never be fully documented as those who reuse the data may accidentally draw the wrong conclusions in data analysis. A reason for deciding against data sharing thus can be the fear that other researchers might not only misinterpret the data but might also be less careful in handling and further sharing the data. One researcher put it as follows: "That's what I get worried about: being reckless with our data. We need to be careful on how we do that. I'm not thinking one's trying to do anything bad, but …"

Pitfalls in Practice and Other Ethical Sharing Dilemmas

As we have seen, researchers may find themselves confronted with different arguments for and against sharing social media datasets. A particularly strong challenge appears to be the direct trade-off between making information as openly accessible as possible on the one side and respecting users' privacy and legal obligations on the other. Researchers sometimes felt stuck within this dilemma:

> "And probably we are going to end up in a situation where we will have some kind of acceptable situation. You know, it is not going to be perfect because with this kind of data I just don't see the perfect situation being possible, especially because there is a lot of personal information there."

Also in many cases there was either little or no practical guidelines or at least none were known to the researchers so that they were trying to work out by themselves "what might be good practice and not". Even if an individual researcher arrived at a solution for his/her current case that seemed to satisfy all ethical considerations, there could be additional external circumstances that might contradict the found solution, including official requirements by funding agencies or other players, or colleagues in collaborative projects possessing differing opinions.

Official requirements by stakeholders like IRBs, funding agencies or journals. Sometimes the decision about whether or not to share research data was not up to just the researchers themselves. Sharing could be formally required by third parties as a condition of funding. Projects might also have promised to make available data in the grant application and would only later notice that sharing would not in fact be possible. Researchers were often uncertain about how to handle funding agencies' expectations about open data in the context of social media:

> "You know two of the major funding agencies in the US the NSF NIH National Institute for Health have mandate such a data has to be public. This is tax payer money and it has to be out there and so one thing is I'm interested in how our researchers are dealing with that."

Some seemed confident that ethical reasons would however be a valid reason not to share datasets:

> "But no one can make you, no one would try to make you publish data that, you would otherwise be ethically or commercially be bound not publish. But it's, I think, it's one of the big ethical dilemmas."

Nevertheless, in some contexts researchers feared that governmental institutions might at some point claim the right to access datasets, e.g. for criminal prosecution. On the other hand we also found cases where researchers wanted to share data, but other stakeholders, e.g. journal publishers, were hesitant to allow them to do so. Several interviewees reported cases where, for example, papers had not been accepted at conferences because of potential legal infringements.

> "We had one conference paper so far that was rejected [...]. I think the paper got mostly good reviews but the program chair, the conference chair said: I am not comfortable publishing it. Because he or she thought that we were violating terms of service of Facebook or some such."

Co-authorship and collaborative work. Often, social media research is done collaboratively, creating a challenge of who among the research team is to decide questions of whether or not to publicly share or archive the underlying research data. This could be particularly difficult in those cases where a semi-official data sharing process had already taken place, e.g. if a researcher obtained a dataset from a colleague who happened to have collected it but would not work with it him/herself. We saw such informal sharing happen in a variety of contexts including, for example, researchers who gave datasets to colleagues for teaching purposes. In these situations, the data receiver's further handling would also need to be considered. It would need to be clarified, for example, whether they would again share the data with others. And in cases where data had been used in research projects, the question arose who would finally decide about whether or not a dataset used for a specific paper should be published or archived. Discussions on research ethics in this context needed to consider options to have the person who initially collected the data to be involved in the decision about finally publishing a dataset – even if he or she was not one of the authors of a resulting publication. In general, there was a lot of uncertainty about how to acknowledge contributions in data collection in collaborative projects and how to define authorship, and this uncertainty yielded the potential for serious conflicts:

> "And when I was using something that somebody else had collected … I think … there's always the question of if you publish something, how do you address that? Do you … is somebody who contributed data always a co-author or not? In what place? So that's a little bit of a new issue for me, that has to be determined."

> "And I started to use some data that had been gathered by one of the other researchers. On the understanding in a team meeting that that's what I would be doing. And then my colleague also … from the same understanding. But clearly it was a kind of miscommunication. And this person became quite upset when I wrote this draft of a paper and shared it with the team. They said, you know: 'You're using my data! That's my data!'"

Finally, there was the possibility that co-authors or project partners might not agree on their preferred mode of balancing the desire to share data with the desire to protect social media users. Although no such case has been reported in our interviews, there is a clear potential for situations in which one researcher is pressured into sharing a dataset which may infringe users' privacy or violate terms of service.

CONCLUSION: TOWARDS ETHICAL SOCIAL MEDIA DATA SHARING

Our study revealed a strong sense of insecurity in many researchers about the topic of data sharing. This insecurity was connected to a lack of clarity with regard to the legal situation, but most often it was caused by a feeling of being in a situation where they were attempting something new. Each project was different and with the use of new methodologies created research that to various extents happened outside or only partially assisted by established research support institutions such as appropriate and helpful guidance by advisors or ethics boards. Although several initiatives and texts exist (e.g. the AoIR guidelines (Ess & AoIR Ethics Working Committee, 2002; Markham & Buchanan, 2012)), we found that decision making happened on the basis of individual considerations; only few examples to follow (e.g. from peers) were seen to be available.

Due to this uncertainty, social media data sharing was often hidden and done informally, even in such cases where it would have been in accordance with legal restrictions and ethical considerations to share at least some of the data. Some researchers even claimed the emergence of a "gray market" in which "everybody has all kinds of stuff on their machines (…). If people ask us for a data set because they are working on something similar (…), then we might share it, but we can never publicly do that." The gray market of social media data could help alleviate inequalities in data access but would not always do so: sharing depended largely on good connections to the "data rich" thus potentially even exacerbating inequalities. But there are also other forms of data sharing emerging (Thomson, 2016), including datasets published openly on researchers' websites, as well as more persistent approaches mediated by professional players such as archival institutions (e.g. at the Internet Archive or at the GESIS Data Archive) or by publishers and conference organizers (e.g. at the ICWSM and TREC conferences) (Weller & Kinder-Kurlanda, 2016). These professional approaches can help to secure long-term accessibility of the data, can support researchers in providing documentation alongside with the actual datasets, and may also provide guidance in legal questions. Archivists are working on solutions in the form of secure, flexible, and controlled access such as usage agreements or data use in safe rooms (i.e. the shared datasets can only be accessed in secure environments) and other controlled access possibilities.

However, other challenges remain. For example, if researchers and archives respect the terms of service of platform providers, they may still be limited in what data they can share (e.g. tweet IDs instead of full tweet texts with metadata). Such requirements limit the ability to fulfil the ethical obligation towards the research community to contribute to high methodological standards (e.g. as tweet IDs only do not guarantee that the full dataset may be re-created after the actual tweets have been deleted). In order to overcome this situation, archiving institutions and other professional stakeholders like publishers will have to increase their efforts to seek the dialogue with social media data platform providers. It may be possible to negotiate better conditions for data sharing if there is a guarantee that sharing will only occur amongst well vetted and ethically reflective researchers. There are already various secure sharing solutions for other research data requiring special protection, such as specially protected data safe rooms or complex usage agreements in which users agree not to share and to protect the data. Secure sharing solutions for social media data could also foster the emergence of sharing guidelines and best practice recommendations. We found that researchers, while willing to find ways to deal with ethical dilemmas of sharing social media data, were, however, often left alone with these issues and needed to resort to individual workarounds. Finally, some ethical decisions will clearly have to be made by the researchers themselves, such as acknowledging co-authorship and deciding about whether to share datasets that are based on collaborative projects.

REFERENCES

Borgman, C. L. (2012). The conundrum of sharing research data. *Journal of the American Society for Information Science and Technology, 63*(6), 1059–1078.

boyd, d., & Crawford, K. (2012). Critical questions for Big Data: Provocations for a cultural, technological, and scholarly phenomenon. *Information, Communication & Society, 15*(5), 662–679. Retrieved from http://doi.org/10.1080/1369118X.2012.678878

Ess, C., & AoIR Ethics Working Committee. (2002, November 27). *Ethical decision-making and Internet research: Recommendations from the AoIR Ethics Working Committee.* Approved by AoIR. Retrieved from http://aoir.org/reports/ethics.pdf

Kinder-Kurlanda, K. E., & Weller, K. (2014). "I always feel it must be great to be a hacker!": The role of interdisciplinary work in social media research. In *Proceedings of the 2014 ACM Conference on Web Science* (pp. 91–98). New York, NY: ACM.

Kirkegaard, E. O. W., & Bjerrekær, J. D. (2016). *The OKCupid dataset: A very large public dataset of dating site users.* Retrieved from http://openpsych.net/forum/showthread.php?tid=279

Markham, A., & Buchanan, E. (2012). *Ethical decision-making and Internet research. Recommendations from the AoIR Ethics Working Committee (Version 2.0).* Retrieved from http://www.aoir.org/reports/ethics2.pdf

Recker, A., & Müller, S. (2015). Preserving the essence: Identifying the significant properties of social science research data. New Review of Information Networking, 20(1–2), 229–235. doi:10.1080/13614576.2015.1110404

Ströbel, L. (2016). Persönlichkeitsschutz von Straftätern im Internet: Neue Formen der Prangerwirkung. *Reihe: Schriften zum Medien- und Informationsrecht, Bd. 17.* doi:10.5771/9783845273747-1

Thomson, S. D. (2016). Preserving social media. *DPC Technology Watch Report.* Retrieved from http://dpconline.org/publications/technology-watch-reports

Weller, K., & Kinder-Kurlanda, K. E. (2014). I love thinking about ethics: Perspectives on ethics in social media research. In *Selected Papers of Internet Research (SPIR). Proceedings of ir15 – Boundaries and intersections.* Retrieved from http://spir.aoir.org/index.php/spir/article/view/997

Weller, K., & Kinder-Kurlanda, K. E. (2015). Uncovering the challenges in collection, sharing and documentation: The hidden data of social media research? In *Standards and practices in large-scale social media research: Papers from the 2015 ICWSM Workshop. Proceedings ninth international AAAI conference on web and social media Oxford University, 2015, AAAI Technical Report WS-15-18* (pp. 28–37). Ann Arbor, MI: AAAI Press.

Weller, K., & Kinder-Kurlanda, K. E. (2016). A Manifesto for data sharing in social media research. In *Proceedings of the 8th ACM conference on web science (WebSci '16)* (pp. 166–172). New York, NY: ACM.

Zimmer, M. (2010). "But the data is already public": On the ethics of research in Facebook. *Ethics Information Technology, 12*, 313. doi:10.1007/s10676-010-9227-5

REACTION BY ALEXANDER HALAVAIS

The authors of this chapter have done an outstanding job of charting not just the obstacles to sharing data, but a piece that is so often left out: the reasons for sharing data in the first place. There are significant continuities between earlier forms of archiving and sharing and those encountered when we move to researching large-scale digital platforms. One of those continuities is the difficulty in understanding the context and process by which the data have been collected.

Of course, in practice, we have reported process – methods – longer than we have shared data. But those methods are rarely explicit or detailed enough to permit the reader to replicate the work. That extends to replicating the collection of data. And while there has been a sea change in the recognition that there is value in sharing data, there has been less consensus around the need to be explicit in sharing the process by which those data were collected. It is true that this would directly eliminate neither the legal restrictions, nor the ethical challenges, nor the growing divide between the data haves and have nots. But as the open sharing of code among developers has shown, wide availability of tools and procedures might make the products of those processes more easily found, assembled, and archived.

Among so much that has come to pass found in Vannevar Bush's half-century old "As We May Think" was the so-far failed prediction that future scientists would wear cameras that would detail precisely their own work. Perhaps the data we should be most effective in sharing is that about the black box that is so often the researchers' own processes.

Alexander Halavais *is associate professor of social technologies at Arizona State University, where he directs the MA in Social Technologies. His work explores the relationship of social media to learning, knowledge, and power.*

REACTION BY BONNIE TIJERINA

This chapter reveals ethical concerns regarding sharing and not sharing social media data. It's clear that more guidance is needed for social media researchers across various disciplines in terms of what data to collect, the method of collecting, and what to share and with whom. Where should more guidance come from? Universities' formal structures, like Institutional Review Boards, don't necessarily have the technical knowledge to understand what data is being collected, how it's collected, how it will be shared. They are not looking into data reuse when considering a research project. Professional associations where researchers look to publish their findings in articles or present at conferences have not been consistent on ethical data practice issues but the incentives for researchers are present. Funding agencies who can set mandates must also provide education and best practices in order for researchers to meet their mandates. Or, should each discipline figure out what is ethical for the type of research they do? For disciplines that do not have a history in considering the ethics of their work, how do those conversations turn into best practices or culture change? There is not one clear place, organization, or resource for researchers. Since this data is by and about humans and there are responsibilities for using and sharing human subjects data, guidance, standards, and best practices are needed.

Bonnie Tijerina *is currently a Researcher at the Data & Society Research Institute in NYC where she focuses on the ethics of big data research, data sharing, online privacy, and the role libraries play in supporting their communities as they navigate the challenges that come with emerging technologies.*

CHAPTER EIGHT

"We Tend to Err on the Side of Caution"

Ethical Challenges Facing Canadian Research Ethics Boards When Overseeing Internet Research

YUKARI SEKO AND STEPHEN P. LEWIS

INTRODUCTION: CANADIAN FRAMEWORK FOR INTERNET RESEARCH

Internet research has gained tremendous momentum over the past few decades. As data collection tools, research sites, communication venues, and community spaces, internet-based technologies greatly benefits researchers to save costs and time associated with reaching diverse populations, obtaining information, and conducting observations beyond temporal and spatial constraints. Despite these unprecedented opportunities, internet research proposes a set of distinct ethical questions to researchers and regulatory bodies that oversee research activities. A number of scholarly publications to date have identified various ethical issues associated with internet research including the changing nature of privacy, confidentiality, informed consent, and data security (e.g., McKee & Porter, 2009). In particular, researchers using internet platforms to study vulnerable and hard-to-reach populations, including individuals diagnosed with Alzheimer's disease (Rodriquez, 2013), sexual minority youth (McDermott & Roen, 2012), and people who engage in self-harm (Seko, Kidd, Wijer, & McKenzie, 2015; Sharkey et al., 2011), have documented unique ethical challenges rising from their studies. Ethical dilemmas pertinent to these studies, along with the practical solutions proposed by these researchers, have contributed greatly to the enrichment of empirical knowledge. Likewise, scholarly associations such as the Association of Internet Researchers (Ess & AoIR Ethics Working Committee, 2002; Markham & Buchanan, 2012) and American Psychological Association (2013), as well as governmental bodies like the U.S. Department of Health and Human Services (2013), have published guidelines to assist internet researchers and ethics reviewers.

Compared to literature on researchers' experiences, little has been written about how regulatory bodies manage internet-based research. One notable exception is Buchanan and Ess's (2009) nation-wide survey of Institutional Review Boards (IRBs) in the United States. Of the 334 IRBs that responded to their survey, 62% did not have guidelines in place for reviewing internet research protocols, 74% did not receive specific training on internet research ethics, and more than half (58%) felt they were not well-equipped to review such protocols. The authors pointed out ample need for preparing practical guidelines and policies for internet research ethics. Nonetheless, the experience of regulatory bodies outside the U.S. remains largely unknown.

Presently in Canada, human subjects research must conform to the *Tri-Council Policy Statement: Ethical Conduct for Research Involving Humans* (TCPS) and be conducted under oversight of an institutional Research Ethics Board (REB) that assesses and monitors the ethical acceptability of the research. Although the original TCPS published in 1998 made no mention of the internet, the debate regarding the ethical issues associated with internet-based research has been steadily evolving over the past few decades. Eysenbach and Till (2001) were among the earliest Canadian scholars to categorize internet studies into three general types consisting of "passive" non-intrusive analysis, "active" participatory research, and web-based data collection via online surveys and interviews. This typology was further elaborated on by Kitchin (2007) who delineated internet research into two discrete categories: 1) web-based research (consisting of two subcategories: 1a) non-intrusive and 1b) engaged) and 2) online research. Claiming that each of these categories is grounded upon disparate assumptions of "human subjects," Kitchin (2007) contended that non-intrusive web-based research (1a) "should not be enveloped under the human subject paradigm" (p. 56) as authors of publicly accessible online material already "relinquish their privacy as a consequence of their participation" (p. 56).

Kitchin's view of public cyber-materials as published "texts" rather than living "human subjects" had a considerable influence on the revision of the TCPS. In 2008, the Social Sciences and Humanities Research Ethics Special Working Committee (SSHWC) under Canada's Interagency Panel of Research Ethics (PRE) issued a discussion paper to address gaps in the 1998 TCPS and made ten recommendations to attend to the ethics of internet-based research. With an extensive reference to Kitchin's typology, the SSHWC took the position that non-intrusive web-research should be exempted from REB review, while engaged web-based research (e.g., participatory observations in chatrooms) and online research (e.g., collecting data via online surveys) would require ethical assessment (Blackstone et al., 2008). However, practical guidance on unique ethical issues – for instance, how to gauge the public-ness of a given online space – was largely absent from the report. Rather, the SSHWC openly admitted its uncertainty by questioning readers: "[...] should we maintain that all information found on the internet is public, or should we subject that assessment to certain criteria (public-private continuum, sensitivity of the theme, etc.)?" (Blackstone et al., 2008, p. 4).

The SSHWC's uncertainty toward internet research was inherited in the 2010 revision of TCPS known as TCPS2 (CIHR, NSERC, & SSHRC, 2014), in which ethical issues pertinent to internet research were discussed only briefly in three sections: research exempt from REB review (Chapter 2, Article 2.2); data security (Chapter 5, Article 5.3); and non-intrusive observations over the internet (Chapter 10, Article 10.2). Notably, the TCPS2 takes a more cautious approach than Kitchin (2007) to "public" online material and encourages that researchers studying publicly accessible websites should carefully assess the sensitivity of the topic being researched and privacy expectation of the site members (CIHR, NSERC, & SSHRC, 2014, Chapter 2, Article 2.2). Nevertheless, the TCPS2 remains largely silent on how exactly such ethical considerations can be translated into practice, and how REBs can evaluate ethical adaptability of internet research involving human participants. Moreover, there are a number of untouched issues including: weighing risks versus benefits in internet research, obtaining free and informed consent over the internet, and establishing robust data stewardship to protect data privacy and confidentiality. Despite recent granting agencies' calls for advancing large-scale digital research (SSHRC, CIHR, NSERC, & CFI, 2013), the latest revision of TCPS2 (CIHR et al., 2014), too, made no amendment to the 2010 version with respect to these issues.

Since the inception of the 1998 TCPS, Canadian scholars have argued that the scarcity of pragmatic guidance in national framework would yield inconsistencies and misconceptions among local ethical decision-making (Tilley & Gormley, 2007). Some have also warned about the problem of an "ethics creep" (Haggerty, 2004) whereby local REBs overextend their power in assessing ethical and methodological acceptability of research. Some internet researchers have also felt uncomfortable having their research reviewed by REBs unfamiliar with internet methodologies and technologies (Kitchin, 2007), while others complained that REBs are likely to "develop their own internal, often opaque, decision making practices" to review internet research protocols, which tend to cause "significant problems and delays for researchers" (Warrell & Jacobson, 2014, p. 24).

With the gap in pragmatic guidelines in the TCPS2, it is essential to explore how local REBs actually provide ethical clearance for and oversee internet research. In what follows, we report findings from a series of semi-structured interviews with members of Research Ethics Boards (REBs) at several Canadian universities. We describe unique ethical challenges REB members had faced when reviewing internet research protocols, and discuss potential gaps in the current national framework and unmet local needs for resources and guidelines. We also address practical solutions local REBs have developed to better review internet research and close this chapter by exploring implications for internet researchers and ethics reviewers across the world.

METHODS

Data Collection

Prior to recruitment, the present study received ethical clearance from the University of Guelph REB. Participants were recruited from university-based REBs in Ontario, Canada, using e-mail addresses presented on university websites. Aiming to interview REB members in charge of protocol review, we emailed initial recruitment notices to contact persons identified on the websites (e.g., REB coordinators, chairs) and asked them to share the invitation with other REB members who they thought might be interested in participating.

A total of 12 REB members from eight universities across Ontario volunteered to participate in this study, which covered two-third of universities in this region – one of the most populated areas in Canada. Participants were from universities of mixed statuses, including small and medium size universities with less than 15,000 students and large size institutions with more than 20,000 students. Interview participants included both voting members (e.g., faculty members) and ex-officio members (e.g., ethics officers), all of whom reporting that they had reviewed research protocols submitted to their REBs. Their positions varied, including board members, ethics officers, and chairs. While some universities with medical programs have distinct medical REBs, our participants did not include members of medical REBs in order to achieve consistent sampling.

Data were collected between June and October 2015 through a series of in-person, semi-structured interviews. To ensure internal consistency, the first author carried out all of the interviews. Interviews lasted between 75 minutes to 2 hours, averaging about 95 minutes. For the purpose of this study, we followed the AoIR's 2012 guidelines for Internet Research Ethics (Markham & Buchanan, 2012) and broadly defined "internet research" as involving both the use of the internet as a *tool* for research (e.g., data collection through online surveys, interviews, mobile apps and crowdsourcing, recruitment through online ads, automatic data scraping) and as a *field/site* for research (e.g., research on how people use the internet, compositional, content or discourse analysis of online materials, analysis of the design and structure of software, code and interface, virtual ethnography).

Data Analysis

All interviews were audio-recorded and transcribed verbatim. To examine the data, we employed thematic content analysis to inductively identify recurrent themes from the interviews, assisted in part by the MAXQDA (version 11) qualitative data analysis software. The analytic procedures outlined by Saldaña (2013) were used to identify prevalent themes and core conceptions. Coding began following the first three interviews to inductively develop a preliminary coding scheme. The first author conducted initial line-by-line coding to develop thematic categories. Each transcript was read at least twice to identify different themes until no new themes emerged. After preliminary coding, the second author provided a detailed review of the coding scheme and preliminary themes emerged during open coding. The two authors then discussed the tentative codes to achieve consensus and collaboratively develop coding structures and a final coding rubric.

In addition, the technique of "member checking" (Harper & Cole, 2012) was employed to ensure the rigor of data. After the interview, we asked each participant to read through the individual interview transcript to confirm the accuracy of the conversation (first member checking). Upon the completion of all interviews and preliminary analysis, participants received a short summary of preliminary findings and were asked again for feedback to determine if the researchers' interpretations matched their experiences (second member checking). We also asked two experts in internet research ethics for comments on the preliminary analysis. Reflecting on the participants' feedback and experts' comments, we finalized the analysis.

RESULTS

Types of Internet Research

All interview participants – regardless of university size – noted the rapid growth of internet research over the past few years. The majority of internet research protocols submitted to the participants' REBs involved online tools for data collection or recruitment, while a handful of studies focused on people's behavior on the internet. Online surveys were the most prevalent type of research mentioned by all interviewees, followed by studies using crowdsourcing platforms (e.g., Amazon's Mechanical Turk, CrowdFlower) for recruitment, data collection and data analysis. Research involving the construction and analysis of large databases (i.e., Big Data analysis) was still in its infancy, but reported to be growing rapidly. The majority of internet research came from Psychology, Business, Education, and other disciplines in which survey methods have been traditionally widespread. However, a few participants observed an increase in the number of internet research protocols from disciplines not traditionally engaged in human subjects research (e.g., History, Engineering). The ease of online data collection, along with the increasing demand for empirical research, has seemingly propelled researchers to employ internet-based methods.

Ethical Challenges Pertinent to Internet-based Research

Despite the increasing volume of research involving internet-based tools, the majority of participants noted that internet research has not proposed challenges *substantively different* from non-internet research. Most internet research protocols fell under a delegated review, as they were seen to involve only minimal risk, and the majority of the interview participants did not see a need for special guidelines or training for reviewing internet-based studies. Instead, a prominent challenge identified in the interviews was the difficulty to translate existing ethics principles into practice. Although many interviewees felt that their REBs have gradually been better equipped with technological knowledge, they still noticed uncertainty among board members regarding the ever-changing digital tools and environments. One participant stated: "*we always say that we can't really write guidelines on how to review research involving the internet, because it's just changing all the time.*" The emergent digital scholarship symbolized by Big Data has also pushed reviewers to another unknown territory. With the absence of empirical assessments on the potential risks associated with Big Data, participants anticipated new challenges facing their boards, as it would "*take some time*" for them to "*fully comprehend the complex privacy implications*" of the growing digital research.

The REB members named several ethical challenges pertinent to this unfamiliar terrain. Some echoed the issues reported in existing literature including participant privacy, data security, and appropriate means of obtaining informed consent (e.g., Buchannan & Ess, 2009). However, there were new concerns that seem to emerge with new technologies such as crowdsourcing services and social media platforms. A few participants mentioned that ensuring voluntary participation and data privacy in crowdsourcing was challenging due to its task-oriented nature, while others concerned with the risk of potential labor exploitation through crowd work wherein many people engage in manual labor for cheap compensation. Some REB members also discussed the increasing risk of re-identification through metadata generated by social media algorithms (e.g., geotags) and information-rich multimedia content posted by users (e.g., selfies, video diaries).

Another common concern identified by participants was the lack of an empirical framework to accurately assess the magnitude of potential harm in internet research and the likelihood of such harm actually occurring in the conduct of the project. Participants commonly addressed that research involving sensitive topics or "vulnerable" populations (e.g., minors, racialized groups, people with health difficulties) often raise ethical concerns, and REBs would request researchers to clarify specific strategies they would employ to mitigate potential harms. However, as the assessment of such risks tends to be based on researchers' experiences and/or reviewers' subjective perceptions rather than empirical evidence, there would occasionally be discrepancies between researchers eager to carry out their research and reviewers who, in the words of one participant, "*tend to err on the side of caution.*" In particular, several participants raised concern with remote and anonymous web-based research that makes it challenging to properly assess risk and deliver timely interventions if needed. One interviewee, in regard to a potential iatrogenic effect of psychological research on the internet, stated:

> We do see people wanting to do research on mental health issues across the internet, and if something happens where you're asking a question about suicide or have you ever tried to hurt yourself, do you know where that person is on the other end of the computer? Can you offer them resources in enough time should something happen, when they go into a crisis situation?

Furthermore, balancing perceived risks and benefits in internet research sometimes posed a conundrum to REB members. Although interviewees unanimously agreed that REBs should conduct ethical assessment from the perspective of research participants and prevent researchers from taking advantage of participants' false sense of privacy or lack thereof, the groundless fear of unknown consequences may hinder their reasonable assessment. Some interviewees framed REB's overestimation of risks as a "*scope creep,*" namely, an unnecessary extension of their responsibilities that would disregard autonomy of study participants:

> I think that REBs in a way sometimes overstep their role when they try to serve a paternalistic role with respect to participants, and deny participants, their right to make bad choices, like posting sensitive information on the internet ... when REBs start to protect people from all possible risks that are out there that's really a scope creep.

Similarly, referring to the ever-expanding demand for REBs to be knowledgeable about privacy and legal issues pertinent to digital research, another participant stated that there is an unreasonable expectation for local REB to serve as a "*privacy board*" beyond their purview:

> [TCPS] just says ... researchers have to respect local laws, the requisite laws, but they don't really tell you what it is, or how to become knowledgeable in those laws ... this is what I'm saying about TCPS is almost inadequate in terms of the privacy context ... we're becoming more the privacy board, not the ethics board.

Gaps in the Current National Framework, Challenges, and Expectations

Interview participants generally favored the current guideline-based, open-ended nature of the TCPS2, as they thought it would provide a greater level of flexibility for local REBs than a statue-driven, regulatory approach. And many emphasized that TCPS2's three core principles (*Respect for Persons, Concern for Welfare*, and *Justice*) would be applicable to any human subject research, including internet-based ones. Nevertheless, quite a few mentioned that TCPS2's open-endedness had become problematic when they tried to apply these core principles to individual research. While the TCPS2 recommends institutions to independently develop and implement research ethics policies and procedures amenable to local needs (CIHR et al., 2014), the lack of shared operational interpretations – for instance, in the words of a participant, "*what 'de-identified' data exactly means in social media research*" – sometime hinders cross-sectorial, inter-institutional collaborations. Currently, Canadian researchers wishing to conduct collaborative studies have to submit the same protocol to each collaborating institution unless these REBs have established official agreements for reciprocal reviews or have delegated ethics reviews to external multi-institutional REBs (CIHR et al., 2014, Chapter 8). Several participants referred to the occasion in which a research protocol their REB approved met denial at another REB. One participant noted:

> Because [TCPS2] is a guideline, and because the very real application issues ... are not addressed by means of interpretations or regulations or anything else, each institution is free to interpret it as it wants. The reality for researchers is that more and more research is multi-site and collaborative. Inconsistency is a roadblock to the research.

The notion that REBs might pose a "*roadblock*" to researchers was, in fact, commonly endorsed across interview participants. Some mentioned that research involving multiple REBs has often caused undue delays, which compelled researchers to see REBs "*not adding to the quality of the research*" but posing "*a hindrance*" or "*a burden*" to them. Others were also concerned that marked inconsistencies in interpretations might not only stir up unwanted antagonism between researchers and their REBs as well as between REBs, but also foster a negative perception among researchers to see REB as "*a bureaucratic quality assurance structure*" designed more to protect "*institutions from lawsuits*" than to protect research participants from harms.

To respond to the increasing demand for multi-institutional research, many interview participants felt that having more shared procedural and adaptable interpretations of the TCPS2, along with a series of nationally recognized best practices, would benefit both reviewers and researchers. Some mentioned that it might prove helpful if the TCPS2 Course on Research Ethics (CORE) online tutorial would include some case studies pertinent to internet research (especially more controversial cases), focusing on how the core principles could be adapted to these specific situations. Others requested that further enrichment of a nation-wide knowledge sharing mechanism for researchers and reviewers be implemented. Webinar series on ethics offered by the PRE were perceived as valuable learning opportunities, which could be extended to include emergent issues such as internet research and digital data management.

Local Best Practices

In order to meet the growing needs of internet-based research, most REBs we interviewed have developed local, university-based guidelines, standard operating procedures (SOPs), and sample forms (e.g., sample information letter, consent form) for affiliated researchers in accordance with the TCPS2 and their institutional ethics policies. With respect to internet research, most commonly mentioned was the guideline for online survey conveying practical guidance for treatment of personally identifying information (e.g., IP addresses) and how to ensure voluntary participation (e.g., by providing an option to skip questions). For researchers proposing to use online survey tools hosted in the United States (e.g., Survey Monkey), many REBs recommend that researchers inform survey participants that responses to the survey may be subject to relevant U.S. laws (e.g., US Patriot Act). Most of these guidelines and SOPs are publicly available on university websites, with some REBs also embedding links to these guidelines on their digital REB application forms, so that researchers can refer to relevant information while completing their REB forms.

Providing tools compliant with ethics guidelines and technical supports was another institutional effort to ensure ethical applicability of research. Some participants said they regularly recommended researchers to use online survey software hosted by their universities or a video chat tool compliant with the Health Insurance Portability and Accountability Act (HIPAA). Researchers wishing to use other tools would be requested to justify their decision and submit detailed security and privacy measures accordingly. Other participants mentioned that they would encourage researchers to consult with IT experts at their institutions, as not all researchers and reviewers possess sufficient technical knowledge to develop adequate data safeguarding plans.

Along with institutional resource provision, many interview participants have formally or informally offered researchers anecdotal tips related to internet research. The most commonly shared tip was to let researchers "*do their homework*" and become familiar with the terms of services and privacy policy for the websites they would study *before* submitting REB applications. Moreover, many interviewees have advised researchers to password protect their research equipment and data with practical guidance how to do so. Many also noted that their boards have occasionally invited internal and external experts to full board meetings to learn new technologies, methods and procedures. These professional development sessions also contributed to the development of practical solutions and local best practices.

In addition to locally grown practices, interview participants also made use of external resources. Some said they had consulted with other university REBs when faced with unfamiliar or ethically challenging research protocols. Others had posted questions on the Canadian Association of Research Ethics Boards (CAREB) list-serv and had consulted the CAREB website for resources. Many had gone through the PRE's online repository for TCPS2 interpretations, and a few had submitted formal requests for interpretation to the PRE. However, the perception toward the PRE varied among interviewees; some viewed the interpretations as helpful to solve ethical dilemmas they faced, while others saw them as too theoretical and thus unhelpful to achieve practical solutions. A couple of participants were also concerned that although the PRE's interpretations were meant to be advisory, in actuality their responses were often taken as official instructions that local REBs must follow. One participant even called the PRE "*the final arbiter*," whose judgment must not be disobeyed. It is worth noting that there is no interpretation regarding internet research, cyber-materials, or social media on the PRE online repository as of March 2016. According to the Secretariat on Responsible Conduct of Research (SRCR) that offers administrative support for the PRE, there were seven interpretation requests in 2015 containing the terms "internet," "social media," or "Mechanical Turk." This represents less than 5% of the requests received (TCPS 2 interpretations, SRCR, February 26, 2016), indicating that not many REBs had yet sought guidance from the PRE regarding internet research.

DISCUSSION

Our findings demonstrate that internet research is presenting several challenges to Canadian REBs, mainly because studies involving emergent online technologies do not always fit well into exiting ethics frameworks. Although few REB members we interviewed considered internet research as posing discrete ethical problems, the speed with which new digital tools evolve and the increasingly innovative ways researchers employ them has nonetheless complicated ethical assessments. Oftentimes ethical challenges pertinent to internet research arise from the lack of consensus as to how a national framework can be applied to individual protocols.

One prominent theme that emerged from the interviews was the difficulty to make accurate risk/benefit assessments of internet research. While the interview participants firmly believed that TCPS2's core ethical principles would apply to internet-based studies – much like any other human subjects research – they still found it challenging to transfer the principles to new and unknown aspects of internet research. Unique ethical issues, such as blurring boundaries between private and public information, increasing risk of re-identification, and the difficulty of ensuring voluntary participation and data security, are inextricably intertwined with unique attributes of internet architectures and applications. Conventional ethics frameworks may not fully capture the convoluted nature of emergent online platforms, wherein users and algorithms constantly generate new forms of identifiable information with an unprecedented speed and scale. Reviewing internet research thus increasingly necessitates up-to-date technical expertise alongside ethical and regulatory knowledge. However, keeping apace with phantasmagoric technologies, site policies, and users' privacy expectations sometimes appears overwhelming to reviewers who may not have such expertise. As a result, reviewers tend to "*err on the side of caution.*"

Striving to attend to growing needs, our interviewees and their institutions have developed a series of local best practices based on their institutional policies, national and professional guidelines, their own experiences and expertise, and dialogue with other REBs, external experts, and national ethics institutions. Most practices and tips were consistent with existing guidelines on internet research ethics (e.g., U.S. Department of Health and Human Services, 2013) and thus assumingly beneficial to researchers conducting research on/through the internet. However, it was nonetheless unclear as to what extent such homegrown wisdoms were shared among board members and with researchers. In the present study, no REB provided reviewers with official training and education for ethical conduct of internet research. Although most REBs mandated reviewers to take the TCPS2 CORE tutorial, the tutorial has no module dedicated to internet research ethics. Consequently, as Zimmer (2010) contends, some REB members may not fully comprehend the magnitude and likelihood of perceived risks pertinent to internet research. Indeed, some interview participants addressed a concern that asking people sensitive questions over the internet – like those regarding suicidal ideation or self-harm – might cause psychological distress and even trigger self-destructive acts, despite research showing no evidence of such iatrogenic effects (Lloyd-Richardson, Lewis, Whitlock, Rodham, & Schatten, 2015). Although the potential harm to participants in internet research is doubtlessly real (e.g., Zimmer, 2010) and researchers must take full responsibilities for participant privacy, confidentiality, and data stewardship, the current lack of shared evidence-based knowledge may lead REBs to overestimate risks while underestimating potential benefits of research.

In a related vein, many interviewees posited that inconsistencies in ethical decision-making from one board to the other would present "*a roadblock*" to cross-sectorial, multi-institutional research. Complications were reported to arise as a result of multiple interpretations and local differences, which consequently caused unwanted tension between researchers and their REBs, as well as between different REBs. Even worse, with confusions and undue delay, researchers may see regulatory oversight as a set of bureaucratic "hoops" that they must "jump through" (McKee & Porter, 2009, p. 31), rather than a necessary mechanism to ensure research meet the ethical standards set by society at large. Such a view not only hinders a healthy collaboration between researchers and their REBs, but also may compromise ethical conduct of research. Just as any human subjects research, there is no one-fits-all solution for internet research; reviewers and researchers must conduct ethical assessments on a case-by-case basis with acute context sensitivity. Nevertheless, our interviews suggested that (inter)nationally recognized best practices on internet research could provide REBs and researchers with a practical mechanism to inform ethical decision-making.

Similarly, there is a clear opportunity for evidence-based and procedural guidelines to facilitate determination about the likelihood and degree of harm involved in internet research in order to avoid unwanted "*scope creeps.*" Some REBs we interviewed have developed individual SOPs and guidelines for determining risk level (i.e., whether a protocol goes to delegated or full-board review), but such measures could be shared more widely in the context of internet research. The TCPS2 in principle only sets out general guidelines and it is beyond the purview of the PRE/SRCR to provide individual REBs with specific, pragmatic advice. Yet, our study revealed that some ethics reviewers recognized the PRE/SRCR as "*the final arbiter*" who ultimately adjudicates how the TCPS2 should be interpreted and implemented to individual protocols. If Canadian funding agencies continue encouraging further development of Big Data analysis and digital scholarship (SSHRC et al., 2013), it is necessary for the TCPS2 to address current gaps in ethics frameworks in order to support ethical conduct of digital research.

In this light, provincial and/or federal efforts to coordinate inter-institutional research under a single REB would be welcomed by researchers working with large-scale digital databases. Current TCPS2 outlines three models for ethics review of multi-jurisdictional research: independent, delegated, and reciprocal (CIHR et al., 2014, Chapter 8). While the independent model has thus far been most prevalent in Canada, delegated and reciprocal models may better ensure consistency across REBs and mitigate the regulatory burden of the review process. Among successful cases is the Ontario Cancer Research Ethics Board (OCREB) that serves as the central review system for multi-center oncology research across the province. OCREB's centralized review process has proven invaluable to streamlining the administrative process and shortening the study start-up times at multiple institutions (Chaddah, 2008). Following this model, regulatory bodies could create a specialized review board for digital science research involving large-scale digital data in a way that enables multiple institutions to collaboratively develop and share robust data sharing and safeguarding measures.

While the present study focused exclusively on Canadian REBs, ethical challenges identified throughout our interview are by no means unique to Canada. As internet-based tools and environments now constitute a significant part of research practices across disciplines and countries, our findings have implications for internet researchers and ethics reviewers in other countries, especially those in which institutional review boards serve as ethical gatekeepers for human subjects research. Two lessons in particular could be drawn from the present study. First, our findings highlighted a growing need for active collaborations between researchers and ethics reviewers. A tendency among researchers to deem review boards as "a roadblock" stems largely from what Larsson (2015) coins an "offline bias" built in to current ethics review process. Ethics frameworks like TCPS2 gear predominantly toward conventional, offline research environments without fully taking into account unique attributes of online tools and environments. This demands internet researchers to adapt "their own descriptions to offline specifics in order to get the point of the research project across in a correct way" (Larsson, 2015, p. 147). Even though internet research may not always pose ethical issues substantially different from offline research, integrating an awareness of online specifics into ethics guidelines would benefit both researchers and reviewers working in the increasingly digitized research landscape. Therefore, scholars wishing to employ internet-based approaches in their studies should strive to establish a collaborative relationship with their review boards to mutually advance their understanding of unique characteristics of online approaches and unique ethical issues pertinent to such methodology. Involving internet researchers within review boards or inviting such researchers as ad hoc reviewers of protocols using online methods may benefit review boards that do not have sufficient expertise and current knowledge regarding internet-based methods. Relevant education and training for reviewers and researchers at local, national, and international level also seem needed to increase knowledge base and decrease inconsistencies across review boards and among board members. Local review boards may also benefit from collaborating more actively with other institutions of similar size and scope or in geographic proximity and consider the development of shared guidance and/or a centralized review system to address internet research and the emerging issues therein.

Second, it is worth considering the other bias in the present review system toward conducting ethical assessments only prior to the inception of research. This "front-end" bias (H. McKee, personal communication, January 5, 2016) among ethics boards let reviewers focus exclusively on initial consent and recruitment procedures while paying little attention to the "back-end" ethical issues that may emerge during and after completion of research projects. Although making sure that potential participants are fully informed prior to taking part in a study is absolutely crucial in human subjects research, the relative lack of ongoing and flexible monitoring mechanism does not allow researchers and reviewers to fully attend to the dynamic nature of internet research, changing technologies, site policies, and security levels. The perception of ethics as "*an ongoing process of reflection, analysis and action* throughout a project" (McKee & Porter, 2009, p. 145, original emphasis) may benefit researchers and reviewers to think through the whole research process and make a sound ethical assessment on an ongoing basis.

Overall, in the current increasingly collaborative research landscape, no researcher or review board should make decisions in isolation; a more collaborative, systematic, and inter-disciplinary framework would benefit scholars to thrive in the era of digital research. It is our hope that our Canadian case study will further the growth of ethical problem-solving for internet researchers in other countries, their ethics review boards, and for the individuals that are studied.

ACKNOWLEDGEMENTS

We thank study participants who generously took time to participate in this study. We are also grateful to Elizabeth Buchannan and Heidi McKee for their expert feedback on our preliminary findings. This study is supported partially by a post-doctoral fellowship granted to the first author by the Social Sciences and Humanities Research Council of Canada [grant number: 756-2014-0412]

REFERENCES

American Psychological Association Practice Organization. (2013). Guidelines for the practice of telepsychology: Legal basics for psychologists. *American Psychologist, 68*(9), 791–800. Retrieved from http://www.apa.org/practice/guidelines/telepsychology.aspx

Blackstone, M., Given, L., Lévy, J., McGinn, M., O'Neill, P., Palys, T., ... De Groote, T. (2008). Extending the spectrum: The TCPS and ethical issues in internet-based research. *Proceedings from the Social Sciences and Humanities Research Ethics Special Working Committee: A Working Committee of the Interagency Advisory Panel on Research Ethics.* Retrieved from http://www.pre.ethics.gc.ca/policy-politique/initiatives/docs/ Internet_Research_-_February_2008_-_EN.pdf

Buchanan, E. A., & Ess, C. M. (2009). Internet research ethics and institutional review board: Current practices and issues. *SIGCAS Computers and Society, 39*(3), 43–49.

Canadian Institute of Health Research (CIHR), Natural Sciences and Engineering Research Council of Canada (NSERC), & Social Sciences and Humanities Research Council of Canada (SSHRC). (2014). *Tri-Council policy statement: Ethical conduct for research involving humans.* Retrieved February 25, 2016 from www.pre.ethics.gc.ca/pdf/eng/tcps2-2014/TCPS_2_FINAL_Web.pdf

Chaddah, M. R. (2008). The Ontario Cancer Research Ethics Board: A central REB that works. *Current Oncology, 15*(1), 49–52.

Ess, C. M., & AoIR Ethics Working Committee. (2002). *Ethical decision-making and Internet research: Recommendations from the AoIR Ethics Working Committee.* Retrieved from http://www.aoir.org/reports/ethics.pdf

Eysenbach, G., & Till, J. E. (2001). Ethical issues in qualitative research on internet communities. *BMJ, 323,* 1103–1105.

Haggerty, K. D. (2004). Ethics creep: Governing social science research in the name of ethics. *Qualitative Sociology, 27*(4), 391–414.

Harper, M., & Cole, P. (2012). Member checking: Can benefits be gained similar to group therapy. *The Qualitative Report, 17*(2), 510–517.

Kitchin, H. A. (2007). *Research ethics and the Internet: Negotiating Canada's Tri-Council Policy Statement*. Halifax and Winnipeg: Fernwood.

Larsson, A. O. (2015). Studying Big Data – Ethical and methodological considerations. In H. Fossheim & H. Ingierd (Eds.), *Internet research ethics* (pp. 141–156). Oslo: Cappelen Damm Akademisk.

Lloyd-Richardson, E. E., Lewis, S. P., Whitlock, J. L., Rodham, K., & Schatten, H. T. (2015). Research with adolescents who engage in non-suicidal self-injury: Ethical considerations and challenges. *Child and Adolescent Psychiatry and Mental Health, 9*(1), 1–14.

Markham A. N., & Buchanan, E. A. (2012). *Ethical decision-making and Internet research (Version 2.0). Recommendations from the AoIR Ethics Working Committee*. Chicago, IL: Association of Internet Researchers.

McDermott, E., & Roen, K. (2012). Youth on the virtual edge: Researching marginalized sexualities and genders online. *Qualitative Health Research, 22*, 560–570.

McKee, H. A., & Porter, J. E. (2009). *The ethics of Internet research. A rhetorical, case-based process*. New York, NY: Peter Lang.

Rodriquez, J. (2013). Narrating dementia self and community in an online forum. *Qualitative Health Research, 23*(9), 1215–1227.

Saldaña, J. (2013). *The coding manual for qualitative researchers* (2nd ed.). London: Sage.

Seko, Y., Kidd, S. A., Wijer, D., & McKenzie, K. J. (2015). On the creative edge: Exploring motivations for creating non-suicidal self-injury content online. *Qualitative Health Research, 25*(10), 1334–1346.

Sharkey, S., Jones, R., Smithson, J., Hewis, E., Emmens, T., Ford, T., & Owens, C. (2011). Ethical practice in internet research involving vulnerable people: Lessons from a self-harm discussion forum study (SharpTalk). *Journal of Medical Ethics, 37*(12), 752–758.

Social Sciences and Humanities Research Council (SSHRC), Canadian Institutes of Health Research (CIHR), Natural Sciences and Engineering Research Council (NSERC), & Canada Foundation for Innovation (CFI). (2013). *Capitalizing on Big Data: Toward a policy framework for advancing digital scholarship in Canada: Consultation document*. Retrieved from http://www.sshrc-crsh.gc.ca/aboutau_sujet/publications/digital_scholarship_consultation_e.pdf

TCPS 2 Interpretations, Secretariat on Responsible Conduct of Research (SRCR), on behalf of the Tri-Council Agencies: Canadian Institutes of Health Research (CIHR), the Natural Sciences and Engineering Research Council (NSERC), & the Social Sciences and Humanities Research Council (SSHRC). (February 26, 2016).

Tilley, S., & Gormley, L. (2007). Canadian university ethics review: Cultural complications translating principles into practices. *Qualitative Inquiry, 13*(3), 368–387.

U.S. Department of Health and Human Services, Office for Human Research Protections. (2013). *Considerations and recommendations concerning Internet research and human subjects research regulations, with revisions*. Final Document, Approved at Secretary's Advisory Committee on Human Research Protections. Retrieved from http://www.hhs.gov/ohrp/sachrp/commsec/attachmentb-secletter20.pdf

Warrell, J., & Jacobson, M. (2014). Internet research ethics and the policy gap for ethical practice in online research settings. *Canadian Journal of Higher Education, 44*(1), 22–37.

Zimmer, M. (2010). "But the data is already public": On the ethics of research in Facebook. *Ethics and Information Technology, 12*(4), 313–325.

REACTION BY MICHELLE C. FORELLE AND SARAH MYERS WEST

In their review of Canadian Research Ethics Boards' approaches to evaluating the ethics of internet studies, the authors trace out a number of important considerations that are especially pertinent in the internet research context: technological change, new consequences for privacy, and assessing voluntary participation. We would like to add an additional consideration that has become especially salient over the past few years: the relationship between internet-based research and the law.

In particular, the role of Terms of Service in shaping online research is deserving of greater scrutiny. For example, a change to Facebook's ToS following the well-known "emotional contagion" study, in which researchers at the company modulated the content shown to users in order to assess the sentiment of their posts, would make this research permissible. But while this change to the terms would make such studies *legal,* this does not necessarily make them *ethical* – ToS are written primarily as a form of protection for the companies, rather than as a code of conduct for the use of their products.

Increasingly, it is becoming clear that there are many instances where the law simply has not caught up to the ethical standards held by academic researchers. In a recent case, the American Civil Liberties Union (ACLU) filed a lawsuit on the behalf of researchers, computer scientists, and journalists to challenge the constitutionality of the Computer Fraud and Abuse Act. This law makes it a federal crime to access computers in a manner that "exceeds authorized access," effectively foreclosing investigations that seek to interrogate the practices of online services for possible discrimination.

Insofar as the authors of this article argue for increased collaboration between researchers and ethics reviewers, we see a similar need for collaboration between both these parties and governmental and legislative rulemaking agencies. The CFAA challenge indicates the necessity of considering how laws and policies can be written to protect and promote ethical research on the Internet. Developing ethical standards for online research, especially standards that work across disciplines and institutions, could provide a valuable resource for informing the legal standards that governments impose on the Internet.

Michelle C. Forelle is a doctoral candidate at the Annenberg School for Communication at the University of Southern California, where she studies how the phenomenon known as the "Internet of things" is changing conceptions of property rights within American culture and legal systems.

Sarah Myers West is a doctoral candidate and the Wallis Annenberg Graduate Research Fellow at the Annenberg School for Communication at the University of Southern California, studying the contested politics of encryption and the history of the cypherpunk movement.

REACTION BY KATLEEN GABRIELS

To what extent are the ethical challenges of internet research unique? Are there crucial and clear-cut differences between online and offline research ethics? These questions, which relate to the results of the study discussed in this chapter, remind me of another prominent discussion: the uniqueness debate in computer ethics. For decades, leading computer ethicists, such as James Moor (1985) and Debora Johnson (2004), have been discussing the (non)uniqueness of ethical issues that arise with computer technologies.

Of course, not every problem related to internet research is unique; for instance, privacy issues existed before the emergence and wider dispersal of the World Wide Web. Yet, the internet magnifies and alters the implications in such a way that privacy requires special consideration.

There are unique ethical issues that deserve special attention while conducting research online: consider, for instance, problems that arise with the scope of audience and distribution, reproducibility, immediacy, and invisibility. Internet research challenges scholars in several ways. Also, as one does not meet research informants face-to-face, it is more difficult to obtain informed consent. For my doctoral dissertation I combined online and offline data gathering with avid residents of the social virtual world Second Life: I recurrently met the informants in-world (as an avatar) and face-to-face. The two fieldsites had a dissimilar character and different conventions. For instance, in order to obtain informed consent and to ascertain that the informant fully understood the research and the research context, I first talked with them through Skype.

In the final paragraphs the authors problematize the ethical assessments that take place in the beginning of an empirical study. However, research is messy, complex, and generally not linear, and questions arise along the winding research road; by confining the ethical review to the inception of the study, these dynamics are disregarded.

Philosopher of technology Peter Paul Verbeek's (2010) notion of "accompanying ethics of technology" might offer a helpful framework here. Verbeek criticizes that ethical assessments generally come down to judging whether a technology is morally acceptable or unacceptable. In his view, ethicists should *accompany* technologies' developmental processes, implementation, and operation and use. In a similar manner, the role of review boards is limited to giving an ethical approval or disapproval in the beginning, instead of reviewing and "accompanying" the entire research process. "Accompanying internet research ethics" might offer an interesting perspective to direct researchers and their research ethical questions not just in the beginning but until completion. Of course, a compelling question is how we can translate this framework into practice, because accompanying internet research ethics would be time consuming and would require significant efforts from ethical committee members. Accompanying internet research ethics demands for an international framework and global efforts, not in the least in terms of collaborations, standards, and debate.

Johnson, D. G. (2004). Ethics on-line. In R. A. Spinello & H. T. Tavani (Eds.), *Readings in cyberethics* (second ed., pp. 30–39). Sudbury, MA: Jones and Bartlett Publishers.

Moor, J. H. (1985). What is computer ethics? *Metaphilosophy, 16*(4), 266–275.

Verbeek, P. P. (2010). Accompanying technology: Philosophy of technology after the ethical turn. *Techné: Research in Philosophy and Technology, 14*(1), 49–54.

***Katleen Gabriels** is currently working as a postdoctoral researcher at the Department of Philosophy and Moral Sciences of the Vrije Universiteit Brussel (VUB), Brussels, Belgium. She is specialized in media ethics and computer ethics.*

CHAPTER NINE

Internet Research Ethics in a Non-Western Context

SORAJ HONGLADAROM

The internet has become an environment for research not only in the West, but also globally. Its ubiquity has resulted in researchers examining it from a large variety of perspectives, and certainly this has given rise to ethical concerns. However, in contrast to traditional empirical research, research based on online data has its own peculiarities that need to be specifically addressed. This specificity, then, needs to be further elaborated when the research is done in non-Western environments, where not only the environment of research ethics but also the vocabularies used to describe it are different.

In this paper I argue that internet research ethics should be sensitive to cultural concerns and address whether the rules and guidelines in internet research need to be changed when the research is done outside of the Western context. Basically my argument is that there are different paths toward the same goal. The goal in this case is protection of the research participants, but how to achieve this goal can vary according to local contexts. In other words, different sets of vocabulary and theoretical tools can be used which vary according to contexts, but they arrive at the same goal. What I would like to argue more specifically is that the rules, regulations, or guidelines of internet research ethics do not necessarily have to be very different when the research is done outside of the West. Certainly there are many differences in internet standards in the West – the US and Europe representing two broad groups within the West that differ significantly in how research ethics should be theorized and practiced. Nonetheless, from the perspective of those from the outside, the differences between the US and Europe, not to mention smaller ones inside either region, seem small in comparison. Thus when I refer to the West in this chapter I mean roughly what similarities there are between, for example, the US and Europe when viewed from a broad perspective. After all, the primary role of the Internet is to bind people together no matter where they live. However, this does not mean that whatever comes from the West should always be accepted as a standard either. What happens, then, is that there should be continual international dialogs on how best to protect the users when they enter online environments and on how the guidelines should be amended as times and circumstances change. What has happened, however, is that some internet researchers in Thailand are not aware that there is such a thing as internet research ethics; they are not aware, that is, of the need to follow the guidelines, and they still largely view online research as not essentially different from typical social scientific research. I focus my examples on Thailand, but the implication is that the conclusion should broadly obtain for other Asian countries also.

The chapter will also provide a reflection on how best to account for a theory behind a set of rules and guidelines of internet research, one that can be accepted internationally. Not only must the content of these rules be acceptable to all parties, but the theory or theories behind them need to be acceptable too. This, I argue, is only possible when, while the content of the theory might differ according to each cultural context, the content of the actual rules themselves stays the same, since there needs to be the same set of internet research ethics rules that is applicable in all countries.

THE NEED FOR THE SAME SET OF RULES

One of the strongest characteristics of the Internet is that it does not seem to respect any international boundaries. Although there have been attempts, notably in China, of erecting censorship walls that filter out information unwanted by the authorities, information always seems to have a way of getting through. An upshot of this is that normative guidelines that arise out of the needs to protect internet research subjects have to cover those in the areas outside of the West too. In other words, these normative guidelines have to be more or less universal. This does not imply that the guidelines are imposed upon the non-West or that the content of the guidelines are those that satisfy the concerns of the West exclusively.

But it does mean that normative guidelines, such as those concerning internet research ethics, should be a result of cross-cultural dialogs where the issues and content comes from diverse sources. This represents a significant conceptual challenge. I have shown elsewhere that normative guidelines tend to create their own conceptual problems when they originate in the context of one culture and are then imported to another cultural environment. There is always a tension between the need to maintain the integrity of the guidelines as *global* on the one hand, and the need to be sensitive to *local* particularities on the other.

However, as the world is getting smaller and more tightly bound together, the balance seems to swing toward the normative guidelines being more global. That is to say, the Chinese and other people in Asia or Africa cannot be expected to come up with their own completely indigenous sets of guidelines for, say, internet research ethics which are completely different from what is commonly accepted as a standard around the world. This does not mean that whatever coming from the West must be accepted everywhere, but it means that, as the Internet is spanning the globe, we cannot as a matter of fact have different sets of guidelines governing internet research that are all completely different. As many research projects are collaborative ones involving people from different countries and cultures, such different guidelines would make collaboration an impossibility. Here examples in other research fields can act as a guide. The UNESCO has published the Universal Declaration of Bioethics and Human Rights (UNESCO, 2005), which is intended to be a global document binding for all member countries. The declaration is a statement of *universal* norms that is accepted by all member countries as an expression of their collective ethical judgments regardless of cultural or religious differences. This is a very serious and difficult challenge, but the fact that the member states of the UNESCO were able to forge such a document shows that global collaboration resulting in one set of universal ethical norms is possible.

Thus, it should also be possible for countries of the world to get together and deliberate among themselves on a comparable document on a set of global guidelines on internet research. Other global documents on research ethics such as the Helsinki Declaration or the Belmont Report in biomedical research ethics should act as clear examples to follow. However, the UNESCO Declaration has been criticized as being shallow and does not contain enough substance to be of any real use.[1] The gist of the criticism is that, as the document is a compromise among member states who come from very different origins, political persuasions, and religious backgrounds, controversial materials were edited out, leaving only a kind of rather vacuous statements that everybody can agree but does not appear to contain any real meaning (Williams, 2005). Nonetheless, if one looks at one of the articles in the Declaration, such as Article 3, then one can see that beneath these high sounding words one can derive substantive measures that can function effectively in the real world. Article 3 says:

Article 3 – Human dignity and human rights

1. Human dignity, human rights and fundamental freedoms are to be fully respected.
2. The interests and welfare of the individual should have priority over the sole interest of science or society (UNESCO, 2005).

We can also see that this Article can also provide a basis for a possible Universal Declaration on Internet Research Ethics, should such a document come into existence. Clause 1 says that human dignity, rights, and freedom need to be respected. This can be a basis for legislation and certainly guidelines for research, internet research included. There can obviously be debates among scholars and practitioners as to what constitutes human dignity and what kind of rights should be respected, but the overall intention of the Article should be clear. It is designed to protect each human individual against any violation of his or her integrity as a *human being*. Any possible *global* guideline for research has to take this into consideration.

Clause 2 of the Article might give rise to more disagreements. It states quite clearly that the interests of the individual take precedence over those of the society or of science itself. In the context of research ethics (internet or otherwise), this is a strong statement. Its intent is to protect each and every individual against their use solely as subjects in a research. In the end, one cannot cite the interests of either society of advancement of science as the sole reasons for undertaking research on a human subject. The Clause thus could provoke conflicts in cultures where the interests of the collective are presumed to take precedence over those of the individual. The literature of biomedical research ethics is also full of cases where a village chief deems it unacceptable for the researcher to approach a member of the village individually without consulting him first (see, for example, Gikonyo, 2008). This is interpreted as not respecting the culture of the tribe or the village where the interest of the group has a priority over that of an individual. Nonetheless, in cases where it is the welfare of an individual that is at issue, the welfare has to be protected and has to be taken as first priority over the sole reason of advancement of science, or the interest of the village or the society. For example, if by doing a particular research project an individual would be irreparably harmed, that would be a reason for terminating the research on ethical grounds. What is important is that Article 3 here is binding for all member states. It is a *universal* norm.

DIFFERENT PATHS TOWARD THE SAME GOAL

The UNESCO Declaration is a good example of how different groups of people can come up with one and the same document that contains normative guidelines that everyone accepts to be binding and ethically significant. What I would like to stress, however, is that the existence of the Declaration does not necessarily imply that different cultures need to accept the same philosophical *theory* leading up to it. What this means is that, while the Declaration is or should be universally binding, the theories behind the document do not have to be one and the same. To the contrary, it is possible for there to be a plurality of theories all of which conclude in (largely) the same set of ethical guidelines such as those appearing in the Declaration. These theories do not agree with one another, but they ultimately point to the same target. This, in a nutshell, is the stance of *ethical pluralism* advocated by Charles Ess and the AoIR Ethics Working Committee (2002, pp. 29–30).

The idea, however, is not exactly the same as Rawls' (2005) view about political liberalism, where parties entering negotiation are advised to leave their metaphysical assumptions behind and enter the negotiating arena only on a purely political basis. What I have in mind is that different parties do not have to leave their metaphysics at home, but they can present their metaphysics in full and argue among themselves about the merit of each metaphysical system trying to convince those who do not subscribe to the same system of thought as they do. For example, Confucians may try to convince Buddhists about the value of the idea of a real existing self, which the latter ultimately deny. For the Confucian, such a view of the self is a lynchpin for their ethical judgment: The self may be relational, but it *does* exist and forms a node in a network of relationships with one's own members of the family and others. The Buddhist, on the other hand, may try to convince the Confucian about the conceptual incoherence of the notion of a substantial self. The debate can continue and can get lively. Nevertheless, both the Buddhist and the Confucian do agree that their different ethical systems point toward largely the same goal. That is, a situation where an individual person is respected and protected when she enters the online environment. After all, both Buddhism and Confucianism put a high emphasis on the idea that persons should be protected from harm (the Buddhist, in particular, has conceptual juggling work to do, for they argue that the individual in the ultimate sense does not exist). For the Buddhist, this is important because harming others is bad karma and for the Confucian harming others will lead to disruption of the cosmos. Buddhists and Confucians, then, have different reasons as to why one should refrain from harming others, but they do agree that harming others is wrong. This can certainly be extended toward the online environment in the context of internet research, too.

The upshot is that both Buddhists and Confucians can fully agree with the content and intention of Article 3 in the UNESCO Declaration. Of course they may criticize how the Article should be interpreted: for example, how one should understand the difficult notion of "human dignity" and so on. But the bottom line is that they agree on what is really the heart of the matter: that one should not harm others. For some such an agreement might require recognition of human dignity, but perhaps the notion might not be needed if human dignity is tinged with a conception of human nature that is derived from one intellectual tradition rather than another. If an intellectual of a culture has a way of protecting human beings from harm in a way that does not require talking about human dignity (for example, Buddhists talk about bad karmas resulting from harming others), then this should be acceptable. This point does not have to be the same as Rawls' political liberalism; in fact all parties, Buddhists, Confucians, Kantians, utilitarians, and so on, can debate among themselves about their theories until they get very tired, but they already largely agree on what is really important, which is the fundamental, first-order ethical judgments.[2] The idea is that when parties come to deliberate on a certain normative issue, it is possible that they could come to an agreement on the first-order level, that is, on the content of the normative issue in question. However, it is possible that the parties employ different vocabularies coming from different traditions to come up with the agreed normative issue. The injunction not to harm others is quite universal among cultures, but different societies and cultures have different ways of characterizing how the normative issue is justified. In other words, the parties agree on the first-order level but disagree on the second-order level of theory and justification. The difference between what I have in mind here and Rawls' political liberalism is that, while Rawls seeks to find a way of political accommodation where the participants leave their metaphysical beliefs behind, I have argued that they should instead bring up their metaphysical beliefs as a way of justifying and theorizing about the putative normative judgments that are intended to be an outcome of the pluralistic dialog.[3]

Thus, it is always possible that there are disagreements at the first-order level. For example, Confucians put much emphasis on family duty (Tang, 1995) – there is a clear duty to produce a son, for example. But for the Buddhists this is not a duty at all, and to claim that one has a duty to produce a son and heir would mean that one is attached to family life, which is an enemy or an obstacle to the kind of life that is conducive to attaining liberation. In this case, whether one has a duty or an obligation to produce the next generation, Buddhists and Confucians cannot find a point where their philosophies can be reconciled, but that does not have to mean that a large part of their ethical judgments cannot be reconciled either.

In the cases where there are disagreements, debates and discussions can certainly continue, and it might be possible in the long run that both parties can come to some kind of agreement. And if there is no agreement, then both parties can recognize this and focus instead on the topics that they can agree on. If the disagreement is on major issues that cannot be passed over, then practical rules would stipulate that the deliberation either be postponed or some kind of compromise be ironed out. Of course this presupposes that the parties involved all share a common interest in seeing the resolution through. This is only possible when the interests of both parties indicate that focusing on similarities is more favorable than focusing on the opposite. Hence, in coming to agreements about basic values that are needed in setting up a global ethical guideline, it is more favorable to all parties coming to the deliberation to focus on the possibility of agreements. This means that the resulting documents or guidelines may appear too thin: The UNESCO document mentioned above has been criticized on this point as we have seen. But as each party can add their own version of theory and rationales to the guideline, the guideline can become thickened and made more suitable to specific locales (Hongladarom, 1999, 2008). In this case the *thin* guideline then becomes usable and appropriate to each locale. This is not always smooth sailing, however. If the clause on the respect of human dignity in the global guideline is interpreted in such a way that there must be a duty to have children (for perhaps to decide not to have children would deprive the unborn of their putative right to be born and thus it is argued their dignity is violated), then there can be substantive debates. If this argument is a serious one (which it certainly appears to be), then there can be a party arguing that human dignity covers the right of the unborn (or, more accurately, the unconceived because the *unborn* may include fetuses or embryos, which is not part of the argument here), and then there will be another party arguing in the opposite way. Rawls' political liberalism tends to downplay such deep and substantive disagreements, but they can play a very important role. In this case it seems to be more beneficial to bring this kind of debate to the table rather than to keep it at home as Rawls seems to suggest. The benefits might include better understanding of each position, as well as a possibility that the global guidelines could be amended later as circumstances change.

What is pertinent in this discussion to internet research ethics is that global guidelines, such as the ones prepared by the AoIR Ethics Committee, are open to change and there does not appear to be any part of the guideline that is permanently fixed. This does not mean that the guideline is invalid and thus lacks any normative force (because some may think that for any normative guideline to have force, its statement has to be fixed objectively), but it means that any content within the guideline can be negotiated and amended. One may object that if a global guideline such as the AoIR Ethics Guideline is open to negotiation, then any protection afforded to an individual is a contingent one and can be revoked at any time. In a way this is true, but the likelihood of a deep seated normative guideline, such as "one should not harm another person either offline or online," is etched so deeply in our human society that it is not practically conceivable that this norm can be changed any time soon. Nonetheless, it is always possible for there to be a change because ultimately everything depends on how a society collectively decides what to value and what not.

Thus, there is a need for the same set of rules of internet research ethics that is applicable throughout the globe. This is necessitated by the fact that research has become a global phenomenon. Universities all over the world, for example, are subscribing to the doctrine of "world ranking" which is administered by a few companies and is focused mostly on publication and citation. This has resulted in an explosion of research works not only in the West, but increasingly also in the developing world, whose universities are struggling to find recognition and to get on the bandwagon. The kind of research that is going to be recognized by the global scholarly community can be none other than one that follows the same set of standards, both in academic excellence and also in research ethics. In medical research, for example, an article cannot be published unless it is demonstrated that the research in that paper has already been approved by the relevant ethical review board.[4] Since research activity has become globalized, universities in the developing countries are also indirectly forced to comply with this standard and practically all have set up their own ethical review committees which have to adhere to international standard. Building up the capabilities of the members of these review committees in developing world universities and research institutes has become a global industry. What this implies is that researchers in Asia and other non-Western countries have to follow these international standards. While it is possible and encouraged for scholars from the non-West to participate in the international meetings that deliberate on drafting these guidelines, most of the activities are still dominated by the West, and those from the non-West often feel left out. This is often because the language and the conceptual tools used in these meetings come from the West. Talks about "human dignity" or "human rights," for example, carry with them long histories in Western philosophy or political thought, something that delegates from the non-West are usually ill-equipped to contribute to. This has contributed to the misconception that the West is equivalent with the global, and that anything coming from the West, especially concerning standards and guidelines, needs to be complied with simply because by doing so one is accepted into the international community. However, for the global to be truly global, members of the deliberative space need to feel that they own the meeting too and that their input is respected. Perhaps the fault lies also partly in the members of the non-West themselves, who sometimes forfeit their opportunities to actively take part and prefer merely to be listeners and followers. In short, members of the research community in the non-West often are on the lookout for any standards and guidelines coming from the West. They are ready to comply with those standards not so much because they understand the reasoning or the theories behind those rules, but because by complying they gain material advantage such as the opportunity to get their papers published in international journals, gaining prestige for their institutions.

Another reason for this situation is that there can be a wide gulf between the philosophy behind the normative guidelines coming from the West and the philosophies of the non-Western delegates. For example, Buddhist Thais typically have a harder time understanding the concept of individual consent than those in the West, as they come from a largely collective culture which seems to favor group decisions rather than individual ones. It is possible that the Buddhist delegates understand the need for individual consent, and, without thinking much about the philosophy behind it, accepts the international norm simply out of practical reasons. Since the delegates do not fully understand the philosophy behind the guidelines, they tend to take up the guidelines and follow them rather blindly without trying to understand the underlying rationales. The reason behind this following is purely technical: They want to be accepted into the international community. An upshot of this is that when a new situation arises which has not been covered before, they do not actually know what to do. Thus, the rationale behind the delegates' accepting the guideline is not even utilitarian. If it were, then the delegates would know what to decide in the new situation. But since they tend to follow the guideline rather mechanically, they do not actually know what to do and, thus, tend to decide in favor of whoever has the most power at a particular time and place.

In conclusion, then, there is a real need for the same set of normative guidelines covering internet research ethics. But there is the problem of participants from the non-Western countries feeling that the guidelines are made by the West and given to the rest of the world to follow. They feel that they need to follow these guidelines because they want the benefits that globalization can bring. This results in a rather mechanical following of the rules without real understanding of the theory behind them. In other words, the subscription to the same set of rules appears to be rather superficial. What is really needed, then, is not only this superficial following of the rules but the following needs to be accompanied by a real understanding of the rationale, which can only happen if the delegates draw upon their own intellectual and cultural resources in the same way as Westerners draw upon the Greek and Christian heritage. Only this can provide the real understanding that prevents the kind of mechanical following of rules mentioned above.

A CASE IN INTERNET RESEARCH ETHICS: AN MA THESIS ON "THE USE OF INTERNET AND THE ROLE OF HOUSEWIFE"

Our discussion of internet research ethics in non-Western contexts can be illustrated by a look at what is actually happening in a research work in an Asian country. Internet research ethics is still a new thing in Thailand. Even research ethics in the biomedical sciences is still being studied and discussed, and not many researchers in the biomedical fields appreciate the important role that ethical considerations play in their research work. As a result, some research that uses the Internet as a venue apparently suffers from lack of attention to ethical concerns. For example, in 2012, the Faculty of Communication Arts, Chulalongkorn University passed an MA thesis on "The Use of Internet and the Role of Housewife" (Ketsomboon, 2012), which looks at how Thai housewives are using the Internet in their daily lives. The research looks at how housewives post their thoughts and share techniques about cooking and other topics in their blogs and finds that housewives use their blogs as a venue for reinforcing the ideal of being a housewife as well as a space where they can be empowered. The researcher looked at the content of some famous blogs for housewives and selected some for content analysis. However, she posted the usernames of the bloggers whose blogs she studied in her thesis, making it possible for the reader to know the blogs of these housewives who participated in the research. And from this step it is relatively easy for the reader to know the real identity of these bloggers. In this case, the topic is mostly not too controversial, as it is mostly about cooking, raising a child, sharing tips about managing the home, and so on. But the researcher apparently was not aware of the potential consequences of her posting the usernames or the blogger names of the housewives, and there is nothing in the thesis that tells the reader that the bloggers have given their consent for the researcher to put their names publicly in the thesis. If her research had been examined beforehand by a knowledgeable ethical review committee, then this situation would not have happened. This shows that there have to be programs of capacity building and awareness raising of the need for ethical guidelines on internet research, something that Thailand or other developing countries have yet to fully establish.

Perhaps a reason why the researcher put up the names of the bloggers she read and interviewed is because there is an atmosphere of trust between the researcher and her subjects. The subjects trust that the researcher will not use their blogger names in a wrongful manner. This may be due to the fact that so far there has not been a scandal or a sensational story arising from abuses of the names that are in the thesis. However, it is possible that someone might find out who the real persons behind the blog usernames are (usually in Thailand bloggers hide their real identity behind their blogger names, which is almost always different from their real names, but it is quite easy to find out who they really are) as well as their private information. After all, the thesis focuses on private information of these housewives, and some of the questions asked include the housewives' reason for using the Internet, and one of the subjects answered that she was stressed by her problems in family life and by her relation with her husband. Moreover, her child was autistic, which caused more problems for her. She, then, was using the Internet to relieve stress. This is all highly private information and should be treated with strict confidentiality. But the researcher did not say specifically that the names used in her thesis were invented; hence it may be possible that she used the subjects' real names. Even though the researcher uses only the first names, and since the researcher tells the reader that the housewives studied were recruited from only three or four websites whose names were given prominently in the work, it is very possible that someone could link the names mentioned in the thesis to the real person.

All this shows that there is a need for capacity building programs for internet researchers in Thailand so that they become more sensitive and more aware of potential ethical problems. However, such a program has to rely more on traditional theories rather than those imported wholesale from the West, as discussed earlier in the paper. Apart from the fact that the traditional theories are easier to relate to and thus easier to understand, relying on traditional theories also supports the philosophical point that normative guidelines do not have to be justified through Western theories only. For example, the MA student here might be required to enroll in a course on research ethics. She, then, learns about the various first-order norms, but she will also learn about the reasons behind those first-order norms, and these reasons might come from the teachings of Buddhism. Going back to Buddhism in the context of research ethics will make a more forceful impact on the student, and she will be more likely to understand the ethical significance of what she is doing. She will also have to study some elements of Western ethical theories so that she will be able to follow discussions in the West on the topic, which might prove to be useful to her later on. After all, Buddhism has a strong emphasis on not harming others, and to see Buddhism in a new context would include seeing that mentioning someone's real name in one's MA thesis would be a breach of her privacy, even though the "real name" in question is a Twitter handle or an invested username in a web chat forum. Then she understands the reasoning behind this guideline through the language of Buddhism, which is already a part of her identity as a Thai.

CONCLUSION

To sum up, I have argued that internet research ethics guidelines should be the same all over the world, but that the vocabulary used to explain them does not have to be the same. This view is in line with what Charles Ess calls "ethical pluralism" which is a middle position between universalism on the one hand and relativism on the other. What I would like to add, however, is that Asians tend to view global ethical guidelines as a ticket for gaining acceptance into the global community without bothering to learn about the reasons behind them. This can be amended if the awareness is grown from the local source, meaning that the vocabulary comes from the traditional and intellectual source of the culture in which a particular researcher is working. Thus, a global guideline such as the UNESCO Declaration on Bioethics and Human Rights could serve as a model for internet research ethics – at least in spirit if the research community prefers to have non-binding guidelines rather than official ones. Furthermore, there needs to be a program of education and capacity building for researchers in the developing countries so that they are really integrated into the new culture of going back to their roots to find that in fact their roots contain valuable resources that can help them integrate with the global normative activities all along.[5]

NOTES

1. See, for example, Benatar (2005); Häyry and Takala (2005); and Williams (2005). These articles are part of the special issue of Developing World Bioethics devoted to responses to the UNESCO Declaration. A defense of the Declaration, on the other hand, can be found in Andorno (2007).
2. I developed this point more fully in Hongladarom (2004).
3. I have argued for this point in the context of bioethics in Hongladarom (2007) and in Hongladarom (2016).
4. Code of Conduct and Best Practice Guidelines for Journal Editors, available at http://publicationethics.org/files/Code_of_conduct_for_journal_editors_Mar11.pdf, published by the Committee on Publication Ethics. See also Uniform Requirements for Manuscripts Submitted to Biomedical Journals: Writing and Editing for Biomedical Publication (updated October 2008), available at http://www.icmje.org/recommendations/archives/2008_urm.pdf.
5. Research for this chapter has been partially supported by a grant from Chulalongkorn University, under the Chulalongkorn Research Fellow Program.

REFERENCES

Andorno, R. (2007). Global bioethics at UNESCO: In defense of the universal declaration of bioethics and human rights. *Journal of Medical Ethics, 31*(3), 150–154.

Benatar, D. (2005). The trouble with universal declarations. *Developing World Bioethics, 5*(3), 220–224.

Ess, C., & AoIR Ethics Working Committee. (2002). *Ethical decision-making and Internet research: Recommendations from the AoIR Ethics Working Committee.* Retrieved from http://www.aoir.org/reports/ethics.pdf

Gikonyo, C. (2008). Taking social relationships seriously: lessons learned from the informed consent practices of a vaccine trial on the Kenyan Coast. *Social Science & Medicine, 67*(5), 708–720.

Häyry, M., & Takala, T. (2005). Human dignity, bioethics, and human rights. *Developing World Bioethics, 5*(3), 225–233.

Hongladarom, S. (1999). Global culture, local cultures, and the internet: The Thai example. *AI & Society, 13*, 389–401.

Hongladarom, S. (2004). Asian bioethics revisited: what is it?, and is there such a thing? *Eubios Journal of Asian and International Bioethics, 14*, 194–197.

Hongladarom, S. (2007). Analysis and justification of privacy from a Buddhist perspective. In S. Hongladarom & C. Ess (Eds.), *Information technology ethics: Cultural perspectives* (pp. 108–122). Hershey, PA: IGI-Global.

Hongladarom, S. (2008, June 24–27). *Global culture, local cultures and the internet: Ten years after.* Presented at the 6th International Conference on Cultural Attitudes toward Technology and Communication, Nimes, France.

Hongladarom, S. (2016). Intercultural information ethics: A pragmatic consideration. In J. Bielby & M. Kelly (Eds.), *Information cultures in the digital age: A festschrift in honor of Rafael Capurro* (pp. 191–206). Wiesbaden: Springer Fachmedien.

Ketsomboon, T. (2012). *The use of internet and the role of housewife* (Unpublished MA thesis). Faculty of Communication Arts, Chulalongkorn University.

Rawls, J. (2005). *Political liberalism. Expanded edition.* New York, NY: Columbia University Press.
Tang, Z. (1995). Confucianism, Chinese culture, and reproductive behavior. *Population and Environment, 16*(3), 269–284.
UNESCO. (2005). *UNESCO declaration on bioethics and human rights.* Retrieved from http://portal.unesco.org/en/ev.php-URL_ID=31058&URL_DO=DO_TOPIC&URL_SECTION=201.html
Williams, J. R. (2005). UNESCO's proposed declaration on bioethics and human rights – A bland compromise. *Developing World Bioethics, 5*(3), 210–215.

REACTION BY ZOETANYA SUJON

As internet research becomes global, the issue of non-Western research ethics becomes increasingly important. The impossible task of balancing universal principles with pluralistic, culturally relativistic practice holds the potential to wrestle with the legacy of colonialism and begin the journey towards a globally inclusive, ethically informed research practice. Yet, how do we engage a truly pluralistic ethical practice without inadvertently taking an intellectual short-cut around the mess and complexity involved in recognizing ethical difference? For example, how do we safeguard research participants when they are defined by oppositional notions of self, of safety and of harm? Western individualism does not sit well with a Confucian or African notion of a relational self or a Buddhist self which can only truly be understood upon reaching enlightenment. When core ethical concepts – like anonymity, public good, privacy – hold fundamentally different meanings, whose responsibility is it to decide which path to take to best protect research participants? Do we take cues from participants themselves, resulting in a potentially endless cycle of research for *each* research project? Or do we follow universal principles across borders, cultures, practices and people regardless of the moments where they are inapplicable in the interests of consistency? Further, internet research straddles many disciplines so how do we decide which is the best to inform our research practice? In non-Western contexts, this is of particular importance as some disciplines, like psychology for example, have clear ethical research guidelines that closely resemble UK and US psychological ethical guidelines.

Part of the question here is not only about *what* ethical principles should be universal, but also about *how* decisions are made about which are the best ethical practices, principles, and philosophies. In discussions of inclusion and non-Western contexts, power is important in determining legitimacy, quality, and ethical standards. All of these moments of questioning come together in different ways in different disciplines and within different cultural contexts. Developing universal research ethics which account for the power dynamics of non-Western cultural particularities is a serious challenge. A challenge that must begin with good ethical decision-making *processes* and an inclusive multi-disciplinary approach sensitive to the inequalities and differences in the West/non-West dynamic.

Zoetanya Sujon is a Senior Lecturer in Media Theory at Regent's University London and HEA Fellow, specializing in new technologies, digital media and culture.

PART TWO

Cases

CHAPTER TEN

Living Labs – An Ethical Challenge for Researchers and Platform Operators

PHILIPP SCHAER

INTRODUCTION

The infamous Facebook emotion contagion experiment (Kramer, Guillory, & Hancock, 2014) is one of the most prominent and best-known online experiments based on the concept of what we here call "living labs". In these kinds of experiments, real-world applications such as social web platforms trigger experimental switches inside their system to present experimental changes to their users – most of the time without the users being aware of their role as virtual guinea pigs. In the Facebook example the researches changed the way users' personal timeline was compiled to test the influence on the users' moods and feelings. The reactions to these experiments showed the inherent ethical issues such living labs settings bring up, mainly the study's lack of informed consent procedures, as well as a more general critique of the flaws in the experimental design (Panger, 2016).

While, to the general public, these kinds of experiments were a reason for outrage over the research practices at Facebook, the fact that nearly every commercial digital platform operator is implementing online experiments of many different flavors was not in the center of the still ongoing discussion. Next to social web platform operators like Facebook, search engine operators like Google or Microsoft are also known to massively invest into online experiments and living labs within their platforms and products (Buscher, 2013).

In this chapter, we describe additional use cases to compliment these: The so-called living labs that focus on experimentation with information systems such as search engines and wikis and especially on their real-world usage. The living labs paradigm allows researchers to conduct research in real-world environments or systems. In the field of information science and especially information retrieval – which is the scientific discipline that is concerned with the research of search engines, information systems, and search related algorithms and techniques – it is still common practice to perform *in vitro* or offline evaluations using static test collections. Living labs are widely unknown or unavailable to academic researchers in these fields. A main benefit of living labs is their potential to offer new ways and possibilities to experiment with information systems and especially their users, but on the other hand they introduce a whole set of ethical issues that we would like to address in this chapter.

Although some questions regarding the ethical challenges that derive from living labs have been discussed before (Sainz, 2012), the topic is relatively new and not much common agreement on the implications and consequences for platform developers exists.

Following an introduction into the field and a broad overview of the possible manifestations of living labs, we present three use cases in this chapter that our research group was involved in over the last years:

- *User motivational studies in a Semantic MediaWiki.* We implemented different user interface variants that we presented to users of a wiki-based research information system. The idea was to trigger different motivation strategies to encourage users to participate more actively in the platform.
- *Ranking studies in an online toy store.* We participated in the 2015 Living Lab for Information Retrieval workshop and retrieval campaign (LL4IR) that allows different research groups to test and compare the effectiveness of their retrieval systems. We computed different ranking results for an online toy store based on historical click data (i.e. usage popularity) and a text-based relevance score (Schaer & Tavakolpoursaleh, 2015).
- *Implementation of a living lab environment into a repository system.* We implemented an application programming interface into an open access repository. The interface allows external collaborators to conduct online retrieval experiments within our own system.

ENABLING IN VIVO EXPERIMENTATION: LIVING LABS AND INNOVATION SYSTEMS

The core idea of living labs goes back to the 1980s but gained more attention in the years after 2006 when the European Commission started funding the living labs movement (Dutilleul, Birrer, & Mensink, 2010, p. 63). In its core living labs are moving from *in vitro* to *in vivo* research settings by gathering research data from living environments like buildings or public spaces (both online and offline).

Researchers are no longer observing artificial laboratory settings but try to observe real-world usage or interactions of people in these research environments that were previously prepared to function as living labs. For example, a store can be wired to record the customers and the employees to learn about their interactions or buying and working patterns.

In market research and innovation management the great potential of these research approaches was picked up quite early and led to including costumers and users early on in the product development process and to more actively involving them in general. As claimed by Chesbrough (2003, p. 41) the traditional model for innovation is becoming obsolete. Innovation is moving from a mainly internal focus, closed off from outside ideas and technologies, to a new paradigm called *open innovation* that is often connected to ideas of living labs and so-called *innovation systems*.

Besides the meaning of living labs as innovation systems, other meanings have evolved over time that are dependent on different foci and use cases. Dutilleul et al. (2010, p. 64) described (among others) four main and distinct meanings of living labs that are present: 1) the already mentioned innovation systems, 2) in vivo monitoring of social systems and the usage of technology within these systems, 3) involving users in the product development process, and 4) organizations developing and maintaining their technological infrastructure and offering services. Living labs are also used in the context of interactive machine learning (Holzinger, 2015), a technique used for content testing at Google, Facebook, and other online platforms. Additional use cases are known to be present in user experience research and ergonomics (Javier & Charles, 2012).

USER MOTIVATIONAL STUDIES USING LIVING LABS APPROACHES

Online communities are highly dependent on their users and their personal involvement in the participation in the community. The activity level is the key concept that makes these communities successful. From the perspective of an online community platform operator we might ask what the central concepts and mechanisms are that make an online community successful. To learn more about the dynamics that drive successful online communities and especially Wiki-based systems we conducted a living labs-based online experiment using the SOFISwiki,[1] a specialized information system that was transformed into a Wiki system.

SOFISwiki is an online platform for a specialized information database that lists social science research projects from Germany, Austria, and Switzerland. The wiki contains more than 50,000 project records from disciplines such as sociology or political sciences. Until the end of 2012 new records for SOFIS were added through an annual survey that was sent out to more than 5,000 social science-related institutions like universities or research and infrastructure institutes. The survey was paper-based and was curated by a team of information professionals and librarians. In late 2012 the new SOFISwiki platform was started, based on a Semantic MediaWiki (SMW) system.

We manipulated the MediaWiki software to include an additional information dashboard right after the users logged into the system. On this dashboard users saw different performance indicators for their own projects and user account (see Figure 1). Each participating user of the system was randomly assigned to one user group. The user groups differed in some aspects of the performance dashboard. During the experiment all activities in the system SOFISwiki of every participating user were logged by the platform to allow us to measure the effects of functionality changes and of different information presented to the users. From the experiment data we were able to positively evaluate the motivational influence of content attribution. So, if users were aware that the good performance of one of their projects in the platform's view statistics was attributed to them (by showing their names and relation), they were more motivated to participate and to contribute more to the platform.

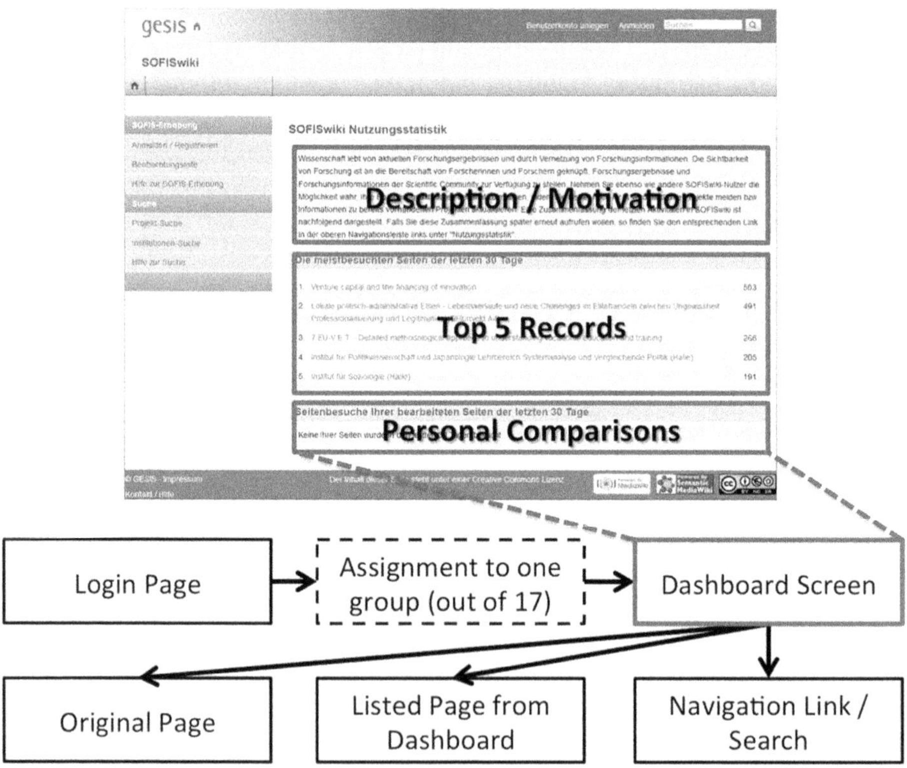

Figure 1. Extended login process for the SOFISwiki experiment. After users logged in they were automatically assigned to one group and were redirected to a personalized dashboard where some performance indicators like numbers of view per project were listed.

Ethical Concerns in the Wiki Setup

Before we started the experiment we released a new version of our terms of use for the SOFISwiki. It included a paragraph on the topic of online experiments and that we would use the interaction data of the platform. This introduces the first ethical issue.

- Although we informed the users about the ongoing (general) changes to the site and the terms of use by showing a notification pop-up, we did not explicitly inform them about every detail of the experiments. But should we not tell the people working on our systems that they are part of an experiment?
- What about the freedom of choice (to not take part in these experiments)? There was no option to opt out of the experiment. Either you were silently accepting the new terms of use and therefore automatically took part in our experiment, or you just had the opportunity to refuse to continue using our system. We did not include a way to simply reject participation in the experiment while still using the platform.
- How much can/should we tell users without spoiling the experiment itself? By telling too much about the motivation behind the experiment itself we would have potentially spoiled the whole experimental setup. Our participants would have been biased because of the background knowledge about our hypotheses and modifications to the system.
- Since Wiki systems tend to be open by design, most of the usage data we showed in the dashboards were publicly available. So the performance indicators are visible as long as you know where to look within the system. We were not able to hide all of this information due to the open nature of the MediaWiki system. Since not every user of the platform uses a pseudonym, one could backlink projects to user accounts and finally to actual persons. A question that might arise here is whether systems that are open by design are a suitable environment for user-centered research, especially when users are not fully aware of the analytical steps that might follow their interactions.

Most of the previously mentioned issues came up late during the experiment or even later during the data analysis phase and we were not able to address these issues at the time when we were running the living lab experiments. We chose to keep a low profile, so we didn't actively announce or comment on the experiment or the ongoing modifications of the platform. This led to a passive behavior or ignorance towards our experiment: The additional steps the users had to perform were silently accepted. Our first level support didn't notice a significantly higher demand for consultation. It seemed as our users just used the platform as usual, regardless of what we were presenting them.

LIVING LABS FOR INFORMATION SYSTEMS AND RETRIEVAL TASKS

The field of information retrieval – summarized as the scientific discipline that is concerned with the research of search engines, information systems, and search related algorithms and techniques – is traditionally heavily dependent on a rigorous empirical evaluation pattern called the Cranfield or TREC paradigm (Sanderson, 2010). In this evaluation technique three essential components are needed: 1) A data set of information objects (most often text documents), 2) a set of topics that describes different information needs, and 3) a set of relevance assessments that judge documents as relevant or non-relevant to the given topics. Obtaining the relevance assessments is a hard and expensive process that relies on human expertise and is an intellectually challenging task. Although some researchers tend to give this task to crowd sourcing platforms like Amazon's Mechanical Turk, most often domain experts are used to judge the search engines results.

To overcome the limitations of the Cranfield paradigm new evaluation techniques were proposed, including online experiments and living labs that allow *in vivo* experiments. Here the meaning of *in vivo* is the possibility for researchers to implement their own algorithms and search methodologies into a live and productive information system. The benefit for the researchers is that they get access to the usage data of real-world users of the information system that are confronted with the results of their search algorithm.

Large search engine companies such as Google or Microsoft use this search engine evaluation technique within their own systems. It has been in use for many years and helps to improve search engines and information systems. The results and the details of these experiments are of course hidden from the public and are only available to the platform developers themselves. Academic researchers are usually not able to participate in these kinds of experiments and to get their hands on the proprietary usage data. By introducing the Living Labs for Information Retrieval initiative (LL4IR) this evaluation paradigm is intended to be open to the academic world. The idea is to find real-world platforms that are willing to implement the LL4IR infrastructure and to open up their platform for the academic community. In this way "living labs are a way to bridge the data divide between academia and industry" (Balog, Elsweiler, Kanoulas, Kelly, & Smucker, 2014). In 2015 the LL4IR initiative received external funding from ELIAS, an ESF Research Networking Programme, and it has established three evaluation campaigns so far.

We were involved within the LL4IR initiative in two different roles: We took part in an evaluation campaign as a research participant, and we implemented the LL4IR API (application programming interface) for our own search engine of the SSOAR system and, therefore, opened up our own system for external research groups (Balog, Schuth, Dekker, Schaer, Chuang, & Tavakolpoursaleh, 2016). The effort to do so was moderate compared to implementing a standalone software solution for different web frameworks and search engines.

Ethical Challenges for Participants of Living Labs

In 2015 we took part in the CLEF LL4IR lab (Schaer & Tavakolpoursaleh, 2015). We worked with the online toyshop REGIO JÁTÉK[2] and implemented an alternative product ranking for their search engine that was based on popularity data of the products. The actual ranking mechanism was a combination of a keyword based search and a mixture of word frequency-based relevance scoring and popularity data extracted from clicks provided by REGIO JÁTÉK. So, popular and highly clicked products from the past were more likely to be ranked higher in the result list due to our approach.

The results of our product ranking were presented using an interleaving method called Team Draft Interleaving. This interleaving technique is different to classical online experimental settings like A/B testing as it presents two different rankings at the same time by interleaving the results of two different ranking approaches. Two advantages are apparent: The interleaved presentation of the results lowers the chance of presenting bad results to the user by interleaving experimental (and potentially bad) rankings and rankings produced by the original productive search engine. Another advantage is that by using interleaved comparisons fewer results presentations are needed to evaluate the systems.

Within this evaluation we were confronted with the following ethical questions:

- Is it okay to be biased in your own implementation? By implementing algorithms that are heavily depending on former popularity, how can we suppress a Matthew's effect where only popular content is getting the most attention? This principle is also known as the rich getting richer principle. If one thinks this through, new products or unpopular products never get the chance to be presented to the users in one of the top positions. This is different to letting users explicitly choose between popularity ranking and relevance ranking based on text features.
- We were aware of some issues in our implementation making it a "bad ranking" but nevertheless submitted the results to the LL4IR campaign just to see whether it had any effect or not. Is it ok to present sub-optimal

search results to users while the main purpose of an evaluation campaign should be to provide them with the best results possible?

The mentioned issues are softened by using an interleaving method and not A/B testing, but still the potential to do "something evil" is inherent.

Ethical Challenges for Platform Operators of Living Labs

After we successfully took part in the evaluation campaign in 2015, we decided to implement the API into our own system, the open access repository SSOAR.[3] We opened the internal search engine for external researchers and took part in the 2016 TREC OpenSearch – Academic Search Edition. Next to CiteSeerX[4] and Microsoft Academic Search[5] we are one of three platforms that provide access to their search engines. By the time of the writing of this article the campaign is still running and no direct results are available. Still, during preparing our system for the TREC OpenSearch, we ran into the following questions:

- Who is responsible for the algorithm and the results? We opened our system and let potential vandals or fanatics present their results. None of the search results provided by the participating researchers are actually controlled by a human assessor.
- What about biased algorithms that present hate-driven, political or religious extremists' content on top of each result list? By opening up the systems one allows others – only on the basis of good will – to decide on the underlying relevance criteria. These might be biased and be based on questionable moral foundations. A ranking algorithm might discriminate in any possible way.

While we believe that the likeliness of such extreme discrimination is very low, we cannot tell if someone will misuse our good intentions. We have no real possibility to check on the validity of the rankings that the external researchers present within our system.

CONCLUSIONS

We introduced the concept of living labs as a possibility to implement in vivo experiments in real-world information systems like wikis and search engines. We implemented different experimental setups using living labs' principles and encountered a number of ethical questions and issues on the way. We were active in both: conducting research using living lab principles and offering living lab services and interfaces for our own platforms. Both scenarios introduced new insights into the methodology and its ethical drawbacks. Many of these were absolutely new to us, and we had not thought of them before we implemented and executed our experiments. Many of these issues are still open questions and are unresolved. In our experiments we mostly choose to simply ignore a lot of these issues – although we were aware of the possible negative outcomes for individuals or the validity of the experiments. We therefore argue to incorporate ethical concerns and best practices into the research design of living lab-based online experiments since up-to-now these are absolutely not a topic within the community. Nobody seems to care. We will try to bring this discussion to the relevant research community e.g. in the LL4IR initiative.

ACKNOWLEDGEMENT

Most of the work presented in this chapter was done during my time with GESIS – Leibniz Institute for the Social Sciences, Cologne, Germany. I would like to thank my former colleagues Narges Tavakolpoursaleh, Simon Bachenberg, Stefan Jakowatz, Annika Marth, and Felix Schwagereit.

NOTES

1. http://sofis.gesis.org
2. http://www.regiojatek.hu
3. http://www.ssoar.info
4. http://citeseerx.ist.psu.edu/index
5. http://academic.research.microsoft.com/

REFERENCES

Balog, K., Elsweiler, D., Kanoulas, E., Kelly, L., & Smucker, M. D. (2014). Report on the CIKM workshop on living labs for information retrieval evaluation. *ACM SIGIR Forum, 48*(1), 21–28.

Balog, K., Schuth, A., Dekker, P., Schaer, P., Chuang, P., & Tavakolpoursaleh, N.. (2016). *Overview of the TREC 2016 Open Search track.* Presented at The Twenty-Fifth Text REtrieval Conference, TREC 2016, Gaithersburg, Maryland. Retrieved from http://trec.nist.gov/pubs/trec25/papers/Overview-OS.pdf

Buscher, G. (2013, November). *IR evaluation: Perspectives from within a living lab.* Presented at the Workshop on Living Labs for Information Retrieval Evaluation @ CIKM 2013, San Francisco, CA. Retrieved from http://living-labs.net/files/ll13/LivingLabsKeynoteGB.pdf

Chesbrough, H. W. (2003). The era of open innovation. *MIT Sloan Management Review, 44*(3), 35–41.

Dutilleul, B., Birrer, F., & Mensink, W. (2010). *Unpacking European living labs: Analysing innovation's social dimensions* (SSRN Scholarly Paper No. ID 2533251). Rochester, NY: Social Science Research Network. Retrieved from http://papers.ssrn.com/abstract=2533251

Holzinger, A. (2015). Interactive machine learning (iML). *Informatik-Spektrum, 39*(1), 64–68. Retrieved from http://doi.org/10.1007/s00287-015-0941-6

Javier, B., & Charles, T. (2012). Ethical issues raised by the new orientations in ergonomics and living labs. *Work 41*(Supplement 1), 5259–5265. Retrieved from http://doi.org/10.3233/WOR-2012-0015-5259

Kramer, A. D. I., Guillory, J. E., & Hancock, J. T. (2014). Experimental evidence of massive-scale emotional contagion through social networks. *Proceedings of the National Academy of Sciences, 111*(24), 8788–8790. Retrieved from http://doi.org/10.1073/pnas.1320040111

Panger, G. (2016). Reassessing the Facebook experiment: Critical thinking about the validity of Big Data research. *Information, Communication & Society, 19*(8), 1108–1126. Retrieved from http://doi.org/10.1080/1369118X.2015.1093525

Sainz, F. J. (2012). Emerging ethical issues in living labs. *Ramon Llull Journal of Applied Ethics 3*(3), 47–62.

Sanderson, M. (2010). Test collection based evaluation of information retrieval systems. *Foundations and Trends in Information Retrieval, 4*(4), 247–375. Retrieved from http://doi.org/10.1561/1500000009

Schaer, P., & Tavakolpoursaleh, N. (2015). Historical clicks for product search: GESIS at CLEF LL4IR 2015. In *CLEF2015 working notes* (Vol. 1391). Retrieved from http://ceur-ws.org/Vol-1391/

CHAPTER ELEVEN

Ethics of Using Online Commercial Crowdsourcing Sites for Academic Research

The Case of Amazon's Mechanical Turk

MATTHEW PITTMAN AND KIM SHEEHAN

Crowdsourcing is the process of collecting needed services (such as information) from a large group of people, generally using digital platforms. Many researchers today collect experimental and survey data from a number of different of online crowdsourcing applications, including Amazon's Mechanical Turk, Prolific Academic, ClickWorker, and CrowdFlower. These online crowdsourcing applications differ in several ways from other online respondent pools. Crowdsourcing applications allow researchers to contract individually with respondents, who are then paid directly for completing surveys or other academic tasks. This is different from panel companies that compensate respondents with points redeemable toward gift cards or entries into lotteries, which do a good job of controlling for important demographic characteristics. Crowdsourcing applications can provide large amounts of data at costs significantly lower than those of panel companies. Academic researchers must weigh several factors, such as budget, desired demographics, nature of task, and anticipated dropout rate, when deciding whether crowdsourcing is an appropriate method for them.

The ethics of crowdsourcing – and online academic crowdsourcing in particular – is a novel and understudied phenomenon. However, it is an area that deserves close attention, as most business analysts believe the micro tasking industry will only increase in scope and size (Olenski, 2015). Levine (1988) wrote that academic research must take the welfare of research participants into account at all times, yet as crowdsourced samples become more prevalent in research studies, academics have raised concerns about whether the research volunteers are paid fairly and treated ethically (Bohannon, 2016). This case will examine Amazon's Mechanical Turk, describe these ethical concerns, and provide possible solutions:

INTERNET-BASED RESEARCH AND MECHANICAL TURK

The internet can be seen both as a research tool and as a research venue (Secretary's Advisory Committee on Human Research Protections, 2013): Amazon's Mechanical Turk is both. Originally designed to assist Amazon employees in categorization tasks, Amazon launched Mechanical Turk (MTurk) publically in 1995 to provide an online interface to connect people who need 'human intelligence tasks' completed with the people who can complete them (Sheehan & Pittman, 2016). Today, some estimates suggest that more than half a million people have registered to work at MTurk, arguably making it the largest source participants in academic research and utilized by researchers in Political Science, Marketing, and Psychology (all researchers must have a US-based billing address).

Researchers use MTurk to recruit subjects (called *Workers* on MTurk) to study the internet and its users: Topics have included online privacy (Coen, King, & Wong, 2016), binge watching and sleep patterns (Kramer, 2015), and effects of age on online activities (Bui, Myerson, & Hale, 2015). Topics unrelated to the internet have also been studied such as cognitive aging and blindness (Stothart, Boot, & Simons, 2015), energy consumption (Yang, Donovan, Young, Greenblatt, & Desroches, 2015), and work-asthma interactions (Harber & Leroy, 2015). A Google Scholar search shows that the number of articles utilizing MTurk for data collection has increased from about 5,000 per year in 2006 to about 15,000 per year in 2015.

Three different entities are directly involved with MTurk academic research: researchers, Workers, and Amazon. Researchers are known as "Requesters" on MTurk and generally post survey links or experimental stimuli. Requesters use MTurk instead of other data collection methods that may either not be generalizable to populations of interest (such as a lab setting with student samples) or may not be affordable (such as an online sample company such as SSI). Samples drawn from MTurk allow for quick data collection at a low cost: In fact, Sheehan and Pittman (2016) found that the low costs of obtaining data are a primary motivator for many Requesters, particularly among graduate students and those in disciplines where grant support is minimal (which includes most of the social sciences). Academic studies that pay 50 cents for a ten-minute survey are common: A sample drawn from an online panel service, such as SSI, would cost at least ten times that amount (Sheehan & Pittman, 2016). Researchers, then, can collect data to generate significant statistical power in surveys with minimal funds. At the same time, a Worker completing a number of academic studies would earn about $3.00 per hour – far lower than minimum wage rates in the United States (Sheehan & Pittman, 2016).

About 80% of MTurk Workers are from the United States, with Workers from India forming a secondary population (Ipeirotis, 2015). Workers are somewhat younger than the United States population but have income and education levels fairly representative of the population as a whole (Sheehan & Pittman, 2016). Workers bring all types of intrinsic and extrinsic motivations to their work: extra income, satisfaction of completing tasks, and flexibility allowing people to work from home to take care of children or elderly parents (Sheehan & Pittman, 2016). Additionally, there is a natural sample bias with participants of a digital platform: Workers are generally understood to be more tech savvy than the average individual. Some researchers might find this bias unacceptable, while others find it advantageous to study emerging issues and challenges of the internet.

The Human Intelligence Task (HIT) is the backbone of MTurk. HITs can range from taking a survey to transcribing audio or identifying images. Amazon, as owner and operator of MTurk, receives a fee for every HIT.[1] It created structural standards such as who can join MTurk as a Worker, operational standards such as who can request tasks, and work standards such as the types of tasks that cannot be requested. Amazon is uninvolved in ensuring that the environment for Workers and Requesters is a positive one: Amazon's terms of service describe its involvement only as a 'payment processor'; Requesters have full power to accept and reject completed HITs (thus they control which Workers do and do not get paid); Amazon will not intervene if Workers believe their work was rejected unfairly (Greenhouse, 2016).

ETHICAL CONCERNS WITH MECHANICAL TURK

Research ethics are generally centered on behavioral norms. Resnick (2008) argued that some of these norms promote the aims of research such as knowledge, truth, and avoidance of error. Other ethical standards promote values essential to collaboration with other researchers and with other research stakeholders: these include trust, accountability, mutual respect, and fairness – key issues raised about research on MTurk. Ethical research norms also help to build public support for research, and research is more likely to be funded if funding agencies trust the quality and integrity of the research and of the researchers. Ethical norms help to ensure that researchers are held accountable to the public. Federal and institutional policies are often derived from these norms and the policies on research misconduct, conflicts of interest, and the human subjects' protections that are necessary in order to ensure that researchers can be held accountable to the public (Resnick, 2008).

Researchers are often faced with tradeoffs between the needs of subjects and the integrity of the research. Johnsson, Eriksson, Helgesson, and Hansson (2015) suggested that abundance of incentives for researchers in the digital sphere (such as low cost and quick data collection) and a shortage of norms can be a challenging combination for ensuring ethical research online, raising the possibility of Worker exploitation. Busarov's (2013) study of MTurk Workers found that about two thirds felt at least somewhat exploited; exploitation was defined as:

> One person makes a profit or gain by turning some characteristic of another individual to his or her own advantage. Exploitation can occur in morally unsavory forms without harming the exploiter's interests and despite the exploiter's fully voluntary consent to the exploitative behavior.

Some aspects of possible exploitation on Mechanical Turk are:

Low Wages

Workers completing academic studies are generally paid poorly. Sheehan and Pittman (2016) found that the majority of academic tasks paid far less than the US minimum wage (e.g. a ten-minute survey with a 50 cent reward equals a $3/hour wage). These low wages occur since academics, particularly those in the humanities and social sciences, generally have limited funds for data collection. At the same time, journals require appropriate levels of statistical power (derived in part from a robust number of participants) for a study's results to be considered valid. Researchers can be put in a precarious position; given the pressure for academics to publish, there is minimal incentive for cash-strapped researchers to pay fewer people a higher payment.

At the same time, institutions do not encourage fair payment. Some academic Institutional Review Boards in the United States question high payments since these may coerce someone to participate or continue in a study that they do not want to do (Sheehan & Pittman, 2016). Amazon itself does not set any payment requirements, unlike other entities that provide research participants (such as Qualtrics).

Partial Work

Most review boards insist that researchers allow participants to exit a study at any time for any reason, without penalty. However, Amazon has set up MTurk to be "all or nothing" – the interface does not allow Requesters to pro-rate or issue partial payment to a Worker who completes part of a task and then withdraws. This suggests MTurk are being penalized for withdrawing. This may damage Workers' interest in academic research and possibly compromise future work at MTurk.

Lack of Transparency

Requesters are able to post requests without identifying who they are or what institution they represent. Workers should be able to decide whether or not they want to work for a Requester based on reputation (Amazon does not provide a way to rate Requesters, but an independent site, Turkopticon, does provide this.); Workers are often unable to identify the Requester's identity or institutional association. This has led to researcher abuse of the MTurk platform. For example, an academic researcher wanted to study whether Requester reputation affected Workers' decisions to complete Requesters' tasks. The researcher created 45 fake Requester accounts, as well as more than two dozen fake Worker accounts at the Turkopticon. The 45 fake "Requesters" were then rated as good, neutral or bad. Then, the researcher posted 45 identical HITs to MTurk – one from each of the 45 fake Requesters, offering a reward of 12 cents for a five-minute survey ($1.44 hourly wage). Workers quickly noticed that different Requesters posted identical HITs; once Workers identified the researcher they demanded an explanation. The researcher stated that he hoped the experiment would go unnoticed and did not plan to mislead Workers, even though he had not provided an opportunity for informed consent. The researcher's institutional review board became involved to examine the research protocol for problems. The researcher also violated Amazon's terms of service by creating multiple profiles, however given Amazon's 'hands off' approach, though, no sanctions against the researcher were taken.

ETHICAL CONSIDERATIONS AND POSSIBLE SOLUTIONS

We argue that MTurk creates an unbalanced relationship between Amazon, Requesters and Workers that is unfair to Workers. Beneficence is a concept in research ethics that states that researchers should have the welfare of the research participant as a goal of a research study (Levine, 1988). The ethical issues described suggest that many Requesters are not considering beneficence when they conduct research on MTurk. A utilitarian perspective on ethics suggests an action or practice is right (when compared with any alternative action or practice) if it leads to the *greatest possible* amount of good or to the *least possible* amount of harm (Mill, 1969). For this parity to be achieved, Requesters, ethics boards and Amazon must work together to create a more balanced environment. In particular, Amazon needs to recognize that many view the company as more than a "payment processor", particularly since July 2015 when the cost of conducting studies increased fourfold on Mechanical Turk in order to "allow Amazon to continue growing the Amazon Mechanical Turk marketplace and innovating (and) … better serve our community of Requesters and Workers (D'Onfro, 2015)."

Payment

As noted earlier, researchers face the challenge of balancing research costs and statistical power given that many academic researchers have limited funds for data collection. Even if it is unconscious, the egoist perspective that prompts researchers to pay as little as possible may prove self-defeating, as meager pay is likely to contribute to worker disillusionment, poor data quality, and ultimately, the decline of MTurk's reputation and viability as a research platform. Institutions differ in their guidelines on appropriate levels of compensation; Duska and Whelan (1975), though, argue that Workers have the right to be compensated fairly (e.g. a minimum wage). Paying appropriately for work completed on MTurk is necessary to respect Workers and to indicate a value for their time, yet it is "unlikely to be painless, especially for younger and underfunded researchers (Williamson, 2016)."

Some ethics review boards consider payments beyond a token 'thank you' as inappropriate incentives that may be unduly coercive. Christine Grady, Chair of the Department of Bioethics for the National Institute of Health, disagreed with this perspective, arguing that coercion defined as a threat of physical, psychological, or social harm in order to compel someone to do something, such as participate in research. She argued that monetary compensation is not a threat of harm but rather an offer of an opportunity, and thus is not coercion (Grady, n.d.). She also argued payments are not an inducement, defining an inducement as an offer one cannot refuse or an influence that is strong enough to compel someone to participate in the research against their own interests in terms of the acceptability of the risks. Workers always have a choice to not participate. A related concern for ethics review boards is that higher compensation might affect the overall nature of the subject pool by including people primarily motivated by money; however, Buhrmester, Kwang, and Gosling (2011) did not find that higher compensation rates distorted the subject pool or affected data quality.

A competitor to MTurk specifically for academic research, Prolific Academic, requires "ethical pricing" of 5 pounds sterling (or $7.50) per hour to participants. Workers support this idea of minimum wage as the floor of ethical compensation; many experienced and skilled Workers will not work for less than $9 per hour (We Are Dynamo, n.d.). Amazon should consider a similar policy, and Requesters must examine their payment policies to ensure Workers are not exploited.

Partial Payments

Amazon should investigate ways to set up the system in order to allow Requesters to provide partial payments so Requesters can be in compliance with ethics review board policies. Amazon's stated responsibility to be a "payment processor" suggest that providing this flexibility is part of its responsibility. Partial payment would also help lessen the problem of unnecessary coercion, since Workers could quit a task when they felt uncomfortable and still be paid for their time.

Transparency

Increasing transparency of academic research to MTurk Workers involves different actions that are relatively straightforward, particularly when Requesters, review boards, and Amazon work to minimize harm to Workers. Researchers should always clearly state who they are and what their affiliation is (currently Requesters can provide a name/affiliation such as "Product Research Lab" for the Requester name). Requesters should also provide informed consent documentation at the start of a survey that describes who the researchers are, as well as the amount of time that a HIT will take so Workers can make an informed decision about accepting work.

Many Requesters, particularly those new to MTurk, look to their institution's ethical review boards for specific guidance on informed consent policies. These boards can assist by creating guidelines that require Requesters identify their names/affiliations in the HIT descriptions. This will allow Workers to investigate Requesters, such as through the Turkopticon, and make a more informed decision about whether they want to participate in the study based on the nature of the research and the academic value they perceive.

Many MTurk Workers complain that academic HITs provide inaccurate completion times (Sheehan & Pittman, 2016), which makes the cost/benefit assessment for Workers very difficult. Requesters should conduct pre-tests with software that contains a timer mechanism and provide this information to Workers clearly.

Amazon can support this increased transparency and signal to Workers that they are important and valued by requiring informed consent protocols in its guidelines for Requesters. Amazon could also leverage their existing capabilities in user rating and provide Workers the ability to rate HITs and requesters. Amazon could integrate ratings collection into existing HIT structures and easily report information on Requesters to Workers, just as they post reviews in the Amazon marketplace.

CONCLUSION: MODELING OF ETHICAL BEHAVIOR

Ethical behavior must be modeled by all entities involved in order to create research with integrity: Bandura and McDonald (1963) found that observing moral behavior being modeled is more effective in changing behaviors than operant conditioning (rewards for appropriate behavior). In emerging digital spheres, where it is difficult to understand appropriate norms and social conventions, modeling by researchers, Requesters, Amazon, and institutional review boards should model best practices for this platform to provide exposure to models of behavior that the individual would not encounter normally (Mejias, 2005). This can also help to create what is called a "shared morality." Bandura explains: "A shared morality … is vital to the humane functioning of any society … Societal codes and sanctions articulate collective moral imperatives as well as influence social conduct" (Bandura, 1991, p. 46).

Halavais (2011) calls for ethical reflection throughout the research process, a practice that moves beyond the idea of traditional guidelines to a more iterative experience of examining issues both in context and in real time. Miller and Boulton (2007) argued that review boards must participate in this process by becoming more aware of emerging research opportunities, learning how researchers have dealt with new ethical issues, and finding ways to integrate others' experiences into improved training for researchers new to these digital platforms. Also, Amazon itself has a responsibility to participate in the moral development of researchers (and everyone who uses Mechanical Turk for their own gain) as it profits from the online environment where ethical decisions must be made.

For Mechanical Turk to realize its potential and flourish as an ethical platform for data collection, numerous changes must be made. These changes involve developing cooperation among the different stakeholders of Mechanical Turk to collaborate to create and maintain an environment where both researchers and participants can flourish.

NOTE

1. In 2015, Amazon raised the fees for Requesters in from 10% to 40% for academic Requesters (or anyone needing more than ten responses to a HIT). The fee for a study paying 0.50 to 200 people increased from $10 to $40.

REFERENCES

Bandura, A. (1991). Social cognitive theory of self-regulation. *Organizational behavior and Human Decision Processes, 50*(2), 248–287.

Bandura, A., & McDonald, F. J. (1963). Influence of social reinforcement and the behavior of models in shaping children's moral judgment. *The Journal of Abnormal and Social Psychology, 67*(3), 274–328.

Bohannon, J. (2016). Psychologists grown increasingly dependent on online research subjects. *Science Magazine*. Retrieved from http://www.sciencemag.org/news/2016/06/psychologists-grow-increasingly-dependent-online-research-subjects

Buhrmester, M., Kwang, T., & Gosling, S. D. (2011). Amazon's mechanical Turk: A new source of inexpensive, yet high-quality, data? *Perspectives on Psychological Science, 6*(1), 3–5.

Bui, D. C., Myerson, J., & Hale, S. (2015). Age-related slowing in online samples. *The Psychological Record, 65*(4), 649–655.

Busarovs, A. (2013). Ethical aspects of crowdsourcing, or is it a modern form of exploitation? *International Journal of Economics & Business Administration, 1*(1), 3–14.

Coen, R., King, J., & Wong, R. (2016, June). The privacy policy paradox. In *Symposium on Usable Privacy and Security (SOUPS)*.

D'Onfro, J. (2015). *Amazon just increased prices on a service you've probably never heard of, and some researchers are really upset*. Retrieved from http://www.businessinsider.com/amazon-mechanical-turk-price-changes

Duska, R., & Whelan, M. (1975). *Moral development: A guide to Piaget and Kohlberg*. New York, NY: Paulist Press.

Grady, C. (n.d.). *Ethical and practical considerations of paying research participants (PDF Document)*. Retrieved from https://www.niehs.nih.gov/research/resources/assets/docs/ethical_and_practical_conside ations_of_paying_research_participants_508.pdf

Greenhouse, S. (2016). On demand, and demanding their rights. *American Prospect*. Retrieved from http://prospect.org/article/demand-and-demanding-their-rights

Halavais, A. (2011). Social science: Open up online research. *Nature, 480*(7376), 174–175.

Harber, P., & Leroy, G. (2015). Assessing work–asthma interaction with amazon mechanical Turk. *Journal of Occupational and Environmental Medicine, 57*(4), 381–385.

Ipeirotis, P. (2015). *Demographics of mechanical Turk*. Retrieved from http://www.behind-the-enemy-lines.com/2015/04/demographics-of-mechanical-turk-now.html

Johnsson, L., Eriksson, S., Helgesson, G., & Hansson, M. G. (2015). Making researchers moral. In D. Mascalzoni (Ed.), *Ethics, law and governance of biobanking* (pp. 261–277). Dordrecht: Springer Netherlands.

Kramer, A. (2015, November). Screening for Sleep Problems: Binge Watching in the Internet Era and its Relationship to Sleep Habits. In *2015 APHA Annual Meeting & Expo (October 31–November 4, 2015)*. APHA.

Levine, R. J. (1988). *Ethics and regulation of clinical research* (2nd ed.). New Haven, CT: Yale University Press.

Mejias, U. (2005). *Moral development and the internet (PDF Document)*. Retrieved from http://blog.ulisesmejias.com/2005/01/02/moral-development-and-the-internet/

Mill, J. S. (1969). *Utilitarianism and on liberty*. In *J. M. Robinson (Ed.), Collected works of John Stuart Mill*. Toronto, ON: University of Toronto Press.

Miller, T., & Boulton, M. (2007). Changing constructions of informed consent: Qualitative research and complex social worlds. *Social Science & Medicine, 65*(11), 2199–2211.

Olenski, S. (2015). *The state of crowdsourcing*. Retrieved from http://www.forbes.com/sites/steveolenski/2015/12/04/the-state-of-crowdsourcing/#533cf34e61bc.

Resnick, D. B. (2008). Increasing the amount of payment to research subjects. *Journal of Medical Ethics, 34*(9), e14. Retrieved from http://www.ncbi.nlm.nih.gov/pmc/articles/PMC3966192/

Secretary's Advisory Committee on Human Research Protections. (2013). *Considerations and recommendations concerning internet research and human subjects research regulations, with revisions (PDF Document)*. Retrieved from www.hhs.gov/ohrp/sachrp/commsec/attachmentbsecletter20.pdf

Sheehan, K., & Pittman. M. (2016). *Amazon's mechanical Turk for academics: The hit handbook for science research*. Irvine, CA: Melvin and Leigh.

Stothart, C., Boot, W., & Simons, D. (2015). Using mechanical Turk to assess the effects of age and spatial proximity on in attentional blindness. *Collabra, 1*(1), 1–7.

We are Dynamo. (n.d.). *Fair payment*. Retrieved from http://wiki.wearedynamo.org/index.php?title=Fair_payment

Williamson, V. (2016). On the ethics of crowdsourced research. *PS: Political Science & Politics, 49*, 77–81.

Yang, H. C., Donovan, S. M., Young, S. J., Greenblatt, J. B., & Desroches, L. B. (2015). Assessment of household appliance surveys collected with amazon mechanical Turk. *Energy Efficiency, 8*(6), 1063–1075.

CHAPTER TWELVE

Museum Ethnography in the Digital Age

Ethical Considerations

NATALIA GRINCHEVA

INTRODUCTION

In the 21st century it is hard to imagine a museum that does not maintain a visible online presence or sustain a digital collection archive. Virtual museum spaces acquaint online "visitors" with museum collections and provide interactive environments for presentational, educational, entertainment, and communication purposes. Online museum spaces may include interactive digital galleries, virtual three-dimensional museum simulators, museum mobile and web 2.0 applications, blogs as well as social network profiles. Most of them allow audiences to interact with digital museum content or communicate with curators or managers through participation in museum blogs, writing comments, and rating posts in social media spaces. In some cases, online audiences are offered to enjoy more "participative" experiences through collecting, curating, or sharing digital objects in online galleries, purposefully designed to accommodate online participation. These audiences' activities create unlimited opportunities for museum ethnographers, who in the digital era can conduct their research beyond physical walls of museums. Whereas video and audio recordings are required to collect evidence of visitor behavior in a museum's physical space, an online environment can provide a perfect recording tool in itself. It instantly traces all of the activities of the users and displays all of the visible records that take form in comments, ratings, posts, uploaded video, audio, text, and image online contributions.

As a digital museum ethnographer, I would like to devote this chapter to sharing my personal experience in addressing ethical considerations while conducting research on museum visitors' behavior in online spaces. My research looks at online museums as important sites of cross-cultural communication. These sites project powerful political and cultural messages across borders and engage not only local but predominantly international audiences. Captivated by the diversity of online museum programs that connect people across the globe, opening up virtual spaces for cross-cultural learning, and immersing online visitors into educational experiences, I traveled the world to conduct a number of case studies. I researched digital spaces of large international museums in Canada, the United States, the United Kingdom, Australia, and Singapore. My ethnographic research revealed that museum online communities as social interactive worlds can be powerful tools of cultural representation or mis-representation, sites of memory and identity construction, and building citizenry or political battlegrounds of resistance and social riots. Online museums can build unique "bridges" among communities for improving intercultural competence and tolerance or, in contrast, can invoke religious and cultural wars. These insights and findings were possible due to immersive ethnographic research within different digital museum spaces. I explored various online museum communities and collected and analyzed a large amount of textual and visual data demonstrating various behaviors of online "museum goers."

Indeed, digital ethnography provides an effective instrument to study and explore human behavior in online communities. It is as immersive, descriptive, and multilateral as the traditional ethnographic approach. Virtual ethnography utilizes similar methods for analyzing and interpreting data, requiring a researcher to become a member of virtual communities in order to observe participants' interactions and communication. Even though digital ethnography within museum online communities provides great insight and depth into a range of visitors' practices and opinions, it also brings many challenges. The majority of these challenges are concerned with various ethical considerations. Based on my extensive experiences, in this chapter I will identify important ethical issues that emerge around digital ethnographic research in online museum spaces. Specific examples from my research projects in different countries will serve as illustrations of various ethical considerations that I faced and addressed while making personal attempts in transferring museum ethnographic tradition into digital realm of museum communities.

ETHICAL DILEMMAS OF DIGITAL MUSEUM ETHNOGRAPHERS

In conventional ethnography, a researcher immerses oneself in the community of interest. Digital museum ethnography transfers the ethnographic tradition of the researcher as an "embodied research instrument" to the social spaces of online museum communities. "In virtual ethnography the travel to a field site is itself virtual, consisting of experiential rather than physical displacement" (Hine, 2000, p. 45). In order to immerse oneself in this imaginary social world existing online around a particular museum content a researcher has to become a part of a museum online community. Even though the majority of online museum spaces are "public" and easily accessible for anyone who wishes to join and contribute, there are some private online communities. These "closed" sites require online registration and disclosure of ones' identity. This process makes a researcher address important ethical questions to avoid unauthorized uses of information that can be mined in these closed environments. The level of access to private online museum spaces can range from an automatic membership granted on the basis of online registration to an officially approved access. In the latter case the access has to be authorized by museum mangers who verify every application. In this situation the ethical concern is raised in regard to the question whether to present oneself as a mere participant or to reveal one's research purposes. Even though it is "easier" to go "covert" since you do not have to deal with numerous questions from museum mangers, it is important to be transparent about one's interests in order to conduct research in a manner that is in adherence with ethical considerations.

An example of this type of "private" online museum community is "Turbinegeneration," a global online network developed by Tate Gallery in 2009 (Tate, 2009). This is a unique program that connects schools, galleries, and artists from different countries to explore international cultures and to exchange artworks online. This collaboration and exchange is facilitated in the online social network created by Tate specifically for the project. The network provides an opportunity for members to create a partnership blog where they can share and develop artwork together. The site also makes it easy to upload photographs, videos, audio, and texts. To ensure better collaboration among partners Tate has developed a free downloadable project pack suggesting a range of activities to initiate and maintain dialogue between schools and artists. The "Turbinegeneration" community is not a publicly accessible platform, where online visitors can easily surf the network. A person must go through a proper registration process that requires disclosure of personal and professional data to get permission to access and interact in the online community. Interested in the powers of this network to connect schools and artists across different countries and collecting statistics on geographical distribution of involved participants I registered with the community as a researcher. In order to become a member of the site, I needed to explain my research objectives and methods to the network managers who eventually approved my access. Having clearly revealed my interests as an online museum ethnographer on my personal profile, I got a "silent" permission from the participants to be a part of their closed community and to collect my data. The network users did not bother contacting me or initiating a dialogue, they simply ignored my profile. At the same time, I was safe to collect my statistics knowing that museum mangers had approved my activities and network users did not protest or express any concerns about my "presence" in their closed community.

Even though the ethical concern of privacy is more critical when a researcher becomes a part of a private museum space, observation in "open" online communities is also rather problematic from the perspective of other ethical questions. Hine (2000) has suggested that "the internet provides an ideal opportunity for covert ethnography, since it is possible to lurk in many online environments" (p. 262). Although this so called "non-obtrusive research" can grant unique opportunities to study online communities as more "natural" settings (Paccagnella, 1997), this research inquiry raises a lot of ethical problems and challenges. "Lurking" presupposes an invisible presence on a site, and many scholars argue that such conduct of research on human subjects is not acceptable since, in this one-way process, a researcher acquires a powerful position to gaze on others, "appropriating their actions for the purposes of research," (Heath, Koch, Ley, & Montoya, 1999, p. 451). On the other hand, the greatest advantage of such a method of data collection is that participants' behavior is not affected by the data collection procedure (Fielding, Lee, & Blank, 2008). Being non-disruptive, this method allows digital researchers to investigate large numbers of online participants. As Hine (2000) reveals, non-obtrusive "lurking" has established itself as a major strand of social science research on the internet. However, if engaged in such a passive method of data collection, a digital ethnographer needs to make sure that the use of collected data on the "public" sites of online museums complies with the terms and conditions of these digital communities.

First, it is important to find out if online museums sites are publicly open spaces where online projects' participants are informed that all their contributions in the form of comments, posts, or visual materials are widely and freely accessible in the public domain of the internet. Many online museum spaces require participants to read and agree with their terms and conditions as a part of registration procedures. In these agreements it is usually specified that participants' contributions automatically become part of a larger internet community. For example, the Singapore Memory Project (SMP), developed by the National Library and Museum Board of Singapore in 2011 to preserve and provide access to the national culture, invites all online participants to agree on their Terms and Conditions before making their contributions to the site. The online memory portal aims to tell a true "Singapore Story" to the world and engages national community in sharing "recollections of historical events, documentation of recent events of significance, as well as personal memories of people, places and activities that resonate with the Singapore psyche" (Elaine, 2011). The Singapore Memory Project Terms and Conditions clearly inform:

> For all memories contributed to this Portal by any and all Parties, the Parties shall grant to the National Library Board (NLB), the perpetual, worldwide, non-exclusive license to digitize, make available to third party(s) and/or members of the public via the internet and/or successive technologies for downloading, printing and shall grant to the NLB and SMP the right to reproduce and republish this Portal's contents in any formats and platforms including print; electronic media; social media platforms; websites; publications; for both NLB's and SMP's internal and external uses and for non-commercial purposes. (SMP, 2011)

In this way, through the registration process on the SMP portal, online participants of the project are informed that their personal "memories," contributed to the site, belong to the public domain of the internet. Furthermore, SMP Terms and Conditions specify that by agreeing with the terms of use participants confirm that they are aware that the content they donate to the project can be used by third parties for non-commercial purposes, including research purposes:

> The afore stated licence grants the NLB the legal right to sub-licence for non-commercial use the contents of this Portal at NLB's sole discretion and on such terms as the NLB may impose on the users. Such non-commercial use includes but is not limited to, use for personal enjoyment, private study and research purposes and/or posting of all content item(s). (SMP, 2011)

Identifying and getting oneself familiarized with terms of use of museum online spaces is the first step in conducting ethnographic research in accordance with ethical norms. It is important to stay well informed about the use of collected data by making sure that one's research activities and further publications don't violate users' privacy rights.

Furthermore, in many cases, museum online communities emerge on third party social networks, like Facebook or YouTube, which offer their own terms and conditions to users. One of such projects that I researched as a digital museum ethnographer is the YouTube Play portal developed by the Guggenheim museum in collaboration with Google in 2010 (Guggenheim, 2010). This project was based on an international online creative video contest that celebrated the creativity, participation, and unique opportunities provided by YouTube, the largest global channel for video sharing. Throughout the project, the museum received more than 23,000 submissions from all corners of the world, out of which 125 were shortlisted and exhibited on the YouTube Play channel. This portal created an online community of fans and followers of the project who actively engaged in online discussions of the videos, shared their own video clips, and communicated with artists. Until today, YouTube Play remains a very popular channel among international online audiences with a constantly growing number of views of the featured videos, as well as an increasing number of online discussions about the video content. Interested in assessing the powerful impacts of global media campaigns upon international online audiences, I researched participants' activities on the YouTube Play portal. Specifically, I focused on content analysis of online users' comments submitted to the videos of the channel.

As a part of the ethics research procedures I consulted the YouTube Terms of Use to ensure that my analysis of the channel's videos and comments does not violate the users' privacy rights. Specifically, the Google Terms of Service clarify for its users:

> When you upload or otherwise submit content to our Services, you give Google (and those we work with) a worldwide license to use, host, store, reproduce, modify, create derivative works (such as those resulting from translations, adaptations or other changes that we make so that your content works better with our Services), communicate, publish, publicly perform, publicly display and distribute such content. (Google, 2014)

These terms of use allow a digital ethnographer a nonreactive data collection, in which, even though online users are aware that their activities in the form of textual and video contributions can potentially be observed, collected and reused, they can't know for sure who is observing them and when. To address ethical concerns of such non-obtrusive "lurking," I took some specific measures to protect the confidentiality and anonymity of the participants' data that I used in my research publications. These measures included avoiding using personal information of online participants, such as their online names, age, nationality, profession, etc. Furthermore, I omitted a discussion of visual/textual user-generated content if it contained personal information on sensitive issues or if it could result in participants' shame or threats to material or psychological well-being.

Although, as Hine (2000) indicates, this "passive" method can appear to be a quite convenient way to collect reliable data based on simple unobtrusive observations, more active engagement with online communities can be very beneficial for online ethnographers (p. 257). Bell (2001) contrasts a covert online-observation methodology with truly ethnographic methods, which emphasize "dialogue with respondents – recasting research as collaboration rather than appropriation" (p. 26). He advocates implementing specific ethical procedures that oblige a researcher to explicitly disclose his or her research interests and goals to other participants within an online community. These ethical obligations have historically been incorporated in traditional ethnographic museum-research activities (such as focus groups and interviews) that comply with the internationally accepted Code of Ethics for Museums, established by the International Council of Museums (ICOM, 2013). However, because virtual ethnography in an online museum space is still a methodological innovation, the professional museum world is experimenting with this new field of research under the guidelines of traditional research practices.

In my research of the mentioned above YouTube Play project moving from non-obtrusive online "lurking" within the channel to conducting traditional interviews with the projects' participants was really beneficial for my research. Specifically, I reached out to 125 finalist artists who participated in the YouTube Play contest and whose video clips were featured on the channel. I presented myself as a digital museum ethnographer, explained my research interests and goals, and requested participants' consent to use the data collected through interviews in my publications. These "open" research methods not only gave me a unique opportunity to gain in-depth insights into the artists' motivations but provided access to the YouTube statistics that I could not have obtained otherwise. For example, the online viewers' social demographics and geographic distribution statistics are not publicly available for YouTube video clips. This is personal data accessible only by the clips' owners. Interaction with artists of the YouTube Play channel in an ethically reflective manner and disclosing my professional identity as a museum scholar allowed me to access this statistical information. The data significantly enriched my research with important geographical and demographical details on the clips' international online audiences. Indeed, conducting research in a traditional ethically reflective manner pays dividends allowing a museum ethnographer to go deeper than a mere online observation of users' activities.

CONCLUDING REMARKS

This chapter started a very important conversation on ethical issues that emerge when conducting research in online museum communities. Even though this paper addressed some basic and critical ethical concerns in digital ethnographic research, it still could not embrace the complexities of ethical problems which are concerned with all the components of an ethnographic study, such as 1) research environment, 2) researcher and 3) research subjects. I was able to sketch some illustrative examples of ethical dilemmas in researching online museum communities mostly relevant to the first component, such as research environment. Online museums, indeed, can be understood as virtual "research laboratories", where users as research subjects can be under constant observation not only by museum managers but also by a great number of museum scholars and ethnographers (Grincheva, 2014). This situation raises a lot of ethical concerns, identified and discussed in this chapter based on my own research experience. It goes without saying that this is only a beginning of the conversation on ethical issues in online museum communities. More detailed and thorough work is required to illuminate the complexity of ethical dilemmas which bother the best minds of museum ethnographers in the age of digital communications. Specifically, it is essential to develop further a discussion on ethical problems with regard to two other research components: the researcher and research subjects. Important questions such as auto-ethnography, "participatory" research design, adequate self-representation in online museum environments, as well as authenticity of online participants' data and interaction with online users require further academic enquiry. In the digital age new generations of museum ethnographers need to be well equipped with comprehensive guidelines on various ethical issues in order to conduct a reliable, but humanistic research online. This research should be respectful to the rights of people who create the social world of the internet.

REFERENCES

Bell, D. (2001). *An introduction to cybercultures*. London: Routledge.

Elaine, N. (2011, August 13–18). *The library as an online community touch-point*. Paper presented at the IFLA World Library and Information Congress, San Juan, Puerto Rico.

Fielding, N., Lee, R. M., & Blank G. (2008). *The Sage handbook of online research methods*. London: Sage.

Google. (2014). *Google terms of service*. Retrieved from http://bit.ly/1qmDqTP

Grincheva, N. (2014). The online museum: A "placeless" space of the "civic laboratory." *Museum Anthropology Review, 8*(1), 1–21.

Guggenheim. (2010). *YouTube Play*. Retrieved April 16, 2016 from http://bit.ly/1ICnS4V

Heath, D., Koch, E., Ley, B., & Montoya, M. (1999). Nodes and queries: Linking locations in networked fields on inquiry. *American Behavioral Scientist, 43*(3), 450–463.

Hine, C. (2000). *Virtual ethnography*. London: Sage.

International Commission of Museums (ICOM). (2013). *Code of ethics for museums*. Retrieved from http://bit.ly/1s8L0RW

Paccagnella, L. (1997). Getting the seat of your pants dirty: Strategies for ethnographic research on virtual communities. *Journal of Computer-Mediated Communication, 3*(1), 1–17. Retrieved from http://bit.ly/1rikypj

Singapore Memory Project (SMP). (2011). *Terms and conditions*. Retrieved from http://bit.ly/1SBhnA4

Tate. (2009). *The Unilever series: Turbinegeneration*. Retrieved from http://bit.ly/1N00kL7

CHAPTER THIRTEEN

Participant Anonymity AND Participant Observations

Situating the Researcher within Digital Ethnography

JAMES ROBSON

INTRODUCTION

Participant anonymity lies at the heart of the majority of ethical research frameworks in the social sciences. Wherever human interactions and human beings themselves are the focus of the research, there is an expectation that researchers should protect their participants from harm by preserving their privacy and ensuring participant data are anonymous (BERA, 2011; British Psychological Society, 2009). This is reflected in the Association of Internet Researchers' ethical framework, which adopts a human subjects model approach. Although acknowledging that some online content can be viewed as public and freely available (see Bassett & O'Riordan, 2002), this framework advocates the need for participant privacy through anonymity in the majority of digital contexts (Ess & AoIR Ethics Working Committee, 2002; Markham & Buchanan, 2012).

However, a key feature of the internet is its "persistence, searchability and replicability" (Jones, 2011, p. 3). Under these conditions it can be extremely difficult to remove all traces from data that may link back to individuals (Zimmer, 2010), making it difficult to ensure privacy and anonymity for research participants. In the context of qualitatively oriented research, one of the key challenges of maintaining privacy and anonymity for participants involves the use of direct quotations taken from accessible online contexts (Beaulieu & Estalella, 2011; King, 1996; Townsend & Wallace, 2016). Online posts and interactions can offer a rich source of qualitative data and directly quoting them can be a very useful and compelling way of presenting findings. This is particularly important when analytical approaches that focus in detail on language and phrasing, discourse analysis for example, are employed. However, it can be possible to trace direct quotations back to their original sources if they are in the public domain, through a variety of methods – the most simple being the judicious use of search engines. As such, significant amounts of information about participants can potentially be discovered.

Therefore, online researchers working in qualitative paradigms, where the collection of rich data related to individuals' online engagement and activity is essential, face significant challenges in protecting participant anonymity. There are a number of ways of overcoming these challenges. The most common of these involve presenting data in a narrative form, fictionalising aspects of the research, creating composite accounts, such as vignettes, and amalgamating specific examples into generic forms (Jones, 2011). Quotations can be paraphrased with all identifying information removed. Although certainly not a fool proof strategy to be used in isolation, paraphrased quotations can also be checked in a variety of search engines to test whether the original source is still easily traceable (Dawson, 2014).

However, these precautions do not necessarily take into account the full complexity of undertaking ethical research in the messy social realities of the real world. This case study, therefore, discusses how a number of practical research decisions, made as part of an emergent ethnographic study of UK teachers' engagement in online social spaces, unintentionally jeopardised participant privacy and anonymity. I made a number of decisions related to the way in which I entered the field overtly and undertook participant observations. I was anxious to engage with participants in an open an honest way, as recommended in much of the literature on ethnography and digital ethnography (Hine, 2008; Hine, 2015), and so I used my real name in my online interactions. The sequence of decisions that led me to use my real name was rooted in methodological and ethical concerns and approved by my ethical review board. However, despite effort being made to protect participant anonymity through anonymization of data and paraphrasing quotations, I later discovered that a search of my own name could lead directly to my interactions with research participants and so to the participants themselves.

Thus, in presenting this case, I aim to describe the complex connection of decisions, features, and contingencies involved in undertaking ethnographic research in digital contexts, some considerations related to entering and participating in the field, and the decision making process I undertook once I discovered participant anonymity had been jeopardised. The chapter concludes with a discussion of a way in which I could have achieved the goal of situating myself in the field openly and honestly without leaving traceable data.

ETHICAL DECISION-MAKING IN MESSY SOCIAL CONTEXTS

I first discovered that I had jeopardised participant privacy when giving a lecture on digital ethnography to a group of graduate students. During this class I shared the findings of a year-long digital ethnography I had undertaken, studying Religious Education (RE) teachers' engagement in online social spaces (Robson, 2016). This study focused on the ways in which teachers constructed and performed professional identity through peer-to-peer online engagement.

The field was conceptualised in multi-sited terms, involving both online and offline contexts, but was centred on a particular online social space used by RE teachers. This was a forum, chosen for the large number of RE teachers using it and the significant role it played in the wider RE community. This forum was open and accessible to the wider public and the content was not controversial. The members of the online community appeared to be very aware that their interactions took place in the public domain and could be seen by non-community members. This was illustrated by the fact that users frequently reminded each other that school students might access the site, that personal details and real names should not be given, and that identifying information relating to schools or pupils should not be shared.

Despite the fact that the forum was publically accessible and users understood it as such (Ess & AoIR Ethics Working Committee, 2002; Markham & Buchanan, 2012), I had discussed the issue of anonymity with a group of participants at the beginning of the fieldwork. Collaboratively we had decided that it was appropriate to protect both their real identities (available to me through offline interviews) and their online usernames. In order to achieve this we agreed that all participants would be provided with pseudonyms, and any quotations taken from the forum would be paraphrased and then checked through Google to see if the source was still accessible.

As in any ethnography, data were gathered through a variety of methods. Narrative-based online and offline interviews formed a key part of this study, alongside textual analysis of time-based samples, questionnaires, and analysis of blogs, news articles, and tweets. However, participant observation formed the primary method of data collection.

Although online contexts can allow for covert observation (Hine, 2015), for many digital ethnographers, particularly those rooted in the anthropological tradition (Boellstorff, 2012; Horst & Miller, 2012), participant observation is the key method by which data are gathered. With the researcher conceptualised as the research instrument (DeWalt & DeWalt, 2002), participant observation requires direct interaction within the online field site. The researcher must engage actively with participants and gain direct experience of the research context (Hine, 2015; Horst & Miller, 2012; Orgad, 2005), adopting a position of open vulnerability within the community (Mills & Morton, 2013). By engaging with participants in an open, honest, and sustained manner, the researcher can develop trust with community members and explicitly discuss the research process, the project's aims and objectives and gain informed consent.

In order to undertake the research in this kind of overt, open, and honest manner, I introduced myself publically to the community of the forum. In keeping with guidance in much of the literature on digital ethnography (Hine, 2015), as well as the value placed on researcher vulnerability in more traditional anthropological approaches to the field, I was upfront about my identity and my institutional affiliation (Walford, 2008). Having been involved in some national policy work and RE specific professional development, I have an existing identity within the RE community in the UK. I, therefore, decided it would be important to use my real name in my online interactions with users so they would know who they were communicating with and the wider community would be fully aware of my identity. By using my real name and by providing a link to the project website in the signature of every post I made, I aimed to remind users in an ongoing way about the project and my identity as a participant observer.

In making the decision to use my real name in the field I considered the possibility of introducing myself at the beginning of the fieldwork, then, using an anonymous researcher account. Users could be encouraged to verify my identity and find out more about the project by directly messaging me through this anonymous identity. However, I deemed this to be problematic in two main ways. Methodologically, it appeared to go against the principles of immersive ethnography. By failing to commit to the field in a fully open and vulnerable way (Mills & Morton, 2013; Walford, 2008), I felt I risked limiting my experience and understanding of it. In a paradigm where the researcher him or herself is the primary instrument of research (DeWalt & DeWalt, 2002), complete with personal and professional history, I felt it was important to be able to interact as *myself* with participants. Being publically open about my identity, including my name and institutional affiliation, seemed to be an important part of that.

Secondly, the community was fluid. By the end of a year of fieldwork, the forum community looked very different to how it did at the beginning – not least because it had doubled in size. From an ethical perspective, I felt that using my real name and linking it clearly with an institution and project website would ensure I maintained an overt, open presence in an ongoing way that could not be achieved by simply introducing myself at the beginning of the fieldwork. Furthermore, statistics showed that inactive users significantly outnumbered active ones. It is arguable that the forum belonged to them just as much as it belonged to the more active, extroverted members. Although this more passive group of community members might not go to the trouble of directly messaging me, I wanted to make it easy for them to find information about the project and me as a researcher. I didn't feel I could achieve this with an anonymous researcher account.

I discussed this reasoning with some participants and the forum manager, who was particularly keen that I should participate in this open and attributable way. Unfortunately, in making the decision to post under my real name, I had not considered my own digital traces in sufficient detail.

However, as I taught the class, I gradually realised that my students, stimulated (I hope) by the topic, had their laptops out and were searching for my name, the subject area, and the project website. They quickly discovered the online social space I had studied and were looking at and analysing my posts and public interactions with other users. All the measures I had taken to preserve the anonymity of my participants by giving them pseudonyms and paraphrasing direct quotations were rendered largely irrelevant by the simple fact that I had situated myself within the field in a traceable way.

This presented an urgent ethical dilemma. My desire to ensure participant anonymity had been jeopardised by my desire to be open and honest with the community I entered. Although rooted in methodological reasoning and ethical concerns, the use of my real name and identity as an academic had led people directly to my participants and their online identities. My students had highlighted this issue and I was consequently faced with the challenge of what to do about it.

As far as I could see, there were two main options. The first was to argue that, in this instance, given the open nature of the space and the relatively uncontroversial content, little harm could be done to the participants through this route of access. Things could, therefore, be left as they were. My second option was to delete my identity on the forum along with all history of my engagement and interactions with participants.

To a certain extent the first option had a certain attraction. It involved maintaining the status quo and seemed rooted in common sense. The majority of the users of the spaces I studied were aware that their interactions were in the public domain and so were deliberately private and cautious about what they shared. As such, it seemed unlikely that any participants could come to serious harm just because an increased number of people viewed their posts. However, the approval I had received from the research ethics board at my institution was based on the principle that I would preserve my participants' privacy and anonymize their data. Although I had undertaken all the measures outlined within my research proposal, participant privacy had still been jeopardised. Therefore, the ethical principles of the research had been compromised. Particularly important was the fact that when I entered the field I had agreed with participants that I would preserve their privacy. Indeed, this was a condition of participation and had been included in all the information about the project. Jeopardising participant privacy, therefore, seemed like a fundamental betrayal of trust.

The second option also appeared highly problematic. Removing all possible public record of my engagement in the online social spaces seemed to go against the nature of open, rigorous research that could be externally validated. Although I had saved digital copies of my interactions (alongside interviews and other textual data I had scraped from the site), completely deleting my profile would permanently remove all records of my time in the field, and so public verification would be problematic. However, and perhaps more importantly, deleting my profile and all the associated posts and activity could not take place within a vacuum. It would involve tampering with other people's posts, leaving a hole in the interactions and discussions we had. This would render large amounts of online material redundant or nonsensical.

This option would essentially involve rewriting the history of the forum. Community identity is, at least in part, defined by its history. Changing the historical records of the forum could be seen as changing the nature of the digital community that populated it. As a participant observer, I had been a community member as well as a researcher, and I felt uncomfortable reducing all my engagement to data generation. To do so seemed to emphasise the instrumental nature of the research process, where a researcher simply enters a community, mines it for data and leaves. This would go against the principles of ethnography, where value is placed on the co-construction of knowledge between the researcher, as the instrument of research, and participants (DeWalt & DeWalt, 2002).

Given that neither scenario appeared satisfactory, I turned to a group of participants to talk through the possible options. After discussing the issues as outlined above, they all agreed that preserving their anonymity was the preferable option. They pointed out that *current* conversations dominated the forum and that archives of historical interactions were rarely accessed. They also suggested, with perhaps painful clarity, that the online social space was a busy community so that, although my participation was important to me, it did not have a particularly significant effect on the majority of community members. As such, concerns over community identity and rewriting history in instrumentalist terms were unfounded.

After this discussion with participants, I deleted my identity in the forum immediately and so removed the danger to participant privacy and anonymity that I had created by situating myself within the field in a traceable way.

CONCLUSION AND LESSONS LEARNED

In this case study I have attempted to highlight the complex connections and tensions between methodological and ethical decision-making in the messy realities of social research and the traceable nature of digital contexts. These connections and tensions present a challenge for anyone undertaking ethnographic research in digital contexts, or adopting any methodological approach that involves the researcher situating him or herself within an online field site. As such, I hope that by highlighting these challenges, the case study will prove beneficial to those working within a qualitative paradigm in digital contexts and help other researchers in their decision making process.

In retrospect, the ethical issues that emerged from this project were rooted in a faulty decision making process that overemphasised particular aspects of my methodological approach without taking into account the traceable nature of digital contexts. While the aim of being overt, open, and honest was important, this could have been achieved in other ways that would not have left searchable digital traces. The most obvious solution would have been to use a named account to introduce myself and remind users of my presence and identity at fixed points (say once a month) throughout the year-long fieldwork period. These posts could then be deleted after a few days and an anonymous researcher account used for active engagement. This would have achieved the aim of ensuring that all community members, both active and more passive users, were aware of my identity and the project in an ongoing manner, and that new community members were informed throughout the fieldwork period. Once the fieldwork had ended, the only historic record would be an anonymous researcher account, which would be difficult to trace.

In many ways situating oneself within the field has always been a difficult and draining task for ethnographers, but moving the field into the digital domain can present fresh challenges. Maintaining awareness of the complex range of methodological and ethical decisions involved in rigorous research in such contexts and managing tensions that emerge are key ethical challenges for anyone involved in qualitative online research.

REFERENCES

Bassett, E. H., & O'Riordan, K. (2002). Ethics of internet research: Contesting the human subjects research model. *Ethics and Information Technology, 4*(1), 233–247.

Beaulieu, A., & Estalella, A. (2011). Rethinking research ethics for mediated settings. *Information, Communication & Society, 15*(1), 23–42.

BERA (British Educational Research Association). (2011). *Ethical guidelines for educational research.* London: BERA.

Boellstorff, T. (2012). Rethinking digital anthropology. In H. Horst & D. Miller (Eds.), *Digital anthropology* (pp. 39–60). London: Berg.

British Psychological Society. (2009). *Code of ethics and conduct.* Leicester: British Psychological Society.

Dawson, P. (2014). Our anonymous online research participants are not always anonymous: Is this a problem? *British Journal of Educational Technology, 45*(3), 428–437.

DeWalt, K., & DeWalt, B. (2002). *Participant observation: A guide for fieldworkers*. Oxford: AltaMira Press.

Ess, C., & AoIR Ethics Working Committee. (2002, November 27). *Ethical decision-making and Internet research: Recommendations from the AoIR ethics working committee*. Approved by AoIR. Retrieved from http://aoir.org/reports/ethics.pdf

Hine, C. (2008). Virtual ethnography: modes, varieties, affordances. In N. Fielding, R. Lee, & G. Blank (Eds.), *The Sage handbook of online research methods* (pp. 257–270). London: Sage.

Hine, C. (2015). *Ethnography for the Internet: Embedded, embodied and everyday*. London: Bloomsbury.

Horst, H., & Miller, D. (2012). *Digital anthropology*. London: Berg.

Jones, C. (2011). *Ethical issues in online research, British Educational Research Association on-line resource*. Retrieved from https://www.bera.ac.uk/wp-content/uploads/2014/03/Ethical-issues-in-on-line-research.pdf

King, S. A. (1996). Researching internet communities: Proposed ethical guidelines for the reporting of results. *The Information Society, 12*(2), 119–128.

Markham, A., & Buchanan, E. (2012). Ethical decision-making and Internet research. *Recommendations from the AoIR Ethics Working Committee (Version 2.0)*. Retrieved from http://aoir.org/reports/ethics2.pdf

Mills, D., & Morton, M. (2013). *Ethnography in education*. London: Sage.

Orgad, S. (2005). From online to offline and back. In C. Hine (Ed.), *Virtual methods: Issues in social research on the Internet* (pp. 51–66). Oxford: Berg.

Robson, J. (2016). Engagement in structured social space: An investigation of teachers' online peer-to-peer interaction. *Learning, Media and Technology, 41*(1), 119–139.

Townsend, L., & Wallace, C. (2016). *Social media research: A guide to ethics*. Retrieved from http://www.dotrural.ac.uk/socialmediaresearchethics.pdf

Walford, G. (2008). *How to do educational ethnography*. London: Tufnell Press.

Zimmer, M. (2010). "But the data is already public": On ethics of research in Facebook. *Ethics and Information Technology, 12*, 313–325.

CHAPTER FOURTEEN

The Social Age of "It's not a Private Problem"

Case Study of Ethical and Privacy Concerns in a Digital Ethnography of South Asian Blogs against Intimate Partner Violence

ISHANI MUKHERJEE

INTRODUCTION

Narrative media provide fertile ground for researchers to conduct digital ethnographies of rich (and sometimes sensitive and protected) textual data within interactive social spaces that may be strictly moderated, informally filtered or largely public. In a "social age" (Azua, 2009) where cultural convergence happens alongside technological convergence within digital communication spaces (Jenkins, 2006), the blogosphere emerges as one such informal network of information and interactions. Blogs operate within this "space of flows," as a form of knowledge (Jenkins, 2006). Digital "produsers" (Bruns & Jacobs, 2006) can control/negotiate media content concurrently, additionally obscuring boundaries between users and producers in a post-democratic, shared social context where ethical boundaries and privacy concerns are constantly being challenged and reimagined.

Within the last decade, blogs have become critical and cultural sites of struggle where technologies of body, mind, society, sexuality, politics, race, and oppression come together in uneasy intersections to complicate the embodied-disembodied schism. While this problematic makes for important social scientific investigation, what it also creates are pedagogical interstices that need to be filled and ethical questions that need to be answered. This chapter will briefly explore certain ethical issues that arose in a study, which had been conducted in the past (Mukherjee, 2013), yet remains relevant to the current and future study of blogs and digital ethics. In particular, by revisiting this case study where ethno-cultural community blogs were explored as social spaces in which groups of concerned, yet unrelated participants challenged patriarchal discourses of intimate partner violence (IPV) against immigrant women within the South Asian American diaspora, this chapter will shed light on various ethical challenges and opportunities that the internet offers as a continuous social site and growing data mine for technocultural research. The case study is cross-disciplinary in scope and seeks to further intersectional research in new media, gender, immigration, and critical ethno-cultural studies. The sample comprising South Asian community blogs were mostly general interest blogs authored by multiple bloggers of South Asian heritage and discussed all issues pertaining to this ethnic group, although the emphasis was on advocating cultural, transnational, and social justice concerns within the South Asian American diaspora (special emphasis on the Indian, Pakistani, and Bangladeshi minority communities). It should however be noted that the study sample represents a microcosm of the larger South Asian blogosphere that covers topics ranging from news, current events, politics, and economic issues to society, welfare, culture, and entertainment concerning South Asians in both home and host nations. Moreover, the case study does not directly involve human subject research in the traditional sense but includes published testimonies from participants within digital social spaces, which may act as identity markers and repositories of information that are by nature private, sensitive, and controversial.

BLOGS AS SOCIAL DATA MINES

Blogs as narrative, social spaces have been and continue to be significant mines of rich textual data. Rhetorical analyses of blogs have been conducted to explore performative capabilities of digital storytelling genres (Lindemann, 2005). Digital ethnographers have mined social data and conducted in-depth interviews of bloggers to study how community, interpersonal dynamics, and cultural identities are negotiated through virtual participation (Hiller & Franz, 2004). A "sense of community" has been identified in blog interactions that work toward creating consensus (Blanchard, 2004). Participants' expectations of online privacy have been distorted, essentially by privatizing public information (via personal, reflective blogs) and making public what has normatively and systemically been rendered private (via community blog sites) (Gregg, 2006; Sink, 2006).

In some cases, political A-list and masculinist blogs have been found to be misogynistic, homophobic and/or ethno-racially bigoted (Adam, 2002; Saresma, n.d.; Wilson, 2005). A-list blogs are a popular and respected category of public, filter blogs (usually among the top 100 non-personal blogs, determined by percentage of readership) that mostly focus on discussions of politics, technology, and/or current events and wield considerable impact on the blogosphere and traditional media (Tremayne, 2007). However, being mostly written and moderated by adult males, A-list or filter blogs often exclude women's and youth perspectives (Herring et al., 2004). Masculinist blogs, a sub-genre of social-gender blogs, are usually moderated by "advocates of traditional gender order, the male rights activists (MRAs) or the masculinists, [and] promote repressive ideas of misogynist, anti-feminist, homophobic and racist ideologies in internet discussion fora and blogs," often using heteronormatively oppressive rhetoric that marginalizes members of "any other gender, sexuality, or ethnic background" (Saresma, n.d., p. 1). At the same time, gender-neutral, gender-empowering, and/or ethno-culturally invested blogs have gained considerable presence in the socio-cultural blogosphere, with related feminist, queer, and critical race discourses supporting such pedagogies (Gregg, 2006; Mukherjee, 2015; Sink, 2006). Moreover, as conscientious acts of political mobilization, civic journalism, opinion leadership, grassroots activism, and/or public intellectualism, it is clear that blogging is accepted and problematized as a socially rife form of digital journaling that gives scholars hope that new media research needs not to be confined to A-list blogs to warrant merit (Papacharissi, 2009).

Identity Performance and Participation: Ethical Challenges for Cultural Blog Research

Digital socialization provides a performance space for participants to negotiate their identities in complex ways and ultimately seek reassurance that their participatory "self" is accepted by others within the online community (Papacharissi, 2002; Turkle, 1997). However, the volatility with which these identities and their associated textual-visual markers are reverse-chronologically presented, given the asynchronous structure of blogging and its (almost) uninhibited accessibility, grants its users the stage to perform their "struggle over identities – interpersonal, social, moral, aesthetic – in uncertain and unstable conditions by making that struggle concrete and accessible" (Langellier & Peterson, 2004, p. 187). This poses an ethical dilemma for digital ethnographers who do want to capture contesting voices and identity disclosures exactly as they are performed online. Yet, they fear doing that exclusively may compromise the objective distance of ethnographers lurking in digital field sites, or even threaten the confidentiality of digital participants and their posts, being data that under present ethical guidelines (as specified by US institutional review boards) do not necessarily have to be sampled using informed consent procedures (IRB, 2015; Markham, 2006).

Reworking Public-private Schisms: Digital Ethnography of Ethno-cultural Blogs

By making the "public personal, as well as the personal public" (Mortensen, 2004, p. 4), it is true that research ethics, involving ethnographic data that are considered culturally relevant on one digital platform, may be rendered ethically ambiguous on another (Gregg, 2006; Sink, 2006). This adaptive function of blogging that contests or reworks dominant hierarchies of public and/or private online interactions helps my research purpose as a digital ethnographer, who is seeking flexibility in methodology and textual fieldwork. Digital ethnography creates situations for ICT researchers to shape ethical considerations along the lines of the methods they use, in particular when their data are textual identity markers for at-risk and/or socio-culturally disenfranchised communities, who have found a polyphonous forum online (boyd, 2005; Gajjala, 2006). Yet, the lack of consistency in ethical guidelines for conducting un-obtrusive data collection on the web makes it difficult for social media researchers to decide whether or not to anonymize blogger identities.

"IT'S NOT A PRIVATE PROBLEM": CASE STUDY ANALYSIS OF SOUTH ASIAN BLOGS AGAINST IPV

This case study is revisiting a previously conducted digital ethnography of ten, purposively sampled South Asian community blogs that, among other social justice concerns, were found to dedicate much of their multi-moderated spaces to the discussion of heterosexual IPV against immigrant South Asian women in the United States. Grounded in postcolonial, gender theories of intersectionality (Crenshaw, 1994; Knudsen, 2006) and social-psychological paradigms of consciousness-raising and action-contemplation (Brown, 1997), the data revealed that blogging about the context, scope and incidence of IPV within South Asian community blogs has made them comparatively safe public spaces for digital natives from this ethnic diaspora to voice their *private* stories of partner abuse, victim blaming, gendered shame, and battered survival.

This study assumed that the sampled blogs had disclosed "internal beliefs, emotions, positions, and opinions" (Mukherjee, 2013, p. 7) of bloggers who had digitized and made publicly available sensitive, powerful, and yet, potentially problematic information, which, if identified (unlikely though it is) by technologically-adept male perpetrators, may have led to more chances of IPV against female survivors/victims of battery. Given the invitational and disclosive nature of the blog fora, it was also assumed that certain bloggers would have self-identified themselves as battered South Asian females living in the US as legally dependent migrants and shared their experiences of IPV in hopes of receiving helpful intervention or information from other blog participants. In the process of data collection and thematic coding it was found that the usernames, accounts, and identities of bloggers, if provided, were not always digitally verifiable given the limitations of the study, and neither was it the investigative intention. A big reason that there was no practical way of confirming if the information provided in the blog posts was indeed factual or the blogger identities were genuine, can be attributed to the controversial and sensitive nature of the research topic. The goal of this study, as is common in qualitative research, was to take an in-depth look at the narrative content of the blogs that created communal empathy and advocacy against gendered violence in ethnic communities, rather than authenticating individual blogger identities.

Moreover, as an observational researcher, I came across many instances of posts where self-identified South Asian females openly discussed their abusive experiences, often in great detail, and also shared important resources with other bloggers to campaign against intimate partner violence. This prompted certain ethical decisions about presenting exemplars in such a way that I could maintain research validity, while still prioritizing the privacy of the vulnerable ethnic group who were blogging about extremely sensitive issues involving domestic violence, misogyny, and ethnic marginalization. The first ethical assumption made was that bloggers and commentators, in particular self-identified survivors/victims of domestic abuse, had provided accurate textual descriptions about their disturbing and/or violent experiences, which otherwise would be difficult to share in their offline socio-cultural spaces, if at all accessible. Second, research ethics demanded that sampled posts (particularly, those containing a good amount of identifiable information) would be reported after being sufficiently paraphrased. Following is an example of a partial, reworded and anonymized blog post that exemplifies the conscious middle ground that was sought to balance contextual validity and user anonymity, while still alluding to the poster's relationship with the South Asian immigrant community.

> I still get shivers down my spine while thinking about it. While I was still pursuing my higher education, my partner of many years had sexually molested me. I remember being ashamed of what had happened and very, very upset. Till this day I try not to think about that horrible experience, but it often comes back to me. It was only recently that I felt liberated when I shared my experiences at the workshop dedicated to adult gender violence in the Sikh immigrant community. I felt very close to my god and my religion when I heard others like me talk about their experiences of abuse and received compassion from others in return. (*The Gurdwara Galleria*, 2012)[1]

The desire for personal, subjective investment in the field site, and the empirically driven quest for research objectivity is often an ethical quandary for scholars of qualitative online research (Hookway, 2008). As an ethically-conscientious digital ethnographer, I collected blog data that were already published and archived in the blogs, as an unobtrusive lurker who did not directly contribute to blog threads, but spent a lot of time in immersive interpretations of "thick" digital artifacts (Geertz, 1973). I am also aware that current scholarship on lurking or non-participant observation as a form of digital ethnography debates whether or not researchers should obtain informed consent from their sample of online participants (Hine, 2008; Markham, 2006; Scharf, 1999). Yet for digital communities that have created publicly accessible forums for civic participation, the desire to increase web traffic and gain prominence comes from the expectation that browsers would actually *lurk* within those spaces for reading, observation, inspiration, and/or research (Hine, 2008; Hookway, 2008; Walther, 2002). Decisions such as these have created, and will continue to pose ethical and privacy challenges for new media researchers and participants alike in this social age of fluid and ambiguous interactions.

Further steps were taken to ensure the optimal privacy of my data and participants. Only those South Asian community blogs that were open to public access and non-password protected were selected for the study sample. For maintaining user confidentiality, I refrained from using screen names associated with blog-generated posts, while also altering the names of sampled blogs and their URLs. Online ethnographers agree that the potential for data obtained from the web to be identified using internet search engines is a compelling ethical challenge for conducting research in our digitally-saturated social age (Hine, 2008; Hookway, 2008; Markham, 2006). To ensure a greater degree of anonymity, I paraphrased textual selections from blogs to make certain that the sampled posts were not traceable using web search engines such as Google, while also taking care to not obscure their intended meanings. Moreover, data collection and thematic coding began after the ethical review board approved the study.

As additional ethical safeguards, I decided not to replicate embedded hyperlinks to external digital sites that were present as a part of several sampled blog posts (for e.g., a post addressed to victims of abuse about seeking support may have provided the hyperlink to the website of an IPV intervention service, thereby increasing the chances of potentially disclosing location and/or identity). Below is an example of a paraphrased blog comment that originally had an embedded hyperlink to a domestic violence safe house's website in North America, but had to be removed to safeguard both blogger and commentator anonymity.

> I believe that the perfect response to your query is communication. As you yourself mentioned, reaching out to related resources and associated groups is most important at the present time (hyperlink to safe house provided). Via this channel more awareness on the issue of domestic violence can be created and spread. I know you are doing a wonderful thing by encouraging these interactions and I believe that a great deal of value will be added though this blog discussion. (*Desis Against Domination*, 2008)[2]

I do realize that networked digital resources such as links to online/offline IPV support services can be very important for understanding the overall content and context of the blog threads, but over time can also lose relevance, be removed by the blogger, be rendered nonfunctional, or worse, become an underlying risk to a vulnerable participant's safety within the blog community, all of which were reasons enough to discount them.

Whatever be the ethical allowances afforded to us as researchers in a social age, which indeed promotes the polysemous mantra that "it's not a private problem" anymore, it is still evident that advocating for unfairly silenced subjects to become publicly mobilized, a lot of pedagogical attention should be paid to how we negotiate privacy issues, the ethical utilization of digital data and copyright concerns. Apprehensions regarding what constitutes private/personal and public/accessible information on social media, and whether digital ethnographers are ethically obligated to get both institutional and participant approval for sampling and reporting textual data from otherwise open, multi-moderated communal blogs are some challenges I encountered throughout the field work and data analyses phases.

CURRENT AND FUTURE CHALLENGES OF BLOG RESEARCH ETHICS

Privacy protection of digital subjects, accurate use of online data and copyright mandates in internet research have raised important ethical questions, including what should be considered public and/or private knowledge, particularly when their boundaries are becoming increasingly distorted. Should social media scholars studying blogs acquire consent from blog authors, moderators or hosting platforms (Blogger, Tumblr, etc.) to sample and quote their published narratives, specifically when the research data are of a sensitive nature? We have pedagogical claims that author/user consent should not be a primary ethical priority for researchers sampling blog data because of the public nature of communal blogs (Walther, 2002). On the other hand, it is argued that since the blogosphere is a widely accessible, public sphere for researchable information, there is more reason for internet scholars to treat data obtained from blogs as private information (Elgesem, 2002; Scharf, 1999). As a methodological compromise, this study adopts a "fair game–public domain" ethical location (Hookway, 2008, p. 105), assuming that blogs being the social and cultural currency of the digital public sphere should cater to the democratic and polyphonous demands of its online participants (boyd, 2005; Gregg, 2006). For a social age that is dominated by social networking, micro/blogging, and image-sharing, there should be an institutional easing of informed consent and privacy protocols to encourage our use of digital data as ethically-viable research practices. Also, when it comes to communal blogs that are not built to be singularly policed or user-filtered, blogging itself becomes a "public act of writing for an implicit audience," where one finds that "blogs that are interpreted by bloggers as 'private' are made 'friends only'. Thus, accessible blogs may be personal but they are not private" (Hookway, 2008, p. 105).

As this case study explains, communal ethno-cultural blogs could be explored as studies of our "selfhood being projected" (Matheson, 2009) through personal storytelling and as a place to challenge normative identification for at-risk migrant, minorities. In a technoculturally-saturated context, Facebook, Twitter, Instagram, Tumblr, Reddit, and personal/communal weblogs are seen as circular, disseminated, non-causal, and socially fluid platforms that are powerful enough to mobilize and initiate political change and collective awareness through postmodern channels of digital storytelling (boyd, 2005). However, it is because of the cyclical nature of digital storytelling that online ethnographic research involving sensitive data that may initially be retrieved from sample shifting, impulsive and often reverse-chronological units of analyses can still end with researchers reporting their findings in static and clinical arrangements. Internet researchers, like me, often face ethical uncertainty when they are unable to capture pertinent digital information because of the volatility and changeability of online information and identities; a methodological blockade that scholars have yet to overcome for addressing ethical shortcomings within several sub-areas of internet studies.

NOTES

1. *The Gurdwara Galleria* is an alias. The names of all the South Asian blogs sampled for this study have been anonymized because of privacy concerns.
2. *Desis Against Domination* is an alias. The names of all the South Asian blogs sampled for this study have been anonymized because of privacy concerns.

REFERENCES

Adam, A. (2002). Cyberstalking and internet pornography: Gender and the gaze. *Ethics and Information Technology, 4*(2), 133–142. doi:10.1023/A:1019967504762.

Azua, M. (2009). *The social factor: Innovate, ignite and win through mass collaboration and social networking*. Boston, MA: Pearson.

Blanchard, A. (2004). Blogs as virtual communities: Identifying a sense of community in the Julie/Julia project. In L. J. Gurak, S. Antonijevic, L. Johnson, C. Ratliff, & J. Reyman (Eds.), *Into the blogosphere: Rhetoric, community, and culture of weblogs*. University of Minnesota: UThink: Blogs at the University Libraries [weblog collection] Retrieved from http://blog.lib.umn.edu/blogosphere/blogs_as_virtual.html

boyd, d. (2005, January 8). Turmoil in blogland. *Salon*. Retrieved from http://www.salon.com/2005/01/08/livejournal/

Brown, J. (1997). Working toward freedom from violence: The process of change in battered women. *Violence Against Women, 3*(1), 5–26. doi:10.1177/1077801297003001002.

Bruns, A., & Jacobs, J. (Eds.). (2006). *Uses of blogs*. New York, NY: Peter Lang.

Crenshaw, K. W. (1994). Mapping the margins: Intersectionality, identity politics, and violence against women of color. In M. A. Fineman & R. Mykitiuk (Eds.), *The public nature of private violence* (pp. 93–118). New York, NY: Routledge.

Elgesem, D. (2002). What is special about the ethical issues in online research? *Ethics and Information Technology, 4*(3), 195–203. doi:10.1023/A:1021320510186.

Gajjala, R. (2006). Editorial: Consuming/producing/inhabiting South-Asian digital diasporas. *New Media & Society, 8*(2), 179–185. doi:10.1177/1461444806061941.

Geertz, C. (1973). *The interpretation of cultures: Selected essays*. New York, NY: Basic Books.

Gregg, M. (2006). Posting with passion: Blogs and the politics of gender. In A. Bruns & J. Jacobs (Eds.), *Uses of blogs* (pp. 151–160). New York, NY: Peter Lang.

Herring, S. C., Scheidt, L. A., Bonus, S. & Wright, E. (2004). Bridging the gap: A genre analysis *of weblogs*. Proceedings of the Thirty-seventh Hawaii International Conference on System Sciences (HICSS-37). Los Alamitos: IEEE Press. Retrieved from http://www.academia.edu/233580/Bridging_the_gap_A_genre_analysis_of_weblogs

Hiller, H. H., & Franz, T. M. (2004). New ties, old internet in diaspora. *New Media and Society, 6*(6), 731–752. doi:10.1177/146144804044327.

Hine, C. (2008). Virtual ethnography: Modes, varieties, affordances. In N. G. Fielding, R. M. Lee, & G. Blank (Eds.), *The SAGE handbook of online research methods* (pp. 257–270). Thousand Oaks, CA: Sage.

Hookway, N. (2008). "Entering the blogosphere": Some strategies for using blogs in social research. *Qualitative Research, 8*(1), 91–113. doi:10.1177/1468794107085298.

IRB. (2015). *Institutional review board* (IRB). Chicago, IL: University of Illinois at Chicago.

Jenkins, H. (2006). *Convergence culture: Where old and new media collide*. New York, NY: New York University Press.

Knudsen, S. V. (2006). Intersectionality: A theoretical inspiration in the analysis of minority cultures and identities in textbooks. In E. Bruillard, B. Aamotsbakken, S. V. Knudsen, & M. Horsley (Eds.), *Caught in the web or lost in the textbook?* (pp. 61–76). Utrecht: IARTEM.

Langellier, K. M., & Peterson, E. E. (2004). *Storytelling in daily life: Performing narrative*. Philadelphia, PA: Temple University Press.

Lindemann, K. (2005). Live(s) online: Narrative performance, presence and community in LiveJournal.com. *Text and Performance Quarterly, 25*(4), 354–372. doi:10.1080/10462930500362494.

Markham, A. (2006). Ethic as method, method as ethic: A case for reflexivity in qualitative ICT research. *Journal of Information Ethics, 15*(2), 37–54.

Matheson, D. (2009). What the blogger knows. In Z. Papacharissi (Ed.), *Journalism and citizenship: New agendas in communication* (pp. 151–165). New York, NY: Routledge.

Mortensen, T. E. (2004). Personal publication and public attention. In L. J. Gurak, S. Antonijevic, L. Johnson, C. Ratliff, & J. Reyman, (Eds.), *Into the blogosphere: Rhetoric, community, and culture of weblogs*. University of Minnesota: UThink: Blogs at the University Libraries [weblog collection]. Retrieved from https://web.archive.org/web/20150606015025/http://blog.lib.umn.edu/blogosphere/personal_publication.html

Mukherjee, I. (2013). *Blogs on domestic violence against immigrant South Asian women: A thematic analysis*. Retrieved from http://hdl.handle.net/10027/10067

Mukherjee, I. (2015). Digi-blogging gender violence: Intersecting ethnicity, race, migration and globalization in South Asian community blogs against IPV. *Ada: A Journal of Gender, New Media, and Technology, 8*. doi:10.7264/N33T9FHP.

Papacharissi, Z. (2002). The presentation of self in virtual life. *Journalism and Mass Communication Quarterly, 79*(3), 643–661.

Papacharissi, Z. (2009). The citizen is the message: Alternative modes of civic engagement. In Z. Papacharissi (Ed.), *Journalism and citizenship: New agendas in communication* (pp. 29–43). New York, NY: Routledge.

Saresma, T. (n.d.). Love as a repressive concept in masculinist blogs. Research project taken from *Populism as Movement and Rhetoric*, funded by the Academy of Finland (SA21000019101). Retrieved from http://www.inter-disciplinary.net/critical-issues/wp-content/uploads/2014/08/saresma_webpaper.pdf

Scharf, B. (1999). Beyond netiquette: The ethics of doing naturalistic discourse research on the Internet. In S. Jones (Ed.), *Doing Internet research: Critical Issues and Methods for Examining the Net* (pp. 243–256). London: Sage.

Sink, A. D. (2006). *Identity and community in the weblogs of Muslim women of Middle Eastern and North African descent living in the United States.* Gainesville, FL: University of Florida. Retrieved from http://etd.fcla.edu/UF/UFE0014380/sink_a.pdf

Tremayne, M. (2007). Introduction. In M. Tremayne (Ed.), *Blogging, citizenship, and the future of* media (pp. ix–xix). New York, NY: Routledge.

Turkle, S. (1997). *Life on the screen: Identity in the age of the Internet.* New York, NY: Simon and Schuster.

Walther, J. B. (2002). Research ethics in internet-enabled research: Human subjects issues and methodological myopia. *Ethics and Information Technology, 4*, 205–216. Retrieved from http://www.nyu.edu/projects/nissenbaum/ethics_wal_full.html

Wilson, T. (2005). Women in the blogosphere. *Off our Backs, 35*(5/6), 51–55. Retrieved from http://proxy.cc.uic.edu/docview/197137490?accountid=14552

CHAPTER FIFTEEN

Studying Closed Communities On-line

Digital Methods and Ethical Considerations beyond Informed Consent and Anonymity

YLVA HÅRD AF SEGERSTAD, DICK KASPEROWSKI,
CHRISTOPHER KULLENBERG AND CHRISTINE HOWES

INTRODUCTION

In 2014 researchers from Facebook and academia conducted a massive-scale experiment on emotional contagion through social networks (Kramer, Guillory, & Hancock, 2014). In the experiment the news feeds of nearly 700,000 Facebook users were manipulated to see whether positive or negative news affected their emotions. The study sparked an intense discussion of ethical guidelines and informed consent in the international research community. Many argued that it breached ethical guidelines by lacking informed consent (cf. Vitak, Shilton, & Ashktorab, 2016). However, another dimension of this episode concerns the limitations of what researchers are allowed to do as compared to other professionals. The core feature of the Facebook platform is to manipulate content using algorithms to optimize it for marketing purposes.[1] Thus, Facebook is allowed to do for *commercial* purposes what researchers are not allowed to do for *scientific* purposes.

As social media is tremendously rich in data, we argue that the question of ethics must be posed in close proximity to the methods and techniques used. Since social media platforms are constructed with the aim of collecting as much user data as possible, we suggest that foreseeable ethical difficulties can be managed by *reducing* the amount of data collected. The perspective of this chapter is that ethical assessments are realized in the application of methods, and that ethical considerations need to be integrated into the hands-on work of collecting, storing, and analyzing data.

This chapter explores how ethical principles can be used to inform and modify digital methods in order to conduct responsible internet research. Rather than abandoning the possibilities that rich data and digital methods offer in instances where informed consent is problematic, we instead discuss how digital tools can be used to achieve anonymization when studying online communities.

We use the case study of a vulnerable, closed Facebook group to illustrate when and how informed consent and anonymity can be achieved and how digitally generated research data urges us to rethink these notions and their relation to data quality. We make use of Jensen's distinction between *found data* – online material that can be found, such as images, texts, and other digital traces left by interacting users; and *made data* – data created by an active research intervention, such as surveys, interviews, and participatory field work (Jensen, 2012). This distinction is important for understanding the ethical implications inherent in various types of data.

The chapter is structured as follows: We begin with a presentation of our data, followed by a discussion of the relevant ethical principles. We, then, consider the ethical considerations taken in the methodological process of studying the closed community. The chapter ends with a discussion of informed consent and anonymization in relation to digital methods.

THE CASE: A CLOSED FACEBOOK GROUP

Our case study is a Facebook discussion group for a community of bereaved parents coping with the loss of a child. This group originates from a physical Swedish peer grief support association and is maintained and moderated by administrators from the association. The community has more than 1,400 members,[2] who produce between 10–40 posts and 100–300 comments per day. The closed status of the group means that only members who have been approved by the administrators are able to access it. Members of this community are peers: They share the experience of having lost a child. In most contemporary Western societies, the death of a child is a near-taboo subject which is so uncomfortable that it is often avoided in everyday encounters (Brotherson & Soderquist, 2002). Moreover, implicit norms require bereaved parents not to grieve for their dead child too openly, too intensely, or for too long. Bereaved parents' grief is thus stigmatized, limiting their opportunities to cope with it.

Social media offers new opportunities for getting in touch with peers in a community where they may talk about their dead children and share experiences and feelings. In a study exploring bereaved parents' use of social media as a resource for coping with the loss of a child, we have conducted surveys and interviews with members of the community. Results show that important functionalities of the group are its closed nature, the shared experiences, and the immediate and constant access to the community through digital and mobile technologies. Members are often in a vulnerable state and perceive the community as a safe haven in which they can share things that cannot be shared outside the group, without being "judged" by the norms of the majority culture. The closed status of the group is regarded as a prerequisite for the community to function (Hård af Segerstad & Kasperowski, 2015a).

When users sign up for a Facebook account, they comply with the conditions stated in Facebook's user agreement, i.e. that all content produced by users is owned by the platform provider and may be sold to third parties.[3] What this entails and the extent of Facebook's practice of monitoring and harvesting their interactions, is not always evident to the user (Zimmer & Proferes, 2014). The everyday interactions of the bereaved parents in the community are informed by high expectations of privacy (Zimmer & Proferes, 2014), which are, in practice, contradicted by Facebook's terms and conditions. Thus, research on this group highlights several ethical principles for responsible internet research.

ETHICAL PRINCIPLES IN RELATION TO STUDYING ON-LINE COMMUNITIES

In our case-study, made data (as in Hård af Segerstad & Kasperowski, 2015a) pose fewer ethical challenges than found data. These different types of data emphasize different ethical considerations and have different implications for the many ethical guidelines for internet research, which have been proposed and discussed on a more or less regular basis since the early 2000s (e.g. Ess & AoIR Ethics Working Committee, 2002; EU, 2015; Markham & Buchanan, 2012). These guidelines are usually formulated in general terms, with the recognition that *in practice* research ethics must be developed in context and cannot be applied universally (Markham & Buchanan, 2012). As Vitak et al. (2016) argue, "discussions of research ethics should be rooted in practice, if we are to have a constructive debate around how to update ethical principles for online research" (p. 10). Principles for internet research emphasize that "the greater the vulnerability" for the subject of research "the greater the obligation of the researcher to protect" (Markham & Buchanan, 2012, p. 4).

Moreover, since "digital information [...] involves individuals" the balance between "rights of subjects" and "social benefits" must be monitored carefully, with ethical considerations continuously addressed in a "deliberative process" during research (pp. 4–5).

In our study of bereaved parents on Facebook, we have undertaken a deliberative process with administrators and moderators of the community, discussing subjects' rights and potential social benefits at length. This has resulted in informed consent from the administrators, but also expectations regarding how the research will benefit the studied community. This highlights the requirement to manage expectations – an aspect of ethical concern which is not commonly addressed. In our study of bereaved parents, the expectation is that the research will produce knowledge that can be used to mitigate or rectify societal issues or inform political decision-making. We have also been engaged in ethical deliberation with colleagues in the international research community (Hård af Segerstad, 2013; Hård af Segerstad & Kasperowski, 2015b). Such ongoing dialog is essential for keeping up with methodological and technological developments in rapidly changing digital environments.

However, the vulnerability of a community in which individuals communicate and share highly sensitive content obliges the researcher to move beyond informed consent given by only administrators and moderators. The biomedical heritage of ethical guidelines is based on harm-reduction principles, where full informed consent is a gold standard, i.e. all participants are informed about the purpose of the study, participation is voluntary, and withdrawal is possible at any time. Following McKee and Porter (2009), we agree that informed consent from all subjects is desirable in cases where vulnerable individuals are under study.

It can be argued that members' expectations of a high degree of privacy, vital for the community to function, set a context for research in which informed consent is required (cf. Vitak et al., 2016). When it comes to data from interviews and surveys this is attainable, however, the issues are more complex when studying the interactional data and content generated by some 1,400 people. These data are produced by human subjects – not a faceless crowd, but vulnerable individuals. As Vitak et al. (2016) argue, the principle of "respect for persons" goes beyond the scope of informed consent and anonymity in the data collection process. Even if this principle is fulfilled, simply asking for consent may lead to unforeseen methodological and ethical consequences.

Vanderhoven, Schellens, Vlacke, and Raes (2014) argued that the need for written informed consent from the participants in their study of teenagers' Facebook profiles was waived, as "obtaining informed consents would have jeopardized the reliability of the study" because the "[t]eenagers could have changed their Facebook-profile [...] before observations took place." Although the researchers took care to make sure that the dataset remained anonymous – by encrypting the real names, merely substituting real names cannot guarantee anonymity (cf. Zimmer, 2010).

Similar issues arise with our data. Additionally, we face ethical problems during the period of data collection because the community is a vital resource for group members' coping strategies. Once the users are aware that they are involved as research subjects, they may adapt their behavior and lose trust in the supporting function of the group.

Access to data has traditionally depended on an interpersonal exchange between researchers and individuals giving their consent, however, such access now tends to go through large, private companies such as Google, Twitter, and Facebook. The members of the closed community on Facebook could be conceptualized as having already given consent in obtaining their Facebook accounts, through *institutional and policy rules of consent* (Beauchamp, 2011). However, for our purposes this is insufficient; we require *autonomous authorization* by every member of the community (Beauchamp, 2011; following McKee & Porter, 2009 a.o.), i.e. each user intentionally agreeing to something which they have adequate understanding of and being free of any internal or external pressures to do so.

Consequences of trying to obtain autonomous authorization (which may include members leaving the group when in need of support) must also be related to the demanding criteria of "full disclosure and complete understanding" as a gold standard of informed consent. These criteria are difficult to meet and it is therefore reasonable to explore if partial informed consent combined with carefully crafted digital methods for anonymization might be a viable route for responsible internet research.

Anonymization is always a trade-off between the comprehensiveness of anonymization and the integrity of the research quality. As discussed in Ohm (2010) one must consider the difficulties of fully protecting anonymized datasets from the possibility of re-identification of individuals. Aggressive suppression, i.e. deleting all direct identifiers (name, social security number, etc.) and indirect identifiers (other information which, when combined, may allow identification of an individual, e.g. year of birth, occupation, postcode, etc.), can render data almost useless for research since the independent variables are more or less removed. To generalize rather than to suppress identification might better balance research possibilities with anonymization. A third alternative is aggregation, which involves using statistics to summarize results, "coarsening" data by decreasing the granularity of personal information (e.g. only providing a person's county rather than their address) or detaching the utterance from the speaker. Yet another possibility is the use of "safe rooms" (cf. Watteler & Kinder-Kurlanda, 2015) in which archives are secured (physically or by using secure software environments). This way, only authorized researchers are allowed to access sensitive data, which in turn makes review of source data possible.

A STEP-BY-STEP DISCUSSION ON RESEARCH ETHICS IN PRACTICE

In this section we discuss how ethical issues must be addressed at all stages of the research process and how they can be re-thought from an integrative perspective.

In this way the often technical hands-on work can be connected back to the ethical issues and overall scope of the research process.

Step 1: Access to Data

A closed group on Facebook is only accessible to approved members, and can thus be regarded as a private, or semi-private, space. As researchers, however, we have to take into account how community members perceive of their privacy (cf. Zimmer & Proferes, 2014).

Closed communities devoted to highly sensitive and private topics, such as child loss, have previously been largely inaccessible to researchers. We have access to this community because one of the researchers is a member. Previous approaches by other researchers have been declined, due to the sensitive subject matter and the bereaved parents' fear of being judged by the norms of the majority culture. In Western societies, for example, a common conception is that the best way to cope with grief is to find closure and "let go" of the deceased (cf. Klass, Silverman, & Nickman, 1996). Many of the respondents in our case study report that they cannot grieve openly and fear that being subject to research would pathologize them (Hård af Segerstad & Kasperowski, 2015a). In our surveys and interviews, members welcomed our research, with some articulating hope that it would contribute to a better understanding of their stigmatized situation outside the closed community. They expressed trust in a researcher who is a peer, even providing administrator status. The association maintaining the group also officially endorses the research (minutes of the annual meeting of the grief support organization, 1 March 2015).

The main ethical problem here is the difficulty of grasping what access to data means in digital environments. As a trusted administrator of the Facebook group, the researcher has access to more information than most users are aware of, complicating the notion of informed consent while relying on a fragile trust-based agreement between community and researcher.

Step 2: Collecting Found Data

There are two main approaches to collecting data from social media platforms, with different ethical consequences. The first involves accessing the material from the perspective of the user interface, referred to as "browsing", "lurking" or "webnography". In this approach, most meta-data is removed by the graphical user interface, and only a limited amount of data can be saved and stored, for example, by creating screenshots, copy-pasting text or saving images. However, this limitation does not preclude the ethical considerations needed to access the personal profiles of users without consent.

The second approach uses another entry point for accessing data. Originally constructed as a way for software developers to create applications and services on top of social media platforms such as Facebook, Twitter, and Wikipedia, the *Application Programming Interface* (API) can be used to extract a large amount of machine-readable data (Batrinca & Treleaven, 2015). However, because this technology was made for programmers rather than researchers, the built-in design choices are based on capacity and cost-related problems rather than ethical standards. Thus, even though APIs are usually restricted to collecting publically available data (cf. Bessi et al., 2015), the very act of collecting data can be problematic, as researchers can build a database of people who subscribe to specific political content, discuss medical information, or belong to vulnerable groups. In this respect, Facebook is a particularly critical case, as they require people to provide "real names and information."[4] Although this policy is not always adhered to (Hern, 2015), the users cannot hide their identity without breaching the terms of service, and the publically available data therefore tend to be accurate.

A crucial problem here is that the default setting for most off-the-shelf software is to collect as much data as possible. This is tempting from a methodological perspective but can lead to ethical dilemmas. Unlike conventional survey methods, data from online environments have a real-life connection, which is difficult to disconnect from the study at hand. For example, as shown in Figure 1, the raw data from Facebook are structured around a unique fifteen-digit ID-number making every individual user traceable both across the Facebook platform and all related web sites and third-party services connected to Facebook. Moreover, the data have a very high resolution, beyond the knowledge of most users. Each post, comment and the like is precisely time-stamped and every image is preserved. In this way, the data are "more real" when retrieved from the API than when viewed by the users themselves.


```
{
"from": {
"name": "Jane Doe",
"id": "234678943234046"
},
"created_time": "2013-04-21T19:32:45+0000",
"message": "This is a Facebook comment.",
"id": "196544587141019_754236",
"user_likes": false,
"can_remove": false,
"like_count": 0
}
```


Figure 1. Data and meta-data from a Facebook comment, retrieved using the Facebook Graph API and stored as a json object.

Using ready-made software or developing your own programs makes it possible to collect hundreds of thousands of interactions with little effort. In the latter case it is possible to collect only the data needed for the research question as a way of minimizing the dangers of surplus data and to obfuscate the data in such ways as to render them less identifiable, by "suppressing identities" or "generalizing identities" (Ohm, 2010).

The *principle of data-minimization* suggests that one should only retrieve the data needed to pursue a specific research question. The benefit of this approach is that the ethical question of sensitive data becomes directly related to the aims and purpose of the study, making it easier to determine the relation between the collection of data and any possible consequences. For example, if the research question asks for the social structure of an online community, the study would need to collect data about user interactions (e.g. who talks to whom). As such studies can potentially reveal sensitive information about specific people, a judgement on whether to collect data or not can be made before operationalizing the research questions further.


```
{
"from": {
"name": "dd3785ad4561af3e97a773d3526469ce6f6028388",
"id": "0d6a50eb4f7b89d338f4a6b58364d26dd0db73e20684a8ebfd837d5e717aa43d"
},
"created_time": "2013-04-21",
"message": "This is a Facebook comment.",
"id": "92222e379b55e71d7427424c3097266b6b73eae19fc7530babaccf7f4ee634cb",
"user_likes": false,
"can_remove": false,
"like_count": 0
}
```


Figure 2. Anonymous Facebook comment. The real name and the identification numbers are replaced with cryptographic hashsums and the exact time stamp is removed (cf. Jones et al., 2013).

While complete anonymization of found data is close to impossible, minimizing the data that can be connected back to a real individual is a viable rule of thumb. There are several strategies for achieving partial "anonymization" of data using encryption technologies that replace identifying information with cryptographic signatures, thus preserving data consistency (e.g. Vanderhoven et al., 2014). In Figure 2, only the content of the Facebook comment is left intact and the timestamp is restricted to the date. The identifying data are replaced with cryptographic hashsums, which preserves data integrity – avoiding duplicate data and preserving the possibility of retrieving what different users say. Even though it is still theoretically possible to reconstruct the source data using only the textual content of a post, this would require direct access to the Facebook database or collection of the same data again.

Step 3: Analyzing Data

When analyzing the collected material, the data minimization strategy outlined above ideally avoids unintentional re-identification of individual users (Vitak et al., 2016; Zimmer, 2010). This is easier to achieve when studying aggregated phenomena, such as frequency of posts, time of day when posts are written, or quantitative patterns of interactions (likes, comments, natural language processing of text corpora), where only the precise units of analysis are extracted from the collected data. But in cases where individual users are the subject of in-depth analysis, the anonymization process is crucial, unless informed consent from each individual has been obtained.

The contradiction between anonymity and analytical clarity (c.f. Ohm, 2010) must be handled with special attention to patterns which can be used to re-identify individuals. For example, there are usually external variables that structure the analysis of natural language in Facebook posts and comments. The analysis might explore at what time of day certain words are used, if there are gender or age differences, or patterns in the turn taking of conversations. Even if the identities of the users have been removed or obfuscated, there is a risk that a determined third party will be able to reconstruct the data and re-identify users. Patterns in metadata can be very revealing in context. For example, knowing what time of the day a person has a lunch break or wakes up might be enough to connect a pattern back to an individual user. This risk increases with small online communities, where participants share intimate experiences and know each other personally.

Step 4: Dissemination/Publication of Data

Once the analysis has been performed, the results and sometimes the source data will be inspected, disseminated, and made publically available. Current science policy is promoting the idea of maximal open data (EC, 2016; NSF, 2015). This has ethical implications for sensitive data, which need to be carefully thought through in each case. These emerging ethical problems should be considered at an earlier stage of the research process. Data extracted from digital environments are, to varying degrees, searchable and traceable once they are made public. Open platforms such as Twitter provide accurate means of searching through online content, whereas Facebook has a more restricted interface, with full-text search only possible within confined parameters. However, the extraction of data from the APIs makes it possible to create independent search functionalities that in turn enable further re-identification of data.

This means that publication of direct quotes must be avoided. In cases where quotes are used, individual permissions must be obtained making sure that research subjects are aware that their anonymity may be breached. Such permission is, however, impossible to attain if the data have already been anonymized in the collection and analysis stages. Another strategy is to use "composite narratives" (cf. Davidson & Letherby, 2014) where direct quotes are rewritten to avoid searchability. However, this strategy involves the modification of data, which necessarily reduces data quality.

Disseminating results to academic peers, especially when attempting to replicate a study or inspect the source data for verification (e.g. by anonymous reviewers), means that all prior steps in the research process are also put to the test in terms of research ethics. The structure of source data is always more sensitive than aggregate and published results. As there might be unforeseen methods of data analysis that lead to accidental re-identification of individuals, it is important to also consider any potential information that can be extracted from the data.

Further ethical issues arise in our case when research subjects explicitly ask us to use their real name and that of their deceased child in publications and disseminations of results. Researchers in death studies have argued that in some cases, anonymity may be disrespectful to both the bereaved and the deceased (cf. Walter, 1996).

The questions of anonymity and informed consent thus also need to be considered in light of what this entails for the research subjects both in the short and long term in relation to their evolving grief process. This affects issues of informed consent of individual members in the community and the expectations of both individuals and the grief association.

DISCUSSION

In this chapter we have discussed the notions of informed consent and anonymity in relation to studying a closed and vulnerable group on social media. We have attempted to tie together methodological considerations and the demand for high-quality data with possible strategies for minimizing harm through the principle of data minimization, where the collection of data is constrained by the specific research questions. We urge researchers to avoid relying on ready-made software solutions, which are often constructed for purposes other than research and thus lack "built-in" ethical considerations. We also argue that general ethical principles must be re-thought and adapted to very specific contexts that change quickly as technology develops.

When working with found data informed consent is difficult to attain and may disturb the community studied as well as affecting data reliability, as individuals alter their behavior due to the presence of researchers. Indeed, found data were never designed to be researched in the first place. When posting information on social media users do not generally consider the possibility of being systematically observed, studied, and disseminated in research outputs. Anonymizing and reducing the data to the bare minimum required to answer a specific research question is viable. However, such approaches need to be carefully monitored throughout the research process and take into account the consequences of dissemination and data sharing that may be required in peer review.

The alternative is to strictly adhere to informed consent in all instances of research. As a consequence, found data will be off-limits for academic and scholarly research, leaving such data (including all phenomena made up by such data) to marketing bureaus, intelligence agencies, and other entities not bound by research ethics. Such a limitation on research could be counter-productive in the long term, as it risks casting a shadow on online behaviors and phenomena that need to be analyzed with proper scientific methods. The challenges imposed upon us by the rapid digitalization of society cannot be met without the increased knowledge produced by responsible research.

NOTES

1. https://www.facebook.com/business/news/update-to-facebook-news-feed, accessed on April 21, 2016.
2. As of April 2016.
3. https://www.facebook.com/terms, accessed on April 26, 2016.
4. https://www.facebook.com/terms, accessed on April 25, 2016.

REFERENCES

Batrinca, B., & Treleaven, P. C. (2015). Social media analytics: A survey of techniques, tools and platforms. *AI & Society, 30*(1), 89–116. Beauchamp, T. L. (2011). Informed consent: Its history, meaning, and present challenges. *Cambridge Quarterly of Healthcare Ethics, 20*(4), 515–523.

Bessi, A., Mauro C., Davidescu, G. A., Scala, A., Caldarelli, G., & Quattrociocchi, W. (2015). Science vs conspiracy: Collective narratives in the age of misinformation. *PLoS One, 10*(2), e0118093.

Brotherson, S. E., & Soderquist, J. (2002). Coping with a child's death. *Journal of Family Psychotherapy, 13*(1–2), 53–86.

Davidson, D., & Letherby, G. (2014). Griefwork online: Perinatal loss, lifecourse disruption and online support. *Human Fertility, 17*(3), 214–217.

Ess, C., & AoIR Ethics Working Committee. (2002). *Ethical Decisionmaking and Internet Research. Approved by AoIR, November 27, 2002.* Retrieved from http://www.aoir.org/reports/ethics.pdf.

EU. (2015). *Opinion 4/2015: Towards a new digital ethics – Data, dignity and technology European Data Protection Supervisor.* Retrieved from https://secure.edps.europa.eu/EDPSWEB/webdav/site/mySite/shared/Documents/Consultation/Opinions/2015/15-09-11_Data_Ethics_EN.pdf

EC. (2016). *Open innovation, open science, open to the world – A vision for Europe.* Retrieved from the European Commission website http://bookshop.europa.eu/en/open-innovation-open-science-open-to-the-world-pbKI0416263/

Hård af Segerstad, Y. (2013). Trust and reliance: Ethical and methodological challenges of studying sensitive topics online. An insider's dilemma. *Paper in the Panel "(Research) Ethics at the Edge: Case-Studies and New Directions" at Internet Research 14.0: Resistance and Appropriation, the fourteenth International Conference of the Association of Internet Researchers.* Denver, CO: AoIR

Hård af Segerstad, Y., & Kasperowski, D. (2015a). A community for grieving: Affordances of social media for support of bereaved parents. *New Review of Hypermedia and Multimedia, 21*(1–2), 25–41.

Hård af Segerstad, Y., & Kasperowski, D. (2015b). Opportunities and challenges of studying closed communities online: digital methods and ethical considerations. *Paper in the Panel "Internet Research Ethics: New Contexts, New Challenges – New (Re)solutions?" Internet Research 16.0: Digital Imaginaries, The Sixteenth International Conference of the Association of Internet Researchers.* Phoenix, AZ: AoIR.

Hern, A. (2015, November 2). "Facebook relaxes 'real name' policy in face of protest." *The Guardian.* Retrieved from https://www.theguardian.com/technology/2015/nov/02/facebook-real-name-policy-protest

Jensen, K. B. (2012). Lost, found, and made. In Volkmer, I (Ed.). *The handbook of global media research* (pp. 433–450). Wiley-Blackwell, Oxford, UK. Retrieved from http://dx.doi.org/10.1002/9781118255278.ch25

Jones, J. J., Bond, R. M., Fariss, C. J., Settle, J. E., Kramer, A. D., Marlow, C., & Fowler J. H. (2013). Yahtzee: An anonymized group level matching procedure. *PLoS One, 8*(2), e55760.

Klass, D., Silverman, P. R., & Nickman, S. L. (Eds.). (1996). *Continuing bonds – New understandings of grief.* Philadelphia, PA: Taylor & Francis.

Kramer, A. D. I., Guillory, J. E., & Hancock, J. T. (2014). Experimental evidence of massive-scale emotional contagion through social networks. *PNAS: Proceedings of the National Academy of Sciences of the United States of America, 111*, 8788–8790. doi:10.1073/pnas.1320040111.

Markham, A., & Buchanan, E. (2012). *Ethical decision-making and Internet research: Recommendations from the AoIR Ethics Working Committee (Version 2.0).* Retrieved from www.aoir.org/reports/ethics2.pdf

McKee, H. A., & Porter, J. E. (2009). *The ethics of Internet research: A rhetorical, case-based process.* New York, NY: Peter Lang.

NSF. (2015). *Open Government Plan (3.5).* Retrieved from The National Science Foundation website www.nsf.gov/pubs/2015/nsf15094/nsf15094.pdf

Ohm, P. (2010). Broken promises of privacy: Responding to the surprising failure of anoymization. *UCLA Law Review, 57*, 1701–1777.

Vanderhoven, E., Schellens, E., Valcke, M., & Raes, A. (2014). How safe do teenagers behave on Facebook? An observational study. *PLoS One, 9*(8), 1–9.

Vitak, J., Shilton, K., & Ashktorab, Z. (2016). Beyond the Belmont principles: Ethical challenges, practices, and beliefs in the online data research community. In *Proceedings of the 19th ACM conference on computer-supported cooperative work & social computing (CSCW'16)* (pp. 941–953). New York, NY: ACM. doi=http://dx.doi.org/10.1145/2818048.2820078.

Walter, T. (1996). A new model of grief: Bereavement and biography. *Mortality, 1*(1), 7–25.

Watteler, O., & Kinder-Kurlanda, K. E. (2015). Anonymisierung und sicherer Umgang mit Forschungsdaten in der empirischen Sozialforschung. *Datenschutz Und Datensicherheit – DuD, 39*(8), 515–519.

Zimmer, M. (2010). "But the data is already public": On the ethics of research in Facebook. *Ethics and Information Technology, 12*(4), 313–325.

Zimmer, M., & Proferes, N. J. (2014). A topology of twitter research: Disciplines, methods, and ethics. *Aslib Journal of Information Management, 66*(3), 250–261.

CHAPTER SIXTEEN

An Ethical Inquiry INTO Youth Suicide Prevention Using Social Media Mining

AMAIA ESKISABEL-AZPIAZU, REBECA CEREZO-MENÉNDEZ, AND DANIEL GAYO-AVELLO

INTRODUCTION

In November 2011, Ashley Billasano, an 18-year-old student, died by suicide. It was one among the 39,518 suicides that took place in the U.S. that year (Kochanek, Murphy, & Xu, 2015) but her case was different. First, she live-tweeted during 6 hours about the abuses she had been suffering and how she was going to put an end to her life (Wallace, 2011). Furthermore – and even though her Twitter account had been shortly removed after her death – a piece of research was eventually conducted on her tweets (Gunn & Lester, 2015). Such a study is not unique; indeed, there is a huge interest in mining social media for clues about the feelings and thoughts of people to eventually prevent suicides (e.g., Abboute et al., 2014; Burnap, Colombo, & Scourfield, 2015; Desmet & Hoste, 2014; Li, Chau, Yip, & Wong, 2014; O'Dea et al., 2015; or Poulin et al., 2014).

This area is more than a fashionable research topic, and it rests on a number of strong facts: First, suicide is among the three leading causes of death among those aged 15–44, and it is a major cause of mortality during adolescence (WHO, 2012). In turn, those cohorts are frequent users of social media and, in some cases – such as those 18–19 – they comprise most of their user base (Duggan, 2015). Moreover, depression – which is among the most common comorbid factors among those who die by suicide (Henriksson et al., 1993) – is correlated with heavy usage of social media (Sidani et al., 2016). Finally, young people tend to consider their problems unique and unsolvable by professionals, but at the same time they share extremely personal information on social media platforms (boyd, 2007).

Still, it is not the goal which is in question but the means from both technological and deontological points of view. It may be laudable a tool to mine social media posts to detect young people who are being abused, bullied, or just feel alone, and whose lives are at peril; however, we cannot help but notice that such a tool would be stalking people and, thus, violating their privacy. Moreover, *quis custodiet ipsos custodes?* Which persons should be granted access to the outcomes of such monitoring tools? Those who are being monitored? Their friends and family? Their teachers? Just mental health professionals? Eventually, one of such tools was developed and freely offered to every Twitter user willing to track the mental health of any of their followees. The fallout after its deployment and eventual withdrawal should teach us a number of lessons.

THE SAMARITANS RADAR FIASCO

In 2014 the Samaritans – a charity working in the British Isles to help people enduring emotional distress or who are under suicidal risk – deployed the so-called Samaritans Radar (Samaritans, 2014a). At first sight, the underlying idea was simple: Any Twitter user could allow Samaritans Radar to monitor their friends' tweets and receive e-mail alerts as soon as they published anything of alarming nature. The rationale the charity offered for such an application was – and still is – sound: Firstly, those who are the most prone to die by suicide – i.e., young people – are also the most avid users of Twitter; and, secondly user generated content can provide clues about the suicidal ideations of their authors. Still, Samaritans Radar suffered of a number of issues that made it not simply unfit for its goal but actually harmful.

Firstly, the algorithm implemented to detect emotional distress in tweets was driven by a keyword list (Kleinman, 2014); that approach is too simplistic and prone to misclassify texts. Secondly, ethical and legal concerns about the processing of personal and intimate information were largely ignored based on the claims that tweets were actually public data and that the app was developed according to Twitter's terms of service (Samaritans, 2014b). Thirdly, Twitter users that were actively tracked by Samaritans Radar were not informed about that, and they were unable to provide or decline consent; that meant that vulnerable people could be potentially targeted not just by their friends, but also by trolls and bullies who were following them on Twitter (Brian, 2014). Because of these flaws, and after a certain amount of public pressure, The Samaritans suspended the application one week after the release and they eventually retired it.

The Samaritans Radar contrasts with the – at the moment of this writing, ongoing – Durkheim Project[1] whose aim seems identical: to detect suicide risk by mining personal data from social networks such as Facebook or Twitter. However, there are a number of important differences in the approach followed by the team behind that project.

To start with, they rely on machine learning rather than on a list of keywords. Moreover, the application requires the informed consent of the patients before accessing any of their social media data. Moreover, the users of the application are the clinicians attending them, and the data are stored and processed complying with the Health Insurance Portability and Accountability Act requirements. Finally, the researchers obtained approval from an Institutional Review Board to conduct and publish research on the topic (Poulin et al., 2014).

Thus, Samaritans Radar (SR) and Durkheim Project (DP) differ at a number of crucial features: 1) the concreteness of their goals – SR is ill-defined while DP aims to predict suicide risk; 2) the targeted population – SR acts like a dragnet while DP is targeted at individuals from a well-defined population; 3) the use (or not) of informed consent; 4) the users of the application – anyone in the case of SR vs. clinicians in the case of DP; 5) the legal and ethical considerations – Twitter's terms of service in the case of SR vs. HIPAA (Health Insurance Portability and Accountability Act) and IRB (Institutional Review Board) in the case of DP; and last but not least (6) their technological approach.

TECHNOLOGICAL AND DEONTOLOGICAL CONSIDERATIONS OF SOCIAL MEDIA BASED SUICIDE PREVENTION

Both aforementioned projects relied on content analysis to determine the suicide risk of social media users, and the same applies to the research briefly mentioned in the Introduction. Unfortunately, it is out of the scope of this chapter to provide a full review of current state-of-the-art, enough to say that both lexicons and machine learning approaches have been used, and that the accuracy of this kind of systems is at best 80% according to the most optimistic reports (O'Dea et al., 2015), but is probably much closer to 65% according to the rest of studies.

Such low accuracy should be a reason for ethical concerns: it means that 20–35% of potentially suicidal social media contents are to be misclassified or, in other words, when using a fully automated suicide watch system a substantial amount of alarms would be false – and, thus, a waste of resources – but much more importantly a relevant number of true alarms would go unnoticed – with mortal consequences.

Such a situation should deserve a deep debate among researchers about which accuracy is acceptable, and under which circumstances we could trust automated systems for suicide prevention. Still, such a debate is not taking place since most of the research is not really aimed to produce viable products – with the exception of the work by Poulin et al. (2014).

Besides, there is another matter that should raise eyebrows among researchers from non-STEM backgrounds: We are referring to the consent of users about their data being collected, analyzed, and finally being used to label them as suicidal or not.

Among the aforementioned research only the Durkheim Project (Poulin et al., 2014) requires informed consent before any social media data is collected. Most researchers simply do not mention informed consent, and a few explicitly stated their reasons for not asking for informed consent, for instance:

> [I]ndividual consent from users was not sought as the data was publically available and attempts to contact the Twitter account holder for research participation could be deemed coercive and may change user behaviour. (O'Dea et al., 2015)

Such a statement reveals that part of the researchers in the field of social media based suicide prevention would not frame themselves as performing research with human subjects but just data analysis. If that was actually the case researchers would be mainly worried about the terms of service of the social media platform – i.e., legal considerations – than about the ethical consideration the human subjects of their research deserve.[2]

Still, we should give those researchers the benefit of the doubt and assume that there can be reasons in which lack of informed consent could be an ethical research approach; indeed, there are three sensible scenarios under which informed consent could be easily obtained or even unnecessary.

The first one is the case of psychological autopsies (Isometsä, 2001) conducted on social media contents. Given that those kinds of studies are conducted only in cases of completed suicide, consent should be granted by those bereaved by suicide. In case of social media contents that would mean requiring consent from "friends" of the deceased in the different social media platforms which – taking into account the current knowledge in the field– could probably be granted to researchers. Of course, it could be that the research is to be conducted only on contents produced by the deceased. Given that there exists a long tradition of analyzing diaries of those dead by suicide (e.g., Chia, 1979; Chia, Chia, & Tai, 2008; Pennebaker & Stone, 2004; Lester, 2009; or Fernández-Cabana, García-Caballero, Alves-Pérez, García-García, & Mateos, 2013) it seems rather natural to perform the same kind of analysis in social media contents, and, indeed, there are some works in that line (e.g., Gunn & Lester, 2015; or Li et al., 2014).

Although it is early to suggest the best way to proceed in such a case, it seems reasonable to warrant the anonymity of the deceased subjects and, thus, to not disclose any excerpt from the social media contents but only aggregated information.

To allow reproducibility, the original data should be shared with other researchers and, thus, some kind of non-disclosure agreement should be signed between the institution the original researchers are affiliated with and those requiring access to the data.

The second scenario corresponds to user generated contents that cannot be linked to any identifiable individual. This implies that research with blogs, Facebook or Twitter data can prove extremely difficult or even impossible at all: Anyone with access to just a couple of posts could use them to pinpoint their original author. Of course, exploiting data from fully anonymous boards such as 4chan[3] may be a daunting task, and pseudonymity – such as that of Reddit[4] – could be much more convenient,[5] and it even allows researchers to track particular individuals by means of their pseudonyms. Needless to say, anonymizing strategies should still be applied before disclosing any data, even before attempting any analysis at all.

The third scenario corresponds to researchers that explicitly reject the idea of looking for informed consent, but we can distinguish here between two different sub-scenarios. In the first sub-scenario we would find researchers that consider their research simple data analysis and not a human subjects research; although such a point of view may be legal by agreeing with the terms of service and End User License Agreement we consider it of dubious ethicality. Certainly, if no identifying information is disclosed, and no harmful actions are performed on the users, such kind of approach could be considered ethical; however, we still disagree because inaction could be harmful for potentially suicidal users detected by an eventual prototype or negligent from the researcher point of view. That caveat, however, is rather moral than ethical, and researchers could avoid it by performing retrospective research, which is easy to conduct on historical social media data – indeed, such an approach was used by Poulin et al. (2014).

The second sub-scenario is actually related with morality; at least as described by Mishara and Weisstub (2005) in contraposition to the "relativistic" and "libertarian" points of view.[6] An extreme moralist position, however, suffers from two severe drawbacks: Firstly, we consider that privacy and anonymity should not be surrendered for the sake of principles, no matter how laudable they are. Secondly, the performance of automated systems means that a substantial amount of fatal inactions would occur, and that is difficult to reconcile with any façade of morality.

Thus, taking into account the current state-of-the-art, at the moment of this writing the most ethical approach to research the field should conform to the following criteria: 1) being retrospective research (the older the data the better) to avoid performing any action on actual at-risk individuals[7]; 2) using data that are *a priori* anonymous or have been fully anonymized; 3) not publicly disclosing any data excerpt, or at most aggregated information; and 4) using NDAs that can be fully enforced by the institution disclosing the data when sharing anonymized data with third parties.

CONCLUSION

We restate the idea that social media mining can be a useful tool for youth suicide prevention. The current body of research shows that it is technically feasible to apply machine learning methods to social media contents to assess suicidal risk. Still, accuracy is to this day far from perfect, and, therefore, a fully automated suicide watch system would be prone to misdiagnoses. Given that the rate of false negatives – with fatal consequences – would be known to every clinician using the system, its application would be ethically flawed *ab initio.*

However, failure to diagnose is not the only challenge faced by researchers working in suicide prevention by social media mining. Even if working with non-real-time user generated content – and, thus, avoiding the chance of harmful actions or inactions, and also the need for informed consent[8] – they would be violating the privacy of people at risk, in addition to disclosing personal information if sharing their datasets with third parties.

Because of that, researchers should be extremely careful when working with user generated contents that could potentially lead to the identification of individuals – e.g., Facebook, Twitter, or blogs – and they should rely on data from anonymous forums or apply strong anonymization techniques on the data. Finally, suicide related social media data should not be publicly disclosed and in case of being shared with third parties they should sign a non-disclosure agreement, and still, the data should be completely anonymized before being shared.

NOTES

1. http://durkheimproject.org/
2. It must be noted that this is not only a trait of social media based suicide research but pervasive to most social media studies: according to Hutton and Henderson (2015) just 5.5% of the papers on the field describe their consent procedures; thus, we may assume there were none, or the terms of service and EULA (End User License Agreement) were interpreted as individual consent.
3. http://www.4chan.org/
4. http://www.reddit.com/
5. See, for instance, the works by Kumar, Dredze, Coppersmith, and De Choudhury (2015), or De Choudhury, Kiciman, Dredze, Coppersmith, and Kumar (2016).
6. Briefly sketched, the libertarians consider that every individual has the right to decide about their death; while the relativistic consider that each self-inflicted death is different and, thus, some of them could be bad and others good; finally, the moralists consider that every life should

be saved by any mean, even at the cost of sacrificing privacy and anonymity. Needless to say, when dealing with suicide prevention – especially among young people – it is difficult to argue that some deaths may be meaningful, much less that someone that may have been abused, bullied, or is underage is exercising their "right to die." In other words, the relativistic and libertarian approaches do not fit with any sensible approach to young people suicide prevention.

7. Needless to say, the ultimate goal of retrospective research in this field should be to fine-tune a system to assess suicide risk of actual individuals in order to avoid fatal *dénouements*. In consequence, a retrospective approach would be just a temporary evasion of the real ethical issues, which could only be dispelled by proper usage of informed consent of the individuals at risk.
8. See Poulin et al. (2014) for a discussion on the needlessness of informed consent when performing retrospective research on social media data.

REFERENCES

Abboute, A., Boudjeriou, Y., Entringer, G., Azé, J., Bringay, S., & Poncelet, P. (2014). Mining Twitter for suicide prevention. In E. Métais, M. Roche, & M. Teisseire (Eds.), *Natural language processing and information systems* (pp. 250–253). Berlin: Springer.

boyd, d. (2007). Why youth (heart) social network sites: The role of networked publics in teenage social life. In D. Buckingham (Ed.), *MacArthur foundation series on digital learning–Youth, identity, and digital media volume* (pp. 119–142). Cambridge: MIT Press

Brian, M. (2014, November 4). Why Samaritans' app to spot depressed tweets does more harm than good. *Engadget*. Retrieved from https://www.engadget.com/2014/11/04/samaritans-radar-flaw/

Burnap, P., Colombo, W., & Scourfield, J. (2015, August). Machine classification and analysis of suicide-related communication on twitter. In *Proceedings of the 26th ACM conference on hypertext & social media* (pp. 75–84). ACM.

Chia, B. H. (1979). Suicide of the young in Singapore. *Annals of the Academy of Medicine, Singapore, 8*(3), 262–268.

Chia, B. H., Chia, A., & Tai, B. C. (2008). Suicide letters in Singapore. *Archives of Suicide Research, 12*(1), 74–81.

De Choudhury, M., Kiciman, E., Dredze, M., Coppersmith, G., & Kumar, M. (2016, May). Discovering shifts to suicidal ideation from mental health content in social media. In *Proceedings of the 2016 CHI conference on human factors in computing systems* (pp. 2098–2110). ACM.

Desmet, B., & Hoste, V. (2014). Recognising suicidal messages in Dutch social media. In *9th international conference on language resources and evaluation (LREC)* (pp. 830–835). Reykjavik: European Language Resources Association (ELRA).

Duggan, M. (2015, August 19). *Mobile messaging and social media 2015*. Pew Research Center. Retrieved from http://www.pewinternet.org/2015/08/19/mobile-messaging-and-social-media-2015/

Fernández-Cabana, M., García-Caballero, A., Alves-Pérez, M. T., García-García, M. J., & Mateos, R. (2013). Suicidal traits in Marilyn Monroe's fragments. *Crisis*.

Gunn, J. F., & Lester, D. (2015). Twitter postings and suicide: An analysis of the postings of a fatal suicide in the 24 hours prior to death. *Suicidologi, 17*(3), 28–30.

Henriksson, M. M., Aro, H. M., Marttunen, M. J., Heikkinen, M. E., Isometsa, E. T., Kuoppasalmi, K. E. E. A., & Lonnqvist, J. K. (1993). Mental disorders and comorbidity in suicide. *American Journal of Psychiatry, 150*, 935–935.

Hutton, L., & Henderson, T. (2015, May). "I didn't sign up for this!": Informed consent in social network research. In *Proceedings of the 9th international AAAI conference on web and social media (ICWSM)*.

Isometsä, E. T. (2001). Psychological autopsy studies – A review. *European Psychiatry, 16*(7), 379–385.

Kleinman, Z. (2014, October 29). Samaritans app monitors Twitter feeds for suicide warnings. *BBC News*. Retrieved from http://www.bbc.com/news/technology-29801214

Kochanek, K. D., Murphy, S. L., & Xu, J. (2015). Deaths: Final Data for 2011. National vital statistics reports: From the centers for disease control and prevention, national center for health statistics. *National Vital Statistics System, 63*(3), 1–120.

Kumar, M., Dredze, M., Coppersmith, G., & De Choudhury, M. (2015, August). Detecting changes in suicide content manifested in social media following celebrity suicides. In *Proceedings of the 26th ACM conference on hypertext & social media* (pp. 85–94). ACM.

Lester, D. (2009). Learning about suicide from the diary of Cesare Pavese. *Crisis, 30*(4), 222–224.

Li, T. M., Chau, M., Yip, P. S., & Wong, P. W. (2014). Temporal and computerized psycholinguistic analysis of the blog of a Chinese adolescent suicide. *Crisis, 35*(3), 168–175.

Mishara, B. L., & Weisstub, D. N. (2005). Ethical and legal issues in suicide research. *International Journal of Law and Psychiatry, 28*(1), 23–41.

O'Dea, B., Wan, S., Batterham, P. J., Calear, A. L., Paris, C., & Christensen, H. (2015). Detecting suicidality on Twitter. *Internet Interventions, 2*(2), 183–188.

Pennebaker, J. W., & Stone, L. D. (2004). What was she trying to say? A linguistic analysis of Katie's diaries. In D. Lester (Ed.), *Katie's diary: Unlocking the mystery of a suicide*. New York, NY: Routledge.

Poulin, C., Shiner, B., Thompson, P., Vepstas, L., Young-Xu, Y., Goertzel, B., … McAllister, T. (2014). Predicting the risk of suicide by analyzing the text of clinical notes. *PloS One, 9*(1), e85733.

Samaritans, The. (2014a, October 29). Samaritans Launches Twitter App to Help Identify Vulnerable People. *Samaritans.org*. Retrieved from http://www.samaritans.org/news/samaritans-launches-twitter-app-help-identify-vulnerable-people

Samaritans, The. (2014b). Samaritans Radar updates – 4 November. *Samaritans.org*. Retrieved from http://www.samaritans.org/how-we-can-help-you/supporting-someone-online/samaritans-radar#4nov

Sidani, J. E., Shensa, A., Radovic, A., Miller, E., Colditz, J. B., Hoffman, B. L., … Primack, B. A. (2016). Association between social media use and depression among US young adults. *Depression and Anxiety, 33*(4), 323…331.

Wallace, R. (2011, November 8). 18-Year-Old Girl Tweets 144 Times before Committing Sui*cide. My FOX Houston*. Retrieved from http://web.archive.org/web/20111111162941/http://www.myfoxhouston.com/dpp/news/local/111108-18-year-old-girl-tweets-144-times-before-committing-suicide

WHO. (2012). *Global Health Estimates*. Retrieved from http://apps.who.int/adolescent/second-decade/section3/page2/mortality.html

CHAPTER SEVENTEEN

Death, Affect and the Ethical Challenges of Outing a Griefsquatter

LISBETH KLASTRUP

INTRODUCTION

In this chapter, I share my experiences and reflections on the ethically most challenging case I have come across in my career as an internet and social media researcher: an imposter creating public R.I.P-pages for people he did not know, apparently in order to harvest as many likes as possible across a range of pages. At the core of this case one central question emerged: What are our moral and ethical obligations, both as researchers and as human beings, when our research gives us important insight into controversial and apparently unethical practices on social media? The question is further complicated if the given practice is not directly relevant to the research project. In my case, the given practice simply did not fit into the journal paper, which came out of my research. Nevertheless, I surmise that what I observed was a form of behavior which is sadly recurrent on social media platforms (notably Facebook at the time of writing), and which other social media researchers may encounter; and accordingly I believe that as researchers in this field we need to identify and carve out more spaces where it makes sense to discuss these practices, both from a research perspective and from an ethical perspective. I certainly was not able to find applicable advice in the existing ethical guidelines for internet research when I became involved in this case. Therefore at the end of the article, I will briefly reflect on how, from an ethical perspective, social media researchers could and should engage with cases similar to mine.

THE CASE

Research Context

Before I describe the case in more detail, a few words on the research context. This case played out in Denmark, one of the smaller Nordic countries. In Denmark, universities do not have ethical review boards, and at that point in time my university did not have a research ethics guideline outlined, nor formulated guidelines on how to deal with human subject research. Nor is there within my own main field of study (the Humanities) any general ethical guidelines outlined for Danish researchers. Rather, in Denmark norms of ethical behaviour are informally regulated between peers and through collegial mentoring. While it is my impression that many Danish internet researchers are aware of and act in accordance with the Association of Internet Research Ethical Guidelines, at the end of the day, judgement in relation to human subject research is still very much in the hands of the individual researcher.

The Beginning

In 2010, as part of my research into Danish user cultures and communities on Facebook, I began looking into Facebook groups and why they were created. As part of my research I studied a so-called "Rest in Peace" (R.I.P.) group, (this was before Facebook pages became popular), created in memory of a young woman who was brutally killed. Reading comments in her R.I.P. group, it struck me how several people explicitly stated that they did not know the girl, but felt sympathy for the family, elaborated on how deeply touched by the case they were, and so forth. I found this phenomenon – people using Facebook to "mourn" people they do not know, including the role the press played in this affective practice – so intriguing that I decided to look into it further when I had time at hand. A few years later, I began researching and looking for similar cases. At that point in time (around 2012–2013), Facebook pages had been introduced and the practice of creating openly accessible "Rest in Peace" (R.I.P)-pages for deceased friends and celebrities was starting to become more widespread. Looking for examples similar to the one I originally studied, I systematically searched through Facebook's own search engine for R.I.P.-pages created to memorialise young people whose death had attracted media attention; and which had therefore also attracted more followers than the average and less public R.I.P.-pages for friends and family only, which I had also come across. In my search for these R.I.P.-pages related to spectacular deaths, it struck me that there was a striking difference between the set-ups of these pages. Some contained a lot of information on the deceased, time and place of the funeral, and several photos of the person and memorial event. It clearly looked like a person with some form of personal knowledge of the deceased had created it. However, other R.I.P.-pages were strangely devoid of information, contained rather few photos, and held no information about the admin behind the pages. Furthermore, as I looked more into these anonymously created R.I.P.-pages, an unusual pattern of behavior emerged. After some time, the administrator would start to post highly irrelevant posts, encouraging the page followers to like and share pages for sports stars, and, not least, explicitly asking them to like a page who purported to be a community for people who "wished that cancer itself got cancer and died," but primarily consisted of posts by the admin sharing uncredited stories about cancer survivors lifted from other sites (and more recently also advertising fanpages for sportstars). It very much looked like the same person was behind several of these R.I.P.-pages because the set-up, the rhetorics, and use of the pages were very similar. Furthermore, it looked like the point of these pages was not just to help memorialise the deceased, but also "to hunt" for likes for a string of other pages. To this day, I do not know whether the purpose behind these R.I.P.-pages was commercial (selling likes or pages for money), or personal (someone for various reasons encouraging and harvesting as many likes as possible). However, at the point in time where the case made headlines in the news, at least, one person with professional expertise (a former Facebook employee) looking into the case stated that this clearly looked like a commercial scheme. That is, pages with many likes (like the given R.I.P.-pages or the pages for sport stars advertised on these) can be used to A) direct traffic to other pages (clearly the case here), and/or B) be sold to other administrators who can then "spam" the huge number of followers of these pages with ads for commercial products and services. Or C) they can be used by the current administrator to post "dark posts" with a commercial content which appear only in some people's feed for a short time until a certain reach is acquired. The admin when confronted by the Danish press in 2014 publicly claimed he did not earn money through his practices. However, in the same interview, he gave false information regarding the number of pages he ran, and claimed he had been hacked by "others" who used them in an unintentional way.

The Discovery

In May 2013, I noticed that on one of these strange R.I.P.-pages a close relation of the deceased repeatedly asked the page creator to contact them, as the family of the deceased were not happy about the page. The admin never responded. In the course of this story, this was then the first time I felt compelled to take action because the close relation was clearly upset about what was going on. With the knowledge I then had, I decided to discover the identity of the industrious page admin, so I could forward it to the given relative. Given that he – to a

Facebook-savy user – had left a very clear trail of links behind him, I was able to follow this trail, which led back to his own profile, revealing his apparent real-life identity. I then sent a private message to the relative who had tried to get in touch with the R.I.P-page administrator, providing the relative with his personal profile name. I hoped that in this way, they could talk to each other behind the scenes and settle things this way. As far as I recall, I also sent a FB-mail directly to the admin informing him of my actions (but I have not been able to retrieve it). At that point, I did not stop to ponder whether the admin – who had by way of his actions become an involuntary part of my research – had the right to be protected as a human subject. He clearly did not want to be identified and had it been a research project, I would have had to respect this wish for anonymity. As is, in the spur of the moment and out of the best intentions, I acted with my heart, not my brains, as I felt I had information which could perhaps be of help to the bereaved family. Following my intervention, nothing happened. The page remained on Facebook.

More time passed, but eventually I decided to pick up the study of R.I.P.-pages in the context of a symposium paper I had promised to deliver on the subject. I was, as stated, also interested in looking at the relation between press coverage of the deaths and the popularity of the R.I.P.-pages, as coverage of the pages by the press seem to increase traffic and engagement with them. I started looking for more cases of popular R.I.P.-pages and following came across more pages seemingly created by the same "griefsquatter" (which was what I had now decided to call him). I decided to leave them out of my research project (not gather data from them), as I began to think of them as scams, not representative of ordinary public R.I.P.-pages. However, I felt both intrigued and revolted by the griefsquatters' practice since the people who used the pages he set up clearly believed the pages had some relation to the deceased's relatives. They often addressed the relatives directly, clearly expecting them to be reading what they wrote. As this appeared to be part of a larger like-hunting scheme with a lot of interconnected pages (the R.I.P.-pages, the sport stars pages, the strange cancer-page), I felt I should do something with this knowledge, but what? I presented my first findings at the symposium and used the opportunity to put forward my dilemma: Should I act on my knowledge about the griefsquatter? The researchers present at that symposium did not have any ready answers at hand. I, then, discussed the case in a private mail to other local internet research colleagues. Suggestions for strategies were either to confront the griefsquatter or to talk to the families of the deceased exploited on the R.I.P.-page to see if they wanted something to be done about it. Personally, at that point, I believed confrontation with the griefsquatter would yield no results (since he never responded when people addressed him); and I was wary of talking to the families already affected – they had literally had grief enough.

Making a Stand and Going Public

Then, one day in late July 2014, a young woman was found dead near a highway, and it appeared to be someone who had been missing for a few days. As part of my research, I started looking for R.I.P.-pages for the deceased as soon as the news story about the tragic death broke. I soon discovered that someone, following the typical pattern of the "griefsquatter", had created a Facebook R.I.P.-page in memory of the missing person. This time, however, police had not yet officially confirmed that the roadside body was that of the missing person. What I saw confirmed my growing suspicion that the griefsquatter strategically aimed at creating these R.I.P.-pages as quickly as possible after a tragic death had made the news in order to make sure that these pages became the "go-to" pages on Facebook for people – strangers as well as gullible friends – who wished to express their support on Facebook. This time, relatives of the family quickly found the R.I.P.-page in question, and pleaded with the administrator to take it down due to the not yet confirmed identity issue. Other visitors to the page pleaded for the same action. The griefsquatter did not respond. Nothing could be done to close the page through official Facebook channels as I soon discovered. You cannot write to Facebook directly to report cases like this, nor can you report more than one page at a time. When you report a page, you can only chose between a preset number of options for reasons for wanting to report it and "elaborate scam" is not one of them. Allegedly, Facebook only takes down public pages if several people report them. So, for instance, if a few family members report a R.I.P.-page as a scam, it is very likely that no action will be taken, and it will likely take some time, before Facebook monitors pay attention to the case.

It was at that point that I found that I had to make a choice. On one hand out of purely selfish interest, I could stand by and observe what happened in real time on the R.I.P-page in order to use in my research. On the other hand, I felt compelled to act now in order to prevent further distress to someone who had just lost someone close to them, as well as that of future families likely to experience something similar. The most proper form of conduct would be to take the long way round by trying to confront the griefsquatter, which I believed would yield no immediate results given that he had previously ignored similar adresses. Furthermore, I had another issue I would like to bring to the public's attention: the Danish press, especially the tabloid press, had begun to regularly refer to and use content lifted from the griefsquatter's R.I.P-pages in their coverage of the death of the young people, they memorised, likely increasing traffic to the pages, and apparently not asking for permission before quoting comments on their walls. I therefore decided to go public with my knowledge of the griefsquatter's practices both in order to have the pages taken down and prevent future pages from being used *and* in order to make the Danish press become more aware of which "sources" they used when they covered these spectacular deaths. I decided to do it on my personal blog (which I run on a domain independent of my university) to make it clear that what I wrote should be read as a personal statement, not as an institutional publication.

A more extensive search revealed that in recent years in total the griefsquatter had created about 15 R.I.P.-pages, some with several thousand likes. The creation of this many pages could not be random. I made the final decision to go public and I decided to publish the public URLs of the pages (many of which had already been mentioned in the press) to substantiate my claims and, admittedly, to enable people to follow the griefsquatter's trails, should they want to. I tried to write a well-argued, factual post, pointing out the problems both of the practice of the griefsquatter and the Danish press, using the very recent case of the premature R.I.P.-page as a striking example of the grief-squatter's practice. I tried to make it very clear in writing that I was not interested in having this particular person personally persecuted. Rather, I wanted to make both journalists and ordinary people aware of his practices so they could pay more attention to their own use of R.I.P.-pages. Finally, I wanted Facebook to make it easy for people to report "scams" like this. I pressed the publish-button and posted a link to my post on my Facebook profile. And hell broke loose.

The Ramifications

It was the late summer, at that time there were no major scandals or disasters going on in the world to occupy the Danish journalists, and people in my network, affected by what I wrote, shared my posts with other people in their own networks. In short time my blogpost went viral – all major Danish newspapers picked up the story, perhaps not surprisingly, *not* focusing on the press's own role in the popularity of the R.I.P.-pages or the difficulty of reporting like-exploitation schemes to Facebook, but centering all attention on the "horrible griefsquatter" (all newspapers adopted my Danish name for him).

What was even worse, the journalists used my list of R.I.P.-pages to track down the relatives of the deceased young people they memorialised, calling them to get their comments on the griefsquatting. Two newspapers even published the entire list. When I found out that the families were being contacted by the press, I personally called those newspapers and had the lists pulled from the online version of the two papers and immediately deleted the list from my blog, but the damage had already been done. I wanted to protect the interests of the families, but it had the unintentional side-effect of also drawing unnecessary attention to them.

I talked to a lot of journalists from the printed press, TV, and radio. I consistently refused to take part in an open exposure of the person I believed was behind the griefsquatter, demanding he remained anonymous because I was worried about the consequences of an exposure and believed he had the right to remain anonymous in the public eye. However, after a few days, one of the more serious Danish newspapers published an interview with the griefsquatter, which they had identified with the help of an anonymous source. In this interview, the griefsquatter's name was anonymized. A little more than a week after I published my blog post, another Danish newspaper, which I had also talked to, published the full name of the man in a lengthy feature. Without my knowledge, they cited me as a source confirming his identity because I had in a conversation a few days earlier said that I recognised his name from my own studies (I had clearly stated this was off the record). They never got back to me before publishing the story. I was devastated. Had I now helped ruin the personal life of the griefsquatter? Would he be persecuted by online mobs now? One could argue, rightly, that I should likely have foreseen that going public with the list of R.I.P.-pages would lead to this, because the press has other standards than researchers. Ultimately, several months after, a commercial TV channel ran a series on bad internet behavior, including an episode in which a well-known Danish researcher (who often appears on TV), confronted the griefsquatter on camera just as he was leaving work. The exposure was total. To this day, I do not know what the repercussions for the griefsquatter have been. He has never gotten in touch with me, and following the TV show mentioned above, I have not seen much discussion of him or his practices online.

What did happen was this: The press, as always, quickly moved on. Soon after the press coverage Facebook took down the most controversial and most popular R.I.P.-pages made by the griefsquatter, including the one which sparked my blogpost. In conversation it was made clear to me that it is too costly to allow people to report pages in their own words, so you still cannot report to Facebook that a string of pages are part of the same scam or scheme. To this day, the minor "fake" R.I.P.-pages are still online, as is a new instantiation of the still very popular griefsquatter's "hub", the anti-cancer page. This page has more than 60.000 followers. It is impossible to track down the owner of this page now, as no information or like-links to other pages are provided. However, I have seen no new examples of "fake" R.I.P.-pages and it is my sense that the Danish press do not refer to R.I.P.-pages of ordinary people as much as they did before my blogpost. The same month as the story went public, a journalist published a piece in the Danish Media Business Journal, in which editors were culled on their principles regarding the use of R.I.P.-pages in news stories. Some newspapers editors stated that they would reconsider their practices of referring to R.I.P.-pages without checking up on the administrator; or that they at least had discussed their use of R.I.P.-pages in articles now.

Post-case Reflections

In hindsight, by going public to a certain degree I got what I had wished for. Both the Danish press and the public became aware of the griefsquatter's practices, and the most popular “fake” R.I.P.-pages were, as stated above, taken down by Facebook. I have no doubt that had I not gone public the pages would still be there, harvesting likes and causing distress. However, even if my intention was to draw attention to a practice, not a specific person, I am also the indirect cause of the public exposure of one individual, whose life is likely to have been affected in a negative way by the exposure my blogpost led to. Furthermore, had I not made the list of the R.I.P.-pages public from the beginning (which I could have refrained from), the families of the deceased would not have been harassed unnecessarily by journalists. Following common research standards, I should have asked for informed consent from the 15 families whose children were memorialised on the fake R.I.P.-pages, before I went public with the list, even if this would have meant that the family in immediate distress over the untimely R.I.P.-page for their child likely would have had to live with it for much longer. I would like to note that following my exposure, families did state either publicly or in communication with me that they were happy the scam had been exposed.

One painful, but obvious, lesson learned from my experiences is: However much you try, as a researcher, you cannot control the press once you go public with a potential sensational story. Their (at least the tabloid press’) ethical guidelines are often different than that of the research community. But going through the press may seem as the only viable option when you want Facebook to take action, as the company is incredibly difficult to get hold of. Every online social service comes with a dark side; people who will exploit the service for their own or commercial purposes. As internet and social media researchers, we know far too little about what takes place behind the scenes and what to do about it, when our research either intentionally or as a side-effect reveals some of the more immoral practices taking place on social network sites. Much literature on ethics and social media originates in specific disciplines, notably health care and law, and within these fields one solution seems to be to apply professional ethical codes from offline practice to similar online practices. However, certain practices and the ethical question they pose arise directly from the affordances of digital social media and confront us with new dilemmas which we will have to figure out on our own. Within the qualitative internet research tradition, questions of how (if possible) and when to obtain informed consent and how to address privacy issues have been at the forefront of ethical discussion. Also in this case general research guidelines for when to ask for informed consent could have served well, even if public exposure would have been postponed. Sometimes, however, choices are not simple: If I had respected the privacy of one person (the griefsquatter), I would have disregarded the violations of privacy of the many (the right to communally grieve and memorialise deceased people in a perceived semi-private space without having to deal with inappropriate content) as well as the implicit violation of privacy which the potential use of a grieving group’s data for commercial purposes also entail.

The study and potential regulation of social media practices requires a global ethics, not just within the research community but also by the social media service providers. As a social media researcher, I believe it is our moral duty to make both the public and the service providers aware of misuse of the services, especially when this (mis)use is causing people grievance. How to publicly address it without harming anyone is still a challenge to be solved, but we should dare more to discuss also the difficult choices with our peers.

CHAPTER EIGHTEEN

Locating Locational Data in Mobile and Social Media

LEE HUMPHREYS

Locational data can be defined loosely as information about where things are. Typically we think about locating places, people, and even things such as cars, keys, etc. Places like countries, cities, or towns are pretty easy to locate because they are mostly defined by representations of space, like maps (Lefebvre, 1991). Places like businesses are also relatively easy to locate because they do not move very often. People and artifacts are more challenging to locate because they move. As such, the changing locational information about people and artifacts in space has been more difficult to attain, but mobile and social media are changing this. People can now share their locations in real time through mobile media whether explicitly through a check-in service like Facebook Places or through default platform settings like Instagram, which automatically tag the location of a social media post was made from.

Wilken (2014) argues situating social media companies as location-based social media platforms helps to understand their financial business models and therefore motivations for evolution and change. In 2015 both Twitter and Facebook attained the majority of their revenue through mobile advertising.[1] So, even though these companies do not describe themselves as location-based social media platforms, technically and, more importantly, financially, they are. Therefore people who are studying such social media platforms can benefit from thinking through aspects and variations of locational data.

As a communication scholar, I make four claims about location data in mobile and social media in this chapter. Increasingly mobile apps are developed, mapping tools employed, and GIS (graphic information systems) data sources accessed as part of humanities and social science research more broadly. First, locational data are becoming easier to collect. Second, locational data are becoming easier to access by some. Third, locations are understood differently by databases versus people. Fourth, different populations have different concerns about locational data sharing. I outline each of the claims below and the ethical implications of them. These claims and subsequent ethical considerations are relevant for those within internet studies who research mobile media as well as for scholars outside of internet studies who use location-based media in service of their own research programs.

LOCATIONAL DATA ARE BECOMING EASIER TO COLLECT

Locational data are increasingly easy to collect because of the high adoption rates of mobile phones. Within the US, 92% of adults own a cellphone and 68% own a smartphone (Anderson, 2015). Ninety-five percent of the world's population is covered by a mobile cellular network (International Telecommunications Union, 2016). While phones break and consistent service may be too expensive for some populations (Gonzales, 2014), the growth of mobile phone adoption has made collecting locational data significantly easier.

Both technological as well as social factors further facilitate locational data collection. While mobile phones are powered on, they regularly emit signals to base stations owned by mobile network operators, like AT&T in the US or BT in the UK (Wicker, 2011). In case people get a call or a text message, the phone mobile networks need to know where mobile phones are so they will know through which base stations to route the call. Therefore mobile network operators attain relatively detailed locational information about a phone's whereabouts as long as it is turned on. Social norms have also emerged in developed countries (Ling, 2012), which encourage people to both keep their phones powered on at all times and to keep their phones on or near them at all times. These social and technical factors together mean that by proxy, mobile network operators know where people are because they know where their phones are.

LOCATIONAL DATA ARE INCREASINGLY EASY TO ACCESS (BY SOME)

Beyond mobile network operators, various smartphone services and apps may also have access to people's locational data. Smartphone app developers can easily request and utilize the location of a phone to better serve up appropriate content, such as weather in the local area or a local map. However, services do not have to immediately utilize locational data to gain access to it. Indeed many apps request locational data when it is not immediately obvious why they would need such information to provide their mobile service. A study of apps permissions on Google Play store (Olmstead & Atkinson, 2015), found that 10 of the top 18 downloaded apps requested locational data. These apps included eBay, Evernote, Facebook, Google Chrome, Google Maps, Instagram, Shazam, Skype, Twitter, and WhatsApp. Adobe, Kindle, Dropbox, Watch ESPN, Gmail, Pandora, Spotify, and YouTube apps did not request such data.

A quick look at my iPhone reveals a variety of apps request my locational data, including calendar, camera, CNN, compass, Facebook, Facebook Messenger, Ithaca Journal (my local newspaper), Maps, MapMyRun, Photos, Safari websites, Apple's Siri, Twitter, and my local grocery store's app. While some of the services include a short explanation of why they request the locational data (such as "to find your nearest grocery store"), many services do not. For example, I have several news apps on my phone, but only CNN and my local newspaper request my locational data and they do not give any explanation for it. Olmstead and Atkinson (2015) point out that such explanations are not as easily available in the Google Play App Store.

Why would companies want such data if they are not using it to customize their content? One potential reason may be because such data might be useful in the future. Locational data is often considered the holy grail of advertising (Cho, 2004). To be able to serve up ads when people are in a place they can immediately act on it, however, typically conjures up images of Tom Cruise's character in Minority Report as he walks through the Gap being solicited to based on retina scanning. While I do not want to suggest news apps that request locational data secretly want to scan our retinas, I do want to suggest that they request locational data in hopes of being able to commoditize locational information through increased targeting and personalization of advertising.

The accessibility of locational data for various apps was initially made possible because locational data are necessary for mobile phones to work. WiFi and satellites have made locational data all the more prevalent because they allow for greater locational precision (Frith, 2015). Therefore, as smartphone adoption continues to increase, locational data become more precise and accessible to companies of all kinds.

Commercial entities are not the only services to build apps. Increasingly, apps are built as part of educational, digital humanities, health, civic, political, and social research programs. Apps are developed as tools for scholarship and outreach.[2] Of course, within the field of information science, human computer interaction researchers and students often develop and design apps to test theories, explore hypotheses, push technological boundaries, and make life easier, more efficient, and enjoyable. Locational data are seen as a way to make content more relevant, useful, and legible (Frith, 2015). Within the academic community, monetary gains are seldom the key drivers of data collection. Nevertheless, data are valuable both financially as well as empirically.

Despite the increase in access to locational data for mobile network operators and app developers, mobile phone users are not always literate in how to access, modify, and manipulate their own locational data. Park and Jang (2014) define mobile-based privacy literacy as both the knowledge about what kinds of data exist and how to access that data as well as the skills to modify default settings or features to enhance privacy. They found that frequent mobile use and being familiar with mobile phones were not highly related to privacy knowledge and skill.

LOCATIONS ARE UNDERSTOOD DIFFERENTLY BY DATABASES VERSUS PEOPLE

The locational data made possible by cellular and WiFi networks are part of databases which link the locational data to other user or customer data (Poster, 1990). Databases understand location as longitudinal and latitudinal coordinates or postal addresses, but people understand location as where they are, were, or will be. For people, locations can be meetings or events. They can be home or work. Locations can be parties or festivals. People understand and experience locations as inscribed with social, cultural, and emotional meanings. Often peoples' understandings of location are defined as "place" (Tuan, 1977).

Therefore locational data are not just in locational databases, but exist in images and texts that circulate online and through mobile apps as well. As people take selfies at tourist attractions or with celebrities, they are presencing themselves (Meese et al., 2015). That is, they are creating images and posts that locate them in particular places at particular times to be shared with their social networks. As people tweet about heading home after a long day at work, they are locating themselves both at work and their future selves at home. Of course home and work are referential locations, that is, one has to know more about me to know where exactly my home is. It would be incomprehensible if I tweeted, "long day at 42.447724°/–76.478072°, headed 42.4734972°/–76.4735724°." Not only do we not speak in latitude and longitude, we seldom speak of places in terms of postal addresses. In a study we did of Twitter (Humphreys, Gill, & Krishnamurthy, 2014), we found that about 12% of public tweets located the person in some way through language. These were not geotagged tweets. While 12% might seem a small percentage, it is important to put that number into a broader context of social media posts. Twelve percent of 500 million posts a day is still 60 million tweets a day that may be communicating where people are, were, or will be.

But why do people purposefully share their locations so much through social media? First, despite globalization and the rise of networks (Benkler, 2006), place still structures our daily lives in many ways. We are always in a place, even if that place is in transit. Mobile communication too has done much to eliminate the geographic barriers for communication, but cellular technology also has made place an even more relevant factor in how we communicate (Donner, 2015). Second, colloquially, locations often stand in for activities. I do not have to tell someone that I am having a beer at a bar. I can just say that I am at a bar. To say that I am having a beer at a bar or shopping at a store is almost redundant. Often the place presumes certain activities and we use that to our advantage when we speak quickly with friends and family. So while people may speak in terms of where they are, people are really sharing what they are doing. This has important implications for the reasons why people share locations. People draw on shared knowledge in their communication, which allows them to locate themselves in places through social meaning rather than postal addresses or latitude and longitude. People share where they are because it says something about them or helps them to coordinate future events and better understand their own life patterns (Humphreys, 2012).

The social and referential ways in which people locate themselves in space also have the inadvertent effect of being very difficult to understand computationally (Humphreys et al., 2014). Most people do not purposefully try to mask their locations when they post information about where they are or where they will be to enhance their privacy (though some do). While social and cultural meanings of places may go missing algorithmically, our patterns of movement and daily routines do not. One could surmise that a particular location is one's home based purely on the amount of time one spends there and when those times are, easily inferred from cellular data. However, the social and referential ways in which people locate themselves in their social media posts are often meant to be read by friends and family, not algorithms.

DIFFERENT POPULATIONS HAVE DIFFERENT CONCERNS ABOUT LOCATIONAL DATA SHARING

In an early study of privacy concerns on location-based social media (Humphreys, 2011), participants were quick to express privacy concerns about potential stalking and not concerns about state or corporate entities accessing their locational data. This suggests that the different ways through which location is understood seem to obscure locational data privacy concerns amongst citizens and consumers. For my participants having their locational data read by people raised stalking concerns, whereas having their locational data in corporate databases did not raise privacy concerns. It should be noted that while I sought out a geographically diverse set of highly active users for my 2011 study, in the end all of my participants were young, white, urban adults between the ages of 20 and 40. At the time of the study, this was the primary demographic makeup of early adopters of mobile social networks.

A study by Yong Jin Park (2012), exploring the privacy literacy skills of students at Howard University, a historically Black college in Washington DC, found different concerns regarding privacy and location sharing than I found (Humphreys, 2011). In particular, his subjects reported concerns about state surveillance of location sharing social media. These findings reinforce earlier studies of privacy concerns among African Americans (Gandy Jr., 1993; Gandy, 1993), which show that African Americans research participants were most concerned about their privacy with regard to the government rather than corporate marketing. I presume the white participants in my 2011 study never mentioned concerns about the government knowing their location because demographically they probably do not have a history of being racially profiled by authorities.

Youth are also likely to have different location privacy concerns than the participants in my 2011 study. Rather than state, corporate, or even stalking concerns, locational data of youth may raise privacy concerns with regard to their parents and peer networks. Youth often use mobile communication as a means of asserting independence from their parents (Vanden Abeele, 2015). Parents may let their children engage in activities outside of their supervision as long as the youth are reachable by their mobile phone. However, parents can also directly track their children's locations through mobile apps, like Friend a Friend. Therefore parental surveillance of youth locational data may lead to consequences regarding where youth are (or are not) supposed to be.

Different populations will have different locational data concerns. Those who are more systematically disadvantaged in society are frequently under greater surveillance than those who are less disadvantaged (Gilliom, 2001; Gonzales, 2014). In most situations, locational data collection and sharing among parties are not transparent. Those monitoring such data are frequently in positions to assert power over those whose locational data are being monitored. Therefore different populations will have different understandings and opinions about locational data sharing and subsequent concerns.

ETHICAL CONSIDERATION OF LOCATIONAL DATA

The four claims about locational data lead to three ethical considerations for internet researchers who are working with locational data. Locational data are becoming easier to collect and access by government, companies, and researchers, but not necessarily by those consumers, citizens, and users who do not have strong technological and privacy skills. Therefore three ethical considerations of locational data need to be addressed.

People Do Not Always Understand When They Are Sharing Locational Data and With Whom

The majority of people in the United States likely do not have the technological literacy to understand exactly how, when, and with whom they are sharing their locational data. Default privacy settings are remarkably powerful (boyd & Hargittai, 2010), so it is likely that people may not realize they are providing access to their locational information through their mobile and social media use. Park and Jang's (2014) study of mobile-based privacy knowledge and skills among teens were relatively low and Park's 2015 study reveals second order mobile digital divides amongst traditionally marginalized youth.

Just Because People Share Locational Data, Does Not Mean They Want to Be Located

There are many reasons why people share their location with others. Sometimes sharing location is a means of connected presencing, where the act of communicating, rather than the content of the communication, reinforces the bonds of the relationship (Licoppe, 2004). Sometimes, sharing one's location is a means of self-presentation (Schwartz & Halegoua, 2015). Sometimes sharing one's location is about self-tracking and documenting one's life (Humphreys, 2012). And sometimes sharing one's location through social media is about memory making and keeping (Özkul & Humphreys, 2015). These are all very different reasons to share one's location other than to be found or located. We cannot assume that if people share locational data, it can be used in whatever capacity we as researchers might want to.

The example of the Girls Around Me app reveals the challenging implications of accessing APIs to combine datasets with locational information. The app combined Facebook relationship status information with Foursquare check-in information to identify potential single girls in the nearby vicinity. The logo of the app showed the outline of a female body in the center of a bull's eye target, suggesting predatory overtones. Foursquare quickly claimed that the app violated its API policy and the app was blocked. Jackson, Gillespie, and Payette (2014) argue the controversy of Girls Around Me reveals the co-constitutive nature of policy, design, and practice of mobile and social media. The open API designs and public/private nature of Foursquare and Facebook user accounts, coupled with the API policies shaped a socio-technical system ripe for such development. As scholars, we need to consider the implications of the policy arrangements, technical design, and social practices when accessing, analyzing, and utilizing locational data in our research.

Locational Data Is Meaningful in Different Ways to Different People

Different demographics and usage communities have different relationships to locational data and to those who may be monitoring or accessing that information. As internet scholars, we need to recognize and consider these differences as we think about accessing and analyzing various kinds of locational data. In some cases, this suggests that locational data from different individuals may need to be treated differently given the various contexts in which it is produced, the histories of inequality, and potential safety concerns that locational data may raise for certain citizens, consumers, and children.

A key consideration for scholars utilizing or studying mobile and social media is to maintain the contextual integrity of how and why locational information was originally shared (Nissenbaum, 2009). As locational data is increasingly added as metadata to various apps, it may go unnoticed by users who may not have the mobile privacy literacy knowledge and skills that Park and Jang (2014) note.

CONCLUSION

Cellular and WiFi technologies have made it easier to locate people through their mobile phones. These data present tremendous opportunity for researchers to study various social scientific questions as well as for various mobile app developers to serve up increasingly relevant information to help customers. However, locational data is complex and can mean different things to different actors. As we move closer to an Internet of Things, we need to continue to think through the social, political, and ethical considerations of locational data from artifacts and systems that can reveal the location of people. Various kinds of locational data need to be understood within their broader socio-technical systems in order to ensure our collective privacy management. Researchers utilizing locational data should consider the contextual understandings and implications of such data by the participants whose data are implicated. As researchers, we need to account for how the interplay between mobile policy, design, and practice may vary depending on the population of study as well as the national and local context of study.

NOTES

1. Facebook Reports Fourth Quarter and Full Year 2015 Results. Retrieved from http://investor.fb.com/releasedetail.cfm?ReleaseID=952040 and Twitter Annual Report 2016. Retrieved from https://investor.twitterinc.com/annuals-proxies.cfm
2. See http://digitalhumanities.unc.edu/resources/tools/ and http://dirtdirectory.org/ for sites developed to help non-technical researchers utilize various digital data in their research.

REFERENCES

Anderson, M. (2015). *Technology divice ownership: 2015*. Washington, DC: Pew Internet and American Life Project.

Benkler, Y. (2006). *The wealth of networks: How social production transforms markets and freedom*. New Haven, CT: Yale University Press.

boyd, d., & Hargittai, E. (2010). Facebook privacy settings: Who cares? *First Monday, 15*(8): np. Retrieved from http://firstmonday.org/htbin/cgiwrap/bin/ojs/index.php/fm/article/view/3086/2589

Cho, C. (2004, August 2). For more advertisers, the medium is the text message. *Wall Street Journal*, p. B1.

Donner, J. (2015). *After access: Inclusion, development, and a more mobile Internet*. Cambridge, MA: MIT Press.

Frith, J. (2015). *Smartphones as locative media*. Malden, MA: Polity.

Gandy, Jr., O. H. (1993). *The panoptic sort: A political economy of personal information*. Boulder, CO: Westview Press.

Gandy, O. H. (1993). African Americans and privacy: Understanding the black perspective in the emerging policy debate. *Journal of Black Studies, 24*(2), 178–195.

Gilliom, J. (2001). *Overseers of the poor: Surveillance, resistance, and the limits of privacy*. Chicago, IL: University of Chicago Press.

Gonzales, A. L. (2014). Health benefits and barriers to cell phone use in low-income urban U.S. neighborhoods: Indications of technology maintenance. *Mobile Media & Communication, 2*(3), 233–248. doi:10.1177/2050157914530297.

Humphreys, L. (2011). Who's watching whom? A study of interactive technology and surveillance. *Journal of Communication, 61*, 575–595.

Humphreys, L. (2012). Connecting, coordinating, cataloguing: Communicative practices on mobile social networks. *Journal of Broadcasting & Electronic Media, 56*(4), 494–510. doi:10.1080/08838151.2012.732144.

Humphreys, L., Gill, P., & Krishnamurthy, B. (2014). Twitter: a content analysis of personal information. *Information, Communication & Society, 17*(7), 843–857. doi:10.1080/1369118X.2013.848917.

International Telecommunications Union. (2016). *ITU Facts and Figures 2016*.

Jackson, S. J., Gillespie, T., & Payette, S. (2014). *The policy knot: Re-integrating policy, practice and design in CSCW studies of social computing*. Paper presented at the Proceedings of the 17th ACM conference on Computer supported cooperative work & social computing.

Lefebvre, H. (1991). *The production of space* (D. Nicholson-Smith, Trans.). Oxford: Blackwell Publishers.

Licoppe, C. (2004). "Connected" presence: The emergence of a new repertoire for managing social relationships in a changing communication technoscape. *Environment and Planning, Society and Space, 22*(1), 135–156. doi:10.1068/d323t.

Ling, R. (2012). *Taken for grantedness: The embedding of mobile communication into society*. Cambridge, MA: MIT Press.

Meese, J., Gibbs, M., Carter, M., Arnold, M., Nansen, B., & Kohn, T. (2015). Selfies at funerals: Mourning and presencing on social media platforms. *International Journal of Communication, 9*, 118–131.

Nissenbaum, H. (2009). *Privacy in context: Technology, policy, and the integrity of social life*. Stanford, CA: Stanford Law Books.

Olmstead, K., & Atkinson, M. (2015). *Apps permissions in the Google Play Store*. Washington, DC: Pew Internet & American Life. Retrieved from http://www.pewinternet.org/interactives/apps-permissions/

Özkul, D., & Humphreys, L. (2015). Record and remember: Memory and meaning-making practices through mobile media. *Mobile Media & Communication, 3*(3), 351–365.

Park, Y. J. (2012). *Mobile literacy among young adults: Evidence for information and location privacy*. Paper presented at the International Communication Association Mobile Communication Pre-conference, Phoenix, AZ.

Park, Y. J. (2015). My whole world's in my palm! The second-level divide of teenagers' mobile use and skill. *New Media & Society, 17*(6), 977–995. doi:10.1177/1461444813520302.

Park, Y. J., & Jang, S. M. (2014). Understanding privacy knowledge and skill in mobile communication. *Computers in human behavior, 38*, 296–303.

Poster, M. (1990). *The mode of information: Poststructuralism and social construct*. Chicago, IL: University of Chicago Press.

Schwartz, R., & Halegoua, G. R. (2015). The spatial self: Location-based identity performance on social media. *New Media & Society, 17*(10), 1643–1660. doi:10.1177/1461444814531364.

Tuan, Y.-F. (1977). *Space and place: The perspective of experience*. Minneapolis, MN: University of Minnesota Press.

Vanden Abeele, M. M. P. (2015). Mobile youth culture: A conceptual development. *Mobile Media & Communication, 4*(1), 85–101.

Wicker, S. B. (2011). Cellular telephony and the question of privacy. *Commun. ACM, 54*(7), 88–98. doi:10.1145/1965724.1965745.

Wilken, R. (2014). Places nearby: Facebook as a location-based social media platform. *New Media & Society, 16*(7), 1087–1103. doi:10.1177/1461444814543997.

CHAPTER NINTEEN

How Does It Feel TO Be Visualized?

Redistributing Ethics

DAVID MOATS AND JESSAMY PERRIAM

INTRODUCTION

What are the ethics of a network graph? Data visualizations like the above present problems for qualitative researchers because they involve data about more users than can feasibly give consent, and they also involve giving over more control in the research process to tools, APIs, and algorithms, while ethical frameworks often assume a heavily orchestrated research process, with the researcher at the helm.

This chapter addresses some of the ethical implications of visualizations utilizing data from social media platforms, drawing on material from two ongoing studies (one which follows nuclear controversies on e-mail lists and Facebook, and another about diet-related hashtags on Instagram). While we cannot hope to offer any programmatic or definitive statements on the matter, we will draw on some insights from Science and Technology Studies (STS) to highlight how ethical issues are distributed between different aspects of the research process and between different types of actors, including non-human algorithms and tools.

Data visualizations range from "… simple pie charts and line graphs to more complex, interactive and emotive illustrations" (Kennedy, Hill, Aiello, & Allen, 2016, p. 715). Of course, plenty has already been said about the ethics (or lack thereof) of infographics (Kennedy et al., 2016) and big data techniques in the private sector (boyd & Crawford, 2012; Savage & Burrows, 2007), but in this chapter we are particularly interested in the kinds of techniques associated with Virtual Methods (Hine, 2005) and Digital Methods (Rogers, 2013) because they

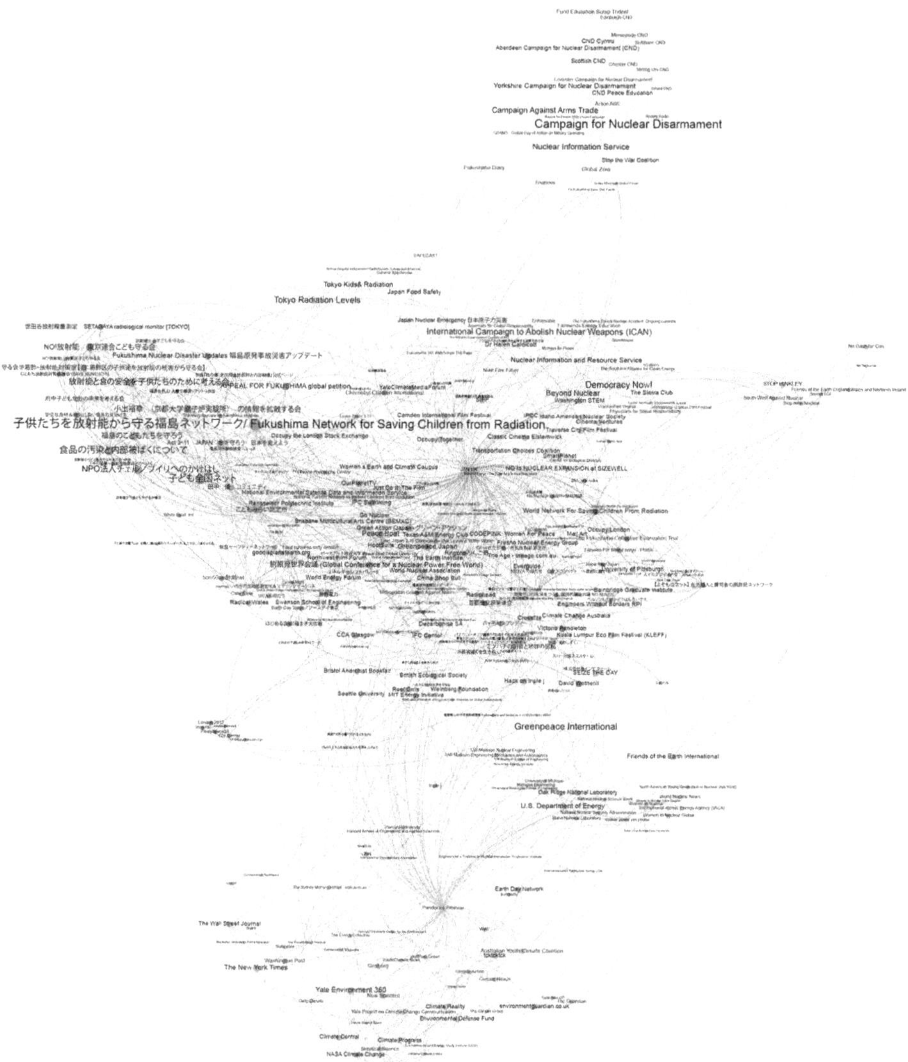

Figure 1. A network of Facebook pages related to nuclear power created with the program Netvizz: https://apps.facebook.com/netvizz/.

are often employed by traditionally qualitative social scientists who have different ethical and methodological concerns.

These include network graphs (of users, hyperlinks, or co-word networks), but also bubble diagrams (Gerlitz & Stevenson, 2009) or stream-graphs (Venturini et al., 2014). However, we will limit our discussion here to networks, as the paradigmatic example. These techniques diverge from existing quantitative methods because, unlike traditional statistics, which are about aggregating cases and abstracting qualities, these visualizations can selectively *highlight* individual users, pages, hashtags, and other digital objects and show relationships between them.[1] These techniques thus add further complications to the challenges faced by both quantitative data analysts and virtual ethnographers dealing with social media data.

In the first section of this paper we will briefly suggest how data visualizations complicate existing online ethics, including situated ethics. We will then offer a tentative framework for thinking through these complications with some insights from STS. Finally, we will provide some examples from our own work and informal discussions with research subjects to illustrate this framework.

COMPLICATIONS TO EXISTING LITERATURE

As many of the other authors in this volume have pointed out, social media data present daunting challenges for existing ethical frameworks, even those grounded in earlier online research. Hard and fast rules about anonymity and consent (Barocas & Nissenbaum, 2014) have given way to more flexible guidelines about (more or less) public and private data (Markham & Buchanan, 2012) even though such distinctions remain highly problematic (Gregory & Bowker, 2016).

Data visualizations exacerbate these challenges because they entail collecting and displaying data from more users than can feasibly give consent. Even if all of the information from data visualizations are anonymized, they can still reveal relationships and patterns which identify users to those familiar with the field. But, if they are entirely anonymized for publication, then, this black-boxes the research, forcing the reader to simply trust the researcher's claims.

Many of these problems stem from the fact that institutional ethics largely emerges from a human subjects research model (Bassett & O'Riordan, 2002). This model assumes a bounded setting like a laboratory or intrusive methods, which actively elicit or produce data (survey, interview, focus group) when what is potentially significant about social media, and more broadly Web 2.0 platforms, is that it is "found" or "transactional" data (Savage & Burrows, 2007), produced as a byproduct of other activities. Now, this does not in any sense mean that these data are "natural" or and any less contrived – only that they are constructed and elicited by a different configuration of actors (private companies, researchers, algorithms, and research subjects).[2] In other words, social media *redistributes* research roles between researchers, platforms, algorithms, and users (Marres, 2012).

So, today ethics is increasingly influenced by the policies and terms and conditions of internet companies (Zimmer, 2010), and practices of ordinary social media users who are actively shaping and re-shaping the field. Ethics are also impacted by often black boxed (Driscoll & Walker, 2014) search algorithms and tools, such as visualization software and clustering algorithms (Jacomy, Venturini, Heymann, & Bastian, 2014), which also participate in defining the parameters of a study.

All of this should incline researchers to a more situated, flexible, and contextually specific version of ethics (Markham, 2006), where we consider scenarios of harm (Zimmer, 2010) for the given case. But precisely the problem with data visualizations is that they do not allow case by case decisions to be made: We cannot evaluate the consequences of representing thousands of data points individually. They often necessitate blanket actions, such as anonymizing entities below certain quantitative thresholds. We could of course limit data visualizations to a scope where each research subject can be carefully considered, but this defeats the very purpose of these tools: to scale up and extend qualitative work.

For example: Vis and Goriunova (2015) created a network diagram related to the viral image of drowned Syrian toddler Aylan Kurdi on Twitter. The visualization depicted the users involved in sharing the image and how it spread. The authors worried that highlighting some users could cause harm, due to the perceived political statement they were making. As Vis and Goriunova explain, "… this report was interested in uncovering broad trends and not in highlighting individual users" (p. 9), but by the same token anonymizing the whole graph makes it meaningless to the reader.

Their solution was to anonymize the graph by default and then only de-anonymize those names which were deemed "public-facing" enough – those speaking in their professional capacity as a journalist, politician etc. as opposed to individual private users. They also cautioned that this public-facingness is not just a property of individuals but depends on the potential audience: They anonymized different names depending on which audiences they were presenting to because individuals have different visibility in different contexts.

Although seemingly arbitrary distinctions like this may be practically necessary in the course of research, in the next section we will explain why it is hard to sustain clear cut categories like "public-facing" or "private" when social media platforms and data visualizations are involved.

DISTRIBUTED ETHICS

Because data visualizations, more obviously perhaps than other types of social research, involve the participation of technologies and devices, it may help to turn to work in STS, which has long argued for considering the social and the technical together. STS is not particularly known for its ethics because it, by its very nature, avoids normative claims or researcher-defined categories,[3] which makes it unhelpful for drafting ethics frameworks. However STS is important for unearthing the politics and power asymmetries in seemingly technical or epistemological matters (Johnson & Wetmore, 2008). STS is helpful because it insists that methods are embedded in larger method assemblages (Law, 2004). Far from the ideal of controlled experimental research, social research is a messy negotiation between technology, researchers, and research subjects all entangled together. It invites us to consider how things like APIs participate in the research process (Marres & Weltevrede, 2013) and by extension the production of ethical issues. Platforms and tools may incline us to certain sorts of research questions as opposed to others and also may selectively make visible certain research subjects at the expense of others.

STS also theorizes how the objects of social research are modulated over the course of a study through chains of transformations (Latour, 1999). For example, data visualizations are highly dependent on the affordances of particular platforms (Koed Madsen, 2013) both in terms of software architectures and user behaviors. Users in social media may be *actively* trying to make themselves visible in certain ways, while online platforms have different ways of ranking and highlighting their actions for certain audiences (Bucher, 2012). In addition, we as researchers make decisions about which data to select and anonymize and data visualization tools have their own standards and protocols, which inform the process. Finally the audiences and readers of research may further disseminate the findings and reframe it in unexpected ways. Thus we should not think of users or platforms as being merely public or private, but consider the various practices by which they might be *publicized* (made visible by users, platforms, visualization tools, researchers, and readers) or conversely concealed or made private.

In other words, the production of research and research ethics is a distributed accomplishment. This, however, is not intended to absolve the researcher of responsibility. To give an analogy: Flying a plane is the work of an socio-technical assemblage, which includes pilots, landing gear, air traffic controllers, communications technologies, and the weather; but the responsibility (socially and legally speaking) more often than not lies with the pilot or the operator (Callon, 2008).

The point is that in making ethical decisions researchers should consider not just their own practices but also the practices of other parties comprising the research assemblage: from the platforms and user themselves, to the scrapers, APIs and visualization tools they employ.

In the next section, we will discuss some concrete examples from our work, in order to show how ethical concerns are distributed up and down the chain of transformations involved in research. We will focus on the problem of privacy and anonymisation, what research makes visible or conceals, a key concern for internet researchers and data scientists, but obviously other concerns like access, trust and the way research subjects are presented are also distributed.

EMPIRICAL EXAMPLES

In this section we will contrast two platforms: one ostensibly private and one ostensibly public to show how these categories become muddled when the full research assemblage is taken into account.

One of the authors was researching anti-nuclear activists online and found that one of the main venues for organizing and sharing information was a traditional e-mail list. This required authorization by admin to join, which in terms of traditional internet ethics would be considered "private" and off limits. Yet, in practice the administrator accepted everyone who applied. Also in practice it should be said that the general tone of the list was public – announcements were meant to be as public as possible. In this case the admin, as the gatekeeper and spokesperson for the group, played a crucial role in defining the possible ethics of the study.

The researcher made a data visualization, manually, that is using a custom scraper, which took only the titles of the posts and the user names and made a network graph to show which users interacted with particular posts. This felt problematic because he was actively collecting data rather than using an existing tool hooked up to and authorized by an API: proceeding without the (tacit) cooperation of the platform or its users.

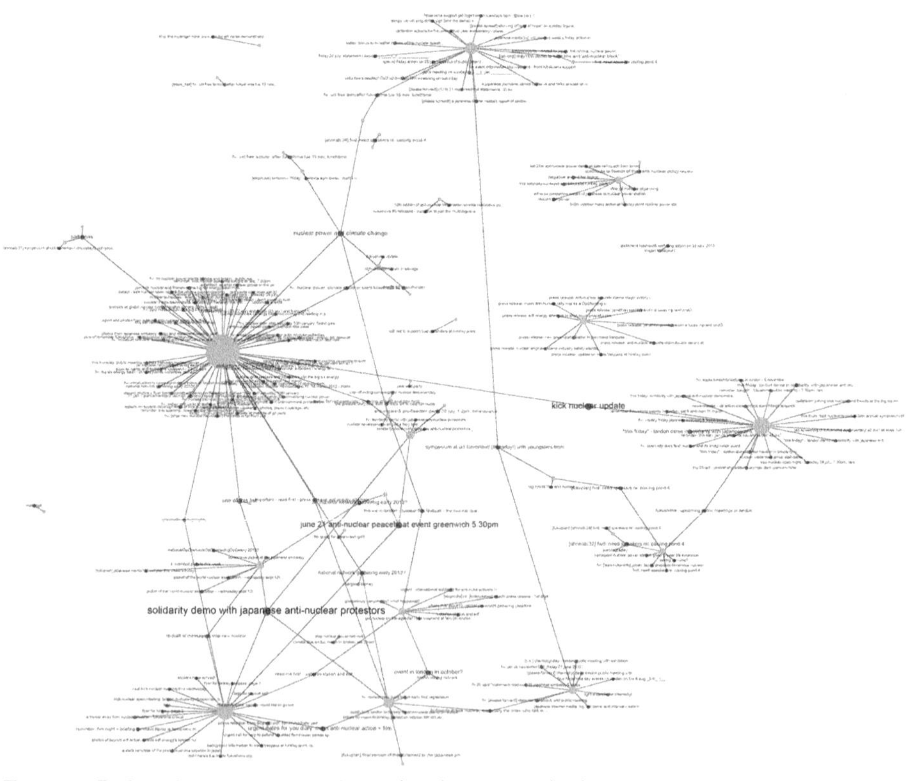

Figure 2. Redacted bi-partite map of users (grey) and posts (red). Size indicates degree or the number of users replying to the post.

However, when speaking to the admin of the list, this seemed to be less of a problem. The researcher showed him the diagram asking him how he felt being visualized. This having elicited a blank stare, the researcher offered, “Does it feel uncomfortable?” The admin mused that it was “a bit creepy”, but went on to say that “it was fine” because he deemed the researcher to be on the right side of the nuclear issue. He then spoke about how nuclear energy companies were no doubt monitoring them in similar ways for different purposes (they had mysteriously anticipated many of their protests).

So firstly, it should be said that ethics becomes different when surveillance itself is part of the case. What happens if the maps get into the wrong hands? The network graph mostly showed the titles of very public posts which were meant to be spread widely, but they also contained arguments between members which possibly revealed tensions within the group. Because the nodes on network graphs are conventionally sized by degree, the number of connections to other nodes, the size of the nodes actually drew attention to the back and forth arguments (Laniado, Tasso, Volkovich, & Kaltenbrunner, 2011), so the visualization software itself can highlight sensitive material. Although the content of the list was very “public facing” due to the permissions, properties of networks and potential uses of the graphs, and the titles of posts and users were redacted from the image above.

The second researcher was undertaking a project examining commonly used Instagram hashtags relating to diet in order to understand how users depicted their relationship to food for a broader study on “obesogenic environments.”[4] In comparison to the prior case study, researching Instagram hashtags[5] in such a way is problematic, not because of the way they expose group dynamics but because of what they inadvertently reveal about individuals (Highfield & Leaver, 2016) with the added difficulty of there being no administrator to act as a gatekeeper or spokesperson for those using the hashtag.

The researcher created a co-hashtag network of #foodporn in order to see the attitudes to food or diet associated with the hashtag as well as a contact sheet of the posted images in order to conduct a visual analysis of the content and identify hashtags that potentially denoted obesogenic lifestyles. The researcher used the Digital Methods Initiative’s tools, which worked despite the fact that the architecture of Instagram in some sense discourages mass scraping and analysis (partly due to limiting the number and size of calls to 500 per hour). Officially, the Platform Policy states that it should not be used to “simply display User Content, import or backup content …” (Instagram, 2016). Instagram’s terms of service lists Instagram users, brands, advertisers, broadcasters, and publishers as intended users but neglects to include academic researchers.

In considering the ethics of this scraping Instagram data, where each and every user could not feasibly be contacted for permission, the researcher instead approached frequent hashtag users about their Instagram data being utilized for visualizations, but very few of those approached responded. One interviewee found the idea of co-hashtag analysis as unproblematic due to the fact that the visualization did not focus on individuals. Still, since hashtags, by their very function, are a means of locating and profiling content, they could help an enterprising troll to locate users with particular eating habits and "fat shame" them.

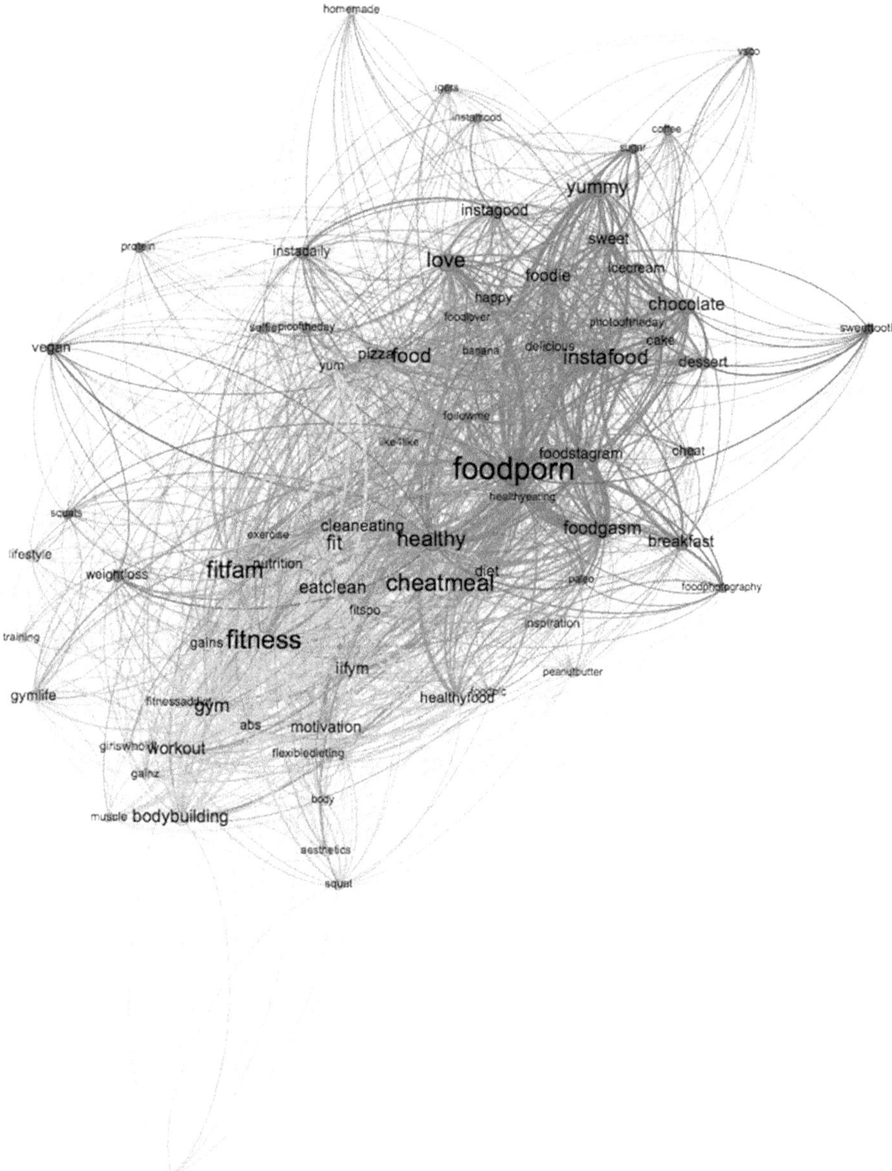

Figure 3. A co-hashtag network displaying hashtags used alongside #cheatday. It depicts fitness and diet related hashtags in green/blue and foodie related hashtags in red.

In relation to the contact sheet of images, their feelings on this were largely dependent on what was being shown. When the images were depictions of food, this was deemed unproblematic, however, other projects have made use of Instagram self-portraits and have created visualizations based on these images (Tifentale & Manovich, 2015) without user consent. For one user pictures containing identifiable people were more problematic because they could be used to stereotype or make judgments about the person behind the portrait, depending on what the users used Instagram for. For exam ple, those who use Instagram to create and maintain social hierarchies (primarily but not limited to teenagers) may have more to lose by being potentially "outed" than casual users.

Just as in the previous case, the decision to display user names or photos depends on scraping tools, user behaviors, the particular features of visualizations and those who might use them after the fact, but with social media platforms there are far more non-human actors involved (APIs, search and ranking algorithms) which influence what is made visible, but which are not as easy to consult or negotiate with. What we can do is draw more attention to these negotiations because issues of access, representation, privacy, and visibility can be empirically interesting, not just unwanted effects.

CONCLUSIONS

The point of the preceding vignettes is that the ethics of research is a tricky negotiation between humans and technologies, researchers, research subjects, and potential readers, and this plays out in unpredictable ways. According to work in STS, all methods are entangled with particular research subjects, settings, and technologies, and inflect research aims in contingent ways, but data visualizations and social media data are an interesting case because they potentially make us *more* dependent on these other actors, devices, and algorithms and make these entanglements harder to ignore.

Our empirical examples dealt with research in two contrasting platforms, one long established and one nominally "social" to show that there are no clear cut distinctions between public and private, only differing practices of making things public which are distributed throughout the research process from data collection to presentation and circulation of findings. If researchers pretend to be fully in control of the research setting, as in a laboratory, then, they may end up neglecting some of the less obvious participants in research.

As we emphasized earlier, this does not absolve the researcher from making tough choices or taking responsibility, we are merely suggesting that the researchers should take into account the entire method assemblage when making decisions. There is no way to ensure that there are no unintended consequences of research, but practitioners can be explicit about these tensions and negotiations rather than trying to contain or suppress ethical trouble.

NOTES

1. Also while survey based statistics are often explanatory, producing causal relationships, these are largely descriptive (Savage & Burrows, 2007) and exploratory (Rieder, 2013).
2. As Marres (2012) notes, there is nothing new about entanglements between the academy and the private sector, or the active role of research subjects, but the balance has increasingly shifted.
3. Though STS researchers do analyze the work that normative claims and categories do in the world e.g. (Slater, 2013).
4. This was done as part of a broader datasprint research project on Oboesogenic Environments at the Technoanthropology Lab, Aalborg University, Copenhagen.
5. Since carrying out this research in late 2015, the ability for researchers to access Instagram data through the API has changed greatly. We therefore, have written this section with reference to data collected before the API change, but acknowledging what the current API and terms of service (in effect from June 2016) allow. Rieder (2016) gives a good overview of the changes to Instagram's API and what they mean for researchers wanting to access Instagram data.

REFERENCES

Barocas, S., & Nissenbaum, H. (2014). Big data's end run around procedural privacy protections. *Communications of the ACM, 57*(11), 31–33.

Bassett, E. H., & O'Riordan, K. (2002). Ethics of internet research: Contesting the human subjects research model. *Ethics and Information Technology, 4*(3), 233–247.

boyd, d., & Crawford, K. (2012). Critical questions for big data. *Information, Communication & Society, 15*(5), 662–679. Retrieved from http://doi.org/10.1080/1369118X.2012.678878

Bucher, T. (2012). Want to be on the top? Algorithmic power and the threat of invisibility on Facebook. *New Media & Society, 14*(7), 1164–1180.

Callon, M. (2008). Economic markets and the rise of interactive agencements: From prosthetic agencies to habilitated agencies. In T. Pinch & R. Swedberg (Eds.), *Living in a material world: Economic sociology meets science and technology studies* (pp. 29–56). Cambridge, MA: MIT Press.

Driscoll, K., & Walker, S. (2014). Big data, big questions| working within a black box: Transparency in the collection and production of big Twitter data. *International Journal of Communication, 8*, 1745–1764.

Gerlitz, C., & Stevenson, M. (2009). *The place of issues. Digital Methods Initiative*. Retrieved from https://wiki.digitalmethods.net/Dmi/ThePlaceOfIssues

Gregory, K., & Bowker, G. (2016). The data citizen. In D. Nafus (Ed.), *Quantified: Biosensing technologies in everyday life* (pp. 211–226). Cambridge, MA: MIT Press.

Highfield, T., & Leaver, T. (2016). *Instagrammatics: Analysing visual social media [PowerPoint Slides]*. Workshop presented at 2016 CCI Digital Methods Summer School, Brisbane, Australia. Retrieved from http://www.slideshare.net/Tama/instagrammatics-analysing-visual-social-media-workshop

Hine, C. (Ed.). (2005). *Virtual methods: Issues in social research on the Internet*. Oxford: Berg Publishers.

Instagram. (2016). *Platform policy*. Retrieved from https://www.instagram.com/about/legal/terms/api/

Jacomy, M., Venturini, T., Heymann, S., & Bastian, M. (2014). Forceatlas2, a continuous graph layout algorithm for handy network visualization designed for the gephi software. *PLoS One, 9*(6), 1–12. Retrieved from http://dx.doi.org/10.1371/journal.pone.0098679

Johnson, D. G., & Wetmore, J. M. (2008). STS and ethics: Implications for engineering ethics. In E. J. Hackett, O. Amsterdamska, M. Lynch, & J. Wacjman (Eds.), *The handbook of science and technology studies* (pp. 567–582). Cambridge, MA: MIT Press.

Kennedy, H., Hill, R. L., Aiello, G., & Allen, W. (2016). The work that visualisation conventions do. *Information, Communication & Society, 19*(6), 715–735.

Koed Madsen, A. (2013). *Repurposing digital traces to organize social attention.* Retrieved from http://hdl.handle.net/10398/8746

Laniado, D., Tasso R., Volkovich, Y., & Kaltenbrunner, A. (2011). When the wikipedians talk: Network and tree structure of wikipedia discussion pages. In *Proceedings of 5th annual conference on weblogs and social media.* Menlo Park, CA: AAAI.

Latour, B. (1999). *Pandora's hope: Essays on the reality of science studies.* Cambridge, MA: Harvard University Press.

Law, J. (2004). *After method: Mess in social science research.* London: Routledge.

Markham, A., & Buchanan, E. (2012). *Ethical decision-making and Internet research. Recommendations form the AoIR Ethics Working Committee (Version 2.0).* Retrieved from http://aoir.org/reports/ethics2.pdf

Markham, A. N. (2006). Ethic as method, method as ethic: A case for reflexivity in qualitative ICT research. *Journal of Information Ethics, 15*(2), 37–54. Retrieved from http://search.proquest.com/docview/1681850245?accountid=11149

Marres, N. (2012). The redistribution of methods: On intervention in digital social research, broadly conceived. *The Sociological Review, 60*(S1), 139–165.

Marres, N., & Weltevrede, E. (2013). Scraping the social? Issues in real-time social research. *Journal of Cultural Economy, 6*(3), 313–335.

Rieder, B. (2013). Studying Facebook via data extraction: The Netvizz application. In *Proceedings of the 5th annual ACM web science conference* (pp. 346–355). New York, NY: ACM.

Rieder, B. (2016, May 27). *Closing APIs and the public scrutiny of very large online platforms.* [blog post] Retrieved from http://thepoliticsofsystems.net/2016/05/closing-apis-and-the-public-scrutiny-of-very-large-online-platforms/

Rogers, R. (2013). *Digital methods.* Cambridge, MA: MIT Press.

Savage, M., & Burrows, R. (2007). The coming crisis of empirical sociology. *Sociology, 41*(5), 885–899.

Slater, D. (2013). *New media, development and globalization: Making connections in the global south.* Oxford: Polity Press.

Tifentale, A., & Manovich, L. (2015). Selfiecity: Exploring photography and self-fashioning in social media. In D. M. Berry & M. Dieter (Eds.), *Postdigital aesthetics: Art, computation and design* (pp. 109–122). New York, NY: Palgrave Macmillan.

Venturini, T., Laffite, N. B., Cointet, J.-P., Gray, I., Zabban, V., & Pryck, K. D. (2014). Three maps and three misunderstandings: A digital mapping of climate diplomacy. *Big Data & Society, 1*(2), 1–19. Retrieved from http://doi.org/10.1177/2053951714543804

Vis, F., & Goriunova, O. (Eds.). (2015). *The iconic image on social media: A rapid research response to the death of Aylan Kurdi**. Retrieved from https://www.scribd.com/doc/293236608/Visual-Social-Media-Lab-The-Iconic-Image-on-Social-Media-a-rapid-research-response-to-the-death-of-Aylan-Kurdi#fullscreen

Zimmer, M. (2010). "But the data is already public": On the ethics of research in Facebook. *Ethics and Information Technology, 12*(4), 313–325. Retrieved from http://doi.org/10.1007/s10676-010-9227-5

PART THREE

Contexts

CHAPTER TWENTY

Negotiating Consent, Compensation, AND Privacy IN Internet Research

PatientsLikeMe.com as a Case Study

ROBERT DOUGLAS FERGUSON

INTRODUCTION

Social networking sites have become an invaluable research tool for researchers today. One type of information that is becoming more accessible through the Internet is personal health information. *Personal health information (PHI)* (Pratt, Unruh, Civan, & Skeels, 2006) refers to documentation about the state of a person's health, normally collected and under the control of health care practitioners or patients. The use of social networking platforms to collect personal health information brings to the fore unresolved ethical dilemmas around: 1) the collection of informed consent online; 2) compensation for participants' contributions; and 3) the ability of researchers to guarantee privacy after data collection. To explore these ethical dilemmas, I reflect on ethnographic fieldwork collected as part of an anthropological study on how people relate to their personal health information. Participant observation was conducted over ten months within the Mood Disorders Community on the American patient social networking site and research platform PatientsLikeMe.com (PLM).[1] My interactions with users of PLM identified: 1) how the site's user agreement failed to ensure participation was full and informed, particularly concerning secondary commercial use of data collected on the site; 2) how some participants perceive their participation on PLM as a form of labor, which underscores the importance of selecting appropriate forms of incentive or remuneration; and lastly 3) how real limitations in the ability of site users and researchers to control the dissemination of personal information in online settings often necessitates users to accept tradeoffs in privacy, or their degree of participation in online settings, in order to gain and retain access to online services such as PLM. I conclude with a brief discussion about how some of these issues might be resolved by future Internet researchers.

PATIENTSLIKEME

PatientsLikeMe.com (PLM) is a social networking site and research platform for patients with various health conditions. Brothers Jamie and Ben Heywood created PLM with their long-time friend Jeff Cole in response to Ben and Jamie's brother Stephen's diagnosis with amyotrophic lateral sclerosis (ALS) in 1998. The site was originally launched in 2005 as an online community for ALS patients. For the Heywood family, PLM's founding was a direct response to a perceived deficit in information and institutional interest in ALS; a condition deemed so rare that it is difficult to mobilize and recoup costs associated with the research and development (Ascher, Jordan, Heywood, & Heywood, 2007). Since its founding, later, PLM expanded to include various other medical conditions, such as mood disorders, cancers, Parkinsons, HIV/AIDS, and multiple sclerosis, before eventually broadening to include "any" patient.

As a social networking site, PLM contains a series of forums in which members can exchange information and informal social support with others on the site. In addition to the forums, PLM offers each member a sophisticated personal health record (PHR) as part of their user profile. Within their PHRs, site members can track and record changes in their health over time, such as diagnoses, symptoms, therapies, and side effects. Data collected through PLM PHR are displayed to members using a series of attractive visualization tools, and members can also print out summaries of their PHR for offline health care providers.

As a researching platform, PLM aggregates and analyzes data collected through the site. Data are available for sale to its researcher clients, which have included several major pharmaceutical companies and the United States' Food and Drug Administration (PatientsLikeMe, 2015). In addition to data, PLM offers researchers a suite of data collection tools (i.e. questionnaires, focus groups), which they can use to interact directly with patient members on the site.

THE SCRAPING INCIDENT

Near the end of my ten months of fieldwork, an incident occurred on the site, which caused members of the site to reflect on the value of their participation and PHI on PLM. A data mining bot was discovered on the site, which was later traced to a New York based marketing firm, Nielsen Co. Upon discovery, PLM sent the firm a cease-and-desist letter requesting that all data extracted from the site be deleted from the marketing firm's servers. In response, the firm agreed to stop scraping the site and offered to quarantine, rather than delete, extracted data to prevent its future use or dissemination (Angwin & Stecklow, 2010).

The story about "the scraping incident" was reported on PLM (Heywood, 2010a, 2010b) as well as by the Wall Street Journal, the latter of which quoted Jamie Heywood stating, "We're a business, and the reality is that someone came in and stole from us" (as cited in Duhigg, 2012, para. 53). Members of the site were quick to notice the way in which PLM made claim of ownership to their PHI contained on the site, which invoked reflections on the nature and value of participation on the site. Overall, members of PLM described several contexts in which their participation violated some of their expectations about consent, compensation, and privacy in comparison to "traditional" research settings.

ETHICAL ISSUES

Ethical Issue 1: User Agreements as Informed Consent

One ethical dilemma that emerged was whether a User Agreement, which explains a website's terms of service, could be an adequate means or substitute for collecting informed consent of individuals online in the context of research. Many members expressed awareness of the fact that their PHI was being collected via the site and used for research purposes, but some members were not fully aware of all the nuances of PLM's for-profit motives despite PLM's disclosure of this information in their user agreement,

> "I sort of knew that PLM [collected] patient data and used it for research, or shared it with certain companies (eg., pharmaceutical and mental health care industries) but surprised to hear they sell it."

Site members' partial awareness of PLM's business model might be explained by the facts that the user agreement is long, full of legal language, non-negotiable, and automated. Thus, it is likely that many individuals did not read the full terms prior to joining the site, which impacts the degree to which their consent is truly informed.

Another ethical dilemma that arises, especially when conducting research with vulnerable populations online, is whether all people can adequately provide informed consent online. As one member identifies, the asynchronous fashion in which user agreements are signed online makes it difficult to assure participation is fully informed and has been consented to:

> "I'm still trying to wrap my head around this whole idea that my life for last two years has been up for sale … There was NO MEETING OF THE MINDS WHEN I SIGNED MY (CONTRACT) AGREEMENT [emphasis in original]. Therefore, there is no contract/agreement. I was mentally ill at the time (as you were aware). And therefore, was unable to fully understand the risk."

The above concern may also apply to several other groups online, including youth, older adults, individuals with minimal computer or technical literacy, and individuals whose first language differs from the language of the website.

Ethical Issue 2: Labor and Compensation

Another ethical issue that the scraping incident brought to the fore is when and how researchers can ethically compensate research participants in online settings. As one participant says:

> "In this day and age, it's not so uncommon and probably not so surprising, but when I take part in Market Research myself I get paid a small amount. Why shouldn't that happen here? … I'm on a disability pension, life is hard enough."

On PLM, some members dedicate large volumes of time and effort to ensure the accuracy of their PHI on the site. In many offline studies, participants are compensated financially in acknowledgement that their participation in research may deprive them of other opportunities to generate income.

On the other hand, research participation is also embedded in an informational gift economy (Mauss, 1954), in which the motivation to participate and give data is connected to larger, non-tangible goals and benefits,

> "If anything I say or post helps to find a cure for bipolar tomorrow or 10 years from now I am happy to contribute to this community."

> "I consider my participation in PLM's site, all of it, a donation of sorts … PLM is an organization I believe in and want to give my time, energy and yes, data to."

The two quotes above demonstrate how research participants are often willing to accept indirect or nonreciprocal forms of compensation when the long-term goals or outcomes of the research resonate with the values, desires, and expectations of participants.

Ethical Issue 3: Privacy and Personally Identifying Information

A third and important ethical issue that members on PLM identified is whether researchers in online settings can adequately protect the privacy of participants in online contexts. This issue becomes increasingly contentious in situations where researchers collect data covertly from searchable spaces online:

> "The fact that we use names other than our real names helps, but really what's to worry? Most of it is friendly [encouragement] and socializing. In my recent situation I did worry some because of a pending medical case so I [temporarily] edited out my bio for [a while] until that clears."

> "In all honesty [-] I think the only way to guard your privacy is to cease posting on any Internet forum, e.g., maintain "lurker" status. Granted, you would still learn quite a bit passively, but would lose out on the opportunity to post questions/comments, which could eliminate more learning opportunities."

Some members see themselves as ultimately responsible for protecting their own privacy online and identify different techniques for mitigating some of the vulnerabilities entailed by their participation. At the same time, members identify that varying degrees of participation entail certain trade-offs that individuals need to consider based on the risks and personal benefits.

DISCUSSION

The above section highlights some of the ethical dilemmas that can emerge as researchers increasingly turn to the Internet and social media as a source for participant recruitment and data collection. Some of the issues identified in this case study are easier to resolve than others.

Issues that emerge around informed consent might be resolved by using a two-step agreement process, in which potential participants are required to demonstrate their comprehension of terms and conditions of their participation. Hypothetically, researchers could require participants to complete a short task (i.e., confirmation questions) that confirm comprehension of the terms and conditions of the research prior to participation online.

The decision whether or not to provide finance incentives in exchange for participation is sensitive. As the above section shows, sometimes direct compensation for research is appropriate and ethical. Internet-based financial services and technologies (i.e., PayPal, Apple Pay, Amazon Wish Lists, etc.) may offer promising avenues for researchers who wish to provide remuneration to participants. On the other hand, sometimes participants are willing to accept less tangible forms of compensation for causes or organizations they value or deem useful. For example, in the case of PLM, many users felt that continued access to the PHR and informal social support available on the site was enough compensation.

Issues surrounding the lifecycle of online data are harder to resolve, especially when data are collected from publicly accessible locations and are personally identifying. In traditional research settings, participants often have the ability to withdraw their participation as well as data. On PLM and other social media platforms, individuals cannot be assured that their information will be permanently removed and inaccessible in the event that a person wishes to stop or not participate in research.

CONCLUSION

In this paper, I argue that the ease and accessibility of personal information, especially about health, makes social media technologies and platforms an attractive tool for researchers. I describe one such platform, PLM, and the ways in which the site's founders attempt to harness the power of the Internet and social media to respond to and participate in the broader health research community. I also describe an incident that resulted in greater awareness of ethical issues (i.e. informed consent, compensation, and privacy) that emerged from use of data collected and contained on the site. I reflect on possible solutions to those ethical issues, some of which may be easier to resolve than others.

NOTE

1. Quotes that appear in this paper also appear in the author's unpublished masters thesis. For full text, see Ferguson (2011).

REFERENCES

Angwin, J., & Stecklow, S. (2010, October 12). "Scrapers" dig deep for data on web. *The Wall Street Journal.* Retrieved from http://on.wsj.com/1zBtmF7

Ascher, S., Jordan, J., Heywood, S., & Heywood, J. (2007). *So much, so fast* [Motion Picture]. Amherst, MA: Balcony Releasing.

Duhigg, C. (2012, February 16). How companies learn your secrets. *New York Times Magazine.* Retrieved from http://nyti.ms/18LN5uz

Ferguson, R. D. (2011). *Crowdsourcing health information: An ethnographic exploration of public and private health information on patientslikeme.com.* (Unpublished master's thesis). York University, Toronto, ON.

Heywood, B. (2010a, May 20). *Transparency, openness and privacy* [Web log post]. Retrieved from http://blog.patientslikeme.com/2010/05/20/bentransparencymessage/

Heywood, B. (2010b, October 2010). *What data do we sell? A continued discussion about "data scraping"* [Web log post]. Retrieved from http://blog.patientslikeme.com/2010/10/21/what-data-do-we-sell-a-continued-discussion-about-data-scraping/

Mauss, M. (1954). *The gift: Forms and functions for exchange in archaic societies.* London: Cohen & West.

PatientsLikeMe. (2015, June 15). *PatientsLikeMe and the FDA sign research collaboration agreement* [Web log post]. Retrieved from http://blog.patientslikeme.com/2015/06/15/patientslikeme-and-the-fda-sign-research-collaboration-agreement/

Pratt, W., Unruh, K., Civan, A., & Skeels, M. M. (2006). Personal health information management. *Communications of the ACM, 49*(1), 51–55.

CHAPTER TWENTY-ONE

The Ethics of Using Hacked Data

Patreon's Data Hack and Academic Data Standards

NATHANIEL POOR

When the data you wanted but could not get presents itself to you thanks to hackers, should you use the data?[1]

A colleague and I study cultural industries and cultural production. We have published research on the topic of *crowdfunding* and have used a variety of data, such as interviews, a survey, and larger scale data we scraped from the web using automated scripts to gather the publically available information on thousands of crowdfunded projects (Davidson & Poor, 2015, 2016). Crowdfunding is when someone has the idea for a project and turns to the internet-based crowd for funding for that project. This is in contrast to funding mechanisms prior to the internet, which included wealthy patrons, arts-focused foundations, government funding, loans, and asking friends and family. In return for funding, backers usually get a copy of the end product or something related to it.

One area of the research we are interested in is the long-term viability of such funding. Could it replace other, more established, but perhaps harder to get artistic funding? We decided to investigate the crowdfunding site Patreon (from "patron"), which is specifically designed to support the long-term funding of creators and their endeavors. I started exploring the site and its structure in August, 2015. However, there was no way to make sure all of the projects would be collected by our automatic web-based collection. An email inquiry to Patreon about viewing all the projects went unanswered. We could not be sure we had retrieved data on all the projects at the site, and as such we would be left with a convenience sample of the projects. We would not be able to draw any conclusions that we could confidently apply to wider contexts or to all the creators on the site. It seemed that this specific line of research was at an end, and we moved on to other related questions.

But a few weeks later, in October, 2015, Patreon was hacked (Goodin, 2015). The entire site was made available, not just all the data on projects, but also private messages, e-mail addresses, passwords, and the code that runs the site. Altogether it totaled approximately 15GB of information. The data we wanted was now available, all of it. Except my colleague and I initially disagreed about if it was appropriate to use it and debated why. He felt it wasn't, I thought it was. Eventually, after my initial excitement wore off, I realized it would not be appropriate to do so.

There are examples of controversial data access by journalists. For example, there was Edward Snowden's release of classified American documents, which falls under the guidelines for journalism and where people have debated the legality and morality of his actions (Adams, 2014). His access was illegal, but for a greater good. Another example was of when employees at Rupert Murdoch's News Corporation in the UK hacked into the cell phones of prominent UK citizens, which was clearly illegal (Fenton, 2012). Both dealt with unauthorized data access.

Certainly, the method the data was gathered under was not legal given US laws and included information meant to be private (such as private messages and passwords). The word "stolen" is not quite appropriate as Patreon still has all the data, "illegal copying" is more accurate. The method by which the data was "collected" tainted all the data.

Some of the data, before the hack, was already public (although perhaps difficult or impossible to get, as retrieving an exhaustive list of every project seemed impossible), and this was the data we were interested in. We would study the same factors as we did previously for our Kickstarter research that was published in a peer-reviewed journal. But this data, if from the hacked data file, is linked to hacking and the release of private data.

But now, with the hack, all the data is public. Were the site users aware of this? Hopefully Patreon sent out a mass e-mail to all of their users informing them about the hack and instructing them to change their passwords. Do the users have an expectation of privacy anymore? Previously they probably did, although perhaps some of the cynical ones who were since proven correct by the hack did not.

We were not going to use any variables for crowdfunding projects we had not used in published academic research, and those variables were good enough to meet academic standards before. We only wanted data that project creators *wanted* to be public, that is, information about their projects. Now that specific data was still public, and it seemed the hack contained the previously public data from *every project*. But should we use it?

I read over the ethics statement of a scholarly group I am a member of, the Association of Internet Researchers, but it didn't address this kind of situation directly. A query to the mailing list resulted in a lively discussion where many people felt it was indeed a gray area, although none said they would use the data outright. One person mentioned how using the data may condone illegal hacking, a valid concern and not something we wanted to do.

Journalists use data and information in circumstances where people did not want the data released, such as with Wikileaks and Edward Snowden. This is a professionally accepted practice, although with the Snowden data, journalists vetted the data first to make sure some types of data were not released, much as we would use only variables we had safely used before. And I could imagine that the Patreon data might be used by academic researchers, specifically security researchers, although they, like we, would make sure not to put any sensitive information in any resulting work. Thus I feel that using such data – at least for some academic areas – meets academic standards. But we are social scientists, not computer scientists or journalists, and our journals, colleagues, and university review committees are based in the social sciences, not computer science.

With my background in media studies, I felt that since we only wanted information that the project creators wanted us to see and that they had already made public, it would be acceptable to use that already public data from the hack. It was public before, but we couldn't get it all, now it was still public and we could get all of it, we just needed to exclude the private data that we had no interest in. With my background in computer science I was reminded of Compaq Computer's famous clean room reverse-engineering of IBM's data: They made sure nothing proprietary was used, and it was legal. Perhaps we could do something similar. Compaq, however, used legal means to get the source data they needed, but in our case the source data was only available thanks to an illegal act, and this was the crux of the matter.

In the end, I downloaded the compressed data file (about 4GB), but I didn't unzip it. I'm not sure what the internal structure of it is, and sorting through it to isolate the parts we want might be more work than it is worth. And I might end up viewing information that was supposed to be private when I try to separate the private from the public in the data, definitely a violation of users' privacy. Overall we realized that just because you can do something, doesn't mean you should.

NOTE

1. A previous, similar, version of this chapter has been published by Data & Society by its Council for Big Data, Ethics, and Society. That version is available at http://bdes.datasociety.net/wp-content/uploads/2016/04/Patreon-Case-Study.pdf

REFERENCES

Adams, A. (2014). Report of a debate on Snowden's actions by ACM members. *SIGCAS Computers & Society, 44*(3), 5–7.

Davidson, R., & Poor, N. (2015). The barriers facing artists' use of crowdfunding platforms: Personality, emotional labor, and going to the well one too many times. *New Media & Society*, *17*(2), 289–307.

Davidson, R., & Poor, N. (2016). Factors for success in repeat crowdfunding: Why sugar daddies are only good for Bar-Mitzvahs. *Information, Communication & Society*, *19*(1), 127–139.

Fenton, N. (2012). Telling tales: Press, politics, power, and the public interest. *Television & New Media, 13*(1), 3–6.

Goodin, D. (2015). *Gigabytes of user data from hack of Patreon donations site dumped online*. Retrieved from http://arstechnica.com/security/2015/10/gigabytes-of-user-data-from-hack-of-patreon-donations-site-dumped-online/

CHAPTER TWENTY-TWO

The Ethics of Sensory Ethnography

Virtual Reality Fieldwork in Zones of Conflict

JEFF SHUTER AND BENJAMIN BURROUGHS

This chapter is a critical analysis of virtual reality (VR) technology in ethnographic fieldwork, specifically the use of VR recording and playback apparatuses such as prosumer multi-camera arrays and Oculus video headsets. Although VR is not a new medium, our purpose is to start a conversation about VR fieldwork and its potential to relay and replay ethnographic findings/recordings within a growing field of digital and sensory ethnography. We begin the process of unpacking what it means for ethnographers to engage with a field site through contemporary VR technology, and how VR transcription and representation of real-time events impact traditional ethnomethodology – in particular, we examine popular claims that VR operates as an empathy machine that shrinks proximity and distance between users and recorded fields of distant suffering.

In July of 2014, Facebook's billion-dollar acquisition of VR firm, Oculus, launched the company into the forefront of revamping virtual reality as an emergent media technology. The Facebook-Oculus deal is just the beginning of a wave of renewed interest and investment in VR as global technology conglomerates ranging from Google to Microsoft invest in a cascade of virtual reality startups. Analysts project this will mature into an 80 billion dollar market by 2025 (Danova, 2015). Yet, VR has been around for nearly sixty years as early VR possibilities explored how "telepresence" or, the experience of being in an environment or community knowingly mediated by communication networks, could reveal more about the human condition (Steuer, 1992). Nascent VR machines paired recordings with tactile interfaces that required audiences to touch and manipulate content beyond the pale of literal tradition. From Sensorama installations to early graphic-oriented computer processing, the impact of early VR experiments shifted print content to multi-modal experiences requiring user-enacted body movements to access information, contributing toward a screen-grabbed, format culture enshrined in present day cyberspace.

Duly inspired by early VR experiments, the present-day structure of Oculus VR interfaces require user bodies to touch and interact with streaming content and, ideally, telescope inside the event at hand. Oculus' first VR hardware release, the Samsung "Gear," requires that users place their Samsung phone directly inside the "Gear" wearable interface; wherein the phone itself becomes an engine and visual portal for experiencing VR content. Google also uses a phone-in-viewfinder technique for their VR device, Google "Cardboard." Oculus' more sophisticated interface, the "Rift," forgoes the use of a phone implant altogether and tethers the wearable VR interface directly to a computer tower, evoking a clinical, cyber-like aesthetic widespread in contemporary computer hardware design.

As Oculus notes on its own website, "Virtual reality has unlimited potential for gaming and entertainment, but it's also a powerful way to drive social change" (Oculus, 2016). And as VR fever shakes the Internet, Oculus' VR for Good Program – a think tank for developers and non-profits to develop impactful experiences across emerging media platforms – is already setting up mentorships with northern California high schools and placing VR recording and transcription technology in the hands of students with the goal of extending opportunities to produce auto-ethnographic projects. Oculus VR for Good Program exec Lauren Burnmaster suggests, "VR will propel social impact in ways we've never seen before" (Nguyen-Okwu, 2016). Furthermore, in a recent article for *Wired*, journalist Angela Watercutter (2015) elucidates a potential humanitarian promise of consumer virtual reality devices: "Taking a page from Roger Ebert's assertion that a movie is an 'empathy machine,' people excited about VR's storytelling potential like to point out that nothing will make a person more empathetic to a protagonist than virtually living in their world. So when that protagonist is actually a resident of a war-torn country, say, or protester in the streets, that potential for empathy is quite sizable."

Recent examples of VR experiences that blur the line between entertainment and social action include *Use of Force*, a VR 360-degree panoramic live-stream that places the viewer in the shoes of 32 year-old Anastasio Hernandez-Rojas as he dies at the hands of United States border patrol agents, and *Clouds over Sidra*, a joint production between global humanitarian non-profit UNICEF and Oculus, which places the viewer in the perspective of 12 year-old Sidra and her life inside a Jordanian refugee camp (Oculus, 2016).

Such VR experiences that mingle activism and entertainment are increasingly popular. For instance, as part of the Samsung VR 360 collection accessible via

Oculus' online store, audiences can stream hundreds of VR 360 panoramic experiences shot and edited by amateur enthusiasts that own prosumer multi-camera arrays. VR enthusiasts can take a vertigo-inducing helicopter flight over the Australian outback, walk the Rue de Rivoli in Paris, explore Egyptian tombs, swim with dolphins, and press olive oil. Often Samsung VR streams will originate from places where conflict and unrest loom in the background. Unlike the filmic VR collaborations described above, Samsung VR streams veer apolitical – each clip represents an enthusiast or filmmaker sharing just a few moments of their physical perspective without crews or executives – though still informative beyond a news headline or cultural treatise.

As researchers experimenting with the possibilities of VR technologies within a growing field of sensory enquiry, we suggest that the very practice of VR data recording using multi-camera arrays and panoramic video stitching redefines the investigator/subject relationship in ethnographic research. Classic ethnomethodology, broadly defined, encourages the researcher to "live in the field" as opposed to doing pre-strategized verbal interviews or laboratory observations (Stoller, 1997). Rather than "report" on phenomena per se, the ethnographer participates in the world they seek to understand – journaling in the field and building a "rapport" with individuals and communities well before developing a laboratory theory (Duncombe & Jessop, 2012). Classical ethnographers smell what their subject smells, eat what their subject eats, and sleep where their subject sleeps (Seremetakis, 1993). Interviews and journal observations ought to exist only as portals to the narratives that circumscribe phenomena in their study. Ideally, this focus on "living in the field" equips an ethnographer with a more reflexive understanding of their studied environment and less preconceived expectations (Silverman, 1993).

However, the increasing use of media recording technologies in ethnographic fieldwork chip away at the idea of "living in the field." Cameras, in particular, are often criticized because they move with and independent of the researcher thus entangling empirical study with added production protocols and arbitrary technology built into the recording medium itself, all of which may effect or color documented content. In other words, recording technologies reassign meaning, place, and even the duration of recorded content according to the wishes of the ethnographer and/or camera operator(s) thereby adding external creative values to otherwise empirical inquiry (Pink, 2009).

Alternatively, if one examines the camera frame beyond its structural power (i.e. the camera operator or producer enforcing their gaze on real-time objects), the critical rift between real-time events and their recordings also operates as a signifier. A field recording may well be embellished; nonetheless, the obvious presence of media technology within a recorded event might also encourage audiences to look closer and critique the content they see, thereby placing a viewer in the position of both camera operator and recorded subject. This is key within the emerging field of sensory ethnography (Pink, 2009). Video compression, camera lens effects, microphone levels and the amount and synchronization of cameras in an array can expose a researcher's signature in their recorded content, thus canceling the power of said researcher by making them complicit and answerable to their own technological exhibitions (just as a movie director's style can so saturate a film that an audience barely notices it exists). By blurring distinctions between real life and virtual interactive space, an audience or researcher engaged in a VR headset (and aware of the obvious array/stitching technologies that produce a VR experience) could exceedingly ignore said technological artifacts and perhaps more significantly *feel* virtual worlds as if they were real-life events (Cranford, 1996). Thus, VR camera arrays and panoramic video stitching could alter the possibility of ethnographic research from hermeneutic recall to the capture, replay, and fetish of VR hardware – solely because headsets are so unnatural and VR production work so apparent one instinctively knows which sensations to ignore and which to engage.

In his provocative work *Ways of Seeing*, John Berger (1980) suggests that image reproduction (as extensions of the photographic medium) both derives from and confirms the suppression of the social function of subjectivity. Audiences expect to read screen events within nominal conventions of viewing, contributing their own knowledge and imagination toward produced narrative structures and particular ideologies. However, operating an Oculus headset replaces human eyes with mechanized eyes, and, in effect, the viewer's gaze extends into unfamiliar visual tropes. Without a visual referent, Oculus' 360-degree virtual environment is scaled to user body movements – thus Oculus users *embody* a virtual environment. Instead of viewing or interpreting virtual space as composition or scape, the user stumbles forward, forming their own unique paths, markers, and sense of location as they go.

Ultimately, there is abundant potential for digital and sensory ethnographers to augment their existing tools along with VR technologies. However, the prospects of VR recording and playback also reveal a future where the presence of the researcher could exist distinctly outside of the events they exhibit. Despite burgeoning consumer appetite for VR entertainment comingled with Facebook-Oculus' self-prescribed social agenda, VR technology and its humanitarian/ethno-research possibilities must keep engendering rigorous open debate.

REFERENCES

Berger, J. (1980). *About looking*. New York, NY: Pantheon Books.

Cranford, M. (1996). The social trajectory of virtual reality: Substantive ethics in a world without constraints. *Technology in Society, 18*(1), 79–92. doi:10.1016/0160-791x(95)00023-k.

Danova, T. (2015, August 12). The virtual reality hardware report: Forecasts, market size, and the trends driving adoption and content development (BI Intelligence, Tech.). *Business Insider*.

Duncombe, J., & Jessop, J. (2012). 'Doing rapport' and the ethics of 'faking friendship'. In T. Miller, M. Birch, M. Mauthner, J. Jessop (Eds.), *Ethics in qualitative research* (pp. 108–121). Los Angeles, CA: Sage Publications.

Nguyen-Okwu, L. (2016, July 27). *Can virtual reality make you a better person?* Retrieved from http://www.ozy.com/fast-forward/can-virtual-reality-make-you-a-better-person/70814?utm_source=dd&utm_medium=email&utm_campaign=07302016&variable=0f0eab2dbe97d3fd121c1a889f2997e1

Oculus. (2016, May 16). *Introducing VR for good – Inspiring social change through the power of VR.* Retrieved from https://www3.oculus.com/en-us/blog/introducing-vr-for-good-inspiringsocial-change-through-the-power-of-vr/

Pink, S. (2009). *Doing sensory ethnography.* Thousand Oaks, CA: Sage Publications.

Seremetakis, C. (1993). The memory of the senses: Historical perception, commensal exchange and modernity. *Visual Anthropology Review, 9*(2), 2–18. doi:10.1525/var.1993.9.2.2.

Silverman, D. (1993). *Interpreting qualitative data: Methods for analysing talk, text and interaction* (2nd ed.). London: Sage Publications.

Steuer, J. (1992). Defining virtual reality: Dimensions determining Telepresence. *Journal of Communication, 42*(4), 73–93. doi:10.1111/j.1460-2466.1992.tb00812.x.

Stoller, P. (1997). *Sensuous scholarship.* Philadelphia, PA: University of Pennsylvania Press.

Watercutter, A. (2015, April 27). How the NY Times is sparking the VR journalism revolution. *Wired.*

CHAPTER TWENTY-THREE

Images of Faces Gleaned from Social Media in Social Psychological Research on Sexual Orientation

PATRICK SWEENEY

In this chapter, I will explore the unique ethical challenges of a group of social psychological research projects that utilize social media profiles and online dating sites to gather images of faces for use as experimental stimuli (e.g. Ding & Rule, 2012; Freeman, Johnson, Ambady, & Rule, 2010; Rule & Ambady, 2008; Rule, Ishii, Ambady, Rosen, & Hallett, 2011; Stern, West, Jost, & Rule, 2012; Tabak & Zayas, 2012; Tskhay, Feriozzo, & Rule, 2013; Tskhay & Rule, 2013). In these studies, images of human faces are selectively downloaded by researchers for use as stimuli in experiments that often ask participants to guess which faces are those of homosexual individuals, and which are those of heterosexual individuals. The images are then kept in databases built to support future research in this area. The use of facial stimuli images in this research raises questions about the ethics of using data that is freely available online, but bound by contextual norms and expectations (Nissenbaum, 2010) about its use. This chapter will outline the procedures of experimental stimuli collection used in these studies, then discuss the ethical challenges that arise in this area of research.

GATHERING FACIAL STIMULI

The images used in these studies were downloaded by researchers from public profiles on social media and dating sites along with associated metadata related to gender, sexual orientation, and location. Some studies in this field of research do not mention where their experimental stimuli came from, but most do include a short description in their methods section of how images were gleaned. Others state they are using a database of faces created for previous research, and provide citation to a previously published study that contains a slightly more robust description of stimuli collection procedures.

Those that do explicitly describe procedures for the collection of facial stimuli are quite similar. The general procedure follows this model: Some person (usually a research assistant) visits a social media site or online dating site, and downloads images of faces that fit that study's criteria for inclusion (facing forward, no glasses or facial hair, etc.), along with the associated metadata such as the gender, sexual orientation, and location of the pictured individual. It is unclear if researchers had to create an account and log into the sites in order to access the images. Missing from all of these narratives is any mention of attempts to obtain informed consent, or discussions of ethical issues beyond blanket statements about data being publically accessible.

ETHICAL CHALLENGES

Several ethical concerns are raised in this practice, including expectations of privacy, valid consent, the unique nature of facial images, and the sensitivity of an individual's sexual orientation in homophobic contexts.

Privacy and Consent

The research conceptualizes the facial images as publically accessible data and thus did not attempt to obtain informed consent from their uploaders, creators, and/or the individuals pictured. While users may be legally bound by a website's terms of service, research has shown that users often "click through" these agreements without actually reading them or understanding their ramifications (Gatt, 2002). Utilizing these images without consent, simply, because they were publically accessible, is similar to the "but the data is already public" argument used as a justification in other ethically challenging uses of social media by researchers (Zimmer, 2010). However, it is likely that the users' contextual norms and expectations (Nissenbaum, 2010) regarding these images did not include harvesting by social psychological researchers for use in experiments on the facial identification of sexual orientation, and instead did not extend beyond their particular use on that particular social media or dating website at that particular point in time.

Unlike the participants who sit in a laboratory and view the images in these experiments, the people depicted and/or those who created the image do not sign a consent form and are not aware that their image is being flashed across a computer screen in the laboratory of a university psychology department. This raises ethical concerns, as the report of the American Psychological Association's Board of Scientific Affairs' Advisory Group on the Conduct of Research on the Internet (Kraut et al., 2004) mentions that definitions of private information are based upon expectations of privacy. In addition, the British Psychological Society's recommendations for ethically conducting Internet mediated research states, "participants may consider their publicly accessible internet activity to be private despite agreeing to the terms of the web service providers' End User Licence Agreements" (2013, p. 7). Whether or not the facial images posted on the social media and dating sites the researchers accessed were intended to be private would greatly impact the ethical nature of these studies.

Faces as Unique Representations of the Self

The particular kind of data used in these studies also contributes to its unique ethical considerations, as faces are a particularly unique and important representation of an individual. They are the most common biometric by which humans identify each other in personal interactions and also are utilized in official representations of identity such as identification cards and passports. The digital information that represents our identity can be seen as "presentations of the self" (Goffman, 1959). These presentations are often subject to attempts to manage the impressions others have of us (Ellison, Heino, & Gibbs, 2006) and are imbued with similar emotional investments in the successful management of those impressions that characterize offline interactions.

Unlike much other data gathered online for research (such as tweets or browsing history), images of a person's face are not traces of a person's activity or a message they have stated about a topic, but represent the person themselves. Indeed, the representations we create of our identities online have been described as "a postmodern performance of the mirror stage" (Nakamura, 2002, p. 37), referencing Lacan's description of the pivotal moment in psychological development when the child forms a sense of wholeness from a previously fragmentary subjectivity by viewing a reflection of their face in a mirror. Facial images that represent a person on the internet can be seen as similarly significant to a person's sense of their self online.

Other scholars have discussed the damage to "feelings of bodily dignity" (Sprokkereef & de Hert, 2012, p. 91) that may occur when parts of a person's body are used by processes outside their control to measure parts of their identity. They argue that when fingerprints, iris scans, and other representations of body parts are abstracted from an individual's embodied experience to be used as a mark of identity, individuals may feel a loss of autonomy and dignity. Faces, more so than other body parts, may convey social meanings around age, gender, race, or health, and thus may have a stronger relationship to feelings of bodily dignity. When used to study potentially sensitive topics such as sexual orientation, this effect may be further intensified.

Sexuality, Sensitivity, and Safety

A person's sexuality is often considered to be a particularly personal and intimate aspect of their life. Non-heteronormative sexualities and genders are often caught in a bind of visibility versus exposure, as the visibility of marginalized people can combat injustice, but can simultaneously expose those same people to violence (Ganesh, Deutch, & Schulte, 2016). For example, apps such as Grindr facilitate connections between community members but have also been used to identify and then arrest, blackmail, or commit violence against the men who use it. Creating databases of heterosexual and homosexual faces removes the ability of the people represented to manage their visibility or exposure. As Ganesh et al. write: "the technical states of 'visible' or 'anonymous' can be considered along a continuum of visibility that has different symbolic and literal meanings for marginalised people, who seek to control and negotiate these states both online and offline" (2016, p. 8). While the individuals represented themselves on online profiles that the images and metadata were sourced from, they had more control over when and where that information is present – there are possibilities of deleting your profile, changing information, or replacing your photo. Research on the topics such as sexuality and with important representations of a person's identity such as the face should take extra care to make sure that participants have as much ability to manage their visibility as possible.

This case is situated in a specific disciplinary context that has longstanding ethical principles regarding interaction with human subjects, but that is struggling to adapt to the blurring of boundaries between public and private domains that occurs on the Internet. This blurring upends many traditional practices across the social sciences and other fields studying social behavior on the Internet, prompting a reevaluation of notions of consent. Going forward, researchers should take special care in using images of faces, particularly when research deals with potentially sensitive topics such as sexuality.

REFERENCES

British Psychological Society. (2013). *Ethics guidelines for conducting Internet-mediated research*. Leicester: British Psychological Society.

Ding, J. Y. C., & Rule, N. O. (2012). Gay, straight, or somewhere in between: Accuracy and bias in the perception of bisexual faces. *Journal of Nonverbal Behavior, 36*, 165–176.

Ellison, E., Heino, R., & Gibbs, J. (2006). Managing impressions online: Self-presentation processes in the online dating environment. *Computer-Mediated Communication, 11*(2), 415–441.

Freeman, J. B., Johnson, K. L., Ambady, N., & Rule, N. O. (2010). Sexual orientation perception involves gendered facial cues. *Personality and Social Psychology Bulletin, 36*(10), 1318–1331.

Ganesh, I., Deutch, J., & Schulte, J. (2016). *Privacy, anonymity, visibility: Dilemmas in tech use by marginalised communities.* Brighton: Institute of Development Studies.

Gatt, A. (2002). Click-wrap agreements: The enforceability of click-wrap agreements. *Computer Law & Security Report, 18*(6), 404–410.

Goffman, E. (1959). The presentation of self in everyday life. New York, NY: Doubleday.

Kraut, R., Olson, J., Banaji, M., Bruckman, A., Cohen, J., & Couper, M. (2004). Psychological research online: Opportunities and challenges. *American Psychologist, 59*(2), 105–117.

Nakamura, L. (2002). *Cybertypes: Race, ethnicity, and identity on the Internet.* New York, NY: Routledge.

Nissenbaum, H. (2010). *Privacy in context: Technology, policy, and the integrity of social life.* Palo Alto, CA: Stanford University Press.

Rule, N., Ishii, K., Ambady, N., Rosen, K. S., & Hallett, K. C. (2011). Found in translation: Cross-cultural consensus in the accurate categorization of male sexual orientation. *Journal of Personality and Social Psychology, 37*(11), 1499–1507.

Rule, N. O., & Ambady, N. (2008). Brief exposures: Male sexual orientation is accurately perceived at 50 Ms. *Journal of Experimental Social Psychology, 44*, 1100–1105.

Sprokkereef, A., & de Hert, P. (2012). Biometrics, privacy, and agency. In E. Mordini & D. Tzovaras (Eds.), *Second generation biometrics: The ethical, legal, and social context.* New York, NY: Springer.

Stern, C., West, T. V., Jost, J., & Rule, N. (2012). The politics of Gaydar: Ideological differences in the use of gendered cues in categorizing sexual orientation. *Journal of Personality and Social Psychology, 104*(3), 520–541.

Tabak, J. A., & Zayas, V. (2012). The roles of featural and configural face processing in snap judgments of sexual orientation. *PLoS One, 7*(5), e36671. doi:10.1371/journal.pone.0036671.

Tskhay, K. O., Feriozzo, M. M., & Rule, N. O. (2013). Facial features influence the categorization of female sexual orientation. *Perception, 42*(10), 1090–1094.

Tskhay, K. O., & Rule, N. O. (2013). Accurate identification of a preference for insertive versus receptive intercourse from static facial cues of gay men. *Archives of Sexual Behavior, 42*, 1217–1222.

Zimmer, M. (2010). "But the data is already public": On the ethics of research in Facebook. *Ethics and Information Technology, 12*(4), 313–325.

CHAPTER TWENTY-FOUR

Twitter Research IN THE Disaster Context – Ethical Concerns FOR Working WITH Historical Datasets

MARTINA WENGENMEIR

In 2010 and 2011 Christchurch and the Canterbury region in New Zealand were hit by a number of devastating earthquakes, which caused the loss of 185 lives, thousands of injuries, and severe damage to transportation, power, and water infrastructures. Similar to other disasters in recent years, such as Hurricane Katrina or the Nepalese and Haiti earthquakes, Twitter was used as a communication tool, to share information, find loved ones, or connect survivors facing the same crisis situation. Analyses of social crisis data offer insights into multiple aspects of the communication process online, for example, how communities were formed, how information was passed on and crowdsourced, what patterns of communications emerged, and where online publics formed (Shaw, Burgess, Crawford, & Bruns, 2013). Despite the benefits of understanding the situational complexities from a local perspective, immediate data collection of social crisis data was impossible to manage for researchers in Christchurch because of widespread power outages. Similar to other social media data, historical data collection comes with a range of ethical challenges attached. This case outlines key challenges faced in the context of a historical Twitter dataset focusing on the Canterbury earthquakes by describing some general concerns surrounding social crisis data, before detailing specifics for historical data extraction from a social science perspective.

VULNERABLE POPULATIONS AND SITUATIONAL CONTEXTS

Disasters pose a disruption to normal life and every day social processes. They leave survivors in shock, influence their behavior, and make them particularly vulnerable (Fischer, 1998). For instance, social media users might not assess what is posted publicly with usual care, in favor of a rapid distribution of information, an instant social connection or an emotional, cathartic reaction in shock. Privacy concerns were set aside in favor of locating help and support, updating friends and family about the personal wellbeing, or to locate loved ones, as other communication channels were out or overloaded. Following the Christchurch earthquakes, people not only tweeted in connection to their own situation but also discussed and reflected on the deaths of victims, voiced their shock and fear through multiple uses of swearwords after the tremors, and posted raw eyewitness accounts publicly on Twitter to make sense of the events. These topics pose privacy concerns which are specific for the situation, as people's choices to communicate publicly and to provide information depend on the context (Nissenbaum, 2009). Crawford and Finn (2015) argue that this context-sensitive data "can be scraped and held on a range of databases indefinitely, opening the risk it could be used in discriminatory contexts in areas such as employment, property and health insurance" (p. 498). For Twitter being a "context-sensitive space" this also means that people might not agree with the use of these public tweets for research at a later point in time (boyd & Crawford, 2012). Further, induced by the rapid nature of events and information flow, users delete tweets because they contain false information, overly emotional and private statements, location information, addresses, e-mails or other contact information. Some of these are still contained and traceable in the data through retweets, for example, false information as starting point of rumors, of collapsed buildings and injuries although the respective user has deleted the original since. The dataset at hand still included personal contact information, such as e-mail addresses and phone numbers, home addresses and location data, as people were trying to find out about the well-being of those missing.

Historical data only gives access to those tweets that have not been deleted before the time of data extraction. Data for this case study was collected four years after the initial earthquake. This delay in historical data collection also meant a longer period of time for people to consider and delete tweets of their own accord. But even though historical data collection allows the consideration and management of tweets by users before data is collected, there might still be users who deleted some of their tweets or whole accounts after a longer period of time.

ACCESS, FILTERING AND STORAGE

Access to historical Twitter data differs from data extraction through the public application programming interfaces (APIs) offered by the platform. Access to historical data is expensive and has to be purchased from data sellers authorized by Twitter. This purchase allows access to the full, undeleted stream of data, the so called firehose, which means more data than can be obtained otherwise, as public APIs only allow access to a restricted amount of data. Access to the firehose also exceeds what would be shown to a Twitter user when searching for information about the earthquakes at the time. Despite the fact that the use of purchased Twitter data is covered by Twitter's terms of service, it places content in a different context to its original one in unfolding disaster.

Purchasing historical data also allows making use of sophisticated filtering techniques, defining a dataset beyond a hashtag and accessing a broad array of data that is publicly available. Seemingly more personal conversations are also included when collecting data beyond a hashtag. Data collection beyond a hashtag generates a larger set but also uncovers @-replies and personal communication among follower networks, which might not be deemed as public by the users.

Tweets connected to a hashtag might be visible a long time after they have been posted, afforded by platform features such as the search function on Twitter (boyd, 2011). Historical data collection even prolongs this period beyond the time frame that data would be accessible through public APIs, which has implications for researchers, when trying to limit exposure to user information in the research process and for research outputs. While the hashtag is arguably used to connect a tweet to a wider public and make it visible, some hashtags only connect micro publics and a very limited number of tweets. There are also alternative uses of hashtags, though, for example, to express emotions or give opinions such as #sadface or #damn. In these cases followers are directed towards a different, more intimate public, which contains a more personal feel. Such specific hashtag combinations make it possible to narrow down and single out tweets in a dataset. They allow connecting tweets to usernames when typed into Twitter's search bar, despite the use of pseudonyms in research outputs. Some tweets can even be found by typing in longer quotes. Tracing information from individual tweets, accounts of deceased people, grieving tweets of their friends and followers and their last conversations on Twitter can be found. Although all these actions have taken place in public, using such data for research purposes creates a different public context, which people might not feel comfortable with.

These risks concerning the traceability of tweets containing sensitive contents have to be managed by the researcher. In disaster research this means the careful consideration of what could be classed as sensitive data for the user and the exclusion of all personal identifiers as well as controlling traceability of tweets when writing about them. Still, aggregation effects can never fully be accounted for as ways in which data can be combined with other data and might reveal something potentially sensitive in the future (Solove, 2013).

In the case of disaster, there are often multiple parties scraping and storing information at the time, producing differing and fractured datasets of the event (Crawford & Finn, 2015). After data has been extracted and remotely stored, deletion of accounts or tweets will have no effect on the dataset, where the information can remain infinitely and potentially resurface at a later point in time. During and after the earthquakes in Canterbury, datasets of differing timeframes were generated and stored by overseas researchers, local and national New Zealand government agencies, disaster response agencies, technical volunteer communities, and local researchers at the University of Canterbury. Twitter's terms of service define restrictions for data to be shared and redistributed, which meant that different datasets could not be brought together. However, parties follow different institutional practices of storing and managing information. This means that each existing set might expose additional information even though another party regulates access to their data in a stricter way (Lambert, 2016).

Twitter datasets from the Canterbury earthquakes highlight some unique ethical challenges in complex disaster contexts, which have been outlined in this section. The option of purchasing historical data adds some further dimensions in prolonging the access to otherwise no longer obtainable data on a larger scale as well as potentially exposing sensitive data, especially in connection with other datasets. A certain distance of data collection to the event can allow self-regulation of users but storing historical data still means that after collection, deleted tweets and accounts still remain. Choices in presenting and cleaning data have to be made from a perspective sensitized for the situation of vulnerable disaster populations, whose risk of exposure is not necessarily outweighed by the benefits of using the data (Crawford & Finn, 2015). The situation of these disaster populations has to be considered in the light of future technologies of obtaining data and insights, too, which have the potential to create aggregation effects that cannot be judged at the current point in time.

REFERENCES

boyd, d. (2011). Social network sites as networked publics. In Z. Papacharissi (Ed.), *A Networked self: Identity, community and culture on social network sites* (pp. 39–58). New York, NY: Routledge.

boyd, d., & Crawford, K. (2012). Critical questions for big data: Provocations for a cultural, technological, and scholarly phenomenon. *Information, Communication & Society, 15*(5), 662–679.

Crawford, K., & Finn, M. (2015). The limits of crisis data: Analytical and ethical challenges of using social and mobile data to understand disasters. *GeoJournal, 80*(4), 491–502.

Fischer, H. W. (1998). *Response to disaster: Fact versus fiction & its perpetuation: The sociology of disaster* (2nd ed.). Lanham, MD: University Press of America.

Lambert, A. (2016). *Disaster data assemblages: Five perspectives on social media and communities in response and recovery*. Paper presented at the 2016 49th Hawaii International Conference on System Sciences (HICSS), IEEE, Kauwai, HI.

Nissenbaum, H. (2009). *Privacy in context: Technology, policy, and the integrity of social life.* Stanford, CA: Stanford University Press.

Shaw, F., Burgess, J., Crawford, K., & Bruns, A. (2013). Sharing news, making sense, saying thanks: Patterns of talk on Twitter during the Queensland floods. *Australian Journal of Communication, 40*(1), 23–39.

Solove, D. J. (2013). Introduction: Privacy self-management and the consent dilemma. *Harvard law review, 126*(7), 1880–1903.

Epilogue

Internet Research Ethics for the Social Age

KATHARINA KINDER-KURLANDA AND MICHAEL ZIMMER

In July 2016, there was a shooting at a shopping mall in Munich in Germany. These attacks were accompanied by a large amount of speculation on online social media platforms so that false information was spread and believed by many. Initially, little reliable information was available to residents from newspapers or on television about highly relevant details such as the number of victims and the type, number, and location of attacks; at the same time, a deluge of information spread via public and semi-public social media platforms. This information's reliability was very difficult to assess, and some of it later turned out to be false. Nevertheless, the rumor that – in addition to the shootings in an outskirts shopping mall – a second attack by Islamist terrorists was underway in the Munich city center led to considerable panic amongst shoppers. Eventually, it was confirmed that there had only been one attack, that the shooter had been motivated by the Breivik attack in Norway some years past, and that he seemed to have suffered from depression.

In an interview with a German newspaper shortly after the Munich shootings, media ethicist Alexander Filipović pointed out how these events showed a lack of what he called "redactional" abilities:

> The redactional society needs to be understood as a utopia: Everybody is able to competently consider t he implications of their public communication and to act accordingly. In fact, we are experiencing the opposite: the post-redactional society. We have no redactions for our public communication. Where this leads we have seen after the attack in Nice, France, and now in Munich. People point their cameras and distribute photos, videos, and false reports furiously fast.[1]

The Munich incident highlights an important issue: The internet still is something surprising and evolving, and, as a result, it is largely impossible to fully oversee its dynamics and complexities. We as scholars (and, in fact, as societies) are trying to understand and even conquer it, often with unintended consequences and rarely without getting it wrong at least some of the time. Filipović's argument draws on Hargreaves (1999) and Hartley (2000), the former of whom argued that "… in a democracy, everyone has the right to communicate a fact or a point of view, however trivial, however hideous" (Hargreaves, 1999, p. 4). John Hartley (2000) showed, following Hargreaves argument, how in the internet age journalism had the potential to become a communicative democracy: While for a long time the right to communicate had been organized in a representative system where members of the public delegated their right to public communication to others (mostly journalists), with the internet "… a more direct form of communicative democracy, that nevertheless makes use of the electronic and broadcast media, is in process of construction and is set to compete with the representative version already found there" (Hartley, 2000, p. 41f.). Theoretically anyone could join in. Hartley therefore saw a new role for journalists in redactional tasks; with 'redaction' referring to the processes of preparing for publication, of revising editing, organizing, rearranging and presenting texts:

> In this context the journalist 'reports to' a privatized, virtualized public whose demands, however, can be expressed directly, in person. A consequence of this altered relationship is that the sense- or sensation-seeking public sets the agenda, not the journalist. (Hartley, 2000, p. 44)

However, this redactional society – where "matter is reduced, revised, prepared, published, edited, adapted, shortened, abridged to produce (…) the new(s)" (Hartley, 2000, p. 44) – has turned out, according to Filipović, to be no more than a utopia that has not actually been realized. Notably, on social media we are currently dealing with the production and distribution of information that can have the status of news without being subject to redactional activities – while traditional newspapers are experiencing huge difficulties. What is more, it is not always easy to assess the reliability of a piece of news, particularly with boundaries between social media and newspapers starting to blur and effects such as personalization taking hold. The literacy skills required to navigate the internet are constantly changing.

These effects, or the "post-redactional society," are the backdrop for our understanding of users' motivations. As researchers, we assess these motivations when studying the internet and when using internet or social media data. However, we have little knowledge of what users are expecting; we cannot assume that they have or have not the redactional abilities that previously used to go along with public communication. What is more, users' abilities and expectations are constantly changing: with every tweet used as an example in a newspaper article, we may assume that amongst users expectations of publicness are changing, or even that deliberate strategies to enhance attention, visibility or invisibility are being employed (Tufekci, 2014; Willson & Kinder-Kurlanda, 2016). Researchers themselves are no different, as our own redactional abilities shape our practices of gathering information, collecting and sharing data, and publishing research results – researchers need to be careful redactors, too, and may often get it wrong as they are challenged to keep up with a constantly moving and very complex target, where research is, as many contributions in this volume note, increasingly shaped by various actors, such as internet companies, social media platform providers, and their users.

The information flows and interactions of users, groups, and crowds on social media are structured by a platform's affordances, making their observation difficult and answering research questions often extremely complex. The ethics of internet research is thus "… a tricky negotiation between humans and technologies, researchers, research subjects, and potential readers, and this plays out in unpredictable ways" (Moats & Perriam, this volume). In the social age, this negotiation particularly includes the following elements and players: platform providers who restrict access to data and police online public spaces; the possibilities for interaction provided by a myriad of resulting platforms with their own logics for structuring communication; advertisers and marketers who collect data for often opaque reasons; and seemingly unpredictable "crowds" of users who may cause content to "go viral." As a result, researchers are faced with unpredictability and risk, especially when publishing their results. There is, for example, the worry that the publication of a specific piece of research may draw unwanted attention to a phenomenon or to certain people or groups – and while this may be an issue for various research fields or topics independently of whether the internet or internet data is the focus – with the internet the publication may have a much wider impact with the researcher "losing control" (as shown, for example, in the case by Klastrup, this volume). Ethical dilemmas facing internet researchers in the social age are thus connected to negotiating the expansion of actors and risks in distributed communicative environments, particularly where actors have unequal power and where there is a loss of control over social media activities, content and communication (Hutchinson et al., this volume).

RESEARCH ETHICS AND INFORMED CONSENT WITH SOCIAL DATA

As Buchanan writes in her introduction to this volume, many concrete challenges for internet research ethics are connected to the new and different types of data and resulting possibilities for (big) data analyses. In the past ethical research practice – and much of the thinking about research ethics – was focused on research where the assumption was that data is mostly generated through researcher interactions such as when conducting interviews or surveys. Social media data, however, is "found" or "transactional" data (Savage & Burrows, 2007; Thomson, 2016), produced for other purposes than research, with a clear or unclear intention, and often even as a byproduct of other activities.

For surveys and other research involving large groups of people, acquiring study participants' informed consent has been an established ethical practice for a long time. When conducting analyses on "found" data or user generated content asking for consent to conduct a specific study is not only rarely feasible but often impossible. Researchers may not even have a way to contact the generators of content or trace data. Therefore mostly, when research data is gathered from social media or other internet platforms, legal release forms provided by internet companies substitute the traditional research participant consent forms. The likelihood that users are even aware that research is covered in these legal release forms, i.e. the terms of service that one accepts when first setting up a user profile, is small (Hutton & Henderson, 2015) – and even if this counts as informed consent users are necessarily not informed about the aims and methods of an individual project.

Questions of data ownership also arise: Who is and who should be allowed to use the data if internet companies and social media platform providers are already doing their own research? This is a particularly important question as research results are used to change and adapt public content on the internet, which may be manipulated or hacked in ways that the public does not necessarily fully understand. Many researchers thus see it as an ethical obligation to work with this kind of data, especially in order to better understand individual users' exposure to news items and other information and to ensure algorithmic transparency, for example, in the production of news (Diakopoulos & Koliska, 2016).

Internet researchers aiming to protect research subjects' interests are often forced to guess users' intentions and to make decisions about how to deal with the research data according to these perceived intentions. They may, for example, decide to anonymize data (a difficult undertaking in most cases) or, alternatively, to recognize authorship by quoting a website and its author. However, such individual decisions are increasingly difficult when dealing with big data analyses, when a blanket decision must be made for all users or data sources. Here, challenges include how to avoid taking a paternalistic stance; a solution could be to allow users to determine by themselves what happens to the data and to aim not to make decisions for the user but to facilitate their decision making. Another challenge is that those who research the internet often do not have a tradition of an ethics discourse in their fields and received little or even no ethical training as part of their academic qualification. This is a question beyond ethics as it touches upon the wider issues of new methodologies that are being developed without an explicit epistemology in the sense of a philosophical underpinning.

As many current questions in internet research ethics are connected to data, its provenance, management, ownership status and explanatory power data repositories and their curators may become more and more important in assisting and guiding researchers, in addition to ethics boards. While many traditional research data archives or repositories are not yet prepared to deal with social media data per se they have established standards, practices and tools for metadata, documentation, data management and ethically and legally reflective data sharing. Newer institution such as web observatories and internet archives, on the other hand, have expertise in the various kinds of internet data and are aware of the specific challenges of new methodologies, but they usually are not as grounded within the established research support communities and their tools as other repositories are. Research data repositories, archives and web observatories, with their unique positioning within the research community (very close to the researchers yet often strongly connected to funding agencies and policy makers), their greater visibility (than an individual research project) may have the opportunity to a) tackle platform providers' often too restrictive data sharing policies which prevent peer-reviewing and thus quality controlling internet data-based research, b) find ways of ensuring transparency of internet research by establishing easy-to-use adapted data management and documentation standards and data citation tools and c) establish more coherent and comprehensive ways of sharing additional material such as web-scraping scripts or other code used for cleaning and analysis in order to leverage the persisting difficulties of sharing data itself.

SO – WHAT TO DO?

The chapters in this book offer extensive reflection about current internet research ethics and suggest some important reframings of well-known concepts such as justice (Hoffmann & Jonas), privacy (Ochs & Matzner), or research validity (Puschmann). They also provide other researchers with concrete case studies to learn from, and – and we believe that this is most important of all – they show that *there is no "ethical research" of the internet in the social age.* Rather, we can really only strive for "ethically-informed" research practices. For one, while ethics can help us by teaching us to think about what we should do or what might be just, it does not *per se* provide solutions or specific courses of action. Rather, ethically-informed research practices come out of processes of deliberation and decision making under great uncertainty, which often may go wrong or seemingly force us towards less-than-ideal options (see, for example, the cases discussed in Hargittai &

Sandvig, 2015). Furthermore, this decision-making process cannot simply be "outsourced" to ethics review boards: In any research project, decision making is eventually dependent on the researcher's individual conscience, but this is even more so in internet research, where often there are few rules or experts. Neither can ethical decision making always be taken care of by blanket rules. For example, if a rule was established that no tweets should be quoted to protect users' privacy and respect the lack of informed consent to research being conducted, this could paternalistically ignore users' carefully crafted public communication targeted at achieving maximum attention – and not acknowledge their authorship. Finally, a researcher will always impact their research environment, no matter how ethically-based their practices might be. As an internet researcher, you might harvest contextually-bound social streams, lurk in online spaces, or impose algorithmic logic on large data sets. These actions, no matter how ethically-informed, have consequences, even if unintended. The important thing is to recognize this condition and to find ways to engage with research ethics as a deliberative process – not to pretend that you have solved the problem and have achieved "ethical research."

We approached *Internet Research Ethics for the Social Age: New Challenges, Cases, and Contexts* with a desire to engage with these difficult ethical discussions and debates, and to help stimulate new ways to think about the novel ethical dilemmas we face as internet and social media-based research continues to evolve. We cannot solve the ethical challenges of internet research in the social age, but with this collection, we hope to have continued the conversation.

NOTE

1. See: Article from 27th of July 2016 in "taz.de – die tageszeitung", retrieved from: http://www.taz.de/!5321764/ (own translation from the German original).

REFERENCES

Diakopoulos, N., & Koliska, M. (2016). Algorithmic transparency in the news media. *Digital* Journalism. Published online: 27 Jul 2016, doi:10.1080/21670811.2016.1208053.

Hargittai, E., & Sandvig, C. (Eds.). (2015). *Digital research confidential: The secrets of studying behavior online*. Cambridge, MA: The MIT Press.

Hargreaves, I. (1999). The ethical boundaries of reporting. In M. Ungersma (Ed.), *Reporters and the reported: The 1999 Vauxhall Lectures on Contemporary Issues in British Journalism* (pp. 1–15). Cardiff: Centre for Journalism Studies.

Hartley, J. (2000, April). Communicative democracy in a redactional society: The future of journalism studies. *Journalism, 1*, 39–48. doi:10.1177/146488490000100107..

Hutton, L., & Henderson, T. (2015). "I didn't sign up for this!": Informed consent in social network research. *Proceedings of the Ninth International AAAI Conference on Web and Social Media (ICWSM)* (pp. 178–187).

Savage, M., & Burrows, R. (2007). The coming crisis of empirical sociology. *Sociology, 41*(5), 885–899. Retrieved from http://doi.org/10.1177/0038038507080443

Thomson, S. D. (2016). Preserving Social Media. *DPC Technology Watch Report*. Retrieved from http://dpconline.org/publications/technology-watch-reports

Tufekci, Z. (2014). Big questions for social media big data: Representativeness, validity and other methodological pitfalls. *ICWSM '14: Proceedings of the 8th International AAAI Conference on Weblogs and Social Media* (pp. 505–514).

Willson, M., & Kinder-Kurlanda, K. (2016). Playing the algorithm: Mobile gamers' everyday (in) visibility strategies. *Proceedings of the Research Conference of the Association of Internet Researchers (AoIR), 2016, Berlin, Germany.*

Contributor Biographies

Elizabeth Buchanan is Endowed Chair in Ethics and Director of the Center for Applied Ethics at the University of Wisconsin-Stout. Her research focuses on the intersection of research regulations and Internet research. She has written and presented widely for over fifteen years to many IRBs throughout the United States, and research ethics boards internationally.

Benjamin Burroughs is an Assistant Professor of Emerging Media in the Hank Greenspun School of Journalism and Media Studies at the University of Nevada, Las Vegas (UNLV). His research focuses on civic streaming, media industries, and social media.

Rebeca Cerezo-Menéndez is an associate professor at the Department of Psychology at the University of Oviedo. Her main area of interest is metacognition and educational data mining.

Amaia Eskisabel-Azpiazu is a Ph.D. candidate at the University of Oviedo; her line of research is at the crossroads of social media mining and the detection of mental health issues.

Charles Ess is a Professor in Media Studies in the Department of Media and Communication at the University of Oslo, and Director of the Center for Research in Media Innovation (CeRMI). His research and publications emphasize cross-cultural and ethical perspectives in Internet Studies, and Information and Computing Ethics.

Robert Douglas Ferguson is a doctoral candidate and researcher at the McGill School of Information Studies. His areas of research include personal information management, personal archiving, and research ethics for information, technology, and design.

Daniel Gayo-Avello is an associate professor at the Department of Computer Science at the University of Oviedo. His main area of interest is social media mining.

Natalia Grincheva is a Research Fellow at the Transformative Technologies Research Unit at the University of Melbourne. She studies digital diplomacy, focusing on new museology and social media technologies, and the "diplomatic" uses of new media by museums in North America, Europe, Russia and South Asia.

Ylva Hård af Segerstad is associate professor in applied information technology at the University of Gothenburg. Her main research interest is in interaction in digital communication technologies, including the role and use of mobile technologies, social media as well as digital methods.

Anna Lauren Hoffmann is an Assistant Professor at the University of Washington iSchool. Her research and writing examines the relationships between data, technology, and human values like respect and justice.

Soraj Hongladarom is professor of philosophy and Director of the *Center for Ethics of Science and Technology* at Chulalongkorn University in Bangkok, Thailand. He has published books and articles on such diverse issues as bioethics, computer ethics, and the roles that science and technology play in the culture of developing countries.

Christine Howes is an associate lecturer in linguistics at the University of Gothenburg. Her main research interest is in interaction in dialogue, which she studies using a range of perspectives, including computational and psycholinguistics.

Lee Humphreys is an Associate Professor of Communication at Cornell University. She studies the perceived uses and effects of communication technology.

Jonathon Hutchinson is a lecturer in Online and Social Media Communication at the University of Sydney. His current research projects explore everyday social media use, the role of social media influencers within co-creative environments, and how social media is used in cyber-terrorism.

Anne Jonas is a PhD Student in the School of Information at University of California, Berkeley. She studies online education, social justice, and critical design.

Dick Kasperowski is an associate professor in theory of science at the University of Gothenburg. His research includes citizen science, participatory practices, open collaborative projects in scientific work, digital methods and governance of science.

Katharina Kinder-Kurlanda is a senior researcher and team lead at the GESIS – Leibniz Institute for the Social Sciences and an Adjunct Lecturer at the Department of Web Science and Technologies at Koblenz University, Germany. Her main research interests are internet research ethics, web science methodology, algorithms and security practices.

Lisbeth Klastrup is an Associate Professor with the Culture & Communication Research Group at the IT University at Copenhagen. She researches social media use and culture in a Danish and global context.

Christopher Kullenberg is a researcher in theory of science at the University of Gothenburg. His main interests include citizen science, quantification in the social sciences and digital methods.

Stephen P. Lewis is an Associate Professor in the Department of Psychology at the University of Guelph. He is current Chair of the Research Ethics Board at the University of Guelph and President of the International Society for the Study of Self-injury. Central to his research is the use of the Internet as a research platform and outreach tool to study self-injury and related mental health difficulties among youth and emerging adults.

Mary Elizabeth Luka is Banting Post-doctoral Fellow at Sensorium Centre for Digital Arts and Technology, School of the Arts, Media, Performance and Design, York University, Toronto, Canada. Her scholarly work focuses on the concept of creative citizenship to investigate how civic, culture and business sectors are networked in the digital age.

Fiona Martin is a Discovery Early Career Research Award fellow and Senior Lecturer in Online Media in the Department of Media and Communications at the University of Sydney. She is the co-author, with Associate Professor Tim Dwyer of Sharing News Online (Palgrave, 2017) and co-editor, with Professor Gregory F. Lowe, of The Value of Public Service Media (Nordicom, 2014).

Tobias Matzner is professor for media studies at Paderborn University in Germany. His research focuses on the development of information technologies and their ramifications for fundamental political concepts like subjectivity, justice, or autonomy.

Mélanie Millette is Assistant Professor at the Département de communication sociale et publique, UQAM, Canada. She studies political uses of social media in the context of Québec and Canada, focusing on online visibility for minorities, and addresses broader political and cultural aspects of social media in the public sphere.

David Moats completed his PhD at Goldsmiths, University of London and is currently a postdoctoral researcher at Tema: Technology and Social Change, Linköping University. His work concerns the methodological implications of 'big data' and particularly data visualizations for social research.

Ishani Mukherjee is a visiting clinical assistant professor in the Department of Communication at the University of Illinois at Chicago. Her research focuses on social media and ethics, digital advocacy, transnational gender politics, critical cultural and globalization studies, and South Asian film studies.

Carsten Ochs is a postdoctoral researcher at the Sociological Theory Department/University of Kassel. His research draws on science and technology studies and sociological theory to investigate forms of privacy, networked practices, and digitized sociotechnical constellations.

Jessamy Perriam is a PhD Candidate at the Centre for Invention and Social Process in the Department of Sociology at Goldsmiths, University of London. Her work looks at the increasing use of social media in demonstrating disruption in everyday life, with a focus on infrastructure and public spaces.

Matthew Pittman is a Communication PhD candidate in the School of Journalism and Communication at the University of Oregon. He studies digital ethics, social media and consumer well-being.

Nathaniel Poor is an independent researcher who studies communication technologies with an eye to the social, historical, and legal issues around them. He is the founder of the Underwood Institute, a non-profit research foundation based in New York.

Cornelius Puschmann is a senior researcher at the Hans Bredow Institute for Media Research in Hamburg. He studies digital media and communication using a combination of traditional and computational methods.

James Robson lectures at Oxford University Department of Education in learning technology and research methods. His research interests include sociology and philosophy of educational technology, online professional engagement and development, and digital research methods.

Philipp Schaer is Professor for Information Retrieval at TH Köln (University of Applied Sciences). His research interests span both computer and information science, with a special interest in the evaluation of all kinds of information systems using offline and online methods.

Yukari Seko is a Research Associate at Bloorview Research Institute, Holland Bloorview Kids Rehabilitation Hospital in Toronto, Canada. Her research interests include visual narratives of pain, digital health promotion, self-harming behaviours, and mental health of youth transitioning into adulthood.

Kim Sheehan is a professor in the School of Journalism and Communication at the University of Oregon. She studies crowdsourcing ethics, advertising and green washing, and anything having to do with culture and new technology.

Aim Sinpeng is a Lecturer in Comparative Politics in the Department of Government and International Relations, the University of Sydney. Her research focuses on online media and political opposition in Southeast Asia.

Daniela Stockmann is Associate Professor in the Institute of Political Science at Leiden University. She studies Chinese politics, political communication, comparative politics, and research methodology.

Jeff Shuter is a PhD candidate in Communication Studies at the University of Iowa. His research examines media production history, machine culture, and the politics of software design.

Patrick Sweeney is a PhD candidate in Psychology and a GC Digital Fellow at the Graduate Center, City University of New York. His work focuses on justice, technology, sexuality, and discourse.

Rebekah Tromble is Assistant Professor in the Institute of Political Science at Leiden University. Her research combines interests in political communication, digital media, research methods, social movements, and Muslim politics.

Jacqueline Wallace is a Post-doctoral Fellow at the Milieux Institute for Arts, Culture and Technology at Concordia University in Montreal, Canada. Her scholarly work looks at the intersection of design, women's work and cultural economies of creative production.

Katrin Weller is an information scientist and senior researcher at the GESIS – Leibniz Institute for the Social Sciences, department of Computational Social Science. Her research interests include interdisciplinary methods in social media studies, altmetrics and web science and she is co-editor of "Twitter and Society" (2014).

Martina Wengenmeir holds a PhD in Media and Communication from the University of Canterbury in Christchurch, New Zealand, which examined the characteristics of communication in online social networks in disaster response and recovery. Her research interests include digital methods and their ethics, as well as the formation of digital publics and communities.

Michael Zimmer is an Associate Professor in the School of Information Studies at the University of Wisconsin-Milwaukee, where he also serves as Director of the Center for Information Policy Research. A privacy and internet ethics scholar, Zimmer's research focuses on digital privacy, the ethical dimensions of social media & internet technologies, libraries & privacy, and internet research ethics.

Digital Formations is the best source for critical, well-written technologies and modern life. Books in the series break new grou multiple methodological and theoretical approaches to deeply prob reformation of lived experience as it is refracted through digital intera in **Digital Formations** pushes forward our understanding of the corresponding implications, between digital technologies and every examines broad issues in realms such as digital culture, electror politics and governance, gender, the Internet, race, art, health education. The series emphasizes critical studies in the context of en digital technologies.

Other recent titles include:

Felicia Wu Song
Virtual Communities: Bowling Alone, Online Together

Edited by Sharon Kleinman
The Culture of Efficiency: Technology in Everyday Life

Edward Lee Lamoureux, Steven L. Baron, & Claire Stewart
Intellectual Property Law and Interactive Media: Free for a Fee

Edited by Adrienne Russell & Nabil Echchaibi
International Blogging: Identity, Politics and Networked Publics

Edited by Don Heider
Living Virtually: Researching New Worlds

Edited by Judith B
& Kathy Walke
The Myths of T
Innovation and

Edited by Knut Lu
Digital Storytel
Stories: Self-re
Media

Theresa M. Senft
Camgirls: Cele
in the Age of S

Edited by Chris Pa
Domingo
Making Online
Ethnography o
Production

To order other books in this series please contact our Customer Ser

(800) 770-LANG (within the US)
(212) 647-7706 (outside the US)
(212) 647-7707 FAX

To find out more about the series or browse a full list of titles, please

WWW.PETERLANG.COM

www.ingramcontent.com/pod-product-compliance
Ingram Content Group UK Ltd.
Pitfield, Milton Keynes, MK11 3LW, UK
UKHW021836100926
8556IPUK00004B/370